LAT. of CAPITOL 38.53 N.

The perpendicular height of the ground where the Capitol is to stand is above the tide of Tiber creek } 78"0

The water of Tiber Creek may be conveyed on the high ground whe the Capitol stands and after watering that part of the City m be destined to other useful purposes

Reedy Branch and that of the Tiber may be conveyed to the Presidents-House

CAPITOL

CAPITOL STREET

NORTH CAROLINA

SOUTH CAROLINA

EAST

KENTUCKY

GEORGIA

DELAWARE

CAPITOL STREET

EASTERN BRANCH

OF MARYLAND WITHIN THE TERRITORY OF COLUMBI

SCALE of POLES

Studies in the History of Art
Published by the National Gallery of Art, Washington

This series includes: Studies in the History of Art, collected papers on objects in the Gallery's collections and other art historical studies (formerly Report and Studies in the History of Art); Monograph Series I, a catalogue of stained glass in the United States; Monograph Series II, on conservation topics; and Symposium Papers (formerly Symposium Series), the proceedings of symposia sponsored by the Center for Advanced Study in the Visual Arts at the National Gallery of Art.

*Forthcoming

The Mall in Washington, 1791–1991

STUDIES IN THE HISTORY OF ART · 30 ·

Center for Advanced Study in the Visual Arts
Symposium Papers XIV

The Mall in Washington, 1791–1991

Edited by Richard Longstreth

National Gallery of Art, Washington

Distributed by the University Press of New England

Hanover and London 1991

Editorial Board
DAVID A. BROWN, *Chairman*
DAVID BULL
NICOLAI CIKOVSKY, Jr.
HENRY A. MILLON
CHARLES S. MOFFETT

Editor
CAROL ERON

Designer
SUSAN LEHMANN

Assistant for Project Management
ABIGAIL WALKER

Editorial Assistant
MEG ALEXANDER

This publication was produced by the Editors Office,
National Gallery of Art, Washington
Editor-in-chief, Frances P. Smyth
Printed by Schneidereith and Sons, Baltimore,
Maryland

The text paper is 80 pound LOE Dull text with
matching cover
The type is Trump Medieval, set by VIP Systems,
Inc., Alexandria, Virginia

Distributed by the University Press of New England,
17½ Lebanon Street, Hanover, New Hampshire
03755

Abstracted by RILA (International Repertory of the
Literature of Art), Williamstown, Massachusetts
01267

Proceedings of the symposium, "The Mall in
Washington, 1791–1991," sponsored by the Center for
Advanced Study in the Visual Arts, National Gallery
of Art, and the American Architectural Foundation of
the American Institute of Architects, 30 and 31
October 1987

ISSN 0091-7338
ISBN 089468-138-9

Cover:
Panoramic View of Washington City, lithograph by
E. Sachse, 1856, looking west from Capitol Hill.
Library of Congress

Endpapers:
Plan of the City of Washington. . ., based on March
1792 plan, drawn by Andrew Ellicott, showing
changes recommended by George Washington and
Thomas Jefferson to L'Enfant plan, engraving by
William Rollinson, 1795. White House Collection

Frontispiece:
Aerial view of Capitol and Mall, looking west, 1985.
Photograph by Dennis Brack

Contents

HENRY A. MILLON
Dean, Center for Advanced Study in the Visual Arts

Preface

I t has been exactly two hundred years since Pierre Charles L'Enfant conceived his extraordinary scheme for the capital city of the United States, which has as its focus a grand ceremonial space. Over the past two centuries the Mall, so designated from its early days, has undergone numerous changes in design and use, all the while retaining its centrality within the life of the city and emerging, in the process, as a vital symbol of national identity.

In October 1987 the American Architectural Foundation of the American Institute of Architects and the Center for Advanced Study in the Visual Arts of the National Gallery of Art jointly sponsored a symposium on "The Mall in Washington, 1791–1991," held at the National Gallery as a bicentenary appraisal of the key element in L'Enfant's plan. The impetus for such a gathering came from the American Architectural Foundation, then preparing an exhibition on "The Plan of Washington, D.C.: Leon Krier and the City Beautiful Movement" to be held at the Octagon Museum in the fall of 1987. First proposed as an informal seminar to discuss recent views of the Mall, the meeting subsequently developed, at the suggestion of the Center for Advanced Study, into a two-day program with presentations both by scholars concerned with the history and development of the Mall, and by architects and landscape architects who have participated in some of its more recent transformations. The American Architectural Foundation and the Center for Advanced Study are grateful to Richard Longstreth, associate professor of architectural history and director of the graduate program in historic preservation at George Washington University, for his many invaluable contributions to the formulation of the symposium program.

This volume of *Studies in the History of Art* contains thirteen of the papers presented at the Mall symposium. They have been edited by Richard Longstreth, who kindly agreed to continue his involvement with the project in this way and to write the introduction. It was not possible, unfortunately, for two papers to be included: Walker O. Cain's "The Museum of History and Technology/National Museum of American History" and Allan Greenberg's "The Classical Imperative."

A special feature of this symposium volume is the set of 140 supplemental reproductions, comprising maps, plans, views, and documentary photographs, and intended to serve as a pictorial reference for the history and uses of the Mall from the eighteenth century to the present. The images were selected by Richard Longstreth. They were assembled with the assistance of Susan L. Klaus and of Sue Kohler of the Commission of Fine Arts, whom the Center is pleased to acknowledge and thank for their essential contributions. The symposium cosponsors are particularly grateful to Janet Annenberg Hooker and to the Morris and Gwendolyn Cafritz Foundation for generous financial support toward the compilation and publication of the pictorial section for the symposium proceedings.

RICHARD LONGSTRETH
George Washington University

Introduction:
Change and Continuity on the Mall

Everyone knows the Mall, that great core of the federal precinct envisioned in the 1791 plan for Washington, D.C., by Major Pierre Charles L'Enfant and realized in varying, sometimes divergent, forms during the two hundred years since that plan was prepared. Probably no other civic space in the country is used by so many segments of society for so many different purposes. Tourists come in droves, but area residents also frequent the Mall, and many use it as a municipal park. Thousands of people work on the Mall or pass through it in the course of their daily business. The Mall long has been heralded as an example of civic design, familiar to historians of architecture and urban development, architects, landscape architects, planners, and others involved with shaping the built environment. Accounts of the Mall's evolution and salient features abound. Yet much remains to be learned about the origins, development, and present configuration of this place. Increased understanding is especially important because the Mall is not a static thing but continues to change and be subject to many proposed changes, ranging from sizable museum buildings to minor commemorative sculpture. What the Mall is and what it should become have long stirred controversy. The intent of both the symposium held at the National Gallery of Art in October 1987 and of this volume is to focus on specific aspects of the Mall's complex history from inception to recent past, building on the distinguished, pioneering research of such figures as John Reps and Frederick Gutheim.[1]

The symposium included scholarly papers addressing the Mall's development through the 1960s as well as papers by architects and others who have figured importantly in the work itself during recent decades. For the historical portion, the focus was on the Mall as a precinct, rather than on individual buildings or monuments.[2] The latter subjects constitute a corpus sufficiently rich to justify a program far more ambitious than the one undertaken on this occasion.[3]

L'Enfant conceived his plan in terms of a matrix for the development of a great city by international standards. Washington may or may not have achieved that rank, but both the L'Enfant plan (pls. IV, V) and the realized form of its major components, such as the Mall, deserve consideration among the significant works of city planning worldwide. Norma Evenson thematically compares a number of these places, from Paris to Brasilia, New Delhi to Canberra, analyzing not only salient physical characteristics, but how the monumental precinct relates to the larger city.

L'Enfant's vision continues to be invoked as the essence of Washington and as a guide for current policy and practice. Indeed the name of L'Enfant is probably cited more often in these contexts than are those of all the others who may have had greater impact on the city as it now exists. The continued, and perhaps even mounting, interest in the French engineer stems partly from the many remarkable aspects of his plan, but also from the fact that so little is known for certain about his design. Some recent interpretations have only heightened the controversy over its precise nature and what L'Enfant conceived as the city in its three-dimensional form. A fresh examination of the plan's features, sources, and iconographic content is offered here in Pamela Scott's paper. Scott's work stands as a major contribution on which future study will depend. Yet the meager extent of surviving evidence promises further debate. Like Pliny's account of his villas, L'Enfant's plan may entice one generation after another to formulate new views without reaching full agreement.[4]

Scott also adds to our understanding of how L'Enfant's plan for the Mall quickly became modified by a succession of architects, most notable among them, Robert Mills. Mills' designs for the area (pls. XXIV–XXVI) and nearby federal properties were the product of a single conception, which was unusually eclectic at the time in proposing that references to several past cultures represented the inheritance of the New World. Indeed, the United States may have been the only country where one could then plausibly advance the idea that this collective inheritance stood as a symbol of the nation itself.

Therese O'Malley likewise breaks new ground in her discussion of Andrew Jackson Downing's 1851 plan (pl. XXVIII) and the development of the Mall as a botanical garden. Downing was no less audacious in his proposal of a naturalistic landscape providing an emblem of the national spirit in the center of the federal city than Mills and L'Enfant had been in their schemes. The fact that Downing's plan at least began to be executed adds to its significance as a precedent. The Mall hence became a proving ground, not only for ideas but for actual work, which would subsequently influence a chain of events whereby the large municipal park would emerge as an essential component of the urban landscape in the United States.

Those portions of Downing's plan and most of the other projects realized on the Mall during the nineteenth century were eradicated in the Senate Park Commission, or McMillan, Plan of 1901–1902 (pls. LVIII–LXXXII).[5] Thomas Hines draws from his past work on Daniel Burnham and the City Beautiful movement to reaffirm the importance of this scheme for

Washington and for the country as a whole. Jon Peterson documents how the new design also provided a catalyst for the transformation of the very idea of what a comprehensive plan was and how the scheme set a new standard that at once influenced the nascent practice of city planning across the nation. Again, a scheme conceived as a national symbol emerged as an agenda for undertakings that would affect the development of communities from coast to coast.

The McMillan Plan has been studied at greater length than have other phases of the Mall's long history; nevertheless, some basic points concerning this scheme beg further inquiry. How, for example, does the comprehensiveness of the McMillan Plan compare to work done in European cities during the second half of the nineteenth century? The Senate Park Commission closely examined the physical evidence of European centers, but did its members learn, too, from the remarkable public works bureaucracy created by Baron Georges Haussmann in Paris, or from the subsequent endeavors of his German counterparts? Hines emphasizes the City Beautiful as an American phenomenon; yet, as it drew primarily from European sources, did it in turn affect work, or at least thinking, abroad? The Senate Park Commission found itself in a highly unusual role: a few designers determining a multifaceted plan for an entire metropolitan region. Daniel Burnham, especially, continued to work in this vein for the remainder of his career. The concept of an architect as the shaper of a city was by no means new; however, Burnham carried the concept to a degree that had little precedent in urban history. To what extent did his example, introduced in Washington and developed further in cities such as San Francisco and Chicago, influence other architects who subscribed to the City Beautiful's tenets, or modernists such as Frank Lloyd Wright, Le Corbusier, and Richard Neutra, for whom designing cities became a fundamental expression of their respective philosophies? Whatever the findings, there is no doubt that the McMillan Plan deserves exploration within a broad, international context.[6]

Implementing the grand design presented in 1902 was, of course, a long, arduous task. Well over half a century passed before the Mall approached the state envisioned in the Mc-

Millan Plan. Among the plan's designers, Charles McKim became a key figure in the ensuing struggle over adhering to its matrix. Without his continued involvement and the tireless behind-the-scenes work of Washington architect Glenn Brown, it is unlikely that the plan ever would have become more than a vision on paper.[7] The years prior to World War I were crucial for resolving the placement of some major components such as the Lincoln Memorial, but it was not until later decades that execution of the overall plan commenced in earnest. David Streatfield's essay documents how Frederick Law Olmsted, Jr. was instrumental not only in developing the original design, but in guiding its execution during the interwar years — a process that entailed numerous changes due to fiscal realities and shifts in taste.

The younger Olmsted, Streatfield emphasizes, has been a sorely neglected figure despite his major contribution to twentieth-century design and planning in the United States.[8] Among the facets of his Washington work that deserve reexamination is his impact on the McMillan Plan itself. McKim generally is given credit for the Mall, but his previous planning work was on a much smaller scale, and neither he nor Burnham had much experience with landscape design.[9] As Olmsted orchestrated the commission's European tour, so he may have been at least an essential adviser in redirecting McKim's superb compositional skills to the demands of working on so ambitious a scheme that employed plan materials as primary design components.

Richard Guy Wilson also examines the implementation process. Rather than concentrating on a single figure, he analyzes events from the standpoint of the different, and often conflicting, groups involved with the federal precinct, emphasizing how vigorous and controversial that process generally has been. Part of the problem, he reminds us, is the divergence of views concerning what constitutes appropriate national symbols. Another factor is that Americans never have been prone to sustaining a single aesthetic over a long period and adhering to the strict controls necessary to achieve a planning objective. In retrospect, it less remarkable that implementation of the McMillan Plan took so long than that the process was sustained.

The impact of the Mall on architectural and planning practice is explored by Robert A.M. Stern, who has contributed to our knowledge of the past as well as to current tendencies in design. Stern reviews a spectrum of projects in the United States dating from the 1900s to the 1980s, emphasizing that the lessons learned, especially since World War II, have not always been positive ones. Nevertheless, he concludes that the Mall may be as potent a source of inspiration today as it was during the early twentieth century.

The fact that work on the Mall remains very much an ongoing phenomenon is underscored in a paper by J. Carter Brown, chairman of the Commission of Fine Arts. Since its founding in 1910, the commission has probably been the most important single force in the Mall's development. Brown delineates what he considers the commission's most significant achievements there during his twenty-year tenure. He also offers, in his capacity as director of the National Gallery of Art, an account of major issues that affected the East Building's design.[10]

Gyo Obata and Jean Paul Carlhian introduce their concerns as architects in creating two major additions to the Smithsonian Institution complex, which collectively defines much of the Mall's architectural character. Dan Kiley has long been involved in landscape designs for the Mall; but rather than focusing on past endeavors, he has chosen to address concerns for future change.

What will happen to the Mall in years hence is a matter of great interest on many fronts. Perhaps for the first time, pronounced departures from the McMillan Plan that amount to redesigning the Mall are being advanced on a theoretical level by Kiley and others, most notably Leon Krier.[11] The Mall now has reached the state where it is almost fully developed; a few "unfinished" parcels remain, yet they are minor compared to the unfinished work of fifty years ago (pls. CXVII, CXVIII). Thus concern in many quarters has shifted from problems of development to those of preservation. Such a shift inevitably rekindles old controversies and generates new ones; to assess the implications, it is essential to examine what the Mall is and what it represents in its current state.

While the history of design in the United

States is marked far more by change than by continuity, the Mall as it now exists has transcended change. L'Enfant's plan was influenced by the classical tradition, but also by picturesque sensibilities in late eighteenth-century France. Not long thereafter, schemes more pronounced in their informality began to be prepared for the Mall, and picturesqueness became the dominant thrust of work executed during most of the nineteenth century. Then a new academic classicism gained the upper hand under the aegis of the Senate Park Commission. By the 1920s, many components of that commission's plan were being realized in a simpler, more relaxed vein; and in work done since the 1960s, a considerably greater range of approaches is evident. Nevertheless, the cumulative result minimizes the differences. Today, one's perception of the Mall, in both its tangible and associative dimensions, is of continuity. Not fully aware of the Mall's complex history, many people refer to the area more as a product of L'Enfant than of his numerous successors, in part because of the desire to believe that all this work has been built on a vision established at the time of the city's founding. And, in contrast to most nineteenth-century proposals for the Mall, the drive to reestablish a continuum, invoking the spirit of the L'Enfant plan as a guide, has shaped much of the Mall's design since 1900.

As a result of the longstanding pursuit of consistent objectives in this century, the Mall's physical character has emerged as sufficiently strong and lucid to embrace deviations. From the Smithsonian Institution Building to the National Gallery's East Building, the area includes over a century's worth of remarkable designs embodying ideas quite different from, yet not necessarily incompatible with, those of L'Enfant and his twentieth-century successors. The Mall can even hold its own against the few architectural banalities that have been inflicted on it; however, any precinct can only tolerate so much intrusion before the underlying spirit is compromised beyond retrieval, leaving little more than an assemblage of varied opinions about design cast in three-dimensional form.

Much of the Mall's visual strength lies in its scale. From the Capitol to Fourteenth Street, the broad, linear space creates a sense of expansiveness commensurate with the bold visions that shaped it, a space that may be said

to be emblematic of the vast reaches of the country itself (pl. CXIX). The utter simplicity of the parts is an essential contributor to this effect; more detailed treatments might at once distract the eye and erode the coherence. The Mall then would become more a collection of things and less a great open forum that allows one to imagine and do so much within its confines.

The best architecture on and adjacent to the Mall acts in concert with its scale and spatial character. From a distance and viewed diagonally, most of the buildings stand as little more than an unobtrusive backdrop (pls. CXX, CXXI). Were the treatment uniform, with scant variation in facades, the effect would be deadening. Many of these works are monuments in their own right, but the pivotal points of focus they provide become apparent primarily at close range. As a result, the sequence appears constantly to change, with moments of emphasis and stretches of neutrality—a varied rhythm that prevents the semblance of mere size.

Then around the Washington Monument, the space opens further to become an enormous field, a plain on which almost nothing is allowed to interfere except the obelisk itself (pl. CXXII). Here definition is replaced by implied limitless expansion. The grassy knoll recedes toward trees that seem distant and unimportant; the shaft meets the ground unceremoniously, without a base. But it is not so much the juncture that matters as the unimpeded vertical thrust, soaring without a visual terminus save the sky.

For all its implicit expansiveness, this central area is only an interlude. The axis continues westward, now more tightly constrained by ranges of trees. Nothing of consequence appears to be on either side; all emphasis is given to the primary axis, guided by the Reflecting Pool and the Lincoln Memorial beyond (pls. CXXIII, CXXIV). This monument to the Great Emancipator might seem a fitting terminus to the whole affair, but it is significant that the sequence neither ends here nor at any other neatly defined place. Instead, the axis pivots and for the first time permits vehicular movement down its center, as it stretches over the Potomac on the Memorial Bridge and approaches the National Cemetery in Arlington, Virginia (pls. CXXV, CXXVI). Once there, the path diffuses amid a setting that is almost entirely picturesque. The axial approach, like Arlington House above, is but a counterpoint to the prevailing landscape, which suggests penetration far into the hinterland.

But it is not in Virginia where the initial break in formal ordering occurs. To the south of the Reflecting Pool, the Mall becomes a park, and the impression is that of a place far removed from any urban constraints (pls. CXXVII, CXXVIII). That spirit continues, if in an altered vocabulary, around the Tidal Basin where the Jefferson Memorial stands as a grand focus, monumental in scale and even somewhat urban in character; but like the much smaller "temples" in an eighteenth-century English park, it is also an integral component of a circuitous, rambling sequence (pl. CXXIX). The Washington Monument is brought into similar service when viewed from one of the most recent and successful additions to the Mall, Constitution Gardens, which lies north of the Reflecting Pool and affords an ingenious balance to the parklike setting to the south (pl. CXXX).

In its parts, its ordering, and its character, the Mall embraces a number of different and potentially divergent aspects of thought and landscape in the United States. Some of the allusions are literal, others abstract. Some of the facets are placid, others highly active. Some are rooted in centuries of tradition, others appear much newer. Not the least of the Mall's salient attributes is that this spectrum of components, this multitude of qualities exist in a compatible relationship. There is ambiguity in places, sometimes tension, but on the whole harmony prevails and to such a degree that one is often scarcely conscious of how varied the particulars are. Indeed, the ensemble seems so straightforward, so logical, so cogently expressed that it easily can be taken for granted, as if it had all been conceived as such from the start. One tends not to think of *when* the Mall was built; of how it embodies phases, tendencies, or movements in architecture, landscape design, and planning; or even of the strong artistic personalities that have contributed to it. As the Mall draws from many historical precedents, as it incorporates many aspects of the landscape into its fabric, so it transcends the specifics of time, personality, and place to embody a nation far greater than the sum of its parts.

All of the Mall's physical qualities would mean little, however, were it not for the abundance of people and activities that continually have been attracted to the precinct (pls. CXXXI–CXL). The relationship between the two is not coincidental. Whether grand or intimate, carefully designed or appearing not to have been designed at all, the Mall's constituent parts allow people, more than buildings, sculpture, or landscaping, to dominate the scene. Americans love space. Since the period of first settlement, a penchant for openness has distinguished rural and components of urban landscapes alike from many counterparts on other continents. On the Mall, even the largest buildings seem to play a minor role, the most pronounced focal points mere punctuation marks set in a well-formed but malleable space. Here orchestrated events involving thousands of people or spontaneous ones with just a few participants are equally fitting. Space here is ever changing—at one point defined, at the next open and casual—but it is seldom limited to a single or even predominating use. In this sense, the Mall's space is neutral, allowing people freely to engage themselves in myriad ways, from revering national heroes to challenging national policy, from learning about artistic and technical achievements to competing in games, from paying homage to the dead to celebrating matrimonial ties, from gathering for mass spectacles to retreating for solitary contemplation.

What may seem to have been an effortless creation is, of course, the product of continuous struggle. Struggle has occurred not only over what has been implemented, but over what has been rejected. There has never been a shortage of ideas to improve the Mall. There have been proposals for more monuments, more buildings, more sculpture, more trees, more water, and more amenities. There also have been proposals for less traffic, less paving, less parking, less formality, less variety, less openness. Much to the credit of the Commission of Fine Arts, its decisions appear to have been right most of the time; yet the process is unpredictable, the proper balance is delicate.

Where does one stop? Does one stop? Should this thing that has been the subject of ongoing change for two hundred years ever be finished? Some critics may argue that in a place such as the Mall, prohibiting significant change in the future would be an artificial and ultimately stifling practice. As the Mall has flourished while experiencing change, so it could become dead or at least less consequential were the process arrested. Such a line of reasoning avoids the fact that many places subject to little physical modification over a sustained period continue to harbor vitality and meaning. Since the Mall itself is almost completed with scarcely any undeveloped space left, additions in most cases would necessitate removing other elements, many of which are landmarks and almost all of which serve good use. Even if the thing changed is a playing field, the loss could be greater than the gain, for the successful relationship between buildings and space, between structured and unstructured use, can easily be compromised. The Mall is not a museum or a Valhalla; it is a living place where diversity of function is as essential to its wholeness as is the diversity of its physical parts.

These characteristics do not imply that the Mall should remain static. Change should occur, but it should be predicated on a compelling purpose and its ramifications should be assessed carefully. Those charged with planning and protection in this quarter have been, and should continue to be, bold enough to resist embarking on pronounced change for its own sake. What the Mall is and what it should be will always be the subject of debate, for it is too important and vital a place for conditions to be otherwise. The history of the Mall is one of major conceptual changes and many minor ones as well. It is vital to understand this complicated legacy in order to understand the place itself; a precinct of comparable richness probably never could be conceived in a single plan or even in a single era. Yet one must also remember that after two centuries of development, the Mall does not bespeak those numerous changes; a sense of continuity in the whole is the overriding force. This sense of continuity is indeed rare in our culture, and is perhaps one reason so many people have long considered the Mall so remarkable a place.

NOTES

1. John W. Reps, *Monumental Washington: The Planning and Development of the Capital Center* (Princeton, 1967). See also: Frederick Gutheim and Wilcomb E. Washburn, *The Federal City: Plans and Realities* [exh. cat., Smithsonian Institution] (Washington, 1976); and Frederick Gutheim and National Capital Planning Commission, *Worthy of the Nation: The History of Planning for the National Capital* (Washington, 1977).

2. Properly speaking, the Mall extends from the Capitol grounds to Fourteenth Street between Constitution and Independence avenues. Yet these blocks form only a portion of the core federal precinct that has been planned as a single entity for generations. To do justice to this reality, while keeping the scope manageable, the authors were asked to focus on, but not necessarily limit themselves to, the Mall itself and the area west of Fourteenth Street and south of Constitution Avenue to the Potomac River. Throughout the volume the entire precinct is referred to as the Mall.

3. Studies of individual buildings include:

Kirk Savage, "The Self-Made Monument: George Washington and the Fight to Erect a National Memorial," *Winterthur Portfolio* 22 (Winter 1987), 225–242.

Kenneth Hafertepe, *America's Castle: The Evolution of the Smithsonian Building and Its Institution, 1840–1878* (Washington, 1984).

Tanya Beauchamp, "Adolph Cluss and the Building of the U.S. National Museum" (Master's thesis, University of Virginia, 1972).

Auditor's Complex: A Synopsis of the Historic Structures Report (Washington, 1979).

Cynthia Field, "The Role of Charles Follen McKim in the Design of the National Museum of Natural History" (unpublished, Office of Architectural History and Historic Preservation, Smithsonian Institution, 1988).

Keith Morgan, "The Patronage Matrix: Charles A. Platt, Architect, Charles L. Freer, Client," *Winterthur Portfolio* 17 (Summer–Autumn 1982), 121–134.

Christopher Thomas, "The Lincoln Memorial and Its Architect, Henry Bacon (1866–1924)," (Ph.D. diss., Yale University, 1990).

Travis McDonald, Jr., "Smithsonian Institution Competition for a Gallery of Art, January 1939–June 1939," in *Modernism in America, 1937–1941*, ed. James Kornwolf [exh. cat., Muscarelle Museum of Art, College of William and Mary] (Williamsburg, Va., 1985), 177–223.

George Gurney, *Sculpture and the Federal Triangle* (Washington, 1985).

Marilyn Sara Cohen, "American Civilization in Three Dimensions: Evolution of the Museum of History and Technology of the Smithsonian Institution" (Ph.D. diss., George Washington University, 1980).

On the architects, see:

John Bryan, ed., *The Drawings of Robert Mills* [exh. cat., American Architectural Foundation] (Washington, 1989).

Keith Morgan, *Charles A. Platt: The Artist as Architect* (New York and Cambridge, 1985).

Stephen Bedford, "The Architectural Career of John Russell Pope" (Ph.D. diss., Columbia University, in preparation).

Richard Guy Wilson, "Arthur Brown, Jr., California Classicist," *Progressive Architecture* 64 (December 1983), 64–71.

Richard Oliver, *Bertram Grosvenor Goodhue* (New York and Cambridge, 1983).

Travis McDonald, Jr., "Modernized Classicism: The Architecture of Paul Philippe Cret in Washington, D.C." (Master's thesis, University of Virginia, 1980).

Elizabeth Grossman, "Paul Philippe Cret: 21; Rationalism and Imagery in American Architecture" (Ph.D. diss., Brown University, 1980).

Carol Herselle Krinsky, *Gordon Bunshaft of Skidmore, Owings, and Merrill* (New York and Cambridge, 1988).

Walter McQuade, *Architecture in the Real World: The Work of HOK* (New York, 1984).

For a thoughtful analysis of commemorative work in the precinct, see: Charles Griswold, "The Vietnam Veterans Memorial and the Washington Mall: Philosophical Thoughts on Political Iconographs," *Critical Inquiry* 12 (Summer 1986), 688–719. Detailed coverage of sculptural work is provided in James Goode, *The Outdoor Sculpture of Washington, D.C.* (Washington, 1974).

4. See, for example, J.L. Sibley Jennings, "Artistry as Design: L'Enfant's Extraordinary City," *Quarterly Journal of the Library of Congress* 36 (Summer 1979), 225–278. See also Donald E. Jackson, "L'Enfant's Washington: An Architect's View," *Records of the Columbia Historical Society* 15 (1980), 398–420. Two significant articles analyzing the influence of George Washington and Thomas Jefferson on the initial planning of the city are: Egon Verheyen, " 'The Splendor of Its Empire': Reconsidering Jefferson's Role in the Planning of Washington," in *Festschrift Herbert Siebenhuner*, ed. Erich Hubala and Gunter Schweikhart (Wurzburg, 1978), 183–206; and Egon Verheyen, "James Hoban's Design for the White House in the Context of the Planning of the Federal City," *Architettura* 11 (1981, no. 1), 66–82. A revealing chronicle of reconstructions of Pliny's villas is contained in Helen H. Tanzer, *The Villas of Pliny the Younger* (New York, 1924).

5. The 1901–1902 plan for the Mall and other public lands in Washington prepared by the Park Commission (Daniel Burnham, Charles McKim, Frederick Law Olmsted, Jr., and Augustus Saint-Gaudens) of the Senate Committee on the District of Columbia has long been known as the McMillan Plan, honoring Senator James McMillan, chairman of that Senate committee and the plan's primary official spon-sor. Following common parlance as well as for brevity, the scheme generally is referred to as the McMillan Plan throughout the text of this volume, and in the figure and plate captions as Senate Park Commission, Plan of 1901–1902. The commission itself, however, is referred to as the Senate Park Commission since McMillan was not a member.

6. A useful comparative study of planning efforts generally is: Anthony Sutcliff, *Towards the Planned City: Germany, Britain, the United States and France, 1780–1914* (New York, 1981). Recently the McMillan Plan has been examined in relation to Burnham's 1909 Chicago plan; see Howard F. Gillette, Jr., "White City, Capital City," *Chicago History* 18 (Winter 1989–1990), 26–45.

7. Concerning Brown, see William Bushong et al., *A Centennial History of the Washington Chapter, American Institute of Architects, 1887–1987* (Washington, 1987), 21–43; and William Bushong, "Glenn Brown, the American Institute of Architects, and the Development of the Civic Core of Washington, D.C." (Ph.D. diss., George Washington University, 1988).

8. Olmsted has only just been the subject of a detailed study: Susan Klaus, " 'Intelligent and Comprehensive Planning of a Common Sense Kind': Frederick Law Olmsted, Junior, and the Emergence of Comprehensive Planning in America" (Master's thesis, George Washington University, 1988).

9. Concerning McKim's work in this vein, see Leland M. Roth, *McKim, Mead, and White, Architects* (New York, 1983), 181–209, 251–259, 279–287.

10. I.M. Pei had agreed to give a paper on the subject; however, several months prior to the symposium, commitments abroad necessitated his withdrawl from the program. J. Carter Brown then agreed to present a second paper.

11. Proposals prepared under Kiley's direction at Harvard are discussed in his paper. Concerning Krier's plan, see: Leon Krier, "Completion of Washington, D.C., Bicentennial Masterplan for the Year 2000," *Archives d'Architecture Moderne* 30 (1986), 7–43; and Christian K. Laine, "City Beautiful: The Critique of the Modern City," in *The Plan of Washington, D.C., Leon Krier and the City Beautiful Movement* [exh. cat., American Architectural Foundation] (Washington, 1987).

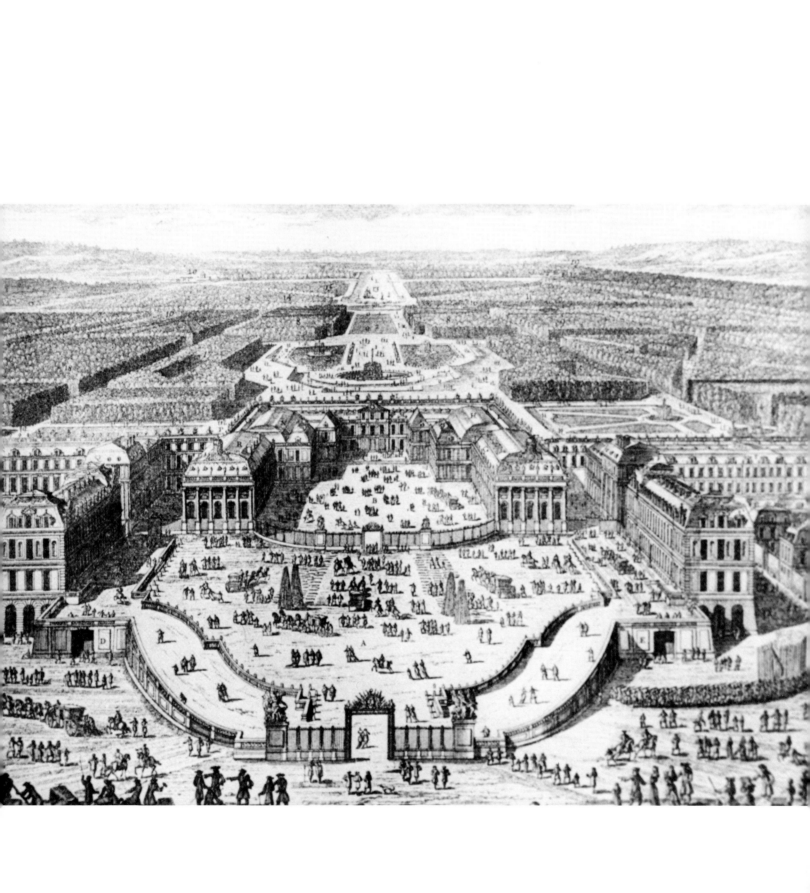

NORMA EVENSON
University of California, Berkeley

Monumental Spaces

Washington is my hometown, and as a child I lived on Capitol Hill. I played on the Capitol grounds and in the Capitol itself The monumental image of Washington embedded itself in my childhood experience and continues to color my memories. Among my recollections also are various plans for extending the Mall as far as the Anacostia River (pls. LXXXIX–XCI, XCV). At that time, I did not realize how far such schemes were from realization, and feared that my neighborhood was threatened with obliteration.

It is in the nature of linear compositions that they suggest their own extension, and it is not unnatural, therefore, that Washington planners periodically would seek to prolong the governmental axis from river to river. I suspect also that some planners may have thought it unseemly that the great ceremonial axis of Washington should terminate so abruptly in a modest residential neighborhood. Actually, during my childhood Capitol Hill was somewhat less than modest, and the extension of the Mall was often given the added justification of slum clearance. Like many decayed urban neighborhoods, however, Capitol Hill comprised a degree of social mixture and a variety of building types. There were some fine old houses, often subdivided into furnished rooms and small apartments, some run-of-the-mill speculators' rows, a few middle-class apartment buildings, and some wretched slums. The worst of these were alley dwellings, rows of narrow brick houses often lacking electricity and inhabited by the poorest black people. Photographers were fond of dramatic juxtapositions showing the alley dwellings with the Capitol dome or some other major federal building in the background. Such images were frequently used as political commentary, evoking a vision of legislators sitting in monumental splendor, oblivious to the misery just beyond their doors (fig. 1).

In terms of urban form, capital cities reflect considerable variety. Some incorporate the governmental function in addition to widely-ranging economic and institutional activity, while others function exclusively as capitals. The monumental aspect of the capital may dominate the city in some cases, or in others appear relatively subdued. Donald Olsen has observed that in the British capital one would "search in vain for the great public buildings, the dramatic vistas, or the striking monuments of Rome, Paris, or Washington," pointing out that, "London rarely attempts to look like a great city, being content to be one." [1]

It is not surprising that people often interpret the monumental aspect of a capital as a reflection of the nature of government and the relation of ruler and ruled. Discussing the early stages of urban evolution, Lewis Mumford dwelt on the intimidating imagery of the citadel, the walled stronghold of the warrior-king: "In the citadel the new mark of the city is obvious: a change of scale, deliberately meant to awe and overpower the beholder. . . . What we now call 'monumental architecture' is first

of all the expression of power. . . . The purpose of this art was to produce respectful terror."[2]

The image of the government center as a walled enclosure persisted in many cultures. In addition to providing the ruler with physical protection, the fortified palace embodied a sense of mystery. Contact between ruler and subject would normally take place only in highly controlled circumstances, emphasizing the distinction between the populace and ruling elite.

One of the most thoroughgoing embodi-

1. Washington, Capitol Hill, aerial view looking west toward Mall, Lincoln Park in foreground
Photograph by Alex McLean, Landslide

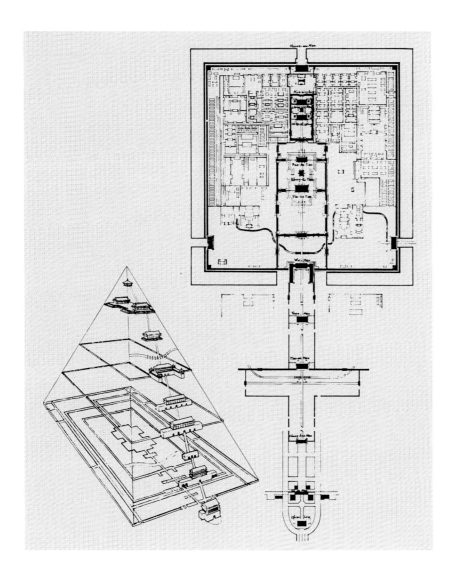

ments of the citadel image is Beijing, as rebuilt
in the fifteenth century. The palace complex
formed a walled axial enclave within a walled
city, with the emperor's audience hall providing the hidden climax of a series of protected enclosures. The sequestered emperor's
elevated status was enhanced by the number
of barriers to be breached in attaining his presence. Throughout Beijing, the imperial authority was reflected in building controls designed to subordinate all architecture to that
of the palace complex (fig. 2).

Although European cities produced their
share of citadels, by the seventeenth century
Western monumentality had come to be characterized by the open, rather than the closed
axis. In Louis XIV's great palace complex at
Versailles, the outer walls were vestigial, and
the power of the king was dramatized through
his visibility, through his public enactment
of the rituals of kingship. The design of Versailles emphasized the palace as the central
focus of extended vistas. Assuming a concordance between physical and social ordering, Versailles might be interpreted as an appropriate expression of centralized authority
and far-reaching bureaucratic control. The
consolidation of power in the new nation-state
had made the fortress-capital obsolete, and at
the same time Louis XIV was building Versailles, he was dismantling the walls of Paris,
replacing them with broad avenues and laying
the groundwork for Parisian expansion (fig. 3).

The scale of baroque design might be linked
in part to the advances of seventeenth-century
astronomy. New telescopes were revealing vast
reaches of outer space, and an expanded perception of distance began to characterize a
new aesthetic. As the universe reflected a single pervasive ordering, so human compositions began to reflect an enlarged sense of spatial control. The increasing use of vehicular
transport, moreover, encouraged the planning
of straight streets providing axial links within
an extended urban fabric. Baroque design provided a geometric framework wherein a series
of widely separated focal points could be visually coordinated. Reversing the outmoded
imagery of the citadel, the new design did not
conceal the center of power, but made it the
dominating element of a clearly-perceived visual hierarchy.

With its formal logic and its easily-comprehended disposition of monumental symbols, such design was to find extensive and
long-lived application. Versailles set the precedent for a type of monumental composition
adopted throughout Europe and, together with
the evolving central axis of Paris, provided an
obvious prototype for the plan of Pierre L'Enfant
for Washington. Symbolically appropriate for
a new republic, the central focus was on the
Capitol, housing the legislature, with the executive mansion placed at a distance and to
one side of the principal axis. As a planned
city, Washington provided opportunity for the
creation of large-scale urban unity: the axial
government complex could be harmoniously
embodied within, and related to, a comprehensively ordered street fabric.

Some of the compositional characteristics of monumental Washington can be found in the city of New Delhi, planned in 1913. Resulting from a decision to move the colonial government away from the commercial city of Calcutta, New Delhi provided a purely administrative center adjacent to an existing Indian city.[3] The initial design effort focused almost entirely on the monumental aspects of the capital, with relatively little attention given to planning the city as a whole. A ceremonial axis was designed to focus on the palace of the viceroy, the representative of the British crown. Sited on an elevation, Raisina Hill, the Viceroy's House (1912–1931) was flanked by symmetrical secretariat buildings. From a large plaza at the foot of the hill, the axial line was extended by a broad avenue flanked by strips of landscaping, bringing to mind L'Enfant's proposed avenue leading westward from the Capitol Hill (fig. 4).

Raisina Hill is far more modest than Washington's Capitol Hill, and the Viceroy's House could never have achieved visual dominance comparable to that of the United States Capitol. The visibility of the palace was hampered, moreover, by an alteration of the sight lines intended by the architect, Sir Edwin Lutyens. Although he meant for the facade to be visible from the foot of the hill, the complex was constructed so that only the dome could be seen from that point (fig. 5).

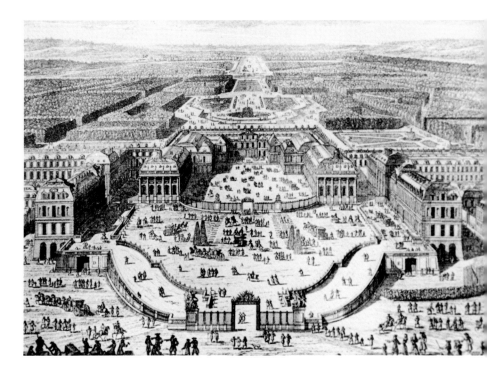

The compositional emphasis on the Viceroy's House dramatized the prevailing hierarchy of the colonial administration. The government center also included the Viceroy's Council House (1913–1928), but this structure was sited below Raisina Hill. Giving additional emphasis to its subordinate role in

3. Chateau of Versailles, seventeenth-century engraving of entrance elevation
From Reginald Blomfield, *A History of French Architecture* (London, 1921)

4. New Delhi, King's Way, looking toward Viceroy's House
Author photograph

government was its placement to one side of the principal axis.

In its overpowering scale, the government center of New Delhi was considered by many to be a perfect expression of imperial dominance. One critic praised the grandeur of the Viceroy's House as remarkably suitable for "the man who, if power be measured by the number of those subject to it, is the most powerful man that breathes." C. Northcote Parkinson, however, employed New Delhi to illustrate his theory that, "perfection of planned layout is achieved only by institutions on the point of collapse." [4]

At the same time New Delhi was begun, a variation on the axial concept could be seen in Canberra, the new capital of Australia. The initial plan (1912) by Walter Burley Griffin was designed to incorporate large-scale features of the landscape, with a so-called "land" axis leading from the capitol hill to a distant mountain, Mount Ainslie.[5] A cross-, or "water-," axis took the form of an artificial lake. Superimposed on this cross-axis was a triangular configuration providing sites for a civic center and commercial center linked to the capitol. Although the scale of the overall composition was grand, its visual effectiveness was diminished for many years by the lack of permanent monumental architecture (fig. 6).

Canberra, like New Delhi and turn-of-the-century Washington, reflected the tenets of Beaux-Arts classicism. By the time the architectural embellishment of the Australian capital was achieved, however, classicism had been superseded, and many buildings along the government axis embodied interpretations of the modern movement.

The permanent capitol, designed in 1980 by Mitchell Giurgola Thorp, reflected what might be viewed as an attempt to "democratize" the image of government. In envisioning the form of the new capitol, the designers sought not to crown the hill as in Washington, but to efface the building into the slope of the land. According to the architects, "the hill is of utmost importance. For centuries man occupied its crest with structures as signs of possession and power. We feel that the hilltop should be left clear of visible constructions. Only the flag . . . should be present as a permanent rallying-point or symbol for the citizens." [6] For maximum visibility, this flag was mounted on an assertive tubular structure of stainless steel (fig. 7).

Although the modern movement in architecture has altered the form of monumental building, large-scale composition often retains basic elements of baroque formality. Such a fusion of tradition and modernism may be found in Brasilia, for which a design competition was held in 1956.[7] The jury indicated that it primarily sought monumental imagery; the new city should look like a capital. As with New Delhi, Brasilia represented the shift of the capital function from a predominantly commercial city to an entirely governmental setting. Although other plans were much more thoroughly developed, the jury described the project of Lucio Costa as the one that "best integrates the monumental elements into the city's daily life as a Federal Capital. . . . The elements of the plan can be seen at once: It is clear, direct and fundamentally simple, as exemplified by Pompeii, Nancy, Wren's London, Louis XV's Paris." [8]

The plan of Brasilia embodies a symmetrical cross-axis, with one axis lined with residential superblocks and the other comprising the government center. The visual unity of the city is maintained by complete architectural control, calculated to give primacy to the monumental core. As in Washington, the center of the axis takes the form of an extended grassy mall leading to the legislative assembly.

The partial concealment of the monumental focal point, occurring by mistake in New Delhi, was consciously designed in Brasilia. Sited on a gentle downward slope, the assembly building is set within a shallow depression, masking the facade, and leaving only the roof level visible from the mall. The architect, Oscar Niemayer, wished not to close the axis visually, but to suggest the extension of space beyond. He pointed out that, "had the Palace been designed in the academic spirit . . . we should have had a tall structure, blocking the view that now stretches out in depth, away and beyond the building, over the esplanade, between the domes, embracing the Plaza of the Three Powers." What is seen from the mall is the profile of the secretariat towers,

7. Canberra, model of temporary Parliament building and new Capitol
From *Architecture in Australia* 69 (September 1980)

together with two sculptural elements projecting beyond the roof of the assembly to mark the legislative chambers below. In the architect's words, "their forms sprout like a symbol of the legislative power" (fig. 8).[9]

The Plaza of the Three Powers lying adjacent to the legislature comprises a rectangular paved space, on opposite ends of which are the Supreme Court (1957–1960) and the Palace of the Planalto (1957–1968) containing the presidential offices. The implied balance of powers, of course, does not reflect political reality. The principal power rests in the executive, and for symbolic accuracy the focus of the composition should have been the pres-

8. Brasilia, view toward
legislative assembly
Author photograph

9. Brasilia, aerial view of
government complex with
Plaza of the Three Powers
NOVACAP

traditional conceptions of monumental building, embodying a massive solidity of form, the
principal buildings of the government complex were conceived as glass-walled boxes
framed with tapering decorative columns. The
overall imagery evokes lightness and fragility
rather than power and permanence.

In their monumental compositions, Washington, New Delhi, Canberra, and Brasilia exhibit an abundance of space that is designed
to permit distant views of architecture, rather
than to accommodate specific use. While providing landscaped areas, these government
malls are generally too remote from the ordinary life of the city to function as recreational parks, and their open expanses seem in
some ways to be intentionally lacking in plea-
surable outdoor amenities. The aesthetic impact derives from the sheer magnitude of scale,
and from the exhilaration of experiencing a
great unbroken vista. Discussing the spatial
isolation of the Canberra government center,
an Australian architectural journal insisted
that, "buildings do not make a place. It is the
sweep of the eye, the relationship of buildings
and trees, the distant views, the reflection of
water, the absence of noise and the clarity of
the light that would make an open National
Place a very valuable asset in the years
ahead." [10]

In terms of its overall symbolism, the baroque axis appears sufficiently flexible to represent any political system, from absolute

idential palace. With its visual emphasis on
the relatively powerless legislature, the design
provides only a symbolic gesture toward democracy (fig. 9).

Brasilia's architecture reflects many attributes of the International style. In contrast to

monarchy to egalitarian democracy. In India, the complex that was viewed as a perfect expression of imperial power accommodated easily to the symbolic requirements of an independent republic. The original arrangement of the buildings, of course, remained unaltered. The Viceroy's House became the headquarters for the virtually powerless president of India, while the newly-powerful legislature persisted in the visually subordinate Council House. Fortunately, both the British and Indians share a taste for spectacle, and the setting designed for imperial ceremony serves the Republic of India equally well as a site for official celebrations.

A similar adaptation took place in Russia at the time of the revolution. The citadel of the Moscow Kremlin became the headquarters for the new revolutionary regime, and the adjacent Red Square was embellished with Lenin's tomb. In this way, the imagery of the past could be juxtaposed with symbols of the new government. Most revolutionary governments have sought more than revolution. They have also sought legitimacy, and visual association with the monuments of the past has provided a means to bolster claims as the rightful heirs of power.

In Beijing, Tiananmen Square, which marks the entrance into the old palace complex, was expanded in 1958 and again in 1976–1977. Intended as a center for great public gatherings, it is the largest square in the world, comprising 123 acres and able to accommodate six hundred thousand people. Just as the tomb of Lenin confronts the Kremlin, the mausoleum of Mao Tse-tung punctuates the axial line of the palace complex, together with the Monument to People's Heroes, an obelisk 118 feet high. Flanking the mausoleum are additional symbols of the revolutionary government, the National Museum and the Great Hall of the People. Despite the gigantic scale of Tiananmen Square, it was filled to capacity during the Cultural Revolution with carefully orchestrated hordes waving banners, shouting slogans and holding aloft the obligatory red books (figs. 10, 11). Although it had been redesigned to provide for officially-sanctioned mass meetings, Tiananmen Square would prove an effective magnet for spontaneous public protest (fig. 12). During the spring of 1989, its sweeping expanse became the stage for a tragic drama in which prolonged demonstrations de-

天安门广场

10. Beijing, Tiananmen Square, aerial view
From People's Republic of China pamphlet

11. Beijing, Tiananmen Square, view of demonstration during the Cultural Revolution

12. Beijing, Tiananmen
Square, student demonstra-
tion, May 1989
Author photograph

13. Nuremberg, Zeplenfeld
From Gerdy Troost, *Das Bauen im
neuen Reich* (Bayreuth, 1938)

ferred his ambition to be architecturally embodied in the domes, arches, columns, and
pediments of antiquity.[11] Among the most
ambitious ceremonial complexes of the time
was the partly-built site of the Nazi party congresses in Nuremberg (fig. 13). The creation
of such architectural ensembles specifically
designed to manipulate crowds into a state
of mass hysteria convinced many modernists
that democratic society had no use for
monumentality.

Much of the ideology of the modern movement in architecture was deliberately anti-
monumental. The futurists, it may be recalled, advocated, "blowing sky-high . . . all
those monuments and monumental pavements, arcades and flights of steps," in order
to create their vision of a contemporary metropolis.[12] Traditional monumental design,
both in terms of architecture and spatial configuration, was frequently condemned as antithetical to the spirit of the modern world and
modern democratic society. John Summerson
once observed that, "all those things which
suggested and supported monumentality are
in dissolution. . . . Monumentality in architecture is a form of affirmation; and affir-
mations are usually made by the few to impress the many. . . . Architecture is no longer
required to give symbolic cohesion to society.
Cohesion is now maintained by new methods
of communication."[13]

In this country, the Beaux-Arts complexes
inspired by the 1893 World's Columbian Exposition at Chicago came to be derided for
their outmoded imagery. Jane Jacobs, describing the impact of the City Beautiful movement, insisted that, "somehow, when the fair
became part of the city, it did not work like
the fair."[14] An example she discussed at length
was the San Francisco Civic Center, which,
she felt, typified the absurdity of assembling
a group of functionally unrelated buildings in
one place solely to create a unified architectural ensemble around an open plaza. There
was ostensibly no reason why the city hall,
public library, opera house, concert hall, convention center, and art gallery needed to be
in the same place, and there were a number
of reasons why they should be separated. In
her book, *The Death and Life of Great American Cities*, she argued convincingly for the
placement of cultural facilities in locations
where they could enliven and enhance their

nouncing government corruption and advocating democratic reforms were brutally
crushed by military action.

Vast monumental complexes often have
characterized authoritarian regimes. The
grandiose plans produced under Stalin for the
embellishment of Moscow and under Hitler
for the rebuilding of Berlin in the 1930s were
seen by many critics to epitomize the dicta-
tors' megalomania. Such plans also exemplified the symbolic adaptability of classicism.
While both leaders regarded their regimes as
the cutting edge of modern society, each pre-

urban surroundings, rather than in the sterile isolation of monumental centers (fig. 14).

Although the appropriateness of traditional monumental imagery in our time often has been questioned, there has been no truly satisfactory replacement. The difficulties some architects have encountered in adapting modern architectural concepts to monumental settings may be seen in L'Enfant Plaza in Washington. This complex provides a contemporary counterpart to the overt classicism of Federal Triangle, and while its hybrid design retains classical elements of symmetry and axiality, the accompanying buildings eschew historical detail. Few would deem its bland and boring ambience an improvement on the traditional imagery dominating the north side of the Mall.

A variant on the design of monumental space was attempted in the early 1950s by Le Corbusier in Chandigarh, the capital of Punjab in India.[15] Although a provincial capital, Chandigarh was intended as a symbol of postindependence India, and was given strong support by the national government. As conceived by Le Corbusier, the composition of the capitol complex was somewhat asymmetrical, employing varied circulation levels, and in-

corporating landscaped earth mounds to define the space. In its architectural concept, the monumental building reflected a notable departure from the idiom of prewar modernism. Characterized by bold sculptural massing and ornamented with ceremonial loggias and porticoes, the government buildings of Chandigarh evoke the timelessness and dignity traditionally associated with monumental structures (fig. 15).

As in many other monumental schemes, however, the scale of spatial composition was based on an architectural conception of vista and the abstract relation of sculptural masses, rather than on human use. As Le Corbusier phrased it, "The question of optics became paramount when we had to decide where to put the government buildings. . . . The geometrical event was, in truth, a sculpture of the intellect." [16] The principal buildings, the Palace of the Assembly (1953–1963) and the High Court (1951–1956), face each other across a 450-meter expanse of concrete which, in the Indian climate, creates an intimidating barrier rather than a link between structures. The lifeless expanse is neither a place of ceremony nor a functional circulation area (fig. 16).

Generally, urban spaces that have retained the greatest attraction over the years are those that have evolved to fulfill some purpose other than the physical separation of buildings. It also seems clear that the successful impact of a monumental space is in many ways dependent on its relation to the surrounding city. In this respect, the Washington government center is far better integrated with the urban fabric than those of New Delhi, Brasilia, Canberra, or Chandigarh. In the latter cities, the spatial impact of a mall is vitiated by its being largely surrounded by space rather than being framed and dramatized. The Washington Mall benefits from a partial juxtaposition with urban surroundings, but these are largely restricted to government offices and public institutions. There is little in the adjacent districts to generate life or bring people into frequent and casual contact with the Mall.

I recently met a European scholar who had been a fellow at the National Gallery of Art's Center for Advanced Study in the Visual Arts. Unfamiliar with Washington, he had requested housing within walking distance of the gallery. The gallery staff doubtless did their best in responding to this extraordinary request, accommodating the visiting scholar in what he contemptuously described as, "some sort of motel," in the southwest redevelopment district. His European experience clearly had not prepared him for the National Gallery's isolation from ordinary urban amenities. Had he been attached to the Louvre in Paris or the National Gallery in London, for example, he would have found himself in the midst of a vital and varied central district.

Of all the monumental capitals, Rome probably encompasses the closest integration of monumentality and intimacy within the fabric of the city. Eleanor Clark once commented on the smallness of many of the spaces, stating that they "give no warnings, so that suddenly the Pantheon or the huge volutes of Sant'Ignazio are crowding right over you; you are not allowed to stand off, it seems you are not allowed to admire at all; it is as though a giant mother were squashing you to her breast." Clark maintained that the streets and squares of the old quarters of the city "do not constitute an *outside* in our sense, but a great withinness, an interior, and running water is its open fire. Even a tourist can tell in a Roman street that he is in something and not outside of something as he would be in most cities. In Rome to go out is to go home." As to the sweeping expanses of Saint Peter's Square, Clark noted that it is "not a place for reasonable individuals to stroll with a happy sense of partaking in the achievement and somehow

16. Chandigarh, view of plaza from High Court toward Assembly Building
Author photograph

corresponding to it, as they would in such a square in Paris. It is a place for people to congregate in the terrific force of their gregariousness, their mass cravings. . . . but when there is no saint being made or other spectacle, it is lifeless. . . . But then as suddenly you find it filled another way; another sequence has begun. It is a sunny winter afternoon, and now even this enormous space has become a living room, or public nursery. The Dome, announcing itself for miles around as the center of the world, is actually presiding like a hen over thousands of babies and mothers and lovers and very ancient people strewn all over the steps of Bernini's colonnade and the awesome area it encloses, not as if they owned it but really owning it. It is where they live. The fountains . . . are as local as a barnyard pump. There is no distance; there is no awe of anything (figs. 17, 18)." [17]

Obviously, those modern theorists who believed the need for monumentality to be past were seriously misjudging modern society. There will always be a desire for special places and buildings, for monuments that commemorate our institutions and our ideals. Yet, the most effective monuments are at the same time familiar, accessible, and part of our lives.

19. Author and friends on
Capitol grounds
From *Evening Star* (Washington, 1936)

artistic merit as well. But it was too late for me to be indoctrinated: I had already learned other lessons. When I was small, the Capitol was my guardian and friend. I was awestruck that human beings could have conceived and built this intricate and gigantic thing. It was like a stone landscape crowned with an iron mountain that I scaled many times. I went to the Capitol for solitude and escape, as a place to dream. To live in intimacy with such grandeur, and to feel personally enhanced by it, was one of the advantages of living in a slum that city planners were itching to demolish (fig. 19).

Capitol Hill is the only area where monumental Washington in any way abuts on the city's ordinary fabric. For most of its expanse, although it provides a superb site for special occasions, the Mall lacks an easy integration with the life of the city. An obvious point of comparison is the monumental axis of Paris. The great linear complex extending from the Louvre along the Tuileries Gardens and the Champs Elysées to the Arch of Triumph provides a recurrent juxtaposition and interaction of the ceremonial and the secular. The Louvre is closely bordered on two sides with busy, high-density mixtures of commerce and

I was attracted to Eleanor Clark's description of Saint Peter's Square, because it reflects what I felt about the Capitol as a child. I owned it. It was where I lived. Of course when I grew older, I was taught to regard such building as social waste and was urged to denigrate its

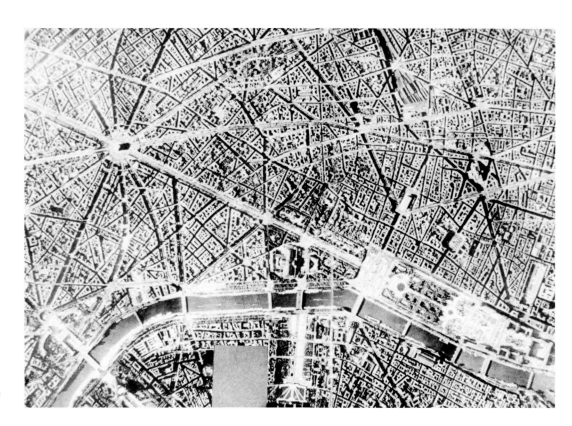

20. Paris, monumental axis
from Louvre to Place d'Etoile
Institute Geographique National

residence. The Tuileries Gardens retain their original role as a pleasure ground, and provide a verdant foil for the closely-packed buildings adjacent. The Place de la Concorde has grandeur of scale while at the same time providing a busy hub for city circulation and transport. Linking the Place de la Concorde with the Arch of Triumph, the Avenue des Champs Elysées also functions as one of the liveliest commercial streets of the city, and one of the most heavily trafficked arteries (figs. 20, 21).

The great monuments of Paris do not sit in tranquil surroundings, yet they suffer no denigration from nearby activity. The scale and dignity of the Arch of Triumph are in some ways enhanced by the counterpoint of street traffic and the nearby cafés and theaters. Monuments sometimes serve us most effectively when they can leaven the bread of daily existence.

In the course of extended stays in Paris, I found the Arch of Triumph forming part of my daily experience of the city. I never intentionally visited the arch; it was simply there. It suddenly loomed up with almost hallucinatory splendor when I emerged from the Métro on my way to have root canal work. I passed it in taxis, glimpsed it while crossing streets. No matter what the circumstances, I was momentarily moved by its solemnity. Surrounded by urban distractions, it embodied an enduring island of memory, and provoked a disquieting layering of sensations. Involuntarily, I found myself pondering such things as madness and nobility, heroism and savagery, life and death, and all while waiting for a traffic light to change in front of Le Drugstore.

One of the most conspicuous, and perhaps controversial, departures from the L'Enfant plan by the Senate Park Commission in 1901 was the rejection of L'Enfant's concept of a major street extending westward from the Capitol, in favor of a swath of grass. Elbert Peets has observed in his analyses of the McMillan Plan that while the architects toured Europe in search of inspiration, they seemed influenced less by the urban imagery of Paris and other cities than the rural atmosphere of the large estates surrounding the great chateaux and country houses (pls. LXX–LXXXII). He once queried, "Is the Mall country, or is it city? Now if the Washington Monument . . . stood in some deserted place, visited only by an occasional pilgrim, it would be glorious to

21. Paris, Arch of Triumph
Author photograph

approach it along a grassy opening between dark and ancient trees and to find it standing alone in a broad meadow. But the Monument is not a hermit." Peets pointed out that, "L'Enfant, when Washington was a forest, dreamed of the Mall as a fashionable Parisian avenue, while the [Senate Park] Commission of 1901, with a big city spreading all about them, dreamed of the Mall as a quiet sanctuary from the city's noise and bustle." [18] The existing Mall must have appeared to the commission a chaotic jumble, marred by the encroachments of a variety of inappropriate urban elements. Apparently obsessed with freeing the government center from contamination, the planners isolated the Mall from the city. As a result, the Mall creates an impressive void, but it is far from the vital urban spine encompassed in the Parisian axis.

The monumental axis of Paris, of course, was not planned as a totality. It developed in piecemeal fashion over centuries, reflecting an overall consistency of vision among those who extended and embellished it. The remarkable balance and contrast of urban components, the fusion of animation and sublimity, that now characterize its spatial sequence are essentially products of the past century, while the Champs Elysées acquired its present image of glamorous modernity during the 1920s. Still evolving, the monumental center of Paris reflects a fortuitous interworking of private and governmental patronage.

In a capital city, the monumental center has multiple functions. It embellishes the urban fabric and, ideally, enriches the lives of those who live there. But it does not belong to the city alone. Monumental Washington belongs to the nation, and its self-containment tends to underline this relationship. For the thousands of tourists who visit Washington, the Mall provides a separate city of shrines. Within a single great composition, the legislative, judicial, and executive headquarters are impressively exhibited, accompanied by major cultural institutions and commemorative monuments to national heroes. Thus the Mall functions in some ways like a monumental theme park, enabling the visitor to "do" Washington without extensive exposure to the rest of the city.

In addition to those visitors who come to see Washington, there are many who come to be seen—demonstrators who create a visual message as they exhibit their numbers on the vast expanse of the Mall. Whatever may have been the specific intentions of the McMillan Plan designers, they created a highly successful outdoor stage for mass assemblage. Just as the Mall provides a focus for tourists adjacent to, but separate from the main fabric of the city, it also can accommodate gatherings that in other cities might prove highly disruptive (pls. CXXXI–CXXXIV). The sort of protest demonstration that in Rome, Paris, or London can block streets, halt traffic, and create a disturbing presence in the city center, can, in Washington, be safely siphoned onto the Mall. As the symbolic locus of government, the Mall provides an appropriate site for symbolic confrontation between the people and their representatives.

Although the McMillan Plan is relatively recent, it has been widely accepted as embodying permanent outlines for the monumental image of Washington. While the rest of the city may evolve subject to the economic and social forces of modern urban growth, presumably the ceremonial core will persist intact. The creation of monumental building is always an act of faith, reflecting confidence in a continuity of social values and aesthetic perceptions. Drawing on the past and attempting to anticipate the future, the architects of the Mall based its composition on what appeared a long-lived and widespread tradition of design. So convincing was their vision that, today, to conceive of an alternative seems an artistic heresy. Nevertheless, all things change in time, and the life of a city can span centuries, even millennia. It is not inconceivable that the city we know will one day be substantially altered and even eclipsed. Meanwhile, the simple clarity of outline, comprehensible hierarchy of focal points, and visual drama of the Mall seem likely to be understood, appreciated, and maintained by many generations.

NOTES

1. Donald J. Olsen, *Town Planning in London: The Eighteenth and Nineteenth Centuries* (New Haven, 1964), 3.

2. Lewis Mumford, *The City in History: Its Origins, Its Transformations, and Its Prospects* (New York, 1961), 65.

3. For detailed discussion, see Robert Grant Irving, *Indian Summer: Lutyens, Baker, and Imperial Delhi* (New Haven, 1981); and Norma Evenson, *The Indian Metropolis: A View Toward the West* (New Haven, 1989).

4. Quoted in Robert Byron, "New Delhi I," *Country Life* 69 (6 June 1931), 708. C. Northcote Parkinson, *Parkinson's Law* (Boston, 1957), 60–61.

5. For discussion, see David Van Zanten, "Walter Burley Griffin's Design for Canberra, the Capital of Australia," in John Zukovsky, ed., *Chicago Architecture, 1872–1922: Birth of a Metropolis* (Munich, 1987), 318–343; Donald Leslie Johnson, *The Architecture of Walter Burley Griffin* (South Melbourne, Australia, 1977), 14–25; and Lionel Wigmore, *The Long View: A History of Canberra, Australia's National Capital* (Melbourne, Australia, 1963).

6. Quoted in "Parliament House," *Architecture in Australia* 69 (September 1980), 40.

7. For discussion, see Norma Evenson, *Two Brazilian Capitals: Architecture and Urbanism in Rio de Janeiro and Brasilia* (New Haven, 1973).

8. Quoted in "Pilot Plan for Brasilia," *Modulo 18* (1960).

9. Quoted in Willy Staubli, *Brasilia* (New York, 1966), 80.

10. "Parliament House," 1980, 56.

11. Anatole Senkevitch has shown that American skyscrapers also had a major influence on Stalin's Moscow, "The Postwar 'Wedding Cake' Skyscrapers in Moscow and Their New York Antecedents" (paper read at the annual meeting of the Society of Architectural Historians, Washington, 1986).

12. Quoted in Reyner Banham, *Theory and Design in the First Machine Age* (London, 1960), 129.

13. John Summerson, *Heavenly Mansions and Other Essays on Architecture* (New York, 1963), 203, 209.

14. Jane Jacobs, *The Death and Life of Great American Cities* (New York, 1961), 25.

15. For further discussion see Norma Evenson, *Chandigarh* (Berkeley, 1966); and Norma Evenson, *Le Corbusier: The Machine and the Grand Design* (New York, 1969), 97–106.

16. Le Corbusier, *Modulor II* (Cambridge, Mass., 1958), 214–215.

17. Eleanor Clark, *Rome and a Villa* (New York, 1974), 53–55.

18. Paul D. Spreiregen, ed., *On the Art of Designing Cities: Selected Essays of Elbert Peets* (Cambridge, Mass., 1968), 94, 92.

PAMELA SCOTT
Cornell University

"This Vast Empire":

The Iconography of the Mall, 1791–1848

Founding a city in the sparsley settled countryside – "the wigwam of empire" [1] – to be the capital of the newly formed United States, rather than designating an area within any existing city, was both a political and symbolic act of great significance for the newly formed nation. From 5 September 1774 until its removal to the federal city on the Potomac on 1 December 1800, Congress had relocated eleven times. Although a federal "district" had been proposed as early as 1783, the site on the Potomac River was not enacted into law until 16 July 1790, following protracted negotiations between regional interests. These debates had been so fractious that President Washington wrote the Marquis La Luzerne on 10 August 1790, that they were "more in danger of having convulsed the government" than any other event. [2] The government's need for jurisdiction over the area containing federal buildings of a civic and military nature was real. Equally important, a national capital conferred on the federal government national and international prestige and added to its symbolic power to carry the Constitution into effect.

Pierre Charles L'Enfant, whom George Washington retained to design the national capital late in 1790 or early in 1791, was cognizant of these issues (fig. 1, pls. IV–IX). His plan for the "federal city" embodied the history of the founding and the early organization of the federal government. Fundamental tenets of the Constitution – the balance of powers inherent in executive versus legislative prerogatives and federal versus states rights – were built into the matrix of his city plan. The spatial complexity of the design, always viewed either as a geometric ideal or as a response to the topography of the site, was also the means of expressing this fundamental iconographic program. [3] The placement of the state avenues to reflect their geographical location within the country and to correlate with certain proposed public buildings embodied the historical forces that brought the federal city into being. Finally, L'Enfant's choice of French prototypes to provide the aesthetic structure for the design was not only a result of his background and training, it probably was intended to commemorate France's contribution to the American struggle for independence.

Many contemporary descriptions of the Potomac valley extolled the unusual natural beauty of the area, [4] and and L'Enfant was particularly sensible of its grandeur and variety. On 22 April 1791, Congressman William L. Smith was taken over the grounds by L'Enfant and quoted him as saying, "Nothing can be more admirably adapted for the purpose [of the federal city]; nature had done much for it, and with the aid of art it will become the wonder of the world." Smith himself found the site of the city "extremely grand and romantic." [5] J. Cartwright's panoramic view done

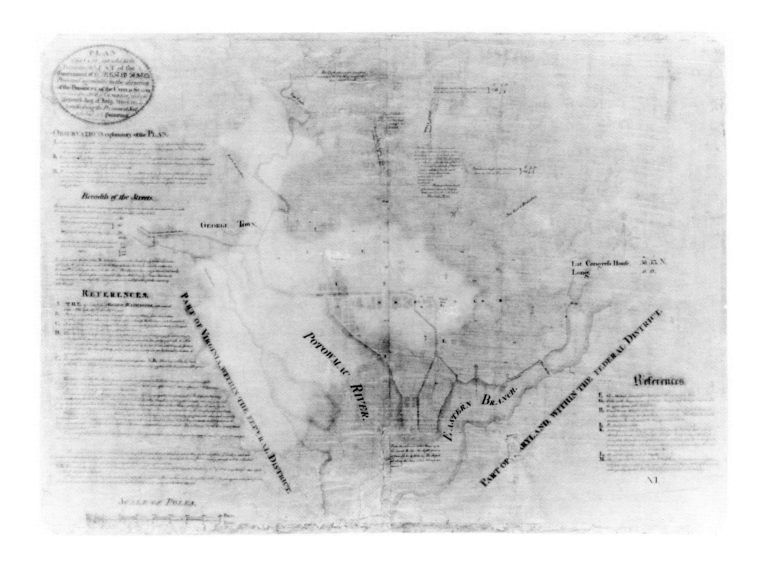

1. Attributed to Pierre Charles L'Enfant, *Plan of the City intended for the Permanent Seat of the Government of the United States . . .*, August (?) 1791 Library of Congress

from a painting of about 1800 by George Jacob Beck depicted the landscape's varied character (pl. XXXVII).

L'Enfant's earliest accounts of the area written to George Washington confirm that he selected the site and visualized the city's elements with a basically picturesque sensibility. He was particularly conscious of the prospects to be had from each major building. On 26 March 1791, in his first report to the president, L'Enfant commented on the importance of placing the public buildings on eminences, as "from these height very grand build[i]ng would rear with a majestic aspect over the Country round and might be advantageously seen From Twenty mile off." In the same letter he noted that a city predicated on

an even grid would be well for level ground "w[h]ere . . . no surrounding object being interesting it become[s] Indifferent which way the opening of a street may be directed," but would not be suitable for the site selected as all the natural, picturesque advantages would be "annilated." He concluded that "such regular plan . . . become[s] at last tiresome and insipide & could never be in its orrigine but a mean contrivance of some cool imagination wanting a sense of the real grand and trewly beautifull." [6] L'Enfant may have been referring to a now-lost design submitted by Joseph Clark, architect of the Annapolis statehouse, to President Washington on 3 December 1790.[7]

More likely L'Enfant was responding to Thomas Jefferson's plan of the city executed in March 1791 (pl. III).[8] As early as August 1790 Jefferson had expressed his thoughts on the spatial relationships within the federal city: the division of city blocks, width of streets, and height of buildings.[9] Presumably these ideas were incorporated some six months later into his design for the entire city. Composed of an even Roman grid, Jefferson's federal city was intimate in scale, but expandable upon a module, a pragmatic response to the reality of available resources. The plan extended to Rock Creek on the west and Tiber Creek on the east, covering only about one-twentieth of the area encompassed by L'Enfant's plan. The focus of Jefferson's city was the "public walks" and the buildings they contained, the capitol and president's house. His major concern was not an extensive urban infrastructure so markedly a part of L'Enfant's design, but rather providing immediately for the most necessary buildings, and giving a sense of a settled city. The public walks, or mall, surrounding and connecting these buildings would have allowed for panoramic vistas of the entire area in an open and natural setting, in contrast to L'Enfant's mall, which was both contained within the urban fabric and complex in its architectural and landscape development.

During his five-year tenure as minister to France, Jefferson had visited numerous public and private gardens throughout Europe and had designed a picturesque garden for his Paris residence, the Hôtel de Langeac.[10] In the spring of 1786, Jefferson toured English picturesque gardens using Thomas Whately's *Observations on Modern Gardening* (1770) as a guide. He responded favorably to the naturalistic phase of the picturesque but found that William Kent's early gardens at Chiswick (completed in 1736) showed "still too much of art." In his 1788 notes drafted for Americans visiting Europe, Jefferson suggested that gardens were "peculiarly worth the attention of an American, because it is the country of all others where the noblest gardens may be made without expense. We have only to cut out the superabundant plants."[11]

These comments, together with the *ferme ornée* that he designed as his own residence, Monticello (1769–1809), suggest that Jefferson's mall, or public gardens, might well have been left in a quasi-natural state with minimal embellishment. The two public buildings would have been the sole visual and symbolic focus in a compact, yet open and natural setting, one indeed picturesque without the aid of art. Jefferson proposed a city modeled on his ideal for an American urban center, small in size and limited in scope, rather than a European city in embryo that would perpetuate the evils he associated with urban life. In a letter to Joseph Priestley dated 9 April 1803, Jefferson said "nature has formed [the federal city] on a beautiful scale and circumstances destine [it] for a great one." His later interest in integrating nature with the human-made in geometric grids for city plans, as well as his influence in mapping the Northwest Territory, suggests the dichotomy in Jefferson's thinking as he attempted to rationalize the American landscape.[12] He may have been influenced by the correlation made between political liberty and the freedom inherent in the picturesque garden, a recurring literary theme beginning as early as 1710, when Joseph Addison dreamed of the place where the Goddess of Liberty reigned.[13]

In contrast, L'Enfant's city was on an immense scale, far beyond the reasonable expectations of the government at that time, because he saw the federal capital as a symbolic representation of the country — "this vast empire."[14] The great extent of L'Enfant's city was unified by a dual system of communication; the unequal grid of streets established private neighborhoods of differing characters while numerous diagonal boulevards, public and ceremonial in nature, directly connected squares and circles throughout the fifty-seven-hundred-acre city.[15] Fifteen of these nodes were identified as squares to be developed by the states with the help of their prominent citizens. Although printed maps depict fifteen state avenues — Kentucky and Vermont were states by June 1791 — L'Enfant originally intended that there be thirteen,[16] representative of the original colonies. He dispersed these avenues, as well as the state squares, so that they would function as separate yet interrelated entities, symbolizing the distinct nature of the states within the nation of united states.

The disposition of the state avenues in the context of the whole city plan was particularly significant.[17] The northeastern states were clustered in the northern segment of the city, the southern in the southeastern quadrant, and the mid-Atlantic states in the center, reflecting not only the country's geography, but also its regional, political, and social alignments. The three prominent regions were represented by their most populous states – Virginia, Pennsylvania, and Massachusetts – having avenues traversing the entire city, with Virginia southernmost and Massachusetts northernmost. Pennsylvania Avenue was given primacy of place, its alignment passing through both the Capitol and President's House, because Philadelphia was the site of the signing of the Declaration of Independence in 1776, as well as of the Constitutional Convention in 1787.[18] Maryland and New Jersey avenues interesect Capitol Square, it seems, because the Continental Congress met at Baltimore, Annapolis, Princeton, and Trenton. Delaware, the fourth of the state streets abutting the Capitol, was presumably so honored because it was the first state to ratify the Constitution and the first to offer a ten-square-mile federal precinct within its boundaries.

New York Avenue passes through the President's Square, for although the state's major city served as a capital for the Continental Congress, an equally important historical association was that George Washington took the oath of presidential office there on 4 March 1789. L'Enfant had renovated New York's City Hall into Federal Hall for this event, as well as for the reception of the First Federal Congress. The decorations he designed for the building – thirteen stars in the frieze, thirteen arrows entwined with olive branches in tablets over the windows, and an eagle in the pediment – indicate L'Enfant's desire to establish an American iconography based on the country's adopted and invented emblems.[19]

The center of L'Enfant's federal city was an immense, T-shaped public park consisting of four interconnected segments, drawing together the public life of the city. The Capitol and the President's House formed the foci, both placed on elevated positions amid extensive gardens sloping down to the central Mall. South of the President's Grounds, separated by the canal, were the Monument Grounds, initially extending in a diagonal line along the Potomac and providing an area for ambassadorial residences. This sector was diminished in scale and altered to a rectangular configuration by the time the maps of the city were engraved in 1792. The Mall itself was composed of a central, tree-lined walkway flanked on both sides by buildings raised on

higher ground; these faced gardens of their own that sloped down to a central promenade.

L'Enfant first described the Mall in a letter to George Washington on 22 June 1791, as a "place of general resort," lined by theaters, assembly halls, academies, and "all sort of place[s] as may be attractive to the l[e]arned and afford diver[s]ion to the idle." [20] The Mall was to be the center of intellectual and artistic life of Washington. Again on 19 August he reiterated the importance of the "publick walk" in giving to the city "a superiority of agreements over most of the city of the world." [21] The official description published in the *Gazette of the United States*, in Philadelphia on 4 January 1792, specified in part:

H. A grand avenue 400 feet in breadth, and about a mile in length, bordered with gardens ending in a slope from the houses on each side: this avenue lead to the monument A. and connects the Congress garden with the
I. President's park and the
K. Well improved field, being a part of the walk from the President's house of about 1800 feet in breadth, and three fourths of a mile in length. Every lot deep coloured red, with green plots, designates some of the situations which command the most agreeable prospects, and which are best calculated for spacious houses and gardens, such as may accommodate foreign ministers, &c.[22]

Plans of numerous buildings, including those on and contiguous to the Mall, were depicted most clearly on the second map published by the Philadelphia engravers Thackara and Vallance in the fall of 1792 (fig. 2, pl. XII).[23] The sixteen C- or E-shaped "houses" paralleling the Mall that are depicted on all the maps of the period may have been intended as residences of government officials, foreign dignitaries, and the wealthy, in the tradition of the French eighteenth-century Parisian *hôtels*, either in addition to, or in conjunction with, L'Enfant's stated cultural usage. In 1795 an anonymous, nineteen-page *Essai sur la ville de Washington* was published in New York describing the city in more detail than, but in concert with, known L'Enfant descriptions.[24] The author of the *Essai* suggested the Mall as the center of the economic and social life of the city, envisaging the buildings lining the Mall as luxurious shops and residences. *Hôtels* lined both sides of the great space, but the facades on the north side facing the canal

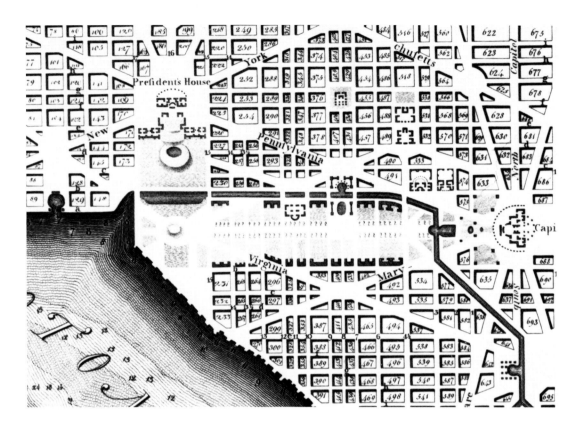

were integrated by an arcade, porticoes, and triumphal arches. The resultant gallery formed both a winter garden nine thousand feet in length and an elegant shopping precinct modeled on the Palais-Royal (1781–1784) in Paris. The central garden was to contain a *pièce d'eau* bordered by *allées* and dense groves of trees. The Mall was to become the meeting place for people of all states of the union and of all countries.[25]

The function of two major architectural elements on the Mall depicted on the second Thackara and Vallance map is elusive. One, on the canal between Seventh and Ninth streets, was identified in the January 1792 description as a fountain, but its scale and architectural complexity suggest a more important function, especially as it was located on the axis of the National Pantheon and the Naval Itinerary Column.[26] The second major element on the Mall proper, at the foot of Tenth to Twelfth streets, was probably for public entertainment and education—possibly a theater or a museum. It was distinguished on the Thackara and Vallance map from the "houses" on the Mall by its size, siting, and more intricate plan.

Located along the northern perimeter of the Mall extending as far as present-day F Street were the proposed sites for the National Pantheon (at F Street, between Seventh and Ninth), Judiciary Square (on E Street between Third and Fourth), a market and exchange complex, a "grand church," the national bank, and a theater.[27] Judiciary Square, the site for the Supreme Court, did not have the prominence of the Capitol and President's House on the plan because the Constitution did not accord the judiciary equal powers with the legislative and executive branches of government. Easy access to these important nodes was by way of the canal and facilitated by three short diagonal streets, the only diagonals not accounted for by the state avenues. These streets linked the governmental functions of the city to its social, intellectual, and commercial aspects, beginning at the Capitol, extending to Judiciary Square and the Mall, then passing through the business sector, and terminating at the President's Grounds.[28] The 1795 anonymous description of Washington emphasized the importance of the city's varied functions to ensure its success, a point reiterated many times by L'Enfant in his correspondence and reports.[29]

Prospects of the Potomac from all buildings

in this central core would have been to the west, the Mall's open end, and according to L'Enfant, would "acquire new Swe[e]tness being had over the green of a field well level and made bril[li]ant by Shade of [a] few tree[s] Artfully planted." [30] It was here at the nexus of the two axes established by the Capitol and president's mansion that L'Enfant placed the bronze equestrian of George Washington voted by Congress in 1783 to commemorate him as commander of the victorious Revolutionary War forces. [31] A national monument, the Monument to Liberty designed by Giuseppe Ceracchi, had been proposed in October 1791. The author of the *Essai* placed it in the President's Grounds, south of the mansion. [32]

The orientation of the Mall — open to the west — implies the future development and growth of the country. Selecting the Potomac site for the capital city was partially predicated on the river's direct link to the western rivers, the means by which the wealth of the

nation could be realized. The eastern end of the Mall was terminated by the Capitol, raised high on Jenkin's Hill, the famous "pedestal awaiting its monument." Emerging from beneath the Capitol was a hundred-foot-wide cascade dropping forty feet to a basin in the canal below. [33] Allegorical statues of great American rivers — the Delaware and the Hudson — situated on the terraces of the Capitol would be the apparent source of this cascade, according to the 1795 *Essai*. [34] At the foot of Capitol Hill, facing the Mall, L'Enfant called for a sculpture group entitled "Liberty hailing nature out of its Slumber," to have been executed by an "eminent Italian sculptor." [35] Liberty Hailing Nature Out of Its Slumber was the iconography of the city: liberty brought the federal city into being, and the city physically and symbolically embodied the country and the history of its founding. [36] The federal government was the agent of civilization, expressed by the federal city carved out of a near

3. Site plan of Versailles, engraving by Abbé Delagrive, 1746
Library of Congress

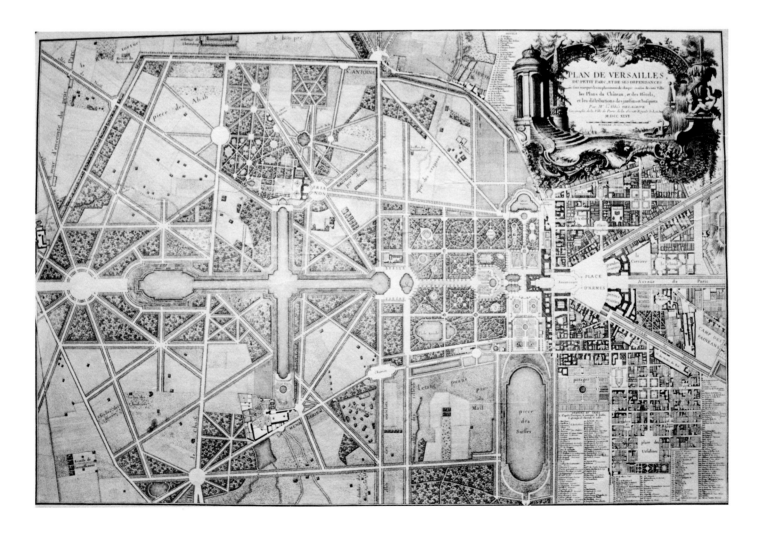

wilderness. L'Enfant almost certainly intended that a large part of the greater public park focusing on the Mall would be planted in the natural, picturesque style of landscape gardening, attested to by his few trees "Artfully planted" on the monument grounds. Not only the country's size, but its pastoral nature affected L'Enfant, as it did Jefferson. It is the fusion of the formal and picturesque elements that gives the L'Enfant plan its unique character.

The major precedents for L'Enfant's plan are found in the French tradition of baroque planning; however, the relationship between L'Enfant's plan and its sources is complex and synthetic. L'Enfant's intention was to create something uniquely American. As his ideological framework was a synthesis of American history and aspirations, so his aesthetic structure was also a synthesis of ideas derived from meaningful archetypes. Versailles may be one such symbolic and formal source, representing the French court of Louis XVI, America's ally during the Revolution, although its layout is more closely followed in the McMillan Plan of 1901–1902. The triangular conjunction of palace and trianons at Versailles and the garden layout with its numerous and

widely-spaced nodes connected by *allées* are most often cited as L'Enfant's immediate inspiration for organizing the large areas encompassed by his plan (fig. 3).

Other French work, rural and urban, probably played an influential role as well. The royal chateau of Marly, the hermitage begun by Louis XIV in 1679, offered an iconographic schema and a landscape not dissimilar to that of the federal city. Marly's site had been selected for its wild, mountainous aspect and its salubrious air (fig. 4). Jules Hardouin-Mansart's design was devised to give to the king and his courtiers both a relaxing, "rustic" environment and a privacy unknown either at court in Paris or at Versailles. The buildings provided a model for an architectural ensemble of separate but interrelated parts based upon a U-shaped plan, with the king's chateau at the head of a terraced parterre and six sets of pavilions for courtiers ranged on either side of a central, sunken basin. The similarities between this complex and L'Enfant's plan are strong: the Capitol takes the place of the king's chateau; L'Enfant's "houses" replace the pavilions; the tree-lined, sunken Mall, the basin.[37]

Mansart's landscape design at Marly was emphatically axial and geometric, hierarchical and emblematic, with numerous diagonals radiating from foci throughout the grounds. Yet the scheme also possessed the beginnings of a picturesque sensibility in the outlying "wilderness" areas.[38] As at Versailles a *patte-d'oie* emanating from the main block of the chateau reinforced the main axis and introduced two new axes while opening up reciprocal vistas. L'Enfant's repeated use of *pattes-d'oie* in his nodes connected by radial streets was directly descended from these large-scale baroque planning devices, but nevertheless, the effect was radically different. Versailles was laid out on a plain; Marly on a smaller plain carved out of a hilly terrain. L'Enfant's plan was superimposed on a landscape irregular in contour both in its elevations and along its primary edges, the shores of the Potomac and Anacostia rivers, and Rock Creek. On paper it was a baroque plan; in reality it had a picturesque aspect, incorporating, indeed taking advantage of, the natural characteristics of the site.[39] L'Enfant was responding not to seventeenth-century French traditions, but to the interpretation of those traditions during his own time.

4. Perspective view of Marly, engraving by Gilles Mortain
From *Les plans, profils et elevations des ville, et château de Versailles* (Paris, 1716)

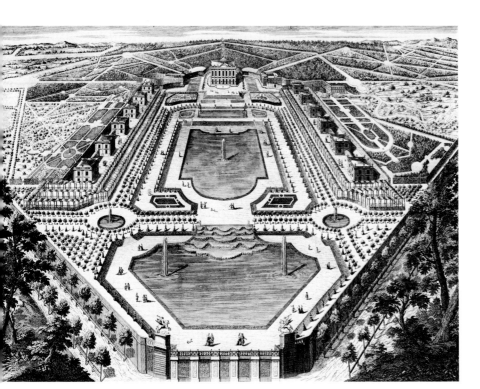

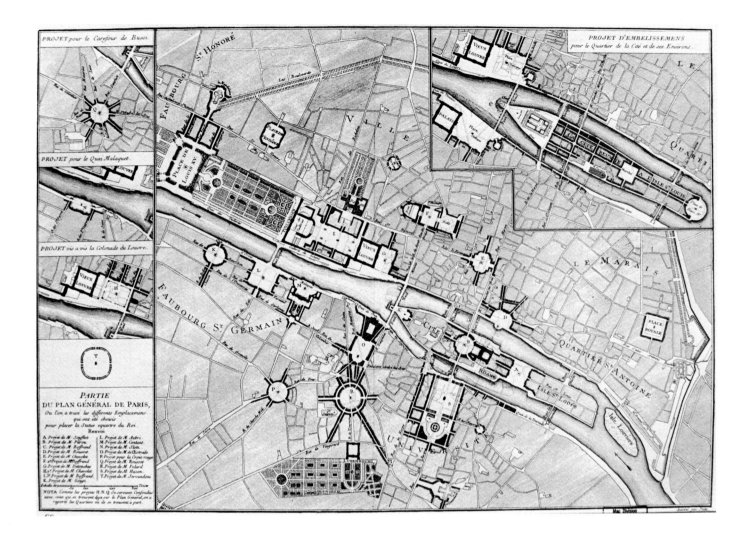

5. Part of the general plan of Paris, engraving by Pierre Patte

From *Monuments érigés en France* (Paris, 1765)

The Paris that L'Enfant would have known, both as it stood and in proposed plans, played at least as significant a role as Versailles and Marly in giving form and meaning to the federal city. Although Washington was a "ready built City out of the Earth" and justifiably partook of ideas frequently applied to landscape architecture, it was still envisaged by L'Enfant as a great city, not "a mere contemptible hamlet."[40] Furthermore, baroque as well as picturesque principles regulating landscape architecture were also applicable to urban design as defined by seventeenth- and eighteenth-century French architectural theory. By 1764, when the Abbé Laugier published his *Observations sur l'architecture*, he was able to define a modern city as one based on a picturesque park in both extent and organization.[41] Squares, intersections, and streets would be varied within a framework of order and hierarchy. The resultant effect would be one of apparent irregularity and accidental conjuction of architectural and urban landscape elements. Pierre Patte's plan of Paris, published in his *Monuments érigés en France* (1765), is a composite of several proposed schemes for a square dedicated to Louis XV and represents the application of Laugier's principles to an existing urban environment (fig. 5). L'Enfant's Washington had a similar, varied effect of irregularly dispersed public spaces. French interpretations and use of picturesque design, still influenced by baroque ordering principles, entailed a higher degree of formal order than contemporaneous English work.[42] The characteristically French balance of varied spatial and architectural effects was more readily integrated into the urban

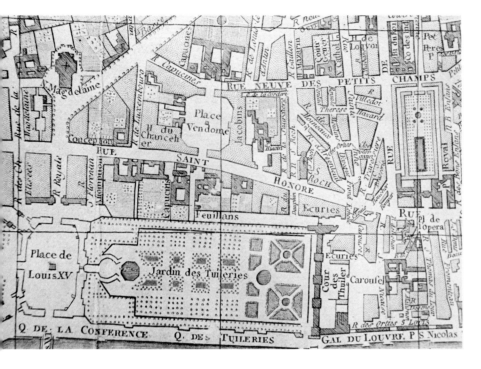

6. *Nouveau Plan Routier de la Ville et Fauxbourgs de Paris*, map by Esnauts and Rapilly, 1790, detail
Library of Congress

7. Guillaume Coustou, statues of *France* and *Amérique*, 1745, Place de la Concorde, Paris
Author photograph

corde in 1795), established a triangular relationship between church and state that was both formal and symbolic (fig. 6). The Place Louis XV, designed by Ange-Jacques Gabriel in 1753, gave definition to these important axes and provided a major open space for Edmé Bouchardon's equestrian statue of Louis XV (1748–1772). L'Enfant's placement of a comparable sculpture honoring George Washington in the same relative position probably was inspired by this arrangement in the governing center of Paris, and the geometric configuration of L'Enfant's Mall suggests more of a debt to Marly and the Tuileries precinct than to Versailles.[43]

The adoption of a French baroque framework, interpreted today as the emblem of absolute monarchism, has occasionally been viewed as an inappropriate prototype for the capital city of a country dedicated to liberty. For L'Enfant, however, forging links between France and America would have been appropriate. France had been midwife to the American Revolution and Louis XVI had provided the troops (that included L'Enfant) who helped to win it. The Treaty of Paris of 1783 ended the Revolution. As L'Enfant commemorated the historical significance of the states in his plan, so he probably alluded to the essential role that France had played in the birth of American liberty in his overt allusions to French architecture and urban planning.

Marly also offered a richly emblematic model in its representation of France's, and America's, place in history. Louis XIV's Paris was seen as a renewed Rome; Louis XIV's Marly was linked to antique villas and gardens through its forms and sculptural program, while at the same time proclaiming France's modern achievements in the arts and sciences.[44] In 1745 a specific American meaning was introduced at Marly when Guillaume Coustou's wild, barely restrained horses representing *France* and *America* were placed in the gardens (fig. 7).[45] Coustou's sculpture symbolized America not as an abstract part of the universe, as traditionally depicted in the four continents iconography, but as part of France's history, for until the 1763 Treaty of Paris expelled France from the North American continent, America had represented France's empire and future.

L'Enfant was not able to carry his ideas for the federal city to completion, as he was forced

The Paris that existed in the 1780s was at least as potent a force for L'Enfant as Patte's ideal Paris. The integration of public and private components, grand and domestic in scale, that was particularly apparent around the Louvre and Tuileries, provided a significant urban model for L'Enfant. Two axes, the first formed by the Louvre, Tuileries, and Champs Elysées, and the second by the Madeleine and Place Louis XV (renamed the Place de la Con-

fabric than the English garden, which, when introduced into cities in the nineteenth century, tended to be self-contained.

to resign his position on 2 March 1792, due to the difficulty he had subordinating himself to the authority of the commissioners charged with bringing the city into being. Thereafter, Washington, Jefferson, and the city commissioners had to concentrate their efforts on completing the President's House and the Capitol for receiving the federal government in 1800. The question of the Mall was again directly addressed on 1 October 1796 when the commissioners of the city, writing to George Washington, urged development of the 289-acre Mall by erecting an "elegant building," which "would add greatly to the beauty and pleasure of the Scene, and would be the means of bringing the whole into more immediate notice and cultivation." On 2 March 1797, when Washington transmitted the official map of the city to the commissioners, the Mall's correctly surveyed boundaries were defined, encompassing 227 acres; its stated purpose was for the health and ornament of the city.[46] Although development of the Mall was neglected during the next half century, there were repeated proposals for its use, generated both by Congress and private groups or individuals. Ad hoc private use is recorded as early as 1804 and 1805 when fairs were held near Center Market.[47] Even as late as 1850 the Mall was used for private cultivation of "grain or vegetables" and for storage of "lumber and firewood and occasionally for rubbish of an offensive and unsightly kind."[48]

A more consequential agenda had begun to unfold on 5 July 1812, when Congress passed an act authorizing the president to lease public reservations for ten years to individuals who would improve the grounds "for public walks, botanic gardens, or other public purposes"; the act included all public sites in the city.[49] George Washington had proposed a botanical garden for the capital as early as 1796, and during the next two decades many people urged its implementation, not only to provide fields for agricultural and botanical experiments but to serve as a pleasure garden.[50] In 1817 a botanical garden imbued with picturesque ideals was proposed by Edward Cutbush, president of the Columbian Institute, Washington's first major intellectual society. Describing Washington as the American city with the greatest "assemblage of sublime views," Cutbush believed that such a facility would stimulate the cultivation of private gardens within the city, serve to promote botanical studies, and exert a moral and didactic influence on society.[51] In 1820 Congress granted the institute five acres at the Mall's east end between Maryland and Pennsylvania avenues. The grounds were fenced in, and two oval ponds, one with an island, were excavated the next year. During the fall of 1823 the ground was drained and partly leveled and gravel walks with borders were laid out,[52] perhaps in response to Charles Bulfinch's 1822 design for enclosing and landscaping the Capitol grounds (pl. XVIII).[53] In this plan Bulfinch indicated that his restrained treatment of the Capitol grounds would appropriately be extended to include the Botanic Garden and the Mall itself. A single row of trees was densely planted to enclose broad, expansive lawns broken only by minor plantings and a hint of a serpentine walk.

Earlier, in 1815, Benjamin Henry Latrobe had also included the east end of the Mall in his picturesque landscape plan for the Capitol grounds (fig. 8). As a component of eighteenth-century aesthetic thought, picturesque design was certainly known to Latrobe, whose education as an architect and engineer was then unparalleled in America.[54] The pleasure he found in the nearly untouched American landscape was expressed in his 1798 "Essay on Landscape," and in a series of watercolor compositions in which he fused the triad of enlightenment aesthetic thought: the beautiful, the sublime, and the picturesque.[55] Within the complex geometric confines established by the streets of the Capitol grounds, Latrobe conceived a succession of picturesque gardens, replete with clumps of trees and broad meadows; for the Mall he designed an artificial lake with an island in the manner of Capability Brown. Yet the overt emblematic structure, so important a part of L'Enfant's heritage and fundamental to the early phase of the picturesque garden in England, was lacking. Latrobe's landscape was nature enhanced and space controlled through an episodic series of intimate landscapes removed from the city by perimeter planting of trees.

For Latrobe a picturesque garden was only one possible solution for developing the Mall. In 1816, in response to congressional interest in reviving George Washington's 1796 scheme for a "National University" in the federal capital,[56] Latrobe designed a walled, U-shaped complex organized on the same principles as

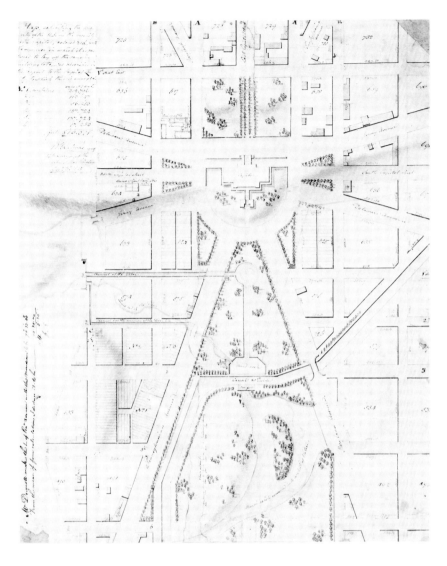

8. Benjamin Henry Latrobe,
Plan of the Capitol Grounds,
1815
Library of Congress

Thomas Jefferson's plan for the University of Virginia (pl. XIX).[57] Placed near the Mall's western extremity, the thirty-four-acre site was planned so that construction could take place over many years. A freestanding, domed church marked the axis of the Capitol as did an amphiprostyle temple that served as both an entrance and an observatory for the university.

The difficulty of developing the Mall with key elements axially aligned with the Capitol is evident in the university plan. A canal running parallel to the Mall had always been envisioned for the practical purpose of draining the swampy area south of Pennsylvania Avenue and allowing easy access to the heart of the city. Latrobe himself was hired by the Washington Canal Company (privately char-

tered on 1 May 1802) to produce designs for the canal, and he completed the drawings in February 1804. Subsequent realization of the canal created an imbalance, for now the Mall's center was not on axis with that of the Capitol. A congressional act approved on 31 May 1832, further reduced the acreage on the north side of the Mall in order to widen the canal, purchased by the city government the previous year, from 80 to 150 feet.[58]

In 1831 Robert Mills, who had moved to Washington in 1829, was hired by the city to redesign the canal, particularly to improve its entrance.[59] He submitted three alternate schemes in which he consciously maintained the axial relationship of the Capitol with the proposed equestrian statue of Washington by dividing the Mall into a grid and thus diminishing the effect of the imbalance (fig. 9). Mills' design was derived from the gardenesque principles of landscape design practiced by Humphry Repton and popularized and expanded by John Claudius Loudon, which called for beds of flowers, shrubs, and trees to be enjoyed on an intimate scale, rather than the parklike settings of the eighteenth-century English garden.[60]

Completion of the Capitol in 1829 and the optimism (and growth of the bureaucracy) associated with Andrew Jackson's presidency spurred many enterprises in the city. The Mall benefited immediately by the improvements to the canal, and projects that were both practical and aesthetic in nature were proposed. In 1830, I. L. Skinner, a civil engineer, suggested that a thirty-acre basin be constructed down the center of the Mall, providing a "highly ornamental finish" to the neglected public grounds as well as supplying the city with water.[61]

The 1826 bequest by the English scientist, James Smithson, to establish an institution "for the increase and diffusion of knowledge among men" had an enormous impact on the Mall. Although his will was not settled until 1838, numerous individuals and organizations wished to participate in forming the institution. Senator Rufus Choate of Massachusetts promoted a great national library, John Quincy Adams an astronomical observatory, and numerous others lobbied for the revival of the National University, a museum, or botanical and agricultural gardens.[62] John McArann, a Philadelphia horticulturist, cam-

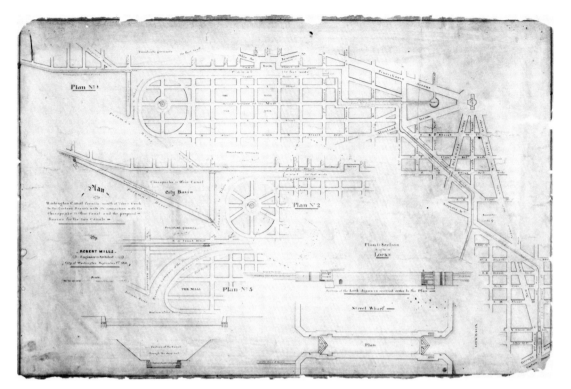

9. Robert Mills, *Plan of the Washington Canal*, 1831
National Archives

10. Robert Mills, proposal for Smithsonian Institution, 1841
National Archives

paigned to interest Congress in purchasing both his botanical collections and his museum of natural curiosities for a national museum.[63] Lieutenant Charles Wilkes' exploring expedition to the South Seas in 1838–1842 resulted in the collection of natural specimens of all kinds that became the nucleus for the national museum. A greenhouse to accommodate the plants collected by Wilkes was erected on the Mall in the Botanical Garden in 1842.[64]

The most significant initiative for the Mall's development to date was launched in May 1840, when the National Institution for the Promotion of Science was founded by Secretary of War Joel R. Poinsett with the expectation of providing a Washington-based organization to receive and administer the Smithson bequest.[65] The following year Poinsett commissioned Robert Mills to design a building for the National Institution and to prepare plans for a botanical garden on the Mall between Seventh and Twelfth streets (fig. 10, pls. XXVI, XXVII).[66] Mills' designs, dated 16 February 1841, could accommodate either a National Institution or a Smithsonian Institution (whichever should be sanctioned by Congress first) and responded to the numerous suggestions that had been advanced concerning its possible functions.

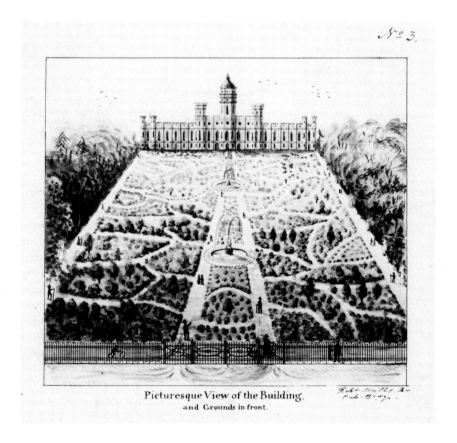

Picturesque View of the Building.
and Grounds in front.

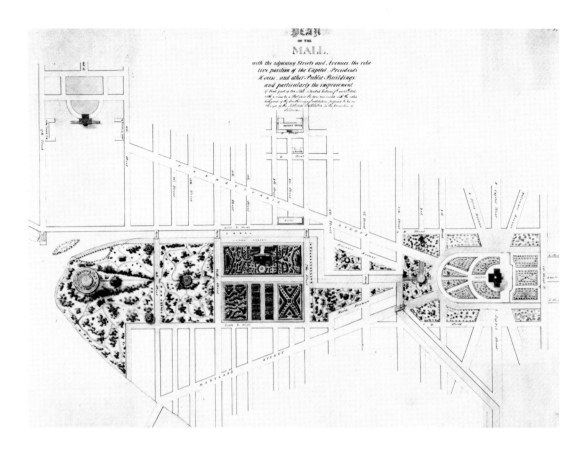

11. Robert Mills, *Plan of the Mall*, 1841
National Archives

With Poinsett's commission, Mills took the opportunity to propose a landscape plan for the entire Mall (fig. 11, pl. xxv). His plan also encompassed the Capitol grounds, and he maintained strict axiality in respect to the center line of the Capitol, organizing both landscape and architectural elements with this central vista as a primary concern. The Mall itself was divided into four segments by three cross streets connecting the northwest and southwest quadrants of the city. A rejuvenated Botanic Garden, at the Mall's east end, was subdivided into several segments by the city canal, one of which seems to have contained a major water element. Mills supplied alternate designs for the grounds of the new institution, one in the picturesque style, the other based on medieval medicinal gardens such as the Oxford Physic Garden. Both schemes contained maze-like parterres, at once formal and informal, with specimen plantings, as a major function of the institution was to supply agricultural and botanical experimentation fields. The western terminus contained an immense circular monument to

Washington on the site of L'Enfant's equestrian statue. The monument grounds, and those adjacent to it, as well as the Botanic Garden, were to be treated as an English picturesque park with serpentine walks, dense planting of clumps of trees, and vistas opening on garden pavilions. The more formal treatment of the institution grounds, in fact the picturesque interpretation of a medieval medicinal or botanic garden, was appropriate within gardenesque theory, which strived for a unity of landscape and architecture. These experimental gardens also provided a transitional zone between the "wildness" of the rest of the Mall and the institution itself, another tenet of gardenesque theory.

Mills described his design for the institution building as based on "ancient English Saxon and Norman" architecture, probably chosen because of the veneration of American educational institutions in the nineteenth century for the great universities founded in the Middle Ages. Sir Christopher Wren's Tom Tower at Christ Church, Oxford (1681–1682) was a likely source for the glazed ogival dome, planned for use as an astronomical observatory. The side aisles were glazed conservatories; the main mass of the building, cut stone. In attaching iron and glass aisles and dome to a medieval revival style of building, Mills may have been offering his (and his contemporaries) interpretation of a proper conjunction between newly-developed technology and historical form, by correlating two skeletal systems of construction.[67] The medieval garden may have seemed to Mills a more appropriate, or correct, visual as well as functional complement for the immediate environs of his institution than the fully developed picturesque garden, or he may have been purposefully proposing a variety of landscape effects for Washington.

Mills' institution design was only one element in an overall iconographic program that he planned for the federal city during the 1830s and 1840s, where he intended to assemble a museum of references to world architecture. His Ionic Treasury Building was a stoa, his Doric Patent Office a temple, and his Corinthian Post Office a palazzo — each having specific architectural allusions within the classical tradition. The medieval period represented by his institution design broadened the referential scope.[68]

L'Enfant's synthesis of French art and American history was revived in 1845 with Mills' original design for the Washington National Monument (fig. 12).[69] Mills designed a 600-foot-tall obelisk surrounded by a circular colonnaded pantheon 100 feet high and 250 feet in diameter, because the Washington National Monument Society mandated that it be the largest monument in the world, because they believed George Washington was the greatest man who had ever lived.[70] Mills' iconographic program was as ambitious as its scale, and as eclectic as its form. The thirty Doric columns of the pantheon base represented the states then in the union. Statues of the signers of the Declaration of Independence were on the exterior behind the colonnade and those of the fathers of the Revolution in the rotunda gallery. The walls of the gallery were covered with a cycle of history paintings recounting the major events of the Revolution, with a monumental statue of Washington in the center. The tetrastyle portico supported a quadriga driven by Washington. From this roof terrace one read the inscriptions and viewed the

sculptural reliefs on the obelisk shaft depicting leading events in Washington's military career.

Mills' design was a conflation of many sources. In 1759 the Comte de Caylus published his reconstruction of the Mausoleum of Halicarnassus (fig. 13), a monument consisting of a colonnaded base and stepped pyramid surmounted by an obelisk, and ornamented with sculptural figures and a quadriga

12. Robert Mills, *Sketch of Washington National Monument* [1845]
National Archives

13. Comte de Caylus, reconstruction of the Mausoleum of Halicarnassus
From *Memoires de littérature, tirés des registres de l'Academie Royale des Inscriptions et Belles-Lettres* (Paris, 1759)

14. Jacques Molinos and Jacques LeGrand, design for a monument to Mirabeau, 1792
From Armand Guy Kersaint, *Discours sur les monuments publics* (Paris, 1792)

described by ancient travelers.[71] Mills' monument was meant to be Washington's tomb, and his intention was probably to associate it with the most famous tomb in antiquity.

Generically related to the Caylus reconstruction of the Mausoleum of Halicarnassus was a proposal for a commemorative monument, to be constructed on the site of the ruins of the Bastille, designed by Jacques Molinos and Jacques LeGrand. The scheme would have been known to Mills through its publication in Armand Guy Kersaint's 1792 *Discours sur les monuments publics* (fig. 14).[72] An obelisk with a colonnaded base, simply adorned with a garland and Phrygian cap, it contained in the center of the rotunda a statue of Mirabeau, one of the most respected intellectual leaders of the French Revolution. Although choice of the Mirabeau monument as a prototype linked two heroes of the two great modern democratizing revolutions — Washington and Mirabeau — it was too plain to convey the full range of historical allusions Mills wanted. He turned to the 1795 proposed Monument to the American Revolution, or to Liberty, to obtain that iconographic richness. Designed by Giuseppe Ceracchi to be one hundred feet high and three hundred feet in circumference, it contained mythological and allegorical figures, portrait sculptures of American heroes and "the goddess of Liberty descended in a great chariot drawn by four horses."[73] Its function as a pantheon dedicated to American Revolutionary War heroes, its rotunda form, and the use of a quadriga all suggest that Mills may have been "reviving" a monument that George Washington himself had sanctioned. Unfortunately no image of it survives. Mills may have derived his immense circular pantheon from a seventeenth-century reconstruction of Hadrian's mausoleum in Rome (fig. 15).[74] In addition to a quadriga (described by ancient authors), the mausoleum was adorned with several sculptural figures and its first circular level was colonnaded with niches cut into the exterior wall. In addition, the enormous scale of Hadrian's mausoleum (now Castel Sant' Angelo) would have justified to Mills the size of his Washington Monument base.

The placement of the Washington Monument off-axis with the Capitol was probably an aesthetic decision, although it is often stated that the siting was due to lack of a stable substructure in the Mall's center. Nowhere in the voluminous records of the society during the monument's design and initial construction is there a record of difficulties locating a specific site within the designated grounds. In fact Mills wrote the society in 1848 that excavation for the foundations need not be as deep as first contemplated. The monument's placement east of the axis of the President's House was probably due to the fact that an extension of the Mall to the west would otherwise have been necessary to accommodate the width of the pantheon base. Not only were time and expense a consideration, but an extension would have interfered with the channel opening to the canal. The monument was aligned with the eastern edge of Lafayette Park, equidistant between the White House and the Treasury Building. The validity of an 1874 report by the Army Corps of Engineers that the foundations of the monument were insufficient to bear the weight of the six-hundred-foot obelisk was contested by other engineers, but the opinion of the corps was accepted.[75]

The preferred location for the national monument by the Washington National Monument Society was on the Mall at Seventh Street next to the canal, decidedly off-axis, as depicted in a lithograph by Charles Fenderich, commissioned by the society in 1848 (fig. 16).[76] A panoramic view of the city as seen from the terrace of the Capitol by E. Weber of about the same date illustrates the visual impact of the monument in relationship to the contemporaneous Smithsonian Institution (fig. 17, pl. XLIV). The Weber view shows that both buildings were meant to be seen in their entirety, visually unambiguous as they filled the void of the Mall on the skyline of the city. In all three editions of Mills' *Guide* to the capital (1834, 1847–1848, and 1854) he described the prospects of the city from the Capitol, either from the terrace overlooking the Mall or from the summit of the dome, indicating that the Capitol was the usual belvedere for viewing the city. The placement of the Smithsonian 300 feet from the center line of the Mall in 1846 would have meant that the view from the Capitol to the monument (chosen in 1845) would have been obstructed, if the monument were placed on the actual axis with the Capitol. Mills himself preferred the central, historically correct location for the monument to Washington, as evidenced by both his 1831 and 1841 schemes.

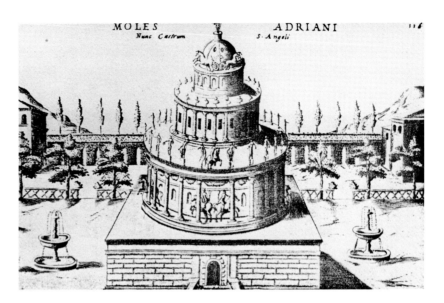

15. Reconstruction of Hadrian's mausoleum, seventeenth century
From Pierre Rodocanachi, *Le Château Sant'Ange* (Paris, 1909)

16. Robert Mills, Washington Monument, lithograph by Charles Fenderich [1848]
Library of Congress

The movement to landscape the Smithsonian grounds and develop the Mall as a picturesque public park, resulting in A. J. Downing's 1851 plan, was begun in 1847 before construction of the monument (pl. XXVIII).[77] Thus work on erecting the Washington Monument commenced with the knowledge that it would soon become one of two major elements in a picturesque garden, and, therefore, its asymmetrical placement would be appropriate. An additional factor to consider in the siting of the monument was the meridian stone erected in 1804 at the intersection of the axes of the Capitol and White House. Although the marker no longer possessed this function in Mills' day, it was conspicuous (thirteen feet tall) and very venerable because Thomas Jefferson was responsible for its erection. To have usurped its place would have been counter to the strong sense of history felt at that time.[78]

Writing to Charles Wilkes in September 1843, Colonel John J. Abert, one of the founding members of the National Institute, stated the most fundamental purpose of the institute, as expressed in the initial meetings:

We then digested a scheme in which we thought all persons could unite, because it was national; which all parties could befriend, because it was national; to which all conditions and branches of service could befriend, because it was national; to which the Government might extend its patronizing hand, because it was national, because it aided and elevated the national character, and because it would furnish a broad platform of national feeling upon which all parties, all sects, all conditions of life could, on principles cherished by all, meet and unite in erecting a temple to national fame.[79]

Ironically, during the period when the country was expanding enormously in size, population, and wealth, sectionalism was seriously divisive of national union.[80] The response of the intellectual community in Washington was to reaffirm national values, embodying them in the two major structures built on the Mall in the 1840s. Symbolically, the plurality of American society was expressed by the Smithsonian Institution, while the history and ideals of the Revolution were embodied in the Washington Monument, a monument to an era rather than to a man.[81] In an address to the Columbian Institute on 6 June 1834, George Watterston reiterated L'Enfant's original thesis: "Nature has done much, in the beautiful outline and splendid landscape scenery she has formed within the limits of our District. It requires but the addition of art, backed by wealth, to render our territory, so far as it concerns mere physical beauty, the Paradise of America."[82] If the essential nature of the picturesque garden was the temporal experience of walking into and through a landscape composition that fused nature, history (or literature), and the arts, then the Mall, with its buildings planned by 1848, represented a physical and political Eden nourished by liberty.

17. *View of Washington City and George Town*, lithograph by E. Weber, 1849, detail
Historical Society of Washington, D.C.

1. The painter John Trumbull used the phrase in a letter to John Adams on 5 February 1791. It is quoted in Kenneth Bowling, "Politics in the First Congress, 1789–1791" (Ph.D. diss., University of Wisconsin, 1968), 198. The events surrounding the Compromise of 1790 and the enactment of the Residence Act, the congressional act which finally settled the question of the site of the federal district, have interested many scholars. These include Bowling, as well as Jacob E. Cooke, "The Compromise of 1790," *William and Mary Quarterly* 27 (October 1970), 523–545; H. Roy Merrens, "The Locating of the Federal Capital of the United States" (M.A. thesis, University of Maryland, 1957); and Donald Sweig, "A Capital on the Potomac: A 1789 Broadside and Alexandria's Attempts to Capture the Cherished Prize," *Virginia Magazine of History and Biography* 87 (1979), 74–104.

2. John C. Fitzpatrick, ed., *The Writings of George Washington*, 39 vols. (Washington, 1939), 31:84.

3. The only biography of L'Enfant is H. Paul Caemmerer, *The Life of Pierre Charles L'Enfant, Planner of the City Beautiful, the City of Washington* (Washington, 1959). Elizabeth S. Kite, *L'Enfant and Washington, 1791–1792* (Baltimore, 1929), reproduced many of the documents of L'Enfant with others involved in founding the national capital. The two most thoughtful interpretive studies of the L'Enfant plan are the first chapters in Daniel Reiff, *Washington Architecture, 1791–1861: Problems in Development* (Washington, 1971), and John Reps, *Monumental Washington: The Planning and Development of the Capital Center* (Princeton, 1967). Reps has also studied the early planning of Washington in detail in *The Making of Urban America* (Princeton, 1965), 240–262; *Town Planning in Frontier America* (Princeton, 1969), 304–343; and *Tidewater Towns* (Williamsburg, 1972), 243–265. Studies of the geometry of the plan include William T. Partridge, "L'Enfant's Methods and Features of His Plan for the Federal City," in *Reports and Plans, Washington Region* (National Capital Park and Planning Commission, Washington, 1930), 21–38; Paul D. Spreiregen, ed., *On the Art of Designing Cities: Selected Essays of Elbert Peets* (Cambridge, 1968), and J. L. Sibley Jennings, Jr., "Artistry as Design, L'Enfant's Extraordinary City," *Quarterly Journal of the Library of Congress* 36 (1979), 225–278.

4. [Alfred James Morrison], *The District in the xvIIIth Century* (Washington, 1909).

5. "Journal of William Loughton Smith, 1790–1791," *Proceedings of the Massachusetts Historical Society* (October 1917), 62.

6. Papers of Pierre Charles L'Enfant, Manuscript Division, Library of Congress.

7. Clark's letter to Washington is in the George Washington Papers, Manuscript Division, Library of Congress.

8. L'Enfant may have been privy to both plans when he formulated his own design. They were officially transmitted to him on 4 April 1791 by Washington.

9. A thorough investigation of Jefferson's plans is included in Julian Boyd's editorial notes for *The Papers of Thomas Jefferson*, 22 vols. (Princeton, 1974, 1982), 19:3–58, 21:3–72, in which he corrects errors made by Saul K. Padover, ed., *Thomas Jefferson and the National Capital* (Washington, 1946). They are also discussed in detail by Reps 1967, 2–5, and Reps 1972, 251–253, and by Paul F. Norton, "Thomas Jefferson and the Planning of the National Capitol," in William Howard Adams, ed., *Jefferson and the Arts: An Extended View* (Washington, 1976), 191–232; Egon Verheyen, " 'The Splendor of Its Empire,' Reconsidering Jefferson's Role in the Planning of Washington," in Erich Hubala, ed., *Festschrift Herbert Siebenhüner* (Wurzburg, 1978), 183–206, and Frederick Doveton Nichols and Ralph E. Griswold, *Thomas Jefferson, Landscape Architect* (Charlottesville, 1978), 38–75.

10. Howard C. Rice, Jr., *Thomas Jefferson's Paris* (Princeton, 1976), 51–54.

11. Quoted in Edward Dumbauld, *Thomas Jefferson, American Tourist* (Norman, Ok., 1946), 151.

12. Jefferson's comments on the superiority of an agrarian ideal for American life are numerous. In a letter to Madison, 20 December 1787, he wrote: "I think our governments will remain virtuous for many centuries; as long as they are chiefly agricultural; and this will be as long as there shall be vacant lands in any part of America. When they get piled upon one another in large cities, as in Europe, they will become corrupt as in Europe." Quoted in Boyd 1955, 442. Jefferson's letter to Priestley is found in his papers in the Manuscript Division, Library of Congress. His later interest in city planning is recounted by John Reps in "Thomas Jefferson's Checkerboard Towns," *Journal of the Society of Architectural Historians* 20 (1961) 108–115.

13. *The Tatler* 161 (18–20 April 1710). Two studies of the relationship between gardening and political thought in the early eighteenth century are Judith Colton, "Merlin's Cave and Queen Caroline: Garden Art as Political Propaganda," *Eighteenth-Century Studies* 10 (Fall 1976), 1–20; and James Turner, "Stephen Switzer and the Political Fallacy in Landscape Gardening History," *Eighteenth-Century Studies* 11 (Summer 1978), 489–496. George Clarke, "Grecian Taste and Gothic Virtue: Lord Cobham's Gardening Programme and Its Iconography," *Apollo* 97 (1973), 566–571, discusses the implied symbolism at Stowe. Carole Fabricant, "The Aesthetics and Politics of Landscape in the Eighteenth Century," *Studies in Eighteenth-Century British Art and Aesthetics*, ed. Ralph Cohen (Berkeley, 1985), 49–81, disputes that there is covert political meaning in gardens such as Stowe.

14. L'Enfant to George Washington on 17 September 1789. Papers of George Washington, Manuscript Division, Library of Congress. L'Enfant's major statements concerning the design of Washington were

contained in a series of letters addressed to Washington beginning on 26 March 1791 (all in the Library of Congress) and the memorials, or petitions, he submitted to Congress between 1800 and 1824. These are in the Library of Congress and the National Archives.

15. There are many unanswered questions concerning the visual evidence we have for L'Enfant's design. Preserved in the Geography and Map Division of the Library of Congress are two unsigned and undated manuscript maps attributed to L'Enfant. The map depicting the layout of the streets and squares is probably the map L'Enfant gave George Washington in August 1791. Richard W. Stevenson, "The Delineation of a Grand Plan," *Quarterly Journal of the Library of Congress* 36 (Summer 1979), 207–224, gives a cogent history of the manuscript plan. In 1887, recognizing the rapidly deteriorating state of the original, the United States Coast and Geodetic Survey published a facsimile of the Library of Congress plan. Beginning in March 1792, engraved maps of Washington were published both in this country and abroad. None was published solely under the direction of L'Enfant (who was dismissed as designer of the city in March 1792). They all differ from the August 1791 manuscript in detail and from one another. Coolie Verner, "Surveying and Mapping the New Federal City," *Imago Mundi* 23 (1969), 59–72, has studied the printed maps and includes a catalogue of sixteen engraved versions published through 1800. Recent interest in the plan has focused on discrepancies between the L'Enfant manuscripts and these early printed plans, denominated the Ellicott plan. These discrepancies are irrelevant for my purposes, as I believe the significance of the plan lies in the relationship of its parts rather than the slight shifts in the streets discernible on the numerous plans.

16. L'Enfant's "Observations explanatory of the plan" was published in several newspapers and journals beginning on 26 December 1791 in *Dunlap's American Daily Advertiser.*

17. The evidence that L'Enfant himself named the state streets is the inherent logic of the plan. There is no written evidence that he did. Thomas Wallcut wrote L'Enfant, probably in January 1792, suggesting that the streets and squares be named for the heroes of the Revolutionary era, both military and civic: draft of letter in Thomas Wallcut Papers, American Antiquarian Society. The city commissioners, the three men appointed by Washington to carry the Residence Act into effect, named the city the City of Washington in the Territory of Columbia and determined that the orthogonal streets be numbered on the north-south axis and lettered on the east-west axis. They reported their decision to L'Enfant on 9 September 1791. Papers of the Commissioner of Public Buildings, Letters Sent; Records of the Office of Public Buildings and Grounds, National Archives, RG 42.

18. Pennsylvania also was the site of the capital more than any other state, with Philadelphia serving four times, Lancaster once, and York once. Its physical position in the country, the "keystone" state,

with six states north of Pennsylvania and six south, is also reflected.

19. A complete study of Federal Hall is Louis Torres, "Federal Hall Revisited," *Journal of the Society of Architectural Historians* 29 (December 1970), 327–338.

20. L'Enfant's "Report accompanying his 1st City Plan to the U.S. President," dated 22 June 1791, has clerks' notations indicating that it was once part of the records of the Commissioner of Public Buildings and Grounds. It is now in the Papers of Pierre Charles L'Enfant. The relevant paragraph is: "To make how ever the distance less to other officers, I placed the three grand departments of States contiguous to the presidial palace and on the way leading to the Congressional House the gardens of the one together with the park and other improvement on the dependency are connected with the publique walk and avenu to the congress House in a manner as must [most] forme a whole as grand as it will be agreable and convenient to the whole city which from the distribution of the local[e] will have an easy access to this place of general resort and all long side of which may be placed play house – room of assembly – accademies and all such sort of places as may be attractive to the larned and afford diversion to the idle."

21. L'Enfant to Washington, Papers of Pierre Charles L'Enfant. L'Enfant often used transliterations of French words: for agreements, read agréments.

22. This description nearly, but not exactly, corresponds to the manuscript map preserved in the Library of Congress. The difficulty arises as the area designated K, obviously referring to the grounds south of the President's House, is not lettered on the extant map, and the only colored areas are the houses lining the Mall. These discrepancies may be due to the difficulty of deciphering the damaged manuscript, but more probably this published description was keyed to another, more complete version of the map.

23. The first map engraved by Thackara and Vallance was that published with the description of the City in the March 1792 issue of the *Universal Asylum and Columbia Magazine*, 656–668.

24. Citoyen des Etats Unis, *Essai sur la ville de Washington* (New York, 1795), 3–4. The author of the *Essai* was probably Stephen Hallet. See Pamela Scott, "L'Enfant's Washington Described: The City in the Public Press, 1791–1795," *Washington History* 3 (1991).

25. *Essai* 1795, 10–12. The Palais-Royal was just becoming popular in 1784 when L'Enfant returned to Paris. For this complex, see Victor Champier and Roger Sandoz, *Le Palais-Royal d'après des documents inédits (1629–1900)*, 2 vols. (Paris, 1900).

26. The central market for the city was eventually located here. The Patent Office Building was located on the site of L'Enfant National Pantheon in 1836. The Naval Itinerary Column, never built, was located by L'Enfant on the banks of the Potomac between Seventh and Ninth streets, SW.

27. Siting of some of these elements is based on the evidence of the January 1792 description in conjunction with the maps themselves, later use assigned by the city commissioners, and L'Enfant's description written to Washington on 19 August 1791: Papers of Pierre Charles L'Enfant. It is not possible to correlate function to location with certainty in all cases.

28. L'Enfant 19 August 1791. "Betwixt these two edifices [Capitol and White House] in the streets from the grand avenu [Pennsylvania Avenue] to the palace [White House] toward the canal there will be a proper stand for shop — for mechanique and every people in various business."

29. *Essai* 1795, 5: "Washington, comme ville fédérale, comme ville de commerce, comme ville d'agrément, peut sous tous ces differens points de vue, offrir des ressources que l'on trouve rarement réunies; il suffit d'étudier cet etablissement sous tous ces rapports, pour en désirer sincerement le succès, & lui assigner d'avance un rang distingué parmi les capitals du monde les plus célèbres."

30. L'Enfant to Washington, 22 June 1791.

31. On 7 August 1783, the Continental Congress resolved that a bronze equestrian of Washington, "in Roman dress, holding a truncheon in his right hand, and his head encircled with a laurel wreath" be erected in the federal district. This statue was to be executed by "the best artist in Europe" under the superintendence of the American minister to France. Quoted in Frederick L. Harvey, *History of the Washington National Monument and Washington National Monument Society*, 57th, Cong., 2d sess., S. Doc. 224, 1902, 13–14.

32. Ceracchi's original proposal, entitled "A Description of a Monument designed to perpetuate the Memory of American Liberty," dated 31 October 1791, is preserved in the George Washington Papers. Correspondence concerning the monument is also in the Jefferson and Madison Papers, Library of Congress. Ceracchi returned to America in 1794 to promote this monument, and as late as 1795 a broadside signed by Washington and numerous prominent citizens solicited funds to erect it. Horatio Gates Papers, New York Historical Society. See Gérard Hubert, *Les sculpteurs italiens en France sons la Révolution, l'Empire et la Restauration, 1790–1830* (Paris, 1964), 25–28.

33. L'Enfant to Washington, 22 June 1791.

34. *Essai* 1795, 7–8. ". . . des cascades d'eau vive fournies par les statues allégoriques des grands fleuves de l'Amérique, tel que la Delaware, l'Hudson, &c. qui peuvent être placées sur la terrasse du Capitole."

35. The first mention of this sculpture group was made by L'Enfant in 1813: L'Enfant Petition for Payment for Surveying City of Washington, 1813, Records of the House of Representatives National Archives, RG 233. Ceracchi is probably the sculptor to whom L'Enfant was referring. L'Enfant noted in this petition that $25,000 had already been subscribed for this and a second major monument, probably Ceracchi's national monument.

36. The author of the *Essai* described the city as "un temple érigé à la liberté" and as a "dépot de l'acte d'union & le sanctuarie des loix," 3–4.

37. In the 1770s and 1780s there had been a vogue for sunken gardens in Parisian *hôtels*, the most famous being Étienne Boullée's Hôtel de Brunoy (1774–1779) and Claude Nicholas Ledoux's Hôtel Thélusson (1778–1783). The Tuileries Gardens themselves were in effect sunken, at least on the western edge where they were enclosed behind the ramparts of one of the walls encircling Paris.

38. Dora Wiebenson, *The Picturesque Garden in France* (Princeton, 1978), 7–8, notes that a wilderness garden was built at Marly as early as 1700.

39. Although some original L'Enfant documents mention "levelling" the streets, the topography of the site chosen precluded a level plain throughout. The picturesque elements in L'Enfant's plan are discussed by J. P. Dougherty, "Baroque and Picturesque Motifs in L'Enfant's Design for the Federal Capital," *American Quarterly* 26 (March 1974), 23–36.

40. L'Enfant to the Commissioners of Public Buildings, dated 30 August 1800: Papers of Pierre Charles L'Enfant.

41. Marc-Antoine Laugier, *Observations sur l'architecture* (The Hague, 1765), 313. Laugier's ideal, in part: "Il faut des places, des carrefours, des rues. Il faut de la régularité & de la bizarrerie, des rapports & des oppositions, des accidens qui varient le tableau, un grand ordre dans les détails, de la confusion, du fracas, du tumulte dans l'ensemble."

42. Wiebenson 1978, 108–121.

43. The relationship between the Governor's Palace and the Capitol at Williamsburg was similar to L'Enfant's design, although there was no diagonal corresponding to Pennsylvania Avenue and the Williamsburg Capitol axis was extended and terminated by William and Mary College, resulting in a basically different configuration. It is not known whether L'Enfant ever visited Williamsburg.

44. Marly is discussed and richly illustrated by Alfred and Jeanne Marie, *Marly* (Paris, 1947). There are two scholarly studies: Gerold Weber, "Der Garten von Marly (1679–1715)," *Wierner Jahrbuch für Kunstgeschichte* 28 (1975), 55–105, discusses the development of the garden during Louis XIV's reign in relation to prior French, rather than Italian, traditions. Betsy Jean Rosasco, "The Sculptures of the Chateau of Marly during the Reign of Louis XIV" (Ph.D. diss., New York University, 1980), convincingly reconstructs an iconographical program based on an antique Roman ideal. Richard Cleary examines the theme of French adoption of Roman elements in "The Places Royales of Louis XIV and Louis XV" (Ph.D. diss., Columbia University, 1986).

45. Coustou's horses are discussed in Wend Graf Kalnein and Michael Levey, *Art and Architecture of the Eighteenth Century in France* (Baltimore, 1972), 40–41. The allegorical allusion of Coustou's horses was identified by A. N. Dazallier d'Argenville, *Vie des fameux sculpteurs depuis la Renaissance des arts* (Paris, 1787), 309. Today Coustou's horses are

on the Place de la Concorde, flanking the entrance to the Champs Elysées.

46. Letterbooks of the Commissioners, Records of the Commissioner of Public Buildings and Grounds, National Archives, RG 42.

47. Harold T. Pinkett, "Early Agricultural Societies in the District of Columbia," *Records of the Columbia Historical Society* 51–52 (1951–1952), 35.

48. Petition signed by forty-four Washington citizens asking Congress to remedy the situation. Committee on Public Buildings and Grounds, Records of the House of Representatives, HR 31A-G17.1, National Archives, RG 233.

49. Copies of Letters Received, Records of the Commissioner of Public Buildings and Grounds, Cited in National Archives, RG 42.

50. Richard Rathbun, "The Columbian Institute for the Promotion of Arts and Sciences," *United States National Museum Bulletin 101* (Washington, 1917), 37–39.

51. Edward Cutbush, *An Address, delivered before the Columbian Institute for the Promotion of Arts and Sciences, at the City of Washington on the 11th January 1817* (Washington, 1817), 17–19.

52. Rathbun 1917, 42–44.

53. Harold Kirker, *The Architecture of Charles Bulfinch* (Cambridge, Mass., 1969), 321–333, discusses Bulfinch's work at the Capitol. Today Bulfinch's gateposts and guardhouses are on the Mall along Constitution Avenue where they were placed after removal from the Capitol grounds when Frederick Law Olmsted's landscaping was begun in 1873.

54. The standard biography of Latrobe is Talbot Hamlin, *Benjamin Henry Latrobe* (New York, 1955). A project to publish the papers of Latrobe has been underway for several years, which, when complete, will survey his work as an architect, engineer, and naturalist. The first publication was Thomas E. Jeffrey, ed., *The Microfilm Edition of the Papers of Benjamin Henry Latrobe* (Clifton, N.J., 1976), followed by individual volumes devoted to various aspects of Latrobe's career.

55. Explicated by Charles E. Brownell, "An Introduction to the Art of Latrobe's Drawings," in *Latrobe's View of America, 1795–1820,* ed. Edward C. Carter II, John C. Van Horne, and Charles E. Brownell (New Haven, 1985), 17–40.

56. Washington's various comments on a national university can be found in the collected writings of Washington concerning his involvement with the national capital; these writings comprise the entire volume 17 of the *Records of the Columbia Historical Society.* A specific history is Elmer L. Kayser, "History of George Washington University," *Records of the Columbia Historical Society* 53–56 (1956), 223–228.

57. Jefferson had settled on the *parti* of his university by 1810, although construction did not begin until 1817. He had exchanged ideas with Latrobe concerning educational institutions, soliciting designs from him for individual pavilions. See William Howard Adams, ed., *The Eye of Thomas Jefferson* [exh. cat., National Gallery of Art] (Washington, 1976), 284–304, and Mary N. Woods, "Thomas Jefferson and the University of Virginia; Planning the Academic Village," *Journal of the Society of Architectural Historians* 44 (October 1985), 266–283.

58. For the history of the canal, see Cornelius W. Heine, "The Washington City Canal," *Records of the Columbia Historical Society* 53–56 (1956), 1–27. On 22 January 1833, Congress was advised to regain from the city title to the entire Mall, as the city had sold lots on the north side of the Mall, thus further reducing the public grounds.

59. The standard biography is H. M. Pierce Gallagher, *Robert Mills: Architect of the Washington Monument, 1781–1855* (New York, 1935). Pamela Scott, ed., *The Papers of Robert Mills, 1781–1855* (Wilmington, 1990) is a comprehensive microfilm edition of Mills' papers accompanied by a guide and index. Mills' 1831 drawing for the Mall is located in the Cartographic and Architectural Archives, National Archives.

60. Repton wrote extensively on his theory and practice; his writings and thought were compiled by Loudon in *The Landscape Gardening and Landscape Architecture of the Late Humphry Repton, Esq.* (London, 1840), a copy of which was in the Patent Office library. Loudon's publications were numerous and readily available in this country. The major study of his life and career is Melanie Louise Simo, *Loudon and the Landscape: From Country Seat to Metropolis, 1783–1843* (New Haven and London, 1988).

61. Skinner's proposals are contained in three reports to the House of Representatives, commencing on 8 March 1830 and ending on 22 April. They are numbered 281, 375, and 376.

62. Efforts are recounted in John Carroll Brent, *Letters on the National Institute* (Washington, 1844).

63. McArann's petition and letters seeking support are in the Records of the House of Representatives, Committee on Public Buildings and Grounds, HR25A-G17.1, National Archives, RG 233. Charles Willson Peale had earlier attempted to sell his museum in Philadelphia to the government. Peter Force Collection, Columbian Institute Papers, Manuscript Division, Library of Congress.

64. Various facets of Wilkes' exploring expedition are examined in *Magnificent Voyagers: The U.S. Exploring Expedition, 1838–1842,* ed. Herman J. Viola and Carolyn Margolis [exh. cat., Smithsonian Institution] (Washington, 1985). A detailed history of the Botanic Garden is given in Therese O'Malley, "Art and Science in American Landscape Architecture: The National Mall, Washington, D.C., 1791–1852" (Ph.D. diss., University of Pennsylvania, 1989).

65. The history of the National Institution (or the National Institute, as it was originally denominated) is recounted in William Jones Rhees, *The Smithsonian Institution; Documents Relative to Its Origins and History, 1835–1899* (Washington, 1901); and in

G. Brown Goode, "The Genesis of the National Museum," *Annual Report of the Smithsonian Institution* (1891), 273–280. Other groups and organizations were also founded around the country to provide possible conduits for the Smithsonian bequest.

66. Mills' Mall drawing is discussed by Therese O'Malley, "The Smithsonian Castle and Its Mall," *Design Action* 2 (1983), 6, and Pamela Scott, "Design for the Mall, Washington, D.C.," in *Drawing Toward Building: Philadelphia Architectural Graphics, 1732–1986*, ed. James F. O'Gorman et al. [exh. cat., Pennsylvania Academy of Fine Arts] (Philadelphia, 1986), 87–88.

67. J. C. Loudon in *An Encyclopedia of Gardening* (London, 1826), 816, illustrated a similar scheme for a large conservatory, but he also showed conservatories in conjunction with classical revival architecture. In this country there was at least one previous instance of correlating cast-iron architecture with medieval forms. See "New Meeting-House of the First Parish in Plymouth, Massachusetts," *American Magazine of Useful and Entertaining Knowledge* 1 (1834), 110.

68. Pamela Scott, "Robert Mills' Washington" (Paper delivered at the Annual Meeting of the Society of Architectural Historians, Washington, April 1986).

69. The basic history of the Washington Monument is Harvey, 1903. The material presented here on the sources and meaning of the design is covered more fully in Pamela J. Scott, "Robert Mills' Washington National Monument" (M.A. thesis, University of Delaware, 1985). A detailed discussion of the Washington Monument is included in Pamela Scott, "Robert Mills and American Monuments," *Robert Mills, Architect*, ed. John M. Bryan [exh. cat., The Octagon] (Washington, 1989). The original papers of the National Monument Society are in the Papers of the Washington National Monument Society, Records of the Office of Public Buildings and Grounds, National Archives, RG 42.

70. Mills' description of the monument was published in a broadside of c. 1845. On 31 October 1833, the constitution of the Washington National Monument Society, a private organization, was adopted. It was written by George Watterston, novelist, journalist, and former Librarian of Congress who conceived that scale was the appropriate symbol of Washington's greatness. Both documents are in the National Archives, RG 42. For Watterston, see William Matheson, *Librarians of Congress, 1802–1974* (Washington, 1977).

71. Comte de Caylus, "Dissertation sur le Tombeau de Mausole," *Mémoires de litterature, tirés des registres de l'Academie Royale des Inscriptions et Belles-Lettres* 26 (1759), 321–334.

72. Armand Guy Kersaint, *Discours sur les monuments publics* (Paris, 1792), plate 4.

73. Description from a broadside in the Horatio Gates Papers, New York Historical Society. Dorothy C. Barck, "Proposed Memorials to Washington in New York City," *The New-York Historical Society Quarterly Bulletin* 15 (1931), 90.

74. The author of this reconstruction is unknown. It was probably based on the one appearing on Étienne Du Perac's 1574 map, *Roma antica nei suoi monumenti*. It has been published by Mariano Borgatti, *Castel Sant'Angelo in Roma* (Rome, 1890), fig. 26, and Emmanuele Pierre Rodocanachi, *Le Château Sant-Ange* (Paris, 1909), 4.

75. Harvey 1902, 65.

76. Selection of the site on the Mall designated by L'Enfant for the equestrian statue to Washington was not automatic, primarily because the Washington National Monument Society was a private organization. Their attempts to induce Congress to set aside some space in the public reservations for a Washington monument began in 1833, with their founding, and culminated in 1848 with the setting aside of Reservation 3 as the monument grounds. In the interim, private individuals offered, or were solicited for, sites throughout the city.

77. For a discussion of the genesis and history of Downing's mall, see David Schuyler, *The New Urban Landscape: The Redefinition of City Form in Nineteenth-Century America* (Baltimore, 1986), 67–77; and Therese O'Malley's essay elsewhere in this volume.

78. Frank L. Culley, "Meridians of Washington," *Geodetic Letter* 1 (March 1936), 56–61.

79. Quoted in Goode 1891, 317.

80. Nullification, whereby certain states questioned the federal government's right to impose tariffs, had the most profound effect, as some states (led by South Carolina) maintained their right to secede from the Union.

81. The inclusive, rather than exclusive, organization of the Smithsonian was shaped by the National Institute. The basic history of the Smithsonian is George Brown Goode's *The Smithsonian Institution, 1846–1896* (Washington, 1897).

82. George Watterston, *An Address Delivered Before the Columbian Horticultural Society* (Washington, 1834), 25.

PATRIOTISM
The highest
object of pub-
lic gratitude

Agriculture
Manufactur-
es & Mechanic-
al Arts

SCIENCE & ART
the rewards
of
Emulation &
Enterprise

Rail Roads,
Canals, Riv-
ers & Harbers

CHARTER
of the
SMITHSONIAN

THERESE O'MALLEY
Center for Advanced Study in the Visual Arts, National Gallery of Art

"A Public Museum of Trees":
Mid-Nineteenth Century Plans for the Mall

During its first few decades, the capital city suffered isolation from other major cities in the country.[1] Washington had a small, impermanent population and lacked the civil and congressional commitments necessary to establish itself as a vital urban center. Not until the 1840s did the city begin to enjoy a relatively stable economic base. Although a period of material prosperity followed, the pre–civil war decades were marked by deep political conflicts. Slavery was becoming an ever greater embarrassment to the democracy. The violation of the principles of natural law on which the nation had been founded, that all men are created equal, was indisputable.[2] Broadsides attacking the active slave trade in Washington, D.C., were among the many products of campaigns launched by the northern abolitionist states (fig. 1).[3] The slavery issue fueled the secessionist movement and threatened the preservation of the Union. This challenge to the federal city generated a desire to strengthen physical symbols of the national image. Notably, in the antebellum period, increased efforts were made to ornament Washington with public gardens in order to counteract the reputation of an unimproved capital and a center of slavery. On the threshold of a civil war, Congress, in unprecedented federal spending, attempted to establish the Mall as a ceremonial core for the city.[4] This essay describes the public park that was planned to bolster the image of a unified republican government committed to popular education and a democratic society.

Between 1840 and 1860 the population of Washington, D.C., doubled. Advances in rail, river, canal, and turnpike links increased trade and communication to such an extent that the small town of the early nineteenth century became the major urban center of the region, surpassing the older settlements of Alexandria and Georgetown.[5] Improvements to the urban fabric could not keep pace with the rapid increase in population and activity. Refuse dumped in the streets and faulty drainage contributed to the unpleasant, often unhealthy atmosphere of the city; neither were federal properties free from the rank consequences of inadequate water and street systems. What is known today as the Ellipse was a fetid swamp created by sewage from the executive mansion. Waste from the Patent Office and Post Office emptied into the canal that ran along the north side of the public grounds that were called the Mall (pl. XLI).[6]

During the late 1840s and the 1850s, improvements were made that focused attention on the physical city: the relocation of the greenhouses and botanic gardens to the foot of Capitol Hill, the extension of the Patent Office, the addition of a portico to City Hall, and congressional appropriations to add two wings and a massive dome to the Capitol.[7] Furthermore, the first two major architectural projects on the public grounds, the Smithsonian Institution and the Washington Monument, were under construction (pl. XL). In 1850, Congress approved a large sum of money to clear the city canal where it passed through the public grounds. After many years of neglect, the Mall finally had become a priority.

Despite the initiation of economic and aesthetic improvements in the late 1840s, Washington continued to experience a crisis caused by slave activity within its boundaries. John Randolph of Roanoke, Virginia, earlier had described the extreme situation: "In no part of the earth, not even excepting the rivers on the Coast of Africa, was there so great, so infamous a slave market, as in the metropolis, in the seat of government of this nation, which prides itself on freedom." [8]

The volume of slave trading conducted in Washington was noted in the *National Intelligencer*, which reported that on one day, 28 March 1836, twelve hundred slaves were offered for sale by three traders. Manacled slaves being led through the streets by a trader with a whip was a familiar scene.[9] This conflict was poignantly pictured as early as 1817, in the frontispiece of a book by Dr. Jesse Torrey, a leading advocate of public education for free blacks, in which slaves were juxtaposed against the Capitol (fig. 2).[10]

The seizure and sale of free blacks often occurred in Washington because the city was a key north-south crossroads and attracted many freed or escaped blacks. At the same time, it was close to southern plantations where the demand for slaves was constant. The expanding cotton industry, which accounted for half of the nation's total exports by the 1830s,[11] increased the dependency on slave labor and intensified its market. It was ironic that agriculture, central to Thomas Jefferson's plan for a new agrarian democracy and the ideal of an American farmer, had become the very institution defending and dependent on slavery.

While the institution of slavery itself was not opposed by all Washingtonians, many, including slave owners, spoke out against the slave trade on the grounds that it was conducted unscrupulously. In an effort to reform conditions, Congress passed the Compromise Act of 1850 which outlawed slave trading in the Federal District. As a result, two large slave pens located across from the new Smithsonian Institution building were removed.[12] Slave ownership was still permitted, however,

which suggests that the appearance of democracy, rather than actual equality, was the foremost objective in the creation of Washington's new public institutions and parks. These public amenities were symbolic gestures of governmental support of public education and entertainment and a show of federal magnanimity. It was hoped that such a display of civic generosity would satisfy both sides of the conflict. A spirit of compromise

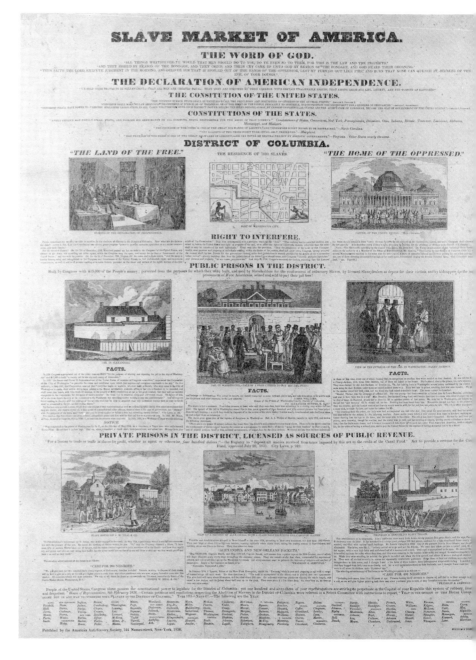

1. *Slave Market of America*, American Anti-Slavery Society, Washington, broadside, 1836
Historical Society of Washington, D.C.

2. *View of the Capitol of the United States, after the Conflagration in 1814*
From Jesse Torrey, *A Portraiture of Domestic Slavery in the United States* (Philadelphia, 1817)

or neutrality characterized the city during this troubled period, since the federal government could not afford to alienate either North or South by aligning itself with a position on slavery: its task was to keep the Union together.[13] Congress, therefore, encouraged cultural and intellectual projects of a civic, democratic character that allowed the city to remain nonpartisan while engendering a strong federal identity.

Developing the Mall as a national park was singularly appropriate at this time because of the pedagogical value placed on public gardens. The concept of gardens as instructive as well as recreational was associated with the movement for popular education that swept the country during the 1840s and 1850s. The proliferation of botanical gardens, museums, public libraries, and free schools was a product of this campaign. The city of Washington, with twenty-three schools by mid-century, was a leader in the free education movement.[14] An interest in educational facilities for advanced artistic and scientific work also increased. A newspaper reporter in 1848 expressed the concern for public education by emphasizing that, "If there be one question set at rest in this community, it is that public opinion has decided that the national metropolis shall be distinguished for the cultivation of the mind."[15]

This viewpoint was expressed in an 1847 depiction of the Mall as an allegory entitled *Elements of National Thrift and Empire* (fig. 3). The inscription identified the elements as "Public Lands; Railroads, Canals, Rivers, and Harbors; Patriotism; Agriculture, Manufactures, and Mechanical Arts; Science and Art, Parents of Emulation and Enterprise." Within a few years, the Washington Monument, the Smithsonian, the city canal, and a landscaped national park would contribute to the realization of this vision of the capital as the city of culture and learning.

Public education was a concept on which all political factions could agree; however, each side supported the movement for different purposes. The southern antiabolitionists claimed education for the white race in order to preserve "its superiority by making its work mental as well as bodily." The abolitionists, epitomized by Henry Ward Beecher, demanded public education because the "broad and radical democratic doctrine of the natural rights of men shall be applied to all men, without regard to race, color, or condition."[16] The crux of their debate was whether "public" included African-Americans or not. Thus, how the public was defined would determine access to educational facilities, and ambiguous meaning was retained in such mottoes as the Smithsonian's "increase and diffusion of

3. *Elements of National Thrift and Empire*, lithograph by E. Weber, 1847, after drawing by J.G. Bruff
Library of Congress

knowledge among men." Both abolitionist and antiabolitionist perspectives equated freedom with education and enslavement with ignorance, concepts that pervaded intellectual and political throught in the period before the Civil War.

With these debates spurring improvement of the city, interest focused on the Mall as the best site for new public institutions and parks. In his 1849 annual report, Ignatius Mudd, commissioner of public buildings, provided a description of the "Capitol Grounds and Mall" that reaffirmed the original identity of the public reservations as national monuments. He wrote that these grounds were an extensive landscape which, when viewed from a favorable point, "cannot fail to strike the observer as the most beautiful and interesting feature of the federal metropolis." Mudd interpreted the appropriations which had already been made for improving the Mall as an indication of "a disposition on the part of Congress to make the public grounds what they were originally designed to be — an ornament and attraction to the capital of the nation." [17]

In October 1850, the year of the Compromise Act, a group of influential politicians and businessmen in Washington approached President Millard Fillmore with the idea of landscaping the Mall. The commission included Joseph Henry, secretary of the Smithsonian Institution, Walter Lenox, Mayor of Washington (1850–1852), and W.W. Corcoran, financier and art collector. [18] Henry was an eminent scientist and administrator. Lenox, a member of one of the oldest Washington families and an advocate of slavery, was a staunch supporter of public schools and libraries for the District.[19] Corcoran has been described as "having had a finger in every Washington economic pie with the probable exception of the tariff." Among the numerous activities that indicated his interest in protecting the city was his role as a major lobbyist for the Compromise Act of 1850.[20] The new Mall initiative was reminiscent of one following the War of 1812, when the removal of the capital was prevented only by the hard work of prominent bankers and local politicians. The retrocession of one-third of the District of Columbia to Virginia in 1846 was considered by many members of the Washington City Council to be the "first step towards destroying the compact by which the seat of government was permanently located in the District, and would result in the removal of the capital to some other place."[21] In the pre-Civil War period, these city leaders, Lenox, Corcoran, and Henry, were concerned not only with preserving the Union but preserving it with Washington as its capital. Although these men represented antagonistic political factions, they joined forces — whether for patriotic, scientific, or financial reasons — in a campaign to strengthen and enhance the city's federal position.

4. *Mount Auburn Cemetery*, Cambridge, Massachusetts, oil by Thomas Chambers, c. 1850
National Gallery of Art.
Gift of William and Bernice Chrysler Garbisch

In his reports as commissioner of public buildings, Ignatius Mudd petitioned Congress to develop the grounds which, since the building of the Smithsonian Institution, had become the focus of efforts to improve the city. He met with some opposition to spending federal funds on District enhancements, but like other champions of city improvements, he attempted to distinguish national from local interests and to assert the position of Washington as a national monument: "The improvement of the public grounds should not be regarded as some are disposed to do, as a mere local objective. These public grounds are the property of the nation, and were reserved at the founding of the city as a means of beautifying and adorning the national capitol."[22]

An 1851 report of the Smithsonian Building Committee records the decision to retain "Mr. Downing, a well-known writer on Rural Architecture, at the request of the President" to prepare a plan for converting "the whole Mall, including the Smithsonian grounds, into an extended landscape garden, to be traversed in different directions by gravelled walks and carriage drives and planted with specimens properly labelled, of all the varieties of trees and shrubs which flourish in this climate . . . if the plan . . . be adopted . . . the Smithsonian lot will form a part of an extended park, of which the Smithsonian building, by its site and picturesque style of architecture, will form a prominent and most attractive feature."[23]

Some money was appropriated and grading of the Mall started before President Fillmore formally asked Andrew Jackson Downing of New York, the preeminent landscape gardener, "rural architect," and advocate of agrarian virtues, to develop a plan for the Mall. Although he had previously avoided government commissions, Downing accepted the Washington project because he wanted to provide one "good example of a *real* park in the United States."[24] He pointed out that rural cemeteries, such as Mount Auburn in Cambridge, Massachusetts, were the only good examples of modern landscape gardening available to the American public.

Mount Auburn was one of several rural cemeteries built in the early 1830s in which picturesque landscape principles were applied in the creations of "gardens of graves" (fig. 4).[25] This new garden type appeared in several American cities during the 1830s — New York,

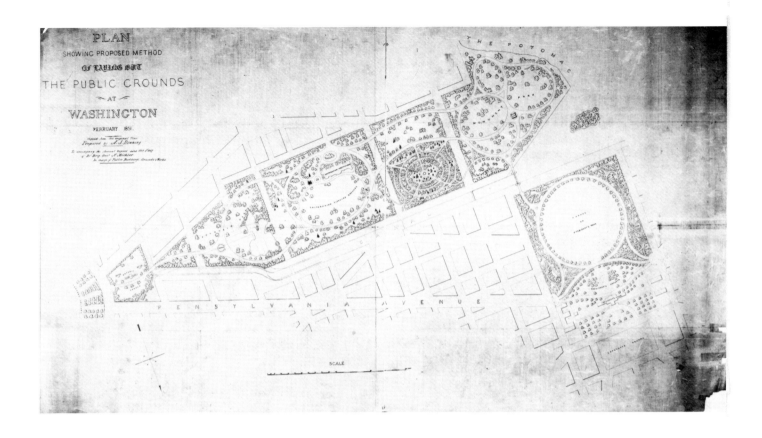

Boston, Philadelphia — offering escape from urban congestion. Rural cemeteries soon became enormously popular, and thousands of people weekly took advantage of new public transportation systems to visit them.

Mount Auburn was a particularly appropriate choice for Downing to cite because it combined the aesthetic and horticultural characteristics that he desired for the Mall. Mount Auburn had been founded by Dr. Jacob Bigelow on behalf of the Massachusetts Horticultural Society for "the purposes of an experimental garden, and to promote the art and science of horticulture."[26] Similarly, Downing's design for the Mall (fig. 5) combined art and science and, in so doing, embodied the goals of the Smithsonian Bequest: the promotion of arts and sciences and the education of citizens in the principles of landscape aesthetics and natural history. Downing presented his plan on 27 February 1851 to the Regents of the Smithsonian Institution, the body that would govern his commission.[27]

Downing's plan for laying out the Public Mall, which connected the Capitol, Smithsonian, and White House Grounds, was a series of six different, but compatible gardens. Downing described his intentions in a letter to President Fillmore on 3 March 1851: "My object is threefold," he wrote: "1st: to form a national park which would be an ornament to the Capital of the United States; 2nd: to give an example of the natural style of landscape gardening which may have an influence on the general taste of the Country; 3rd: To form a collection of all the trees that will grow in the climate of Washington, and, by having these trees plainly labelled with their popular and scientific names, to form a public museum of living trees and shrubs where every person visiting Washington would become familiar with the habits and growth of all the hardy trees."[28]

Downing's six "scenes," as he called the parts of his plan, were to serve as didactic units, exemplifying various garden types. His design was similar to Robert Mills' plan for the Mall of 1841 (pl. xxv) in that it encompassed the entire public grounds, and contained a sequence of linked units, each one appropriate to a different functional and architectural component of the Mall. Down-

5. Andrew Jackson Downing, *Plan Showing Proposed Method of Laying Out the Public Grounds at Washington*, 1851, copy by N. Michler, 1867
National Archives

6. Andrew Jackson Downing,
"Landscape Gardening in the
Graceful School"

From Downing, *A Treatise on the
Theory and Practice of Landscape
Gardening . . .* , 2d ed. (New York and
London, 1844). Dumbarton Oaks,
Trustees for Harvard University

7. Andrew Jackson Downing,
proposed suspension bridge
over Washington Canal, 1851

From Downing, "Explanatory Notes
to Accompany the Plan for Improving
the Public Grounds at Washington,
D.C.," 1851. National Archives

missing from Mills' proposal, which had been
a rare experiment for him in garden planning.

The "Explanatory Notes" that Downing
submitted with his plan provide an opportunity to compare the Mall project to his published theory on garden design. A prolific author of books and articles on rural affairs,
Downing expounded his ideas about the
methods and meaning of landscape design in
a body of widely read works. In his popular
*Treatise on the Theory and Practice of Land-
scape Gardening Adapted to North America*,
Downing defined two types of gardens in the
"natural," or "modern," style which he called
the "beautiful" and the "picturesque." [29] The
"beautiful" school of landscape gardening he
regarded as appropriate to architecture in the
classical modes. This type was illustrated in
the *Treatise* by a view which included an It-
alianate house (fig. 6). With this garden type,
according to Downing, "Trees are planted sin-
gly or in open groups, to allow full expansion"
and viewing of specimen trees. [30] In his plan,
Monument Park at the western edge of the
Mall was in the beautiful style, planted exclusively with American trees disposed in
groups around Mills' obelisk and proposed
pantheon dedicated to Washington. A suspension bridge, seen in a sketch in his letter to
the president, crossed the canal at Monument
Park and led to President's Park (fig. 7). [31]

The principal architectural ornament
Downing designed for the Mall, a marble arch,
was intended to mark the main entrance to
the newly improved grounds (fig. 8). The
scheme related to the classical architecture of
the President's House and the Treasury Building. Its proposed location, just south of the
Treasury Building on Fifteenth Street at Pennsylvania Avenue, was to reestablish the visual
link from the White House to the Capitol, a
view that had been blocked by the siting of
the Treasury Building in 1836. Although
Downing rarely used a classical monument
type, such as the triumphal arch, he believed
that: "To the scholar and man of refined and
cultivated mind, the *associations* connected
with Grecian art are of the most delightful
character." [32] Downing linked the "Grecian
style" specifically with the "agitation of politics and a life passed chiefly in public." [33] He
saw "no positive beauty in a straight or level
line" in this mode. However, he claimed, "It
is often interesting as expressive of power." [34]

ing's drawings, however, were much more
competent, illustrating greater skill and experience in landscape design. They showed a
gracefulness in design and delineation that was

Downing believed that classical architecture was indeed appropriate for major public facilities, including this new entrance to the executive mansion grounds. Again he used the "beautiful" style in the President's Park, laid out as a parade ground for military reviews and public celebrations. The large circular open space was to be surrounded by an avenue of elms, a carriage drive, and a series of footpaths winding through shady groves.[35]

In contrast to the Monument and President's parks, the Smithsonian Pleasure Grounds—in the area between Seventh and Twelfth streets surrounding the new Smithsonian building—were to be planted according to Downing's "picturesque" school. This style was illustrated in the *Treatise* by a garden surrounding a bracketed gothic villa (fig. 9). Downing had written that the picturesque style was required for a garden with an architecture of bold projections, deep shadows, and irregular massing. This formula described quite accurately James Renwick, Jr.'s Smithsonian Institution Building, (1847–1855), the exterior of which was completed in 1851 (fig. 10). In the picturesque school, according to Downing, "trees and shrubs are often planted closely together and intricacy and variety as in wild nature are all indispensable." In his "Explanatory Notes" the Smithsonian garden was proposed to be "thickly planted with the rarest trees and shrubs, to give greater seclusion and beauty to its immediate precincts." [36]

If Downing's plan showed a concern with the symbolic and aesthetic functions of celebrating the agrarian republican union, it was also concerned with the practical considerations of introducing the citizenry to the principles of horticulture and arboriculture.[37] As a professional nurseryman, Downing worried about the depletion of cultivated land owing to ignorant husbandry. Therefore he repeatedly called for public education and experimental gardens and incorporated instructional elements in his designs. In an 1838 issue of Hovey's *Magazine of Horticulture*, he had written: "The way is preparing, and the necessity is beginning to be strongly felt in the public mind for such a garden, through the means of a general increase of taste for botany and all branches of agriculture, horticulture and rural pursuits." [38]

Implementing this instructional objective on the Mall, Downing planned a sixteen-acre

8. Andrew Jackson Downing, proposed entrance arch to President's Park, 1851
From Downing 1851. National Archives

9. Andrew Jackson Downing, "Landscape Gardening in the Picturesque School"
From Downing 1844. Dumbarton Oaks, Trustees for Harvard University

10. James Renwick, Jr.,
Smithsonian Institution
Building (1847–1855), north
elevation
From Robert Dale Owen, *Hints on
Public Architecture* (New York, 1849)

Evergreen Garden between Twelfth and Fourteenth streets on the north side of the Mall to be planted with native and foreign trees laid out in such a manner to "show every tree in detail." [39] The idea of specimen planting derived from the "gardenesque" style promoted by the English landscape theorist John Claudius Loudon, whose work Downing followed closely and helped to popularize in this country. Downing wanted to introduce 130 new species and varieties of evergreens beyond the few known in Washington in order to create a winter garden for Congress in session, when the population of Washington was at its peak.

In designating a Fountain Garden to be located between Seventh and Third streets, Downing incorporated part of the city canal to form a fountain and pond. The canal itself was to be rerouted in order to provide more open ground for parkland. A serpentine drive would lead around these water features into the next and last "scene," the Botanic Garden. This garden was to be a continuation of the old Columbia Institute Garden, which had been started in 1820. A large greenhouse, flanked by two smaller structures that had been moved from the Patent Office, was already in place (pl. LV). Now the Botanic Garden was to be expanded to accommodate the collections brought back from the Wilkes Exploring Expedition. [40]

Suitably developed, these grounds at the foot of Capitol Hill would complete what could be perceived as a physical representation of the Union, that is, the federal government located on the eastern seaboard seen in relationship to the recently annexed transcontinental states and territories.[41] Radial roadways stretched unchecked westward from the Capitol grounds, as seen in a contemporary view of the Mall (pl. XLV). The spirit of Manifest Destiny was felt in the open-ended arms which created the image of the city, "vaguely realizing westward," as Robert Frost later described it.[42] A sense of union in the city's configuration had been evident in Pierre Charles L'Enfant's plan for the city as well (pls. IV, VI). L'Enfant had dedicated various city squares to each of the original states and linked them with radial streets to the ceremonial center, thereby contributing to the physical embodiment of the idea of the Union in the city plan.[43]

Downing's design should be seen as a series of botanic gardens and arboreta that continued a tradition of experimental and exotic gardens for the Mall emphasizing the didactic and practical value of the landscape. His approach grew out of a continued faith in, and ardent advocacy of, agrarian capitalism: "Trade and commerce are not the great interest of the country, that interest is as everyone admits, agriculture."[44] Downing believed botanic gardens, designed for both aesthetic and scientific purposes, were a necessary part of the agrarian utopia the Founding Fathers had hoped to establish. He drew on this tradition of agrarian idealism to convey the strength of the Union because it signified a history of commitment to popular education and national interests. The reaffirmation in Downing's plan of the nation's ceremonial core was expected to strengthen the city's image as the federal capital.

Downing's design was a physical expression of his belief in American democracy because his gardens would be instruments of public education and edification. In his writing on American society, Downing spoke optimistically about the equality of men that would be established for the first time in the United States. Every educated citizen, he believed, would be able to participate in the democratic system. He wrote: "America has been reserved the greater blessing of solving for the world the true problem of all humanity: that of the abolition of all castes, and the recognition of the divine rights of every human soul."[45]

Sympathetic to the popular movement for

public education, Downing attempted to create a public school of natural history and landscape art on the Mall. In his letter to President Fillmore, Downing wrote that: "The public grounds at Washington . . . would undoubtedly become a Public School of instruction in every thing that relates to the tasteful arrangement of parks and grounds, and the growth and culture of trees, while serving more than anything that can be derived to embellish and give interest to the Capital."[46]

In creating a park with labeled plants as a setting for monuments, museums, and research institutes, as well as for federal buildings, Downing envisioned a perfected environment that would benefit society by educating, refining, and elevating the people. He believed that republican America should accept its responsibility to provide such an environment for its citizens: "The true policy of republics is to foster the taste for great public libraries, sculpture and picture galleries, parks and gardens, which *all* may enjoy, since our institutions wisely forbid the growth of private fortunes sufficient to achieve these desirable results in any other way."[47]

For Downing and his supporters, the public park — as well as art galleries, public libraries, and other such institutions of popular enjoyment and refinements — "takes up popular education where the common school and ballot box leave it, and raises up the working man to the same level of enjoyment with the man of leisure and accomplishment."[48] He believed the refining influence of intellectual and moral culture could equip the common man with the stature necessary to fully participate in the democratic system.

Downing shared with many of his contemporaries a conviction that the perfected environment would produce the perfect citizen, one who practiced the principles of scientific agriculture and the arts of landscape gardening, and who could ultimately support the republican Union. In this respect, he was professing a theory of environmental determinism that had a long tradition in Enlightenment thought. Earlier in the century, J. Hector St. John de Crèvecoeur described the influence exerted by the environment on human character: "Men are like plants, the goodness and flavor of the fruit proceeds from the peculiar soil and exposition in which they grow. We are nothing but what we derive from the air we breathe, the climate we inhabit, the government we obey, the system of religion we profess, and the nature of our employment."[49]

There were contradictions in Downing's philosophy of social order. Although he opposed slavery, he did not consistently support total equality. Downing wrote about the "indistinguishable rights of a superior organization in certain men and races of men which Nature every day reaffirms."[50] Much of his architectural and landscape theory was addressed to members of the middle class who could depend on "invisible hands" to manage their rural cottages and villas. Downing and his republican contemporaries were not convinced that all men were created equal. They believed, however, that with the improvement of the landscape for the public, America in time would contribute to that ideal. This outlook, at once idealistic and compromising, was embraced during this period by many Washingtonians living in a city that has been described accurately as the "eye of the hurricane."[51] Their reaction to the crises of slavery and secession was to display through public architecture and gardens, an *image* of democracy and national achievement.

Downing's approach to urban park design was informed by the recognition that America's rural population was not increasing at the rate of urban populations.[52] His design therefore responded to what he saw as inevitable in the development of American society — the growth of cities and the need to adjust by protecting and providing green open space and contact with nature within the city structure.[53] He understood that although it was "needful in civilized life for men to live in cities . . . it is not . . . needful for them to live utterly divorced from all pleasant and healthful intercourse with gardens and green fields.[54]

Like L'Enfant, Downing knew that the improved Mall served as a symbol of the nation, though L'Enfant's perception of the country as a powerful, new empire differed from Downing's romantic concern with the individual experience of American nature. L'Enfant had laid down his monumental radial and grid plan in order "to take possession of and improve the whole district," and "to turn a savage wilderness into a Garden of Eden."[55] By the 1840s and 1850s, with increasing urbanization, the concern had shifted from conquering the natural environment, the "savage

wilderness," to relieving what a writer in 1846 called "the wilderness of bricks" that was beginning to choke the young city.[56] Downing's design for the Mall was oriented to an intimate scale, emphasizing the varied topography, plant material, and the engagement of the individual spectator (fig. 11). Downing specifically described the relationship between L'Enfant's plan and his own: "The straight lines and broad avenues of the streets of Washington would be pleasantly relieved and contrasted by the beauty of curved lines and natural groups of trees in the various parks. By its numerous public buildings and broad avenues, Washington will one day command the attention of every stranger, and if its unimproved public grounds are tastefully improved, they will form the most perfect background or setting to the city, concealing many of its defects and heightening all its beauties."[57]

In order to provide the "healthful intercourse" and "relief" from straight lines and broad avenues, Downing designed an irregular landscape of rolling terrain, varied gardens, and changing vistas. He was contrasting by style the Mall as a construct of rural scenery against the symmetrical classical federal buildings and straight broad avenues. At this point in the city's development, the densest concentration of governmental, residential, and business activity lay between the White House and the Capitol (fig. 12). Pennsylvania Avenue, lined with poplar trees that Thomas Jefferson had planted in 1803, was the principal artery, creating a monumental civic link between the two oldest federal buildings, the Capitol and the White House. The Mall area was separated from the city streets to the north by the Washington Canal. The area just north of the Mall, known as the "island," consisted of scattered dwellings, markets, and small industrial buildings. The "island" created a transitional zone between the relatively dense urban center and the open public grounds.

With its picturesque, naturalistic character, Downing's plan contrasted markedly with the urban area. This "romantic association" of rural picturesqueness, as opposed to classicism, would exert, according to Downing, an "enchanting influence, by which the too great bustle and excitement of our commercial cities will be happily counterbalanced by the more elegant and quiet enjoyments of country life."[58] The serpentine paths and roadways would in-

vite a slower pace than the straight streets outside the public gardens. Spectators could stop to read the labels identifying the plants and, while they enjoyed the scenery, learn of new varieties that would thrive in the city.

For all its qualities, the plan had critics, especially in Congress, who disputed its importance. Perhaps they considered it a smoke-screen to distract attention from the larger issues of the day. Perhaps, too, increased urbanization and industrialization undermined the validity of an agrarian utopia as the most powerful symbol of the nation. Certainly the escalation of tensions that would result in the Civil War deterred nonunionist leaders in Congress from supporting the effort to ornament the national capital at Washington.[59] In response to the mounting criticism and difficulties in funding, Downing wrote to Joseph Henry restating his commitment to the project: "I have a great interest in the work in Washington and if you gentlemen who have influence in Washington will stand by me I will make the Capital "blossom like the rose —

I would serve the government in this matter with all my soul — but . . . I would not beg either for office or its continuance. If the government or Congress do not recognize in me the man that they need, then I do not wish to serve them."[60]

Before Downing's death in 1852, the federal government appropriated only enough funds for landscaping the grounds immediately around the Smithsonian.[61] Without Downing's leadership and perseverance, his vision for the Mall only persisted in a diluted version. In 1854 the integrity of the very design was undermined when Congress permitted the Baltimore and Ohio Railroad to run tracks across the foot of Capitol Hill. Fragmentation of the Mall continued so that by the end of the century, the Mall consisted of a series of seven separate parks or gardens, each representing different governmental bureaus, each with its own architect and gardeners, and each responsible to independent congressional committees (pls. LIII–LVII).[62]

In spite of the incohesiveness in the devel-

11. *Washington, D.C., with Projected Improvements*, lithograph by B.S. Smith, Jr., 1852, showing Robert Mills' design for the Washington Monument and Andrew Jackson Downing's plan for the Mall
Library of Congress

12. *View from the Capitol to the White House along Pennsylvania Avenue,* engraving by J.B. Neagle, 1834, after drawing by J.R. Smith
From Conrad Malte-Brun, *A System of Universal Geography* (Boston, 1834)

opment of the Mall after Downing's death, Frederick Law Olmsted wrote in 1882 that "in no other planted ground near Washington is there, or does there promise to be, any tree beauty to compare with what has already been attained in it." [63] In addition to its importance to Washington, the design of 1851 served as a model of landscape gardening for parks and squares throughout the country. In Washington, it remained the guiding plan for the Mall until the early twentieth century. Up to that time admirers, including Frederick Law Olmsted, petitioned Congress to complete the Mall according to Downing's scheme. The design, according to Olmsted, was planned as a composition of natural scenery appropriate to a national seat of learning: "It is historically important," he wrote, "not only because it was the only important public work of Andrew Jackson Downing," but also because it was "the only essay . . . made under our Government in landscape gardening." [64]

Downing's design was significant for several other reasons as well. First, it established

a standard for the Mall as a showcase of horticultural and artistic achievement and as a place for popular instruction. Second, it established the romantic, naturalistic style for the Mall which would prevail throughout the nineteenth century. Finally, it reclaimed the total expanse of public grounds as originally intended by L'Enfant, and in doing so, reaffirmed the triangular geometry of the monumental core, the White House, the Washington Monument, and the Capitol, which had been allowed to deteriorate while the Mall remained undeveloped. The national park proposed by Downing offered solutions to the problems of the capital city at mid-century: it provided an antidote to the rapid urbanization and increased population that the city was experiencing; it promoted an image of "democracy" through the public and didactic character of the park at a time when the true meaning of the word was hotly debated; and it ornamented the capital city in such a way as to promote the artistic and scientific achievements of the country.

In Downing's plan for the Mall, neoclassical federal buildings and monuments were to express the strength and authority of the federal government. At the same time, these classical monuments were to be linked by a nonmonumental, naturalistic public park. The romantic Mall enhanced the ceremonial core of the city because it balanced the monumental buildings with public gardens planned for the benefit of individual citizens. Together the classical and picturesque characteristics of the Mall contributed to the comprehensive expression of a unified nation and a democratic popular government. These values empowered the Mall, with its national park and cultural institutions, as a symbol for the endangered Union in the years preceding the Civil War.

Downing championed the idea of a national garden in an essay written while he was at work on the design for the Mall, when the seat of the federal government needed to project an image of republican strength. In words that remained vital throughout the nineteenth century, Downing expressed a persistent American desire to create a cultured and democratic environment: "The higher social and artistic elements of every man's nature lie dormant within him, and every laborer is a possible gentleman, not by the possession of money or fine clothes — but through the refining influence of intellectual and moral culture. Open wide, therefore, the doors of your libraries and picture galleries, all ye true republicans! Build halls where knowledge shall be freely diffused among men, and not shut up within the narrow walls of narrower institutions. Plant spacious parks in your cities, and unloose their gates as wide as the gates of morning to the whole people. As there are no dark places at noon day, so education and culture — the true sunshine of the soul — will banish the plague spots of democracy; and the dread of the ignorant exclusive who has no faith in the refinement of a republic, will stand abashed in the next century, before a whole people whose system of voluntary education embraces . . . not only common schools of rudimentary knowledge but common enjoyments for all classes in the higher realms of art, letters, science, social recreations, and enjoyments." [65]

NOTES

1. I am indebted to Susan B. Taylor for her assistance in preparing this article.

2. Daniel Webster in his famous "Seventh of March Speech" invoked the law of nature as the authority for excluding slavery from the West. Quoted in Holman Hamilton, *Prologue to Conflict* (New York, 1964), 77.

3. Robert V. Remini, *The Revolutionary Age of Andrew Jackson* (New York, 1976), 93.

4. Constance Green, *Washington: A History of the Capital*, 1800–1950 (Princeton, 1962), 199.

5. Frederick Gutheim and the National Capital Planning Commission, *Worthy of the Nation: The History of Planning for the National Capital* (Washington, 1977), 50–51.

6. Green 1962, 212.

7. Green 1962, 200.

8. Quoted in the Junior League of Washington, *The City of Washington: An Illustrated History*, ed. Thomas Froncek (New York, 1977), 170.

9. Henry C. Celphane, "The Local Aspect of Slavery in the District of Columbia," *Records of the Columbia Historical Society* 3 (1900), 235–237. See also W.B. Byran, "A Fire in an Old Time F Street Tavern and What It Revealed," *Records of the Columbia Historical Society* 9 (1906), 198–215.

10. Jesse Torrey, *A Portraiture of Domestic Slavery in the United States* (Philadelphia, 1817), frontispiece. The inscription reads: " . . . the old capital then in ruins, a procession of men, women, and children following a wagon and bound with ropes and some iron chains." Torrey advocated that slaves be taught to read, a proposal first seriously considered in Washington, D.C. He is discussed in Byran 1906. Egon Verheyen brought this image to my attention.

11. Remini 1976, 98.

12. Green 1962, 180.

13. Remini 1976, 98.

14. Allan C. Clark, "Walter Lenox, the Thirteenth Mayor of the City of Washington," *Records of the Columbia Historical Society* 20 (1917), 167–193.

15. Quoted in Green 1962, 170.

16. Quoted in Rush Welter, *American Writings on Popular Education: The Nineteenth Century* (New York, 1971), 208, 219, 141–151. Welter attributes the major challenge to the liberal democratic vision of education during this period to southern apologists who used the fact of Negro slavery as grounds for denying that education and democracy were compatible.

17. Commissioner of Public Buildings, *Annual Report*, 1849, 31st Cong., 1st sess., Doc. 30, 6–7.

18. Commissioner of Public Buildings, *Annual Report*, 1850, 31st Cong., 2d sess., H. Ex. Doc. 47, Ser. 599, 9, 114. See also Wilcomb E. Washburn, "Vision of Life for the Mall," *Journal of the American Institute of Architects* 47 (March 1967), 52.

19. Green 1962, 108; Clark 1917, 182.

20. Hamilton 1964, 130–132.

21. Green 1962, 174.

22. Commissioner of Public Buildings 1850, 12.

23. *Annual Report of the Board of Regents of the Smithsonian Institution*, Special Session, Miscellaneous no. 1, Report of the Building Committee, March 1851, 83.

24. Wilcomb E. Washburn, "The First Attempt to Humanize the Mall: Andrew Jackson Downing's Plan of 1851" (Washington, 1967), manuscript version, 18.

25. Jacob Bigelow, *A History of the Cemetery of Mount Auburn* (Boston and Cambridge, 1860), 18.

26. *A Catalogue of Proprietors in the Cemetery of Mount Auburn* (Boston and Cambridge, 1855), 98.

27. For a discussion of the influence of Downing's plan on the public park movement, see David Schuyler, "The Washington Park and Downing's Legacy to Public Landscape Design," in George B. Tatum and Elisabeth Blair MacDougall, eds., *Prophet with Honor: The Career of Andrew Jackson Downing, 1815–1852* (Washington, 1989), 291–311.

28. Andrew Jackson Downing, "Explanatory Notes to Accompany the Plan for Improving the Public Grounds at Washington, D.C.," 3 March 1851, Records of the Commissioners of Public Buildings, Letters Received, RG 42, LR, vol. 32, National Archives, Washington, D.C. This letter was printed in Washburn 1967 and in John W. Reps, "Downing and the Washington Mall," *Landscape* (Spring 1967), 6–11.

29. Andrew Jackson Downing, *A Treatise on the Theory and Practice of Landscape Gardening Adapted to North America* (New York, 1850), 4th ed., 78. See George B. Tatum, "Nature's Gardener," in Tatum and MacDougall 1989, 45–60.

30. The term "graceful," which appeared in the early editions of 1841 and 1844, was changed to "beautiful" after the second edition. See Ann Gilkerson, (unpublished essay, Harvard University, 1985) for a comparison of the 1844 (2d) and 1850 (4th) editions. See also Roger Stein, *John Ruskin and Aesthetic Thought in America, 1840–1900* (Cambridge, Mass., 1967).

31. Washburn 1967, n. 6. Washburn noted that these sketches were found in a copy of the "Explanatory Notes" by Downing, the original of which is lost. It is unclear who made the copy and sketches, but perhaps N. Michler, who copied the entire plan of 1851 in 1867, was also responsible for the sketches.

32. Downing 1850, 381.

33. Andrew Jackson Downing, *Rural Essays*, ed. Frederika Bremer (New York, 1856), 103.

34. Downing 1856, 107.

35. Downing, "Explanatory Notes," quoted in Washburn 1967, 60.

36. Downing, "Explanatory Notes," in Washburn 1967, 61.

37. Downing's most successful book was the *Fruits and Fruit Trees of America*, which appeared in fourteen editions between 1845 and 1856. He also edited John Lindley's treatise on horticultural classification, which brought the "natural system" of taxonomy to a popular audience in America.

38. *Magazine of Horticulture* 3 (1838), 9–10.

39. Downing, "Explanatory Notes," in Washburn 1967, 60. See also Andrew Jackson Downing, "Study of Park Trees," *The Horticulturist* 6 (September, 1851), 427. "Even in our ornamental grounds, it is too much the custom to plant trees in masses, belts, and thickets: by which the same effects are produced as we constantly see in ordinary woods: that is, there is picturesque intricacy, depth of shadow, and seclusion, growing out of masses of verdure: but no beauty of development in each individual tree: none of that fine perfection of character which is seen when a noble forest tree stands alone in soil well suited to it, and has nothing else to do but grow into the finest possible shape that nature meant to make."

40. The Great United States Exploring Expedition of 1838–1842, led by Lieutenant Charles Wilkes, traveled to the polar regions, the South Pacific, the coast of Oregon, Washington, and British Columbia, mapping and collecting scientific specimens of everything encountered. The yield was of a magnitude far greater than anticipated. See William Stanton, *The Great United States Exploring Expedition* (Berkeley, 1975). See also *The Magnificent Voyagers*, Smithsonian Institution, Museum of Natural History (Washington, 1985).

41. In 1848 the Treaty of the Guardian of Guadalupe Hidalgo was signed, adding large areas of the West and Southwest to the Union, making the United States transcontinental. See Green 1962, 177.

42. Robert Frost, "The Gift Outright" (1942), quoted in Robert J. Gangewere, ed., *The Exploited Eden* (New York, 1972), 42.

43. For the iconography of L'Enfant's plan, see Pamela Scott's essay elsewhere in this volume.

44. Downing 1856, 391.

45. Quoted in David Schuyler, "The Washington Park and Downing's Legacy to Public Landscape Design" (1987), manuscript version, 1–2.

46. Washburn 1967, 61.

47. Andrew Jackson Downing, "Public Cemeteries and Public Gardens," *The Horticulturist* 4 (July 1849), 12.

48. Downing 1856, 152.

49. J. Hector St. John de Crèvecoeur, *Letters from an American Farmer* (London, 1782), 71.

50. Carl Cramer, *The Hudson* (New York, 1939), 247.

51. Green 1962, chap. 7.

52. Downing 1856, 391. "The rural population of the older states is either at a standstill, or it is falling off, or it increases very slowly in proportion to the population of those cities and towns largely engaged in commercial pursuits."

53. Downing, *The Horticulturist* (July 1849), 10–11.

54. Downing, *The Horticulturist* (August 1851), 148.

55. L'Enfant to the "Comissionaries of the City of Washington," 30 May 1800. Quoted in H. Paul Caemmerer, *The Life of Pierre Charles L'Enfant* (Washington, 1959), 398.

56. From an American Art Union declaration, 1846. Quoted in John William Ward, "The Politics of Design," in Laurence D. Holland, ed., *Who Designs America?* (Garden City, 1966), 64.

57. Washburn 1967, 61.

58. Andrew Jackson Downing, *A Treatise on the Theory and Practice of Landscape Gardening Adapted to North America* (New York, 1841), 408.

59. A debate recorded between the senators from Tennessee and Kentucky reveals a conflict of interest that was probably due to the Tennessee gentleman's reluctance to spend money on the federal city of Washington. Similarly, Sam Houston was charged with having deliberately obstructed the hearing of reports from the Commissioner of Public Buildings and Grounds in order to prevent discussion on the Mall. Houston was that same year elected president by Texans, indicating an obvious lack of interest in the East Coast capital.

60. Quoted in Washburn 1967, 21.

61. Downing died in 1852 in the burning of the steamer *Henry Clay* on the North River in New York. The catastrophe was described, curiously enough, in a letter to President Millard Fillmore by Robert Mills, who proposed a method of protecting steamers from fire by providing a cavity of steam surrounding the furnace. Mills did not mention Downing by name but refers simply to the "hecatomb of victims." Quoted in H.M. Gallagher, *Robert Mills* (New York, 1935), 208–209.

62. Gutheim 1977, 96.

63. Frederick Law Olmsted, *Park Improvement Papers: A Series of Seventeen Papers Relating to the Improvement of the Park System of the District of Columbia* (Washington, 1902), 235.

64. Olmsted 1902, 235.

65. Downing 1856, 152–153.

THOMAS S. HINES
University of California, Los Angeles

The Imperial Mall:
The City Beautiful Movement and the
Washington Plan of 1901–1902

"The Washington work is a stupendous job," Daniel Burnham wrote to a friend in April 1901, "and it appeals to me as nothing else ever has." Burnham was referring to the task of the Senate Park, or McMillan, Commission, of which he was chair, to reevaluate and in effect to replan the central part of Washington. The scheme was the most significant event in the capital's development since the original design of Pierre L'Enfant in 1791.

The McMillan Plan of 1901–1902 formed the keystone of the City Beautiful movement, the dominant motif and motivating force in American urban design from 1893 to 1917. Like the larger Progressive movement with which it became identified, the City Beautiful movement developed in the 1890s from a theoretical base which had been adumbrated in various sporadic stages throughout the nineteenth century. The City Beautiful reached its apogee in the first decade of the twentieth century and had largely spent its force by the time the United States entered the European war in 1917, although certain legacies of the vision persisted through the 1930s.

To call the City Beautiful an American movement, however, demands an immediate qualification since it was integrally and inextricably connected with European developments, contemporary and historical. It had subtle connections, for example, with the coeval English Garden City movement, but unlike Ebenezer Howard's idea, the City Beautiful was urban-oriented rather than arguing for alternatives to the city. It was American in that it was primarily conceived and implemented in the United States. The term *City Beautiful* seems not to have penetrated deeply or even to have been translated widely into other national vocabularies, though its reverberations were global – back through Europe to such far-flung nations as India, Australia, and the Philippines. It was chiefly an ambitious, and at times naive, effort on the part of civic-minded and aesthetically oriented Americans to achieve for their own raw cities something approaching a "cultural parity" with the great urban centers of an older, grander European civilization. Not surprisingly, the American movement used those cities as the models for its own efforts. Moreover, countless images of ideal urban forms, both in Europe and the United States, provided a major source of inspiration. Particularly from the example of artists and architects of the Renaissance and baroque eras, City Beautiful planners nurtured the conviction that environmental aesthetics strongly affected the quality of life.

Like the City Beautiful movement, the contemporary Progressive movement, whatever its failures and contradictions, effected significant changes in the political, economic, and social fabric of American life. Since Progressivism developed concurrently with the work of Louis Sullivan and the Chicago school and of Frank Lloyd Wright and the Prairie school, it has been tempting for some political and social historians with a slight knowledge of architectural history and for architectural historians with an equally slight sense of social and political history to link them and associate them as comfortable correlates of one another. Progressive, liberal, even at times radical change in the political and social spheres should have welcomed, it frequently has seemed, such avant-garde architecture as a logical cultural corollary. Yet the actual identification of the Chicago and Prairie schools with the Progressive movement in politics was relatively slight compared with the more integral involvement of the architects and planners of the other, "conservative" Beaux-Arts persuasion that composed the City Beautiful. The key to this connection was less a commitment to a "style" than to a scale — a growing commitment, in Daniel Burnham's case, to the design of whole environments rather than merely to individual buildings.

The central ideological conflict in the acceptance or rejection of the City Beautiful idea was the issue of invention and innovation versus continuity and tradition. On the one hand was the idea of newness, cultural nationalism, and the quest for a new and uniquely American culture, which suggested that a reliance on Europe, the Old World, and the tried and true traditions of the past was little more than a timid return to the womb, a mark of American immaturity and insecurity. On the other hand, there was the belief that the sometimes frantic quest for Americanness, the obsession with New World originality, the almost xenophobic horror of things European, itself reflected another kind of insecurity, and that, in fact, it was the very sign of maturity to acknowledge that America was not and should not be culturally isolated from the rest of the world, present or past. It was argued that America, like modern Europe, was also heir to the traditions of Western culture and entitled to recall them, celebrate, and use them.

Most sensitive observers of late nineteenth and early twentieth century America — residents, visitors, and expatriates alike — believed that its cities were ugly. "Unsightly," "undignified," "grotesque," and "chaotic" were the favored terms of disdain. "One of the most depressing impressions of my childhood," wrote Edith Wharton in her memoir, *A Backward Glance*, "is my recollection of the intolerable ugliness of New York, of its un-

tended streets and the narrow houses so lacking in external dignity ... this low-studded rectangular New York cursed with its universal chocolate-covered coating of the most hideous stone ever quarried, this cramped horizontal gridiron of a town without towers, porticoes, fountains or perspectives, hide-bound by its deadly uniformity of mean ugliness." [1]

With varying degrees of explicitness, American cities were inevitably compared to the great European centers, especially by journalists, novelists, and members of the traveled leisure class. In his long, nonfiction essay, *The American Scene*, and especially in his novels about Americans abroad, Henry James frequently compared cities of the old world with those of the new. To one young American of *The Ambassadors*, Paris "hung before him this morning, the vast, bright Babylon, like some huge, iridescent object, a jewel brilliant and hard, in which parts were not to be discriminated or differences comfortably marked. It twinkled and trembled and melted together and what seemed all surface one moment seemed all depth the next." [2]

Yet in Henry Blake Fuller's 1895 novel, *With the Procession*, the artistic young Truesdale Marshall, just returned from a prolonged grand tour, looked on his native Chicago as "a hideous monster — a piteous floundering monster, too. It almost called for tears. Nowhere a more tireless activity, nowhere a more profuse expenditure, nowhere a more determined striving after the ornate ... yet nowhere a result so pitifully grotesque, gruesome, appalling. 'So little taste,' sighed Truesdale; 'so little training, so little education, so total an absence of any collective sense of the fit and the proper! Who could believe, here, that there *are* cities elsewhere which fashioned themselves rightly almost by intuition ... ?'" Fuller's fellow Chicago novelist, Robert Herrick, appreciated on the other hand the brightly hellish vitality of many American cities but described them ambivalently as being either "squalidly ugly or infernally beautiful." [3]

These critics of America's urban "ugliness" and "vulgarity" constituted an aesthetic and architectural analogue to such muckrakers as Ida Tarbell, Henry Demarest Lloyd, and Lincoln Steffens in the political and economic spheres. [4] By calling attention to the polluted urban environment via the printed word and the personal crusade, these aesthetic muckrakers, working with similarly aroused architects and civic leaders, began to appeal to the consciousness of a larger constituency and to embarrass it into realizing that in civic amenities, as in social and political equity, America was somehow woefully "behind."

The Marshall family in Fuller's *With the Procession* spoke symbolically for the American urban situation. "We are steady and solid," Fuller had them protest, "but we are not precisely in society, and we are far, very far indeed, from any attempt to cut a great figure. However, do not misunderstand our position; it is not that we are under, nor that we are exactly aside; perhaps we have been just a little bit behind. Yes, that might express it — just a little bit behind." "How are they to catch up," Fuller himself inquired, "how rejoin the great caravan whose fast and furious pace never ceases, never slackens?" This was, in effect, the question posed by the actual aesthetic reformers of the day, and the answer that slowly appeared seemed chiefly to call for harnessing and redirecting the very energies that had powered the nation's already abundant economic drive. As another of Fuller's grittier and more determined heroines admitted: "Keep up with the procession is my motto, and lead it if you can." [5]

Few observers of any persuasion denied the prodigious growth of American cities in the nineteenth century. While the total population of the United States increased from 31.4 million to 91.9 million between 1860 and 1910, the number living in incorporated communities of over twenty-five hundred increased from 6 million to 45 million. By 1910, 46 percent of the total population lived in such municipalities, as opposed to 20 percent in 1860. During these years the number of cities of ten to twenty-five thousand population increased from 58 to 369, while the number of cities of over one hundred thousand rose from 9 to 50. [6] These statistics formed the underpinning of the City Beautiful impulse. How was one to respond to these almost "instant" cities? Admittedly, they had been there in smaller forms, some for a long time, but they had grown so large so quickly that now they simply overwhelmed the imagination. How, in addition to solving the basic political, economic, and social demands of urbanization, did one deal with the more subtle problems of image, spatial focus, and urban identity?

Indeed, most of the leading urban muckrakers and reformers of the 1890s and thereafter would have supported the sentiment later articulated by Lewis Mumford that "contrary to the convictions of census statistics, it is art, culture, and political purpose, not numbers, that define a city." All the things, Mumford contended, "that have helped bring the city into existence came to nothing if the life that the city makes possible is not its own reward. Neither augmented power nor unlimited material wealth can atone for a day that lacks a glimpse of beauty, a flash of joy and a sharing of fellowship." [7]

Henry Fuller's "procession" provides an apt metaphor for the City Beautiful movement, not only on a social level but on an architectural level as well. However eclectic it became in its borrowings and whatever the style of particular buildings within its plans, the thrust of City Beautiful planning was predominantly baroque in its emphasis on processional sequences of spaces and buildings arranged as a unified group. For its parallax effect, such planning depended on the individual's movement through space from one specific point to another. "It was one of the great triumphs of the Baroque mind," Mumford has suggested, "to organize space, make it continuous, reduce it to measure and order, and to extend the limits of magnitude embracing the extremely minute; finally to associate space with motion and time." [8] The impact of this arrangement on the individual, both consciously and unconsciously, was at its best powerful, impressive, and moving. Whether the moral effect was stimulating and inspiring or overpowering and oppressive depended — in the baroque era as well as in the twentieth century — on an infinite number of personal, social, political, temporal, and spatial variables. The single most important catalyst in the launching of the City Beautiful was the 1893 World's Columbian Exposition at Chicago (figs. 1–3). [9] More than anyone could have suspected at that time, the White City would become a microcosm of the City Beautiful movement — both on pragmatic and ideological levels. Beyond creating a spectacular ensemble, the builders of this temporary city groped with some of the problems of cities in the real world — from the arrangement of streets, sidewalks, waterfronts, and bridges to the problems of transportation, sustenance, and sew-

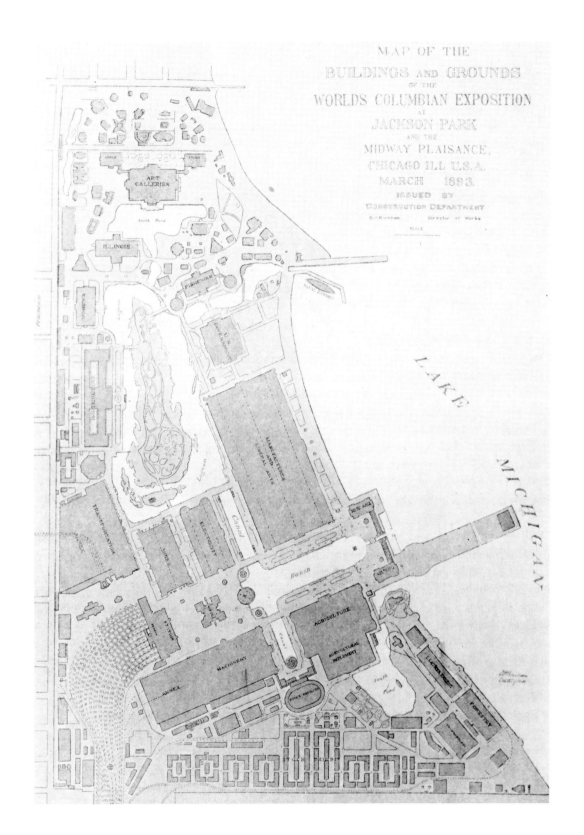

1. *Map of the Buildings and Grounds of the World's Columbian Exposition . . . ,* Chicago, 1893
From Daniel H. Burnham and Edward H. Bennett, *Plan of Chicago* (Chicago, 1909)

2. World's Columbian Exposition, Chicago, 1893
Avery Architectural and Fine Arts Library, Columbia University

3. World's Columbian Exposition, Chicago, 1893
From Burnham and Bennett 1909

age. While the relatively informal lagoon area to the north reflected the picturesque aesthetic that had characterized the earlier work of Frederick Law Olmsted, Sr., who was one of the fair's planners, the Court of Honor to the south formed the seminal image of the City Beautiful mentality.

Meeting in Chicago for several crucial planning sessions during the early months of 1891, the board of architects confirmed Burnham and Olmsted's tentative overall scheme, which included the formal and architecturally unified central court. The board quickly determined the size and exact location of the key elements and also agreed on a maximum height and a uniform cornice line for the buildings. These decisions led with seeming inevitability to a consensus in favor of designing in the classical tradition. The choice was reinforced by the pressing need to build quickly in a readily understandable idiom. Several of the architects had studied at the Ecole des Beaux-Arts and had acquired their penchant for classicism there. All were acquainted with the formal, ordered, and axially oriented imperatives associated with Beaux-Arts design — a perspective that would dominate most City Beautiful architecture. Sculptors and painters sympathetic to Beaux-Arts aesthetics were enlisted to embellish the buildings and open spaces. "I feel this to be the greatest chance for architecture ever known on the continent," Burnham wrote to a friend. His mood was confirmed by the much-quoted proclamation of sculptor Augustus Saint-Gaudens that it was "the greatest meeting of artists since the fifteenth century." [10]

As director of works, Burnham pushed the work forward with a power and determination that more than confirmed his reputation as an organizer, executive, and architectural impresario. He would later serve as a prototype for the fictitious Tom Bingham in Fuller's *With the Procession*, an architect-builder of "breadth and poise . . . habituated to the broad treatment of big matters." Fuller's description of another of the novel's characters applied equally well to the Burnham-Bingham type: "one of the big, the broad, the great, the triumphant with . . . a Roman amplitude and vigor, an Indian keenness and sagacity, an American ambition and determination . . . one who baffles circumstances and almost masters fate . . . one of the conquerors, in short." [11]

And conquer he did. The fair, with all its myriad and vexing problems, was completed on time — in less than two years. To the work force, the commissioners, and the numerous amazed spectators, Burnham seemed the ideal, benevolent dictator. It was, curiously enough, that particular role of authority that was forgotten in later years by civic promoters and by Burnham himself, as they sought to transplant the autocratically ordered Court of Honor and its similarly ordered European precedents to the cumbersomely "democratic" American urban scene.

Yet in 1893, the results seemed remarkable. The white ensemble of classical buildings, especially impressive when floodlighted at night, had much the "twinkle" and "iridescence" that Henry James had found in Paris. It was reminiscent in fact of Thomas Cole's great mid-nineteenth-century painting, *The Consummation of Empire*. In the very year that historian Frederick Jackson Turner announced the "end" of the American frontier at one of the fair's numerous professional "congresses," American urban reformers gleaned from the White City a suggestive vision of things to come. Olmsted had feared that the architects' decision to make the court buildings "perfectly white" would create a blinding effect. Yet the whiteness of the fair shortly became an important symbol of purity and freshness in the moral crusade against the dark "ugliness" of the actual urban landscape.

Visitors came from every part of the world. A total of 21 million paying visitors turned over gate receipts of $10 million. The masses of plain people were especially titillated by the naughty belly dancing of "Little Egypt" and the new and terrifying Ferris Wheel of the Midway Plaisance, but they also marveled at the architectural spectacle. Novelist Hamlin Garland spoke for them in recording the "stunned" awe of his untraveled mother who "sat in her chair visioning it all yet comprehending little of its meaning. Her life had been spent among homely small things and these gorgeous scenes dazzled her, overwhelmed her, letting in upon her in one mighty flood a thousand stupefying suggestions of the art and history and poetry of the world." Journalist Henry D. Lloyd was certain that it revealed to such people "possibilities of social beauty, utility, and harmony of which they had not been able even to dream. No such vision could otherwise have entered into the prosaic drudgery of their lives," he believed, "and it will be felt in their development into the third and fourth generation." The whole enterprise indeed prefigured Burnham's own later exhortation: "Make no little plans. They have no magic to stir men's blood." [12]

Both Henry Adams and William Dean Howells saw the fair's planned grouping of buildings, streets, bridges, parks, waterways, and service facilities as a suggestive model for the planning of the larger society. Theodore Dreiser, in his autobiographical *Newspaper Days*, recalled that the fair had "caused me to be swept into a dream from which I did not recover for months." Fuller's Truesdale Marshall of *With the Procession* visited the site shortly after returning from Europe. " 'It *is* good,' he assented, 'better than I could have thought — better than anybody over there could be made to believe,' " as he "met halfway the universal expectation that the spirit of the White City was but just transferred to the body of the great Black City close at hand, over which it was to hover as an enlightenment — through which it might permeate as an informing force. 'Good!' he thought. 'There's no place where it's needed more or where it might do more good!'" In Robert Herrick's novel, *The Memoirs of an American Citizen*, the protagonist had a similar but more optimistic view: "The people who could dream this vision and make it real," he suggested, "would press on to greater victories than triumph of beauty." Similar sentiments were echoed in a prophetically named children's book by Frances Hodgson Burnett, *Two Little*

Pilgrims' Progress: A Story of the City Beautiful.[13] On another key, it was ironically prophetic that one of the common laborers who silently worked to create this fantasy was a man by the name of Elias Disney, the father of Walt.

Among major contemporary critics, only Montgomery Schuyler voiced even partial dissent from the favorable consensus. As a temporary summer festival, he acknowledged, the White City was quite splendid. His reservations involved its relevance to future American architecture, especially its probable stimulus to yet another classical revival. In 1893, Louis Sullivan was relatively silent, though in time he became the fair's bitterest critic. In his *Autobiography* of 1924, the tragically depressed and impoverished Sullivan deplored the fair's "retrograde" neoclassicism which, he believed, had "penetrated deep into the constitution of the American mind, effecting there lesions significant of dementia." The naive visitors, he asserted in retrospect, had "departed joyously, carriers of contagion, unaware that what they had beheld and believed to be truth was to prove, in historic fact, an appalling calamity." Yet for most observers the fair was a symbol of light and promise. Though one among several influences on the development of the City Beautiful, the exposition was undoubtedly its most significant catalyst.[14]

The impact of the Chicago fair was heightened and attenuated by the subsequent expositions which continued throughout the next two decades to present new ideas and to confirm the messages proclaimed by the White City. From Buffalo (1901) to Saint Louis (1904) to San Francisco (1915), the major fairs of the period served as a laboratory of the developing City Beautiful, both suggesting and reinforcing the movement's evolution. In 1898 and 1899, fleeting reenactments of the Court of Honor theme occurred as Philadelphia and New York staged "peace" celebrations to commemorate the recent victories of the Spanish-American War. Each featured triumphal Roman arches and rows of large, white, freestanding columns, beneath which would pass the ceremonial procession.

The 1890s also saw the merging of goals and activities of different groups working toward different aspects of urban reform: political, social, economic, aesthetic. By the decade's end, certain facts were becoming apparent even to the most aesthetically indifferent urban activist: first, that increased beauty and convenience of the physical enivronment could have beneficent psychological effects on its inhabitants; second, that "municipal art" evoked and enriched the urban spirit and the civic patriotism that seemed crucial to urban reform of any type; and third, that the problems of the city were interrelated; those wishing to improve the quality of urban life in one area had to begin thinking of the city as a whole. The depression of the mid-1890s and the Spanish-American War did inhibit some aspects of American urban reform; but with economic recovery and, in 1901, the inauguration of Theodore Roosevelt as president, the Progressive and City Beautiful movements entered their heyday.

If the Chicago fair was the single most important catalyst for the City Beautiful, the McMillan Plan became the movement's most significant model. Building on L'Enfant's plan for Washington and the baroque tradition from which it emanated, the new scheme paid homage to those monumental precedents while updating them in response to the contemporary needs of the federal government and the federal city.[15] The primary axis and centerpiece of L'Enfant's plan had been the mall or "grand avenue" stretching from Capitol Hill to the banks of the Potomac some two miles away. The perpendicular secondary axis crossed from the President's House to the river as it curved southeastward. The monument to George Washington was to mark the convergence of the two axes while not obscuring the river vistas from the Capitol and and White House. Broad thoroughfares radiated from both of those buildings into the outlying city — the most important being Pennsylvania Avenue, which connected the two major nodes and formed an architecturally promising triangular precinct between them and the Mall.

The nineteenth century had seen significant erosions of L'Enfant's concepts. Owing to difficult but not insoluble soil and foundation problems, the huge obelisk erected to honor Washington had been built slightly but disconcertingly off center, south and east of the point of axial convergence. L'Enfant's "mall" existed only on paper, with the area between the Capitol and the Washington

Monument containing a railroad terminus, informal gardens, and other constructs viewed as heterogeneous clutter (pls. LVI–LIX). The Smithsonian Institution buildings (1847–1855, 1879–1881); the State, War, and Navy Building (1871–1888); and the enormous Library of Congress (1886–1897) possessed an exuberant Victorian presence in the otherwise restrained, classical government center.

Indeed, Washington at the turn of the century did not escape any more than most American cities the criticism of visitors and citizens alike that it was "ugly" and infelicitous. Henry James found the capital an "oddly scattered" place, presenting "a general impression of high granite steps, of light, gray corniced colonnades . . . contending for effect with slaty mansard roofs and masses of iron excrescence, a general impression of somewhat vague, empty, sketchy fundamentals, however expectant, however spacious, overweighted by a simple dome and overaccented by a single shaft. The back of the scene . . . might have been but an immense painted, yet unfinished cloth." [16]

Yet in Washington, even earlier than in other cities, came rumblings of discontent and proposals for reform. One of the discontented was Glenn Brown, secretary of the Washington-headquartered American Institute of Architects (AIA), who in 1898 proposed that the AIA solicit and sponsor schemes for the capital's improvement that would coincide with the approaching centennial of the government's removal to the District of Columbia. Designs from various architects were then collected and published, though without any discernible effect on events except as they served to raise public consciousness. A much-favored AIA suggestion, however, to the effect that a commission of experts be appointed to study and report on conditions and possibilities was ultimately realized in 1901. Senator James McMillan, the sympathetic chairman of the Senate Committee on the District of Columbia, sponsored the legislation creating such a board, to be financed by Senate contingency funds.

With the advice of his secretary and architectural advisor, Charles Moore, McMillan appointed Burnham head of a three-man planning committee, which was also to include the young landscape architect, Frederick Law Olmsted, Jr., whose famous father had worked with Burnham at the World's Columbian Exposition. Burnham and Olmsted were to name the third member of the commission, and they selected Charles McKim, also an important figure at the Chicago fair. Later, deciding that the commission should include a sculptor, they arranged for the appointment of Augustus Saint-Gaudens, yet another veteran of the exposition staff. The four commissioners gave their time and talent as a public service, accepting reimbursement only for expenses. Though not officially a member of the commission, Charles Moore served as full-time secretary and administrative assistant for the project. In addition, he became the commission's unofficial reporter and historian, contributing numerous articles and memoirs on the Washington work as well as writing early, firsthand biographies of both Burnham and McKim. Moore's "power is very great," Burnham wrote to a friend, "although he keeps in the background." [17]

Moore's characterization of himself and his commission colleagues revealed a keen perception of their personalities and the part of each in the total enterprise. "Daniel Burnham . . . never hurried and never rested," he later recalled. His "mind worked on a grand scale. He saw things in the large." McKim, on the other hand, "always acquiesced; he never contradicted; but when his logical mind began to work, quite hesitatingly he would offer suggestions which seemed only an expansion of the original idea, or perhaps a little better way of arriving at the intended result. Olmsted, being younger and possessing a brain fertile in expedients, offered many variations on the themes." Describing himself in the third person, in the Henry Adams manner, Moore, "at the outset . . . ventured to suggest that the ideas were too overpowering to receive consideration in Congress, but he was silenced if not then convinced by Burnham's downright assertion that it was the business and duty of the Commission to make the very finest plans their minds could conceive. The future, he maintained, would prove even those plans all too small; and that the time [if ever] to compromise was after the large plans had been made." [18]

Burnham's convictions epitomized his credo to "make no little plans," but they also embraced a high Republican class consciousness that would likewise pervade his later thought.

"My own belief," he wrote to "Rick" Olmsted, "is that instead of arranging for less, we should plan for rather more extensive treatment than we are likely to find in any other city. Washington is likely to grow very rapidly from this time on, and be the home of all the wealthy people of the United States." [19]

In attempting to recover the spirit of L'Enfant's ideas and the older precedents that had inspired his Washington proposals, the commissioners believed research trips to Williamsburg and Europe were of crucial importance. In the decaying colonial capital of Virginia, they observed the relationship of Capitol and Governor's Palace sites, which had presaged the similar cross-axial relationship of Capitol and White House in Washington. And in the summer of 1901, they crisscrossed the European continent savoring its riches and reflecting on its lessons for Washington — both of L'Enfant's era and of their own. Their pilgrimage in general, and their specific itinerary, reflected the reverence of the City Beautiful mentality for the culture of the Old World: ancient, Renaissance, baroque, and modern Rome, from the Forum of the Caesars to Michelangelo's Campidoglio and Bernini's Saint Peter's Square; the Versailles and Paris of Le Nôtre and of Haussmann, with the spaces and monuments of intervening epochs: the Place de la Concorde, the Etoile, the Champ-de-Mars, the Champs Elysées; the baroque palace gardens and the mid-nineteenth-century Ringstrasse development of Vienna; and countless other examples of landscaping and urban design from Budapest to Berlin to London (figs. 4–7).

Moore later recalled the influence of specific European places on the Washington work and on the developing City Beautiful movement: "Paris revealed itself as a well-articulated city — a work of civic art. Versailles, Fontainbleau, Hampton Court, examples of the use of a long stretch of water, tree-lined, furnished ideas for the basin . . . Vaux le Vicomte, Compiègne, Schönbrunn, Hatfield House . . . gave inspiration for the treatment of the mall." Yet in Rome, most of all, the Americans "were brought face to face with things eternal. All that man had done to express his nature in highest terms had been gathered there during the ages. The fleeting,

4. Basin of Latona, Versailles
From Charles Moore, ed., *The Improvement of the Park System of the District of Columbia* (Washington, 1902)

5. Avenue de Beaumont,
Compiègne
From Moore 1902

6. Fountain in front of Villa
Medici, Rome
From Moore 1902

the transitory, the ephemeral, the self-assertive, the struggle for originality, all seemed to drop out of mind, leaving a desire to discover and to use in the work of a new nation those forms which have satisfied age after age of men."[20]

The European trip both refreshed and intoxicated the commissioners, who set to work immediately on their return to integrate the influences absorbed abroad with the realities and imperatives of the Washington assignment. Since their return, Burnham wrote to a

7. Memorial Walk, Thiergarten, Berlin
From Moore 1902

and will be ready to fill in when we meet" later in the month. He then turned it over to Moore for emendation and final editing.[22]

There was constant communication and interaction among the various members over most aspects of the project. Usually the criticism was friendly and constructive, and the work went smoothly, despite its geographical fragmentation. Occasionally, however, honest disagreements appeared, some caused by the peculiar financial pressures of the undertaking. Accustomed to operating in the grandest manner in all their other pursuits, and feeling justified because they were charging no fees, Burnham and McKim, in particular, failed to accept the scarcity of resources in the Senate Contingency Fund, raising further the ire of penurious congressmen. "We have out of our pockets now furnished Three Thousand Dollars toward paying Curtis" for the models, Burnham wrote to Moore in late August, "and this sum has been expended. Cannot you from this time on pay his bills? Mr. McKim is worried over the matter."[23]

Burnham also had words with Moore over the style and editing of the final report, revealing again his peculiar mixture of dreamy romanticism and tough-minded pragmatism. "I do not think the report should be elaborate," he wrote to Moore on 30 August 1901. "It should depend for its acceptance on the accuracy of its statement, and the good sense of its recommendations." He trusted "that the final draft will be shorn of every unnecessary word." Moore's tentative final draft, however, displeased Burnham for what he deemed to be excessive aridity and austerity. Much of the commission's original excitement and enthusiasm, Burnham argued, had been sacrificed in the acknowledged desire for clarity and directness. Writing to Moore in early 1902, Burnham the promoter, the man of the marketplace, questioned the artistic and intellectual biases of his colleagues: "You have taken the color out of the report and made it a dead level statement of facts . . . While I sympathize with you and the Harvard dislike of highly colored statements, I doubt very much whether you are entirely right in this case."[24]

The ensuing argument revealed the conflict of democratic values and elitist noblesse oblige in Burnham's make-up. "A skillful lawyer appealing to a judge in chambers," he suggested to Moore, "does not care to go beyond un-

friend, they had "been at it, hot and heavy. Again has come the old joy of creating noble things . . . Our happiness has at times seemed almost too full . . . of the dream-visions. The parks, the roads, the great mall with its avenues, woods, fountains, and statues, the distant vistas in the hills, the monumental bridges and arches, all of which we are allowed to play with for the nation, have brought back the day dreams of youth and we stop at nothing, developing our themes to ever nobler heights, each man raising the thoughts of the others, and altogether we have risen where I never hoped to tread in this existence."[21]

Throughout 1901, Burnham commuted often between Washington, New York, and his Chicago office, where he supervised the work on the design of Union Station. In Boston and New York, Olmsted, Saint-Gaudens, and McKim supervised the completion of the drawings and models. George C. Curtis of Boston was in charge of making models; William T. Partridge, a young draftsman in McKim's firm, prepared most of the final drawings. Olmsted's office had general advisory responsibility for landscaping details, especially in the outlying parks throughout the District. Burnham himself blocked out the rough draft of the report with the help of a Chicago writer, W.H. Harper. The report, he wrote to Olmsted on 9 September, was "now in skeleton form,

adorned statements of precedence and does not feel that his case is helped much by argument, especially of a sentimental kind, but would not the same man before a jury take the other tack? When appealing to the ordinary untrained mind, he would know that legal argument, standing by itself, would avail him little, and he would be wise therefore to deal . . . not on his own but on their plane of thought and understanding. If you expect this report to be copied in part or in whole by the newspapers of this country, as I supposed was your intention, should it not dress the statements up in colors that will appeal to the ordinary citizen who is not much moved by cold facts, but is carried forward by feelings?" He believed indeed that, "We should not write this report in a style that would appeal to us as individuals, if by taking the other course we can awaken a much needed sympathy, a sympathy which will be the parent of all that can be brought to support the objects we have in view." If they were trying "to raise the enthusiasm of the people, very few of whom are trained to appreciate cold statements of facts, it should have plenty of color." The final report contained the necessary balance between the "color" and the "directness" Burnham desired — as well as a compromise between his personal preferences and those of his colleagues. Certainly the section of the

Viewing the Exhibit in the Hemicycle.

8. Staff working on exhibition of models of the Senate Park Commission Plan of 1901–1902, Corcoran Gallery, Washington, 1902
From John W. Reps, *Monumental Washington: The Planning and Development of the Capital Center* (Princeton, 1967)

9. President Theodore Roosevelt and his party visiting the Senate Park Commission Plan exhibit at the Corcoran Gallery, 1902
From Reps 1967

final report that dealt with Arlington Cemetery was not lacking in "color" or emotion: "The interest excited by the drills at the cavalry post," it read, "the superb view from the heights, and the feelings of patriotism awakened by the vast field of the heroes dead, known or un-named, all call for such a treatment of the entire reservation as shall not diminish

10. Senate Park Commission,
Plan of 1901–1902, *Model of
the Mall, Showing Treatment
Proposed, Looking West*
From Moore 1902

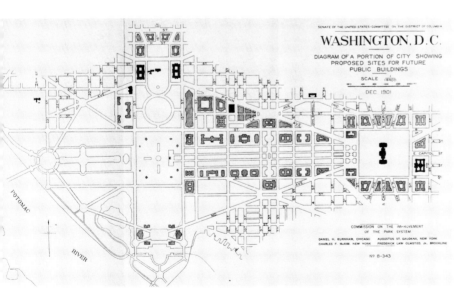

11. Senate Park Commission,
Plan of 1901–1902, *Diagram
of a Portion of the City Show-
ing Proposed Sites for Future
Public Buildings*
From Moore 1902

but rather enhance the effect produced on the visitor." [25]

The commission's synthesis of visions and realities was announced via printed report and graphic display in an exhibit of drawings and models at Washington's Corcoran Gallery in early 1902 (figs. 8, 9). President Roosevelt, members of the cabinet and Congress, as well as the larger public, greeted it with amazement and with general approbation. They saw before them essentially a revival, an enlargement, and in several crucial ways, a departure from L'Enfant's seminal design.

In an effort to restore the Washington Monument as the nexus of the Capitol and White House axes, the line from the Capitol was redrawn to bisect the off-center monument and extend westward through the then-marshy backwaters of the Potomac to the designated site of a future Lincoln Memorial (figs. 10, 11; pls. LX–LXIX, LXXI–LXXIII). This line would form the new spine of the grand mall of land and water courses, bordered by elms and embellished by statuary and plantings (fig. 12, pl. LXXVII). The secondary axis of necessity then had to pass slightly west of the existing monument and to extend from the White House to another proposed shoreline site ultimately occupied by the Jefferson Memorial (figs. 13–15). In those extensions of axes and ultimate closures of vistas, the 1901–1902 plan departed from the relative openness of L'Enfant's, which had sought to exploit in a more visible, explicit way the city's interaction with the river that curved around it. It was symptomatic of the City Beautiful's urbanizing values that McKim, Mead, and White in their concurrent renovations at the University of Virginia were closing off with buildings the south edge of the "Lawn"—a vista that Jef-

ferson had intended to keep open (pls. LXXX–LXXXII).[26]

Government buildings designed to complement the neoclassicism of Jefferson's and L'Enfant's era were to line the Mall and encircle Capitol Hill and the White House, likewise tending to seal off official Washington from the neighboring commercial and residential districts. Pennsylvania Avenue, among other major thoroughfares, was to be broadened and the triangular area between it and the two primary axes reserved for a more intense governmental development (pl. LXVIII). With Burnham's prodding the Pennsylvania Railroad had agreed to relinquish its holdings in the Mall area and to build a new, handsome, and architecturally compatible Union Station north of Capitol Hill (fig. 16). As a counter-

12. Senate Park Commission, Plan of 1901–1902, *View Showing Proposed Treatment of Basin, Terraces, and Capitol Approaches, Head of Mall,* rendering by Henry McCarter
Commission of Fine Arts

13. Senate Park Commission, Plan of 1901–1902, *View of the Monument and Terraces from the White House*
From Moore 1902

14. Senate Park Commission, Plan of 1901–1902, *View in the Monument Garden, Looking toward the White House*
From Moore 1902

15. Senate Park Commission, Plan of 1901–1902, *View of the Washington Common and Public Playgrounds, Showing Proposed Memorial Building, Baths, Theater, Gymnasium, and Athletic Buildings*
From Moore 1902

point to the formally treated areas of the government center, Olmsted, in a style and manner worthy of his father, promoted the development of a far-reaching park system of naturalistic design (pl. LXIII).

Although the plan elicited a generally favorable, often enthusiastic response in official and popular circles, the scheme was not without its critics — both at the time of its submission and throughout the first half of the century as it slowly attained fulfillment. Some congressmen thought the plan overly visionary and had serious doubts concerning the accuracy of the cost estimates, which ranged from $200 million to $600 million. Others objected to specific proposals, such as one removing the Botanic Garden from the Mall at the foot of Capitol Hill, where greenhouses

UNION STATION
WASHINGTON, D.C.
1906

had stood for more than sixty years. Since the focus of the plan involved a westward extension from the Library of Congress, east-side Washingtonians objected that their section would continue to be slighted. Strong opposition existed for years to locating the Lincoln Memorial in what then was only a marshy backwater of the Potomac, where as one wag suggested, the structure "would shake itself down in loneliness and ague." Representative Joseph Cannon, the arch-conservative from Illinois, was the plan's most vicious and enduring critic. "So long as I live," he told Elihu Root, "I'll never let a monument to Abraham Lincoln be erected in that God-damned swamp." [27]

In addition to the closure of L'Enfant's river vistas, the character of his envisioned mall had changed from a grand processional avenue, such as the Champs Elysées, to a *tapis vert* that was similar to elements at Versailles and to the Schönbrunn Palace gardens in Vienna. No suggestions were made for underpassing the Mall as the senior Olmsted had done in New York's Central Park, with the resulting and endless criticism that the Mall was a "dividing" rather than a "uniting" urban space. Though the plan adumbrated the "Federal Triangle" that would arise in succeeding decades, little attention was paid to the corresponding area north of Pennsylvania

Avenue. The recommendation to surround and perhaps even to fill Lafayette Square, north of the White House, with administrative office buildings would have reared a foreboding wall around an area too intimate and domestically scaled to contain such mass. More technical problems were involved with the commission's insufficient study of strength factors surrounding the stepped, sunken plaza beneath the Washington Monument, one area of the Mall that would remain into the late twentieth century stylistically incompatible with its surroundings. Sufficient attention on a more symbolic level was also lacking in the commission's failure to provide appropriately for the location and housing of the judiciary, one of the three branches of government that had neither in L'Enfant's plan nor in subsequent efforts received consideration equal to the executive and legislative branches. Some thought the appropriate site would be at the west end of the Mall or the south end of the cross-axis. Ultimately, however, a new Supreme Court building was proposed for the northeast side of Capitol Hill, in the shadow of Congress. [28]

One attitude of the commissioners that would influence and reflect a prevailing City Beautiful obsession was the emphasis on stylistic "uniformity" and adherence as far as possible to the classical canon. This was a

16. D.H. Burnham and Company, Union Station, Washington (1903–1907), aerial perspective rendering, 1906
From Reps 1967

partially understandable response to the plan-less, heterogeneous, and frequently irrational departures from the L'Enfant plan during the nineteenth century. Yet had the commission been given its way, it would have demolished the best as well as the worst of the capital's nineteenth-century heritage – a tendency apparent throughout most City Beautiful planning. Though he circumspectly avoided such potentially explosive specifics in the report itself, Burnham told an astonished congressman that he trusted that one day the Library of Congress could be demolished, and he later confided to a friend that the commission planned ultimately "to wipe out the Smithsonian Institution." [29]

Despite such questionable recommendations, the plan of 1901–1902 was a momentous if continually controversial contribution to American urban planning. It was the first large effort to retrieve and restore the historic capital of the Founders, one of the earliest major attempts in the history of the republic to reestablish for any city a sense of continuity with its origins and with the national heritage, as expressed in architectural forms. It also spoke boldly for an impulse that was gaining national momentum.

Numerous popular periodicals reproduced the drawings, carrying the commission's concepts to the nation as a whole and to foreign countries as well. Members of the commission also helped to publicize the plan with articles, lectures, and interviews. Burnham discussed it at the Chicago Art Institute and wrote an article for *Century Magazine* linking the plan to the incipient Progressive movement – a reform of the landscape, he suggested, to complement the burgeoning reforms in other areas of society. [30]

Yet the House of Representatives, influenced by the hostile Joseph Cannon, officially ignored the plan, since Senator McMillan earlier had made the "politically egregious error" of failing to obtain House concurrence before appointing the Senate Park Commission. For that reason the commission could obtain no further funds and officially ceased to exist shortly after it presented its work in 1902. With the death of Senator McMillan in the summer of that same year, the plan lost its most important governmental supporter. Encouraged by the interest of presidents Roosevelt and Taft, however, Burnham and McKim continued making unofficial contributions of time and support. Charles Moore also retained his important affiliation with the Senate Committee on the District of Columbia. [31]

Despite the continued opposition in the lower house on other aspects of the plan, Congress took prompt action on the Union Station project and the removal of the old terminal from the Mall. Congress also provided for a number of important new facilities including House and Senate office buildings, new quarters for the Department of Agriculture, and an imposing complex by McKim, Mead, and White for the Army War College. The attempt to disregard the commission's plan in the placement of the new Agriculture Building led to an especially bitter fight and test of strength. Only by winning President Roosevelt over to their position that the structure's siting should respect the new line of the Mall were McKim and Burnham able to save their scheme. The Washington plan, Burnham wrote to Moore, would "persist in spite of all the Joe Cannons in the world" (fig. 17). [32]

The formal landscaping aspects of the proposals received little attention until 1910 when President Taft created a permanent Fine Arts Commission and appointed Burnham its first chairman. Under the leadership of Burnham and his successors, the commissioners became "virtually the executors of the Plan of

17. *Group of Le Nôtre – McKim Tree Butchers and Nature Butchers*, cartoon by Clifford K. Berryman
From *Evening Star* (Washington, 14 January 1908)

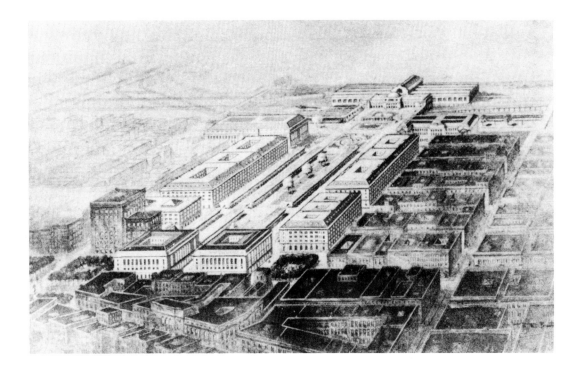

1901," and despite repeated skirmishes with Congress, by the end of World War I the commission had "made itself the arbiter of public taste in the Capital." The Lincoln Memorial reached completion in 1922, located virtually as the Senate Park Commission had intended it. On its completion someone asked the ancient Cannon what he thought of the memorial, and his answer seemed to vindicate the commission's long and bitter struggle. "I have been in many fights," Cannon replied. "Some I have lost—many I have won—it may have been better if I had lost more. I am pleased I lost the one against the Lincoln Memorial." [33]

Further building and landscaping programs in the spirit of the plan reached significant fulfillment during the administrations of Calvin Coolidge, Franklin D. Roosevelt, and Lyndon Johnson. Indeed, despite the slowness of execution, the McMillan Plan has made far too strong an impact on Washington and the nation for it ever again to be ignored or forgotten. The plan's ultimate efficaciousness derived from a number of factors peculiar to a national capital and not always transferable to other cities. While expensive in the aggregate, the cost of the Washington work represented, at any one time, only a minuscule percentage of the national tax base supporting it—hardly comparable to the pinch on urban

taxpayers of municipal bonds for purely local improvements.

This reality was complemented by the positive factors of national pride and patriotism—sentiments heightened by rigorous promotional campaigns to develop a capital that would evoke and reflect the nation's image and aspirations as the United States rose to greater prominence in the early twentieth century. In L'Enfant's day, the political and architectural allusions had been to republican Rome. In the era of McKinley, Roosevelt, Burnham, and McKim, the rhetoric and rationale were unabashedly imperial. Despite its intrinsically national attributes, the McMillan Plan and the continued campaign to promote its realization profoundly influenced ambitions to improve and embellish other American cities. During the early twentieth century the Washington example was especially effective in inspiring and confirming the development of state capitals, new and old, from Saint Paul, Minnesota, to Harrisburg, Pennsylvania, from Jackson, Mississippi, to Madison, Wisconsin, as well as in affecting the replanning of such larger metropolises as Cleveland, San Francisco, and Chicago (figs. 18, 19).

Washington, Burnham asserted, would become "a demonstration of the sense and soul

18. Group Plan Commission (Daniel H. Burnham, John M. Carrère, and Arnold W. Brunner), proposed Civic Center, Cleveland, 1903
From Group Plan Commission, *Report on a Group Plan of the Public Buildings of Cleveland* (Cleveland, 1903)

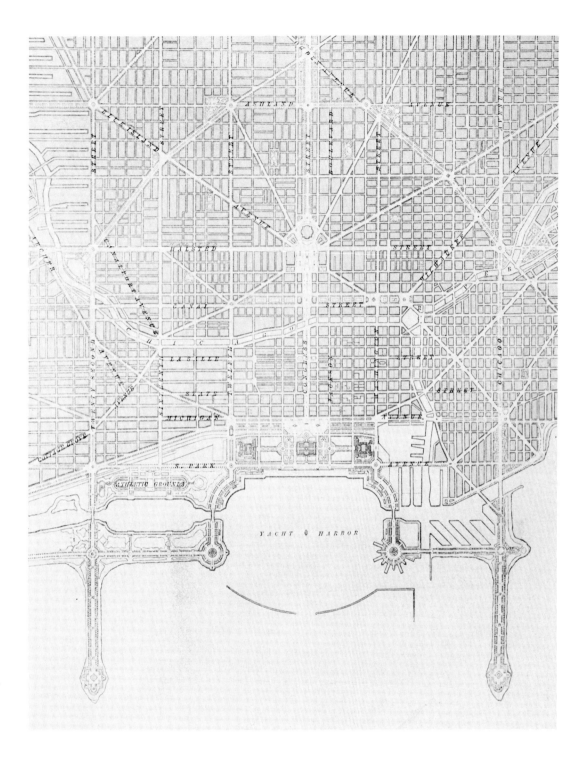

19. Daniel H. Burnham and Edward H. Bennett, Plan of Chicago, 1909, proposed lakefront development
From Burnham and Bennett 1909

of landscape art, so magnificent that the capitals of Europe shall confess it; so simple that the rawest county seat in the newest State . . . shall grasp and apply. The general plan is the thing." [34] The look and layout of twentieth-century Washington, therefore, owed as much to the architects and planners of the City Beautiful as to L'Enfant and the Founding Fathers. Burnham and the other commissioners of 1902 were, in fact, as certain as the first generation had been that noble architecture and sensitive urban design were essential components of a healthy environment, and indeed of what Jefferson himself had called "the pursuit of happiness."

NOTES

I dedicate this paper to the memory of my cousin and friend, Hope Howard Hart (1898–1986), who welcomed me at Union Station in June 1956, guided me then on my first tour of Washington, and continued through the years to educate and inspire me.

Portions of this paper appeared in variant forms in Thomas S. Hines, *Burnham of Chicago: Architect and Planner*, 2d ed. (Chicago, 1979); and in Hines, "The City Beautiful Movement in American Urban Planning," *Transactions of the Royal Society of British Architects* 7 (London, 1985), 28–43.

1. Edith Wharton, *A Backward Glance* (New York, 1934), 54–55.

2. Henry James, *The Ambassadors* (1902; reprint, New York, 1930), 62.

3. Henry Blake Fuller, *With the Procession* (1895; reprint, Chicago, 1965), 72–73; Robert Herrick, "The Background of the American Novel," *Yale Review* 3, new series, (January 1914), 224–225; Guy Alan Szuberla, "Urban Vistas and the Pastoral Garden: Studies in the Literature and Architecture of Chicago (1893–1909)" (Ph.D. diss., University of Minnesota, 1972).

4. See for example, Henry Demarest Lloyd, *Wealth Against Commonwealth* (New York, 1894); Ida Tarbell, *History of the Standard Oil Company* (New York, 1904); and Lincoln Steffens, *The Shame of the Cities* (New York, 1904).

5. Fuller 1965, 5, 58.

6. Charles N. Glaab and A. Theodore Brown, *A History of Urban America* (New York, 1967), 107–108.

7. Lewis Mumford, *The City in History: Its Origins, Its Transformations, and Its Prospects* (New York, 1961), 113–125.

8. Mumford 1961, 113.

9. See, for example, William H. Wilson, *The City Beautiful Movement in Kansas City* (Columbia, Mo., 1964); Jon A. Peterson, "The Origins of the Comprehensive City Planning Ideal in the United States, 1840–1911" (Ph.D. diss., Harvard University, 1967).

10. Burnham to James Windrim, 9 February 1891, Burnham Papers, Art Institute of Chicago; Charles Moore, "Interview with Daniel Burnham," unedited manuscript notes, Charles Moore Papers, Library of Congress, published in a slightly different form as "Lessons of the World's Fair: An Interview with the Late Daniel H. Burnham," *Architectural Record* 33 (January 1913), 36. Hines 1979, 73–124. Unless otherwise noted, the material in the following paragraphs about the Chicago fair is derived from this larger study. For more detailed information and citations, see the notes for chapters four and five therein.

11. Fuller 1965, 42, 97.

12. Hamlin Garland, *A Son of the Middle Border* (New York, 1917), 460; H.D. Lloyd to Burnham, 26 March 1895, Lloyd Papers, Wisconsin State Historical Society, Madison. For a full discussion of the Burnham motto, see Hines 1979, 401 n.8.

13. Henry Adams, *The Education of Henry Adams* (Boston, 1918), 339–343; William Dean Howells, *Letters of an Altrurian Traveller, 1893–1894* (reprint, Gainesville, Fla., 1961), 22–26; Theodore Dreiser, *Newspaper Days: A History of Myself* (New York, 1922), 249; Robert Herrick, *The Memoirs of an American Citizen* (New York, 1905), 192; Frances Hodgson Burnett, *Two Little Pilgrims' Progress: A Story of the City Beautiful* (New York, 1895).

14. Montgomery Schuyler, "Last Words about the World's Fair," *Architectural Record* 3 (January-March 1984), 291–301; Louis H. Sullivan, *The Autobiography of an Idea* (1924, reprint, New York, 1956), 321–325.

15. The basic document in the study of the redevelopment of Washington is the report itself: Charles Moore, ed., *The Improvement of the Park System of the District of Columbia*, 57th Cong., 1st sess., 1902, S. Rept. 166 (hereafter Moore 1902). For a more detailed treatment of Burnham's role in this work, see Hines 1979, 139–157, 352–355; John W. Reps, *Monumental Washington: The Planning and Development of the Capital Center* (Princeton, 1967), the most detailed treatment and critique to date; and Edmund G. Bacon, *Design of Cities* (New York, 1967), 222, which is especially suggestive in its brief comparison of the L'Enfant and McMillan plans.

16. Henry James, *The American Scene* (reprint, Bloomington and London, 1968), 332–364.

17. Charles Moore, *Daniel H. Burnham, Architect, Planner of Cities*, 2 vols. (Boston and New York, 1921), 1:135–140; 147–149; Moore 1902, 13. Burnham to William H. Brown, 7 October 1901; Burnham to Charles Moore, 24 August 1901, Burnham Papers.

18. Charles Moore, *The Life and Times of Charles Follen McKim* (Boston, 1929), 182, 188.

19. Burnham to Frederick Law Olmsted, Jr., 15 April 1901, Burnham Papers.

20. Moore 1921, 1: 156. In the *Life and Times of Charles Follen McKim*, 192, Moore wrote: "Some things seemed to them self-evident: that the problems in Washington must be worked out along Roman rather than Parisian lines; that simplicity, directness and the subordination of ornament to structural uses should prevail . . . Also that the effects produced by tree-crowned terraces should be sought where the configurations of the land permitted . . . More than this it was determined that the fountain and not the man-on-horseback is the proper ornament for Washington, and that the heat of our capital requires that the city should be filled with running water even as is Rome."

21. Burnham to "Old Man" [Lyman Gage?], 24 October 1901, Burnham Papers.

22. Burnham, 24 October 1901; Burnham to Charles F. Weller, August 1901; Burnham to Charles McKim, 3 August 1901; Burnham to Charles Moore, 23 August 1901; Burnham to William T. Partridge, 9 September 1901; Burnham to Frederick Law Olmsted, Jr., 9 September 1901, 15 October 1901, Burnham Papers; Burnham's diary, noted 16, 19–20 August; 15, 23, 26–29 September, 18–26 October, and 3–6 December as days that he spent in the east conferring with his colleagues, Burnham Papers; Reps 1967, 99–107. I disagree with Reps' emphasis on McKim as the leading figure in the Washington project. He apparently drew this impression partly from Glenn Brown's account of the story, which has the same emphasis. I also disagree with Reps' conclusion that Olmsted and Moore wrote the report almost alone. Its ideas, I believe, were truly a joint effort similar to the pooling of ideas by Burnham, Root, Codman, and Olmsted for the Columbian Exposition. Burnham's diaries and letters indicate that he contributed substantially to the rough written draft of the report. At least Burnham believed himself to be in charge; in 1911, he wrote: "I was chairman of the Washington Commission, and everything there was under my direction" (Burnham to H.A. Horwood, 27 February 1911, Burnham Papers).

23. Burnham to Charles Moore, 23 August 1901, Burnham Papers; Reps 1967, 103–104.

24. Burnham to Charles Moore, 30 August 1901, 1 and 10 February 1902, Burnham Papers.

25. Burnham to Charles Moore, 1 and 10 February 1902, Burnham Papers; Moore 1902, 58.

26. Bacon 1967, 222. George Humphrey Yetter, "Stanford White at the University of Virginia: Some New Light on an Old Question," *Journal of the Society of Architectural Historians* 40 (December 1981), 320–325; Leland M. Roth, *McKim, Mead, and White, Architects* (New York, 1983), 195–199.

27. Reps 1967, 139–154; Hans Paul Caemmerer, *The Life of Pierre Charles L'Enfant, Planner of the City Beautiful, the City of Washington* (Washington, 1950), 325; Philip Jessup, *Elihu Root*, 2 vols. (New York, 1938), 1:279–280.

28. Reps 1967, 133–138.

29. Reps 1967, 133–138; Burnham to H.M. Pettit, 30 June 1904, Burnham Papers.

30. Robert W. Wrigley, "Daniel H. Burnham, Architect and City Planner," *Journal of the American Institute of Planners* 35 (March 1961), 70–71; Moore, "The Improvement of Washington City," 623, 625–628; Daniel H. Burnham, "White City and Capital City," *Century Magazine* 63 (February 1902), 20; Moore 1921, 168–170.

31. Constance McLaughlin Green, *Washington, Capital City, 1879–1950* (Princeton, 1963), 133.

32. Green 1963, 141–142; Moore 1921, 1:205–229.

33. Reps 1967, 159.

34. Burnham 1902, 619–620. In a letter to Moore that same year, Burnham urged that he forward the Washington drawings for exhibition in Chicago, Saint Louis, and New York. "The value of this sort of thing," he wrote, "will not be alone the influence on Congress which may be needed, but also the influence in each city for the sake of good public work." Burnham to Moore, 5 March 1902, Burnham Papers. For an example of the widespread promotion and commendation of the Washington plan, see "Burnham Plan Liked," *Chicago Record-Herald*, 12 December 1904, and "Capital to Awe All; Washington in Ten Years Will Be Most Beautiful City in the World," *Chicago Record-Herald*, 17 December 1904. In "To Beautify Washington," *New York Times*, 13 November 1901, one notice stated: "The country knows of the Park Commission and the results of its work will no doubt be seen in many cities of the country, modeled after its initial development of the nation's capital."

JON A. PETERSON
Queens College of the City University of New York

The Mall, the McMillan Plan, and the Origins of American City Planning

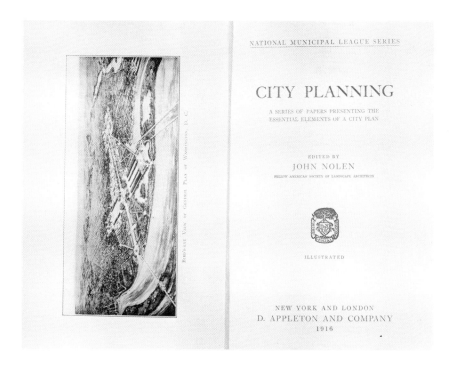

1. Frontispiece and title page from first edition of John Nolen's *City Planning* (New York and London, 1916) Frances Loeb Library, Graduate School of Design, Harvard University

In 1916, D. Appleton and Company published one of the first books on city planning written in the United States. Entitled *City Planning*, it appeared in the midst of the so-called City Practical era of the American planning movement, during which the costly monumentalism of the preceding City Beautiful period was supplanted by a more down-to-earth agenda. Indeed, the book's editor, John Nolen, a prominent landscape architect and consultant in the then-novel planning field, stressed practicality. Everything from land subdivision to water supply and rapid transit, from public buildings and parks to residential and industrial decentralization, was discussed by various specialists. Such topics, the book's subtitle suggested, represented the "essential elements of a city plan." [1]

But for one puzzling feature, Nolen's book would not merit attention in this collection of essays on the Mall: its frontispiece. Opposite the title page, occupying a position of conspicuous honor, was a reproduction of a painting of Washington, D.C. (fig. 1). It depicted the capital city as it would have appeared from four thousand feet if the plans of the United States Senate Park Commission of 1901–1902 (often remembered as the McMillan Commission) had been carried out (pls. LX–LXXXII). Especially highlighted in the painting was the proposed ceremonial core of Washington. This was a kite-shaped expanse of public domain anchored by the Capitol to the east, the White House to the north, the suggested Lincoln Memorial site to the west, and another commemorative site later taken by the Jefferson Memorial to the south. Significantly, this illustration was doing repeat service. Fourteen years earlier, it had appeared as the frontispiece of the Senate Park Commission report. [2]

Why this illustration, itself so emblematic of the City Beautiful, retained a position of such high honor in a book seemingly devoted to the City Practical, raises a fundamental

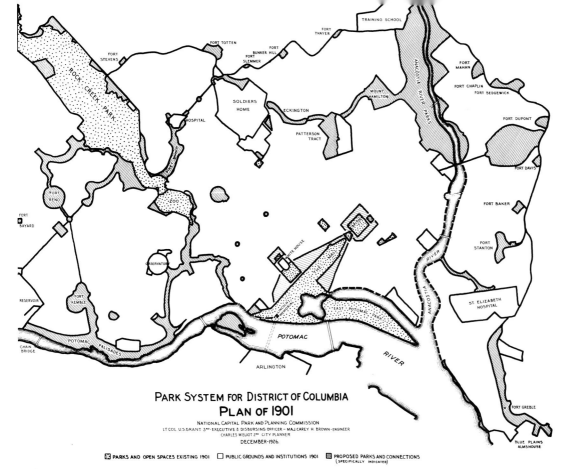

2. *Park System for the District of Columbia, Plan of 1901*, drawn by Charles W. Eliot II, National Capital Park and Planning Commission, 1926

From *Work of the National Capital Park and Planning Commission* (Washington, 1928). Frances Loeb Library, Graduate School of Design, Harvard University

PARK SYSTEM FOR DISTRICT OF COLUMBIA
PLAN OF 1901
NATIONAL CAPITAL PARK AND PLANNING COMMISSION
LT. COL. U.S.GRANT 3ʀᴰ·EXECUTIVE & DISBURSING OFFICER - MAJ·CAREY H. BROWN·ENGINEER
CHARLES W.ELIOT 2ᴺᴰ·CITY PLANNER
DECEMBER·1926.

PARKS AND OPEN SPACES EXISTING 1901   PUBLIC GROUNDS AND INSTITUTIONS 1901   PROPOSED PARKS AND CONNECTIONS (SPECIFICALLY INDICATED)

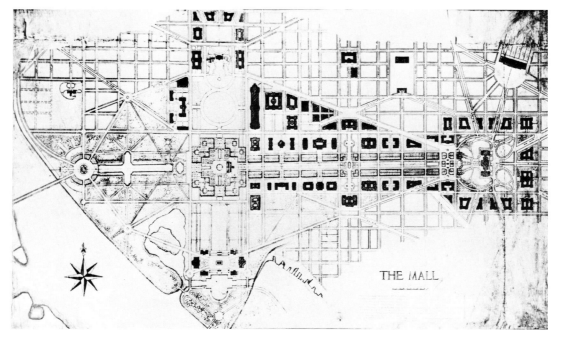

3. Senate Park Commission, Plan of 1901–1902, *The Mall*

From National Capital Park and Planning Commission, *Plans and Studies: Washington and Vicinity* (Washington, 1929). Frances Loeb Library, Graduate School of Design, Harvard University

THE MALL

question: what was the connection between the stunning plans of the Senate Park Commission for Washington and the national movement for city planning in the United States at the opening of the twentieth cen- tury? Nolen's book offers no explicit answer. He and his contributors neither explained the frontispiece nor said much about Washington. Thus, to understand Nolen's intent and to an- swer the question, both the McMillan Plan itself and its relationship to the broad history of the planning movement in the United States must be explored.

THE MALL AND THE McMILLAN PLAN

Published early in 1902, the McMillan Plan profoundly influenced American experience in two distinct ways. First, it reinterpreted Pierre L'Enfant's original design of the city by combining proposals for a system of parks, parkways, and shore reservations throughout the District of Columbia (fig. 2) with a grand design for the immense public grounds at the core, retaining the Mall as the centerpiece (fig. 3).[3] In so doing, the scheme laid the basis for the baroque monumentality and landscape spaciousness so intrinsic to the public image of the national capital today.

The second influence of the McMillan Plan was its catalytic role in initiating the national movement for city planning in the United States. The plan's bold scale and the public idealism it embodied inspired people in other cities to undertake similar actions. Within less than a decade an entirely novel field of public endeavor known as city planning had taken root. Although it would never fulfill all the hopes expressed for it, city planning represents one of the most distinctive innovations in American public life made by Progressive Era reform. It is this second, broader impact of the McMillan Plan that accounts for its frontispiece status in 1916 and that must now be explained.

Prior to the twentieth century, the term "city planning" did not yet exist in the ordinary language of American local governance. There were no "city planning" commissions or departments. No one was called a "city planner." No books, articles, or pamphlets had "city planning" in their titles.[4] Furthermore, no substitute terms existed. Even more important, no similar activity took place on a sufficiently competent, recurrent basis to generate such terms. In a fundamental sense, then, city planning itself did not yet exist, either in concept or in fact, although certain developments prefigured it and contributed to its later emergence.

If city planning was an early twentieth-century invention, what was invented? Ever since the term first came into usage around 1907–1908, it has possessed a certain malleability and looseness of meaning.[5] This quality, while it bedevils the historian, reflects the compelling, if equally malleable, principle that lay at the heart of the new field. As phrased by Nolen and other pioneers in the movement, this was the comprehensive city planning ideal. Without question, it is the key to understanding early twentieth-century city planning history, including the role of the McMillan Plan in originating the movement.[6]

In the decade following the publication of the McMillan Plan, the comprehensive city planning ideal expressed a growing commitment to a generalist form of urban planning. The urban fabric, it was believed, should be shaped by means of a coherent, omnibus program framed in advance by experts. For most of the pioneers, this objective meant devising a general scheme of a forward-looking, often visionary nature. Perfectly expressed, such a plan would be citywide in scope, multipurpose in conception, and integrated in formulation. It would chiefly address existing cities, not *de novo* townsites, and would emphasize almost exclusively the physical city. Usually it would take the form of an expert's report filled with diagrams, maps, and pictures illustrating the intended results. Daniel Burnham's *Plan of Chicago* (1909) is its most celebrated expression (fig. 4). Nolen's 1913 plan for Erie, Pennsylvania, offers another example (fig. 5).

If modern planning arose from the growing acceptance of this generalist or comprehensive conception of the shaping of cities, then it was the absence of such a conception that is crucial to understanding its nineteenth-century antecedents. Nineteenth-century planning for established urban centers was fragmentary, not comprehensive—at least not comprehensive in the sense just expounded. The point is not that American cities had never made farsighted provision for their physical betterment, but rather that such provisions, when made during the nineteenth century, did not manifest a generalist planning ideal of the sort that took root thereafter. Before the McMillan Plan the term "comprehensive" as applied to planning had other meanings.

Fragmentary planning reflected the economic and political realities of the nineteenth century, during which a new, dynamic urban-

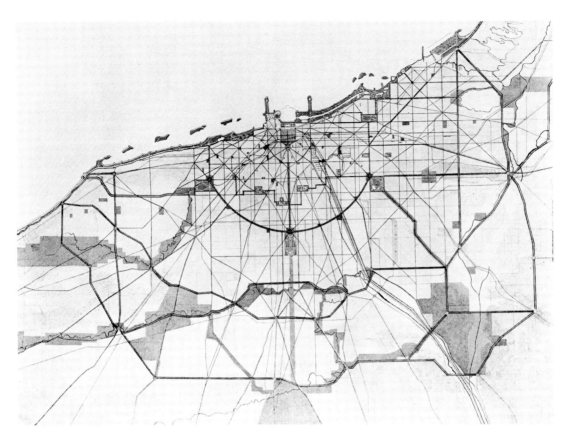

4. Daniel H. Burnham and Edward H. Bennett, *Plan of Chicago*, 1909, proposed system of streets, boulevards, parkways, and parks
From Burnham and Bennett, *Plan of Chicago* (Chicago, 1909). Frances Loeb Library, Graduate School of Design, Harvard University

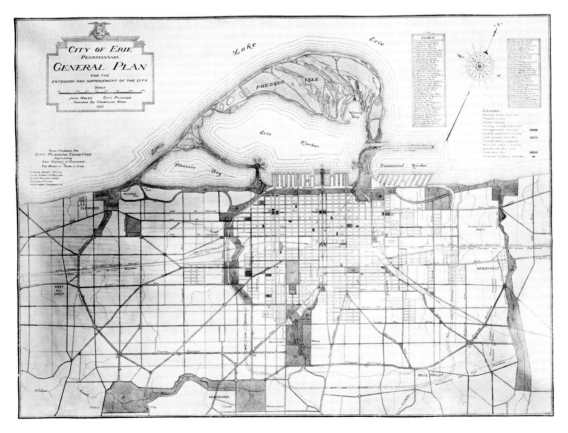

5. John Nolen, plan for Erie, Pennsylvania, 1913, showing proposed parks, boulevards, harbor improvements, belt-line railroad, and other features
Cornell University Libraries

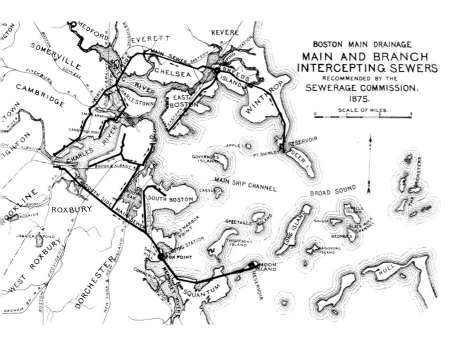

6. Metropolitan sewerage plan for Boston, 1875; a bold example of fragmentary planning meant to eliminate sewage pollution from the flats and estuaries bordering central Boston

From Eliot C. Clarke, *Main Drainage Works of the City of Boston* (Boston, 1885)

ism had emerged. Gone were the small, maritime cities founded along the Atlantic seaboard during the colonial era. In their place had arisen massive commercial-industrial centers increasingly enmeshed in an expanding national market economy. Big, congested, and highly concentrated in form, these great cities had expanded, often at a chaotic pace, through rapid surges of market-based growth. By its nature, such growth had been piecemeal and ill-coordinated.[7]

Local governmental authority had exerted little control over nineteenth-century urban growth. Strict judicial interpretation of municipal powers and the legal subordination of city to state government usually had precluded sweeping action.[8] Typically, power to plan the environment had been granted for quite special purposes such as parks, sewers, and water supply. For example, the sewers of New York City had been built one by one in response to property-owner petitions until 1865, when the New York State legislature authorized the Croton Aqueduct Board to plan sewers.[9] As a result of such initiatives, components of the city, such as a public park or the water supply, might be planned but not the city as a whole. Although fragmentary planning had been limited and special-purpose in nature, it had not necessarily been

trivial and unspectacular. A sewerage plan such as that prepared in 1875 for metropolitan Boston illustrates how the conception of this work could be bold and its scale colossal (fig. 6).

COMPREHENSIVE PLANNING AND THE McMILLAN PLAN

Nineteenth-century urban planning was sometimes described as "comprehensive." What was meant by this older use of the term is crucial to understanding the McMillan Plan and its role in American planning history. Prior to the twentieth century, the concept of comprehensiveness was predicated on the realities of piecemeal growth and limited public authority, and referred to the completeness and thoroughness with which a project was developed before its execution. For example, the governor of Massachusetts appointed a panel of experts in 1881 to devise "a comprehensive plan" for the drainage of a vast territory northwest of Boston.[10] Five years later the Park Commission of Worcester, Massachusetts, boasted that its plan for a park system was "comprehensive and wide-reaching" and thus "worthy of the city."[11] Finally, in 1896, the Regents of the University of California called for a "permanent and comprehensive plan" for a new University of California at Berkeley (fig. 7).[12]

In these and similar instances, the word *comprehensive* modified the word *plan*, denoting qualities of broad-minded and matured consideration. "Comprehensive plan," in short, applied to any of a great variety of urban schemes that were fully worked out in advance. Thus in the late nineteenth century, a park system might be "comprehensively" planned. And so might an institutional complex as at Berkeley, or a suburban site, or a public water supply.

Almost never subject to a comprehensive plan was the city itself. With only rare exceptions, no one advocated shaping the overall growth of existing urban centers.[13] For that idea to gain wide acceptance, the city would have to be seen as so interconnected that only a generalist approach to its development could produce a fully satisfactory result. Not even Frederick Law Olmsted, Sr., who is often celebrated as the premier urban planner of nineteenth-century America, advocated anything

so ambitious or idealistic. Olmsted argued vigorously for the comprehensive planning of park systems (fig. 8) and suburban fringe districts; yet he resisted broader application of the concept as impractical.[14] The built-up parts of cities, especially the business core, he argued, lay beyond significant change—as the 1666 London fire demonstrated.[15] More fundamental still, Olmsted shared with elite reformers of his era a distrust for the spoils system of politics and the rank corruption and incompetence of much city government.[16] For Olmsted, realism precluded a generalist approach.

Nonetheless, between the Civil War and the mid-1890s, several developments prefigured more sweeping forms of urban planning. But significantly, they did not generate a planning movement. A brief examination of two such episodes suggests the constraints on generalist planning then at work. It also suggests that historical circumstances play a major role in determining the nature of urban planning during any given era.

A first example of Gilded Age constraints on generalist modes of planning is provided by a massive public works program begun in Washington, D.C., in 1871. Spearheaded by Alexander "Boss" Shepherd, a newly created, powerful Board of Public Works upgraded the

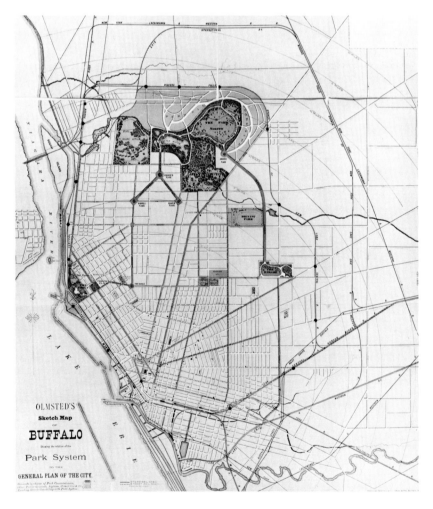

OLMSTED'S
Sketch Map
OF
BUFFALO
Showing the relation of the
Park System
TO THE
GENERAL PLAN OF THE CITY.

city, using a "comprehensive plan" devised by a panel of five experts, including Quartermaster General Montgomery C. Meigs and Frederick Law Olmsted. The plan emphasized street improvements, drainage, harbor facilities, and public markets. In practice, however, Shepherd stressed massive street betterment, but not always according to plan.[17] No sooner did construction begin than evidence of shoddy work, mismanagement, arbitrary power, and corruption surfaced. By 1873, the out-of-town press had dubbed Shepherd's Board of Public Works Washington's "Tammany."[18] Despite lasting improvement to the city, the entire effort collapsed in 1874, reinforcing the lessons then recently taught by the fall of the Tweed Ring in New York. To the reform-minded, fiscal stringency, not better planning, appeared to be the answer.[19] Comprehensive planning, even when attempted along early twentieth-century lines, was premature under Gilded Age conditions. Incompetent execution and an unsympathetic audience precluded its development as a civic ideal.

In an entirely different vein, reflecting elite culture near the end of the Gilded Age, the World's Columbian Exposition of 1893, held in Chicago, kindled much talk of planning but no planning movement (fig. 9). For all its apparent perfections, the fair had resulted from an evolutionary process impossible to duplicate in cities. As P.B. Wight, the Chicago architect who daily viewed the construction of the fair, observed: "Neither the Grand Court nor the whole plan of the Park was the result of a simple comprehensive plan. . . . No body of men could have conceived all its varied features, and recorded them all on paper before executing any of the work. . . . It was absolutely necessary to begin the work on a tentative and elastic plan, which was modified and enlarged from time to time until the whole ground was covered."[20]

Then as now, American cities lacked the authority over their own development that would have been necessary for evolutionary planning, as exemplified by the Chicago fair, to succeed on a citywide scale. As the fair's chief of construction, Daniel Burnham had orchestrated all physical aspects of the undertaking from design to construction, from engineering to policing and maintenance, from bidding on contracts to hiring and firing workmen.[21] In Washington not even Boss Shepherd had exercised comparable power. Any attempt to incorporate such absolute authority into the fabric of municipal democracy was out of the question.

When the architects and artists who shaped the Chicago fair returned to their home cities

seeking ways to exploit its brilliant after-image, none advocated a movement to shape the city as a whole. Rather, as the history of public art activism in the 1890s makes clear, they championed small, practical projects such as courthouse adornment, or they proposed big, but still fragmentary schemes such as waterfront parks or civic building groups.[22] A Cleveland plan for the Lake Erie waterfront (1899–1900) illustrates this tendency (fig. 10). The wish for more sweeping transformation of cities was no doubt present, but Gilded Age realism still held the upper hand.

The McMillan Plan imparted a novel meaning to the words "comprehensive planning," and even more important, that new meaning soon gained acceptance. A major reason was the plan itself. By a remarkable convergence of events, too complex to detail here, the Senate Park Commission brought together two previously distinct realms of public planning, each representative of the fragmentary character of nineteenth-century urban development.[23] Specifically, the commission drew on the vital tradition of citywide park-system design which had evolved in the United States since the Civil War (fig. 11); and in an unprecedented fashion, the commission employed this tradition to advance aspirations for civic art emerging among the American architectural elite (fig. 12).[24] Consequently, the McMillan Plan combined a citywide park system of immense sophistication with a visually spectacular scheme for the ceremonial core of Washington (pl. LXIII). These combined modes of planning became the means for addressing other issues, such as locating a new union railroad terminal, clearing a slum in what is now the Federal Triangle, providing a city playground system, bridging the Potomac River, and preserving Civil War fortifications.[25]

Charles Moore, secretary to the Senate Park Commission and the major writer of its report, would rightly describe the plan as "the most comprehensive ever provided for the development of an American city."[26] No doubt Moore employed the word comprehensive in its old sense. But his emphasis on the superlative signaled a shift in meaning. Thus, when admirers of the scheme began to call for "comprehensive plans" elsewhere, they wanted something that reflected the same bold idealism and imaginative sweep. Soon, the old words functioned as a compound noun—a term

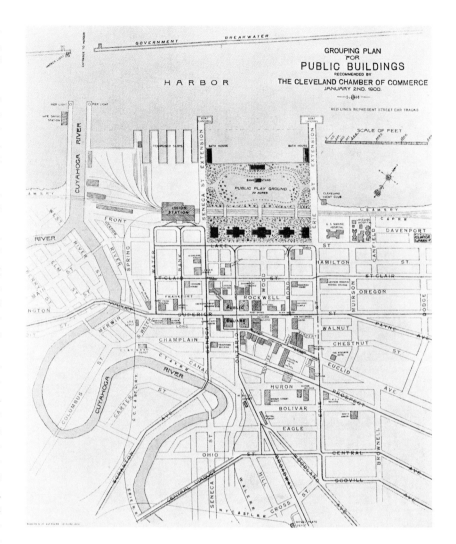

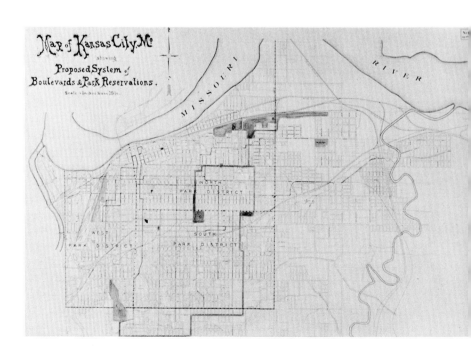

in its own right – denoting a novel conception of planning, qualitatively distinct from nineteenth-century practice.

The question that remains is why the McMillan Plan had this influence. The plan itself is part of the answer. The breadth and complexity of its proposals, their patriotic aura, their resonance with the original L'Enfant plan, their evocation of great epochs of European civilization, their consummate professionalism and manifest urbanity – all contributed to their public appeal. Even more crucial were the historical circumstances. At the beginning of the twentieth century, a national mood and an economic climate exceptionally favorable to a new vision of urban planning had taken hold. It was an upbeat age; many people were open to possibilities never seriously considered by previous generations.

THE BIRTH OF A NEW PLANNING IDEAL

What had changed by 1902 that enabled the McMillan Plan to inspire a national movement for comprehensive city planning? At least three interrelated circumstances contributed to the change: such planning now had a receptive audience; for urban progressive reform had transcended Gilded Age constraints, establishing a mood supportive of public idealism; and finally, urban America had entered what Carl Condit has rightly called "perhaps the greatest creative period in the evolution of the modern city and modern urban technology." [27]

Only a highlighting of these circumstances is possible. First, the audience. All across the nation, especially in major cities, but also in many smaller communities, a diffuse, rather inchoate drive to upgrade the appearance of urban centers had taken root as the economic depression of the mid-1890s lifted. This was the City Beautiful movement. As of 1902, it had yet to become a planning movement. Drawn from the upper ranks of local society, including businessmen and many women, its leaders crusaded to enhance the beauty of their home communities, even if in practice this meant no more than cleaning up vacant lots, planting street trees, regulating billboards, or waging now-forgotten wars against public spitting. Modest, piecemeal improvement, as in Harrisburg, Pennsylvania, typified much local effort (figs. 13, 14). In big cities, especially New York, the same impulse often inspired grander schemes, such as waterfront esplanades, bridge approaches, and civic sculpture. But everywhere, enthusiasm for concrete action, not general urban plans, propelled the movement forward.[28]

The much publicized McMillan Plan offered inspiration to City Beautiful leaders, especially on the national level, by suggesting a new way to direct their efforts. Local energies, so prone to haphazard results, might now be focused by asking experts to devise schemes of comparable breadth and public spirit. Charles Mulford Robinson, the most prolific of the City Beautiful advocates, immediately embraced comprehensive planning for precisely these reasons.[29] Charles Zueblin, a spellbinding platform lecturer for the City Beautiful cause, also endorsed the new ideal with alacrity. In his September 1902 presidential address before the American League for Civic Improvement, he discoursed on "A Decade of Civic Improvement." "No city," he proclaimed, "should be content with anything less than a comprehensive plan incorporating the best accomplishments of the last ten years."[30]

New York City advocates of public art responded the fastest of all. Only four days after the McMillan Plan went on display in Washington, the *New York Times* editorialized on "The Art of City Making."[31] Those who had seen the plan, the editors reported, agreed that it "would make Washington 'the most beautiful city in the world.' What a tantalizing prospect this must be for an artistically sensitive New Yorker!" Tantalizing indeed. Within a month, the Fine Arts Federation had made the McMillan Plan the basis of a campaign for a public improvement commission.[32]

13, 14. A piecemeal beautification project, before and after, in Harrisburg, Pennsylvania, about 1900–1905
Frances Loeb Library, Graduate School of Design, Harvard University

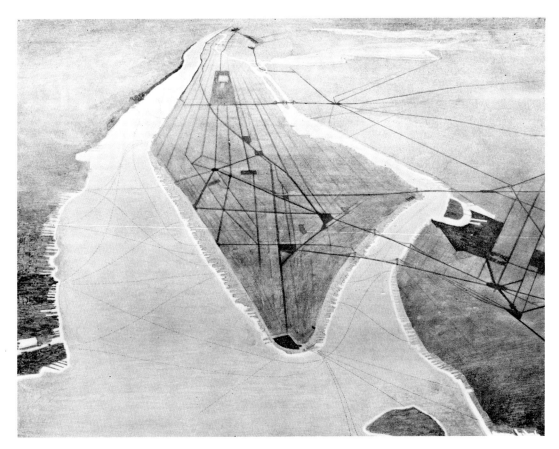

15. New York City Improvement Commission Plan, 1907, aerial view looking north, emphasizing street openings in lower Manhattan and boulevard links between the major boroughs

From The Report of the New York City Improvement Commission (New York, 1907). Frances Loeb Library, Graduate School of Design, Harvard University

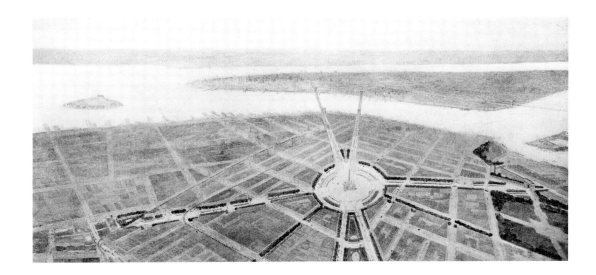

16. New York City Improvement Commission Plan, proposed bridge plaza, Brooklyn, 1907

From Report of the New York City Improvement Commission, 1907. Frances Loeb Library, Graduate School of Design, Harvard University

After a struggle, New York got its commission and, in time, its comprehensive plan (figs. 15–16). Meanwhile, San Francisco civic leaders contacted Daniel Burnham as early as May 1903, and soon enlisted him to frame a general plan for their city.[33]

Why City Beautiful leaders found the new planning concept so compelling also stems from the emergence of urban progressive reform with its summons to public idealism. For all its baffling diversity this wider movement, just then attaining full force, had identified the city as the critical arena in which the future of the nation was being determined.[34] Already, reformers had devised a host of solutions – political, educational, moral, and environmental – to the city's ills. No one person or organization possibly could have coordinated all these strands of activity, but the leitmotif running through most of them was that public life and public values must be revitalized if the waste, incompetence, and socially neglectful materialism of the Gilded Age were to be transcended. It was believed that devotion to the civic good – what was called the new citizenship or new civic spirit – had to be accorded a more central position in American life.[35]

The McMillan Plan appealed to this socially affirmative mood. It suggested a novel way to mount a concerted attack on the perceived failings of the city and to ennoble public life. A general plan was seen as more than a practical scheme; framed by independent experts, it would also be a unifying and beautiful expression of the public interest.[36] To a reform generation unembarrassed by public idealism, the McMillan Plan suggested a rational means by which to steer human progress, and to symbolize the higher order of civilization toward which they believed they were already moving.

In 1902 none of these ideas seemed impractical. The nation had entered an era of unprecedented city building. The national economy was booming. Municipal purse strings, tight since the mid-1870s, had loosened around 1890, only to tighten again during the mid-1890s depression. Now they loosened once more.[37] By 1902, not only had many great urban public works, initiated a decade or more earlier, come to fruition, but private construction also was booming. The new century seemed bright with the promise of even more ambitious endeavors.

The drive for public improvement is well illustrated by Chicago, where the celebrated Sanitary and Ship Canal opened in 1900. Ten years in the making and one of the biggest public works projects of the nineteenth century, the canal directed the city's sewage wastes away from Lake Michigan into the Mississippi River Basin.[38] Within the next five years businessmen began constructing a unique freight tunnel network under the traffic-clogged, downtown streets.[39] Concurrently, the South Park District started building its renowned

playground system, featuring community-center fieldhouses located on plots ranging from five to sixty acres.[40] A Special Park Commission also projected a park system of unprecedented regional scale, much of it later realized as the Cook County Forest Preserves.[41] And while all this was happening, Chicago traction companies were completing "one of the best rapid transit systems in the world."[42] The list of improvements in Chicago was extensive, as it was in other cities as well.[43]

Such an era provided a special opportunity for comprehensive planning as suggested by the McMillan Plan. Here was a novel means by which to coordinate, focus, and systematize the prodigious city building energies then at work. Between 1904 and 1909, at least thirty-seven towns and cities would consult various architects, landscape architects, and other advisers for suggestions about general improvement.[44] Daniel Burnham, drawing on his experience with the Chicago fair and the McMillan Plan, would produce schemes for San Francisco, Manila and Baguio in the Philippines, and Chicago. Charles Mulford Robinson would author eighteen reports for communities as diverse as Jamestown, New York; Denver, Colorado; and Honolulu, Hawaii. And a young landscape architect, John Nolen, would launch his planning career just as this burst of pioneer activity got underway.[45]

The McMillan Plan only initiated this process. As the new movement took hold, its underlying principle was more broadly applied. Initially, most schemes did no more than blend antecedent forms of fragmentary planning from the nineteenth century with piecemeal beautification and improvement ideas then current – parks and park systems with playgrounds and waterfront improvements; civic building groups with public art; railroad station design with street beautification. By 1909, however, functional issues, especially traffic circulation, claimed major attention as both planners and clients grappled with the practical needs of cities.[46]

Unlike the limited-purpose planning of the late nineteenth century, the new planning ideal gave license to an expanded agenda. Logically, there were no limits to comprehensive planning as then conceived; in principle, it could be applied to any or all aspects of the physical city. This possibility, however theoretical, imparted extraordinary flexibility. As early as

1909, a Boston-area Metropolitan Improvements Commission prepared a scheme in which transportation issues all but eliminated any concern for beauty.[47] Yet the report, despite its radical discontinuity with prior schemes, was regarded as part of the new movement.[48] By World War I, issues of private land use, previously ignored by beautifiers, would gain prominence in city planning literature.[49] Beauty had become one of many goals; functional objectives now received priority.

Concurrently, planning leaders deepened — as well as broadened — the meaning of their new ideal. Comprehensive planning now meant more than the making of generalist plans of ever greater scope; it became the concept that undergirded planning as a unified field of public endeavor and body of practical knowledge. The term expressed the planners' belief that the physical city must be seen as a complex organism whose interconnections must be systematically understood and acted upon in order to achieve farsighted, socially beneficial change.

In retrospect it is apparent that the McMillan Plan catalyzed a movement which in turn quickly evolved beyond beautification. The underlying ideal of comprehensive city planning increasingly sustained the conviction that diverse forms of practical knowledge and experience, previously pursued in fragments, should now be brought together as a coherent public agenda to master the urban environment. It was precisely this societal ideal that had never taken hold in the nineteenth century. The emergence of comprehensive planning in the early twentieth century comprises one of the great events in the history of American urbanism.

Come 1916, it is little wonder that Nolen, when he edited his book, selected a frontispiece that paid unspoken homage to the McMillan Plan. Nor is it any wonder that Nolen would ask his mentor and colleague, Frederick Law Olmsted, Jr., to write the introductory essay explaining the root principles of city planning. Olmsted was then president of the National Conference on City Planning, an annual forum begun in 1909 to discuss planning issues. Like Burnham, he too had been a member of the Senate Park Commission and had subsequently framed several general plans for American cities.

City planning, Olmsted explained, attempted "to exert a well-considered control on behalf of the people of a city over the development of their physical environment as a whole." It reflected "a growing appreciation of a city's organic unity, of the interdependence of its diverse elements, and of the profound and inexorable manner in which the future of this great organic unit is controlled by the actions and omissions of to-day.... Nothing which may conceivably become a part of the city or affect the city's future can logically be excluded from its field." In short, the new field rested on "the new social ideal of unified and comprehensive city planning." It appealed, he confessed, to "our hopeful idealism." [50]

By 1916 the principle that had been nurtured since the appearance of the McMillan Plan had become the firmly acknowledged basis of city planning. Whether it could survive the deeper traditions of piecemeal growth and limited public authority that had long rendered American urban planning a fragmented art remained to be seen. At the time Nolen assembled his book, city planning had already shifted its focus toward the City Practical in search of an effective response to this challenge, but it was far from yielding the compelling ideal of comprehensiveness on which its entire endeavor rested.

NOTES

The author wishes to acknowledge the Frances Loeb Library, Graduate School of Design, Harvard University, which made available many of the photographs for this paper.

1. John Nolen, ed., *City Planning: A Series of Papers Presenting the Essential Elements of a City Plan* (New York, 1916).

2. Charles Moore, ed., *The Improvement of the Park System of the District of Columbia*, 57th Cong., 1st sess., 1902, S. Rept. 166 (hereafter Moore 1902).

3. Moore 1902.

4. For the novelty of the term "city planning," see Frederick Law Olmsted, "Introduction" in Nolen 1916, 1. For a rare nineteenth-century use of the phrase, see Horace Bushnell, *Work and Play; or Literary Varieties* (New York, 1864), 336. In the late nineteenth and very early twentieth centuries, the term "city plan" referred to the official map of a city. For example, see Andrew Wright Crawford, "The Development of Park Systems in American Cities," in American Academy of Political and Social Science, *City Life and Progress* (Philadelphia, 1905), 17.

5. The emergence of "city planning" can be traced through the monthly "Notes and Comments" section in *Architectural Record* 21–23 (January 1907–June 1908).

6. Jon A. Peterson, "The Origins of the Comprehensive City Planning Ideal in the United States, 1840–1911" (Ph.D. diss., Harvard University, 1967).

7. For case studies that discuss market-based growth, see Eugene P. Moehring, *Public Works and the Patterns of Urban Real Estate Growth in Manhattan, 1835–1894* (New York, 1981); Christine Meisner Rosen, *The Limits of Power: Great Fires and the Process of City Growth in America* (New York, 1986); and Sam Bass Warner, Jr., *Streetcar Suburbs: The Process of Growth in Boston, 1870–1900* (Cambridge, 1962).

8. Ernest S. Griffith, *A History of American City Government: The Conspicuous Failure, 1870–1900* (New York, 1974), 211.

9. Moehring 1981, 38. For the American planning concepts associated with nineteenth-century sanitation, see Jon A. Peterson, "The Impact of Sanitary Reform upon American Urban Planning, 1840–1890," *Journal of Social History* 13 (Fall 1979), 83–103.

10. "The Metropolitan Drainage System for Boston," *American Architect and Building News* 9 (4 June 1881), 266.

11. The Parks Commission of the City of Worcester, *Annual Report* (Worcester, Mass., 1887), 21.

12. Samuel E. Moffett, "A Western City of Learning," *Harper's Weekly* 41 (11 September 1897), 906.

13. For a rare instance, see Robert Morris Copeland, *The Most Beautiful City in the World: Essay and Plan for the Improvement of the City of Boston* (Boston, 1872).

14. For examples of Olmsted's use of the term "comprehensive," see: Olmsted, Vaux, and Company, *Preliminary Report Respecting a Public Park in Buffalo, and a Copy of the Act of the Legislature Authorizing Its Establishment* (Buffalo, 1869), 12; Frederick Law Olmsted and John Charles Olmsted, *The Projected Park and Parkways of the South Side of Buffalo* (Buffalo, 1888), 9, 16. For commentary on Olmsted's ideal of comprehensive planning, see David Schuyler, *The New Urban Landscape: The Redefinition of City Form in Nineteenth-Century America* (Baltimore, 1986), 130–133, 172–179.

15. Frederick Law Olmsted, *Public Parks and the Enlargement of Towns (1870)* (New York, 1970), 12–13. For similar views, see H.W.S. Cleveland, *Landscape Architecture as Applied to the Wants of the West* (Chicago, 1873), 49–50.

16. Geoffrey Blodgett, "Frederick Law Olmsted: Landscape Architecture as Conservative Reform," *Journal of American History* 62 (March 1976), 869–889.

17. William H. Maury, *Alexander "Boss" Shepherd and the Board of Public Works*, GW Washington Studies, no. 3 (Washington, 1975), 6–9; Constance McLaughlin Green, *Washington: Village and Capital, 1800–1878* (Princeton, 1962), 345, 349.

18. Green 1962, 351.

19. Green 1962, 358–362; Seymour J. Mandelbaum, *Boss Tweed's New York* (New York, 1965), 59–104.

20. P.B. Wight, "The Great Exhibition Reviewed," *American Architect and Building News* 42 (14 October 1893), 22.

21. Thomas S. Hines, *Burnham of Chicago: Architect and Planner* (New York, 1974), 92, 94.

22. Jon A. Peterson, "The City Beautiful Movement: Forgotten Origins and Lost Meanings," *Journal of Urban History* 2 (August 1976), 417–428.

23. For a detailed analysis of this convergence, see Jon A. Peterson, "The Nation's First Comprehensive City Plan: A Political Analysis of the McMillan Plan for Washington, D.C., 1900–1902," *Journal of the American Planning Association* 51 (Spring 1985), 134–150.

24. Albert Fein, "The American City: The Ideal and the Real," in *The Rise of an American Architecture*, ed. Edgar Kaufmann, Jr. (New York, 1970), 51–111; Richard Guy Wilson, "Architecture, Landscape, and City Planning," in *The American Renaissance, 1876–1917* [exh. cat., Brooklyn Museum] (New York, 1979), 74–109.

25. Peterson 1985, 134–150.

26. Moore 1902, 16.

27. Carl W. Condit, *The Port of New York: A History of the Rail and Terminal System from the Grand Central Electrification to the Present* (Chicago, 1981), XI.

28. Peterson 1976, 415–434.

29. Charles Mulford Robinson, "What the Smallest Town Should Do," *Public Improvements* 7 (July 1902), 108. See also Robinson, *Modern Civic Art or the City Made Beautiful* (New York, 1903), 271–286.

30. Charles Zueblin, "A Decade of Civic Improvement," in American League for Civic Improvement, *Nation-Wide Civic Betterment* (Chicago, 1903), 18.

31. "The Art of City Making," *New York Times* (19 January 1902), 8.

32. Editorial, *American Architect and Building News* 75 (15 February 1902), 49.

33. Judd Kahn, *Imperial San Francisco: Politics and Planning in an American City, 1897–1906* (Lincoln, Neb., 1979), 80–84.

34. Ernest S. Griffith, *A History of American City Government: The Progressive Years and Their Aftermath, 1900–1920* (New York, 1974), 9, 32; Paul Boyer, *Urban Masses and Moral Order in America, 1820–1920* (Cambridge, Mass., 1978), 189–190.

35. Charles Zueblin, *A Decade of Civic Development* (Chicago, 1905), 1–11; Boyer 1978, 252–276.

36. Robinson 1903, 280–286; Zueblin 1905, VI.

37. Joel A. Tarr, "Building the Urban Infrastructure in the Nineteenth Century: An Introduction," in Public Works Historical Society, *Infrastructure and Urban Growth in the Nineteenth Century*, no. 14 of *Essays in Public Works History* (Chicago, 1985), 77–78.

38. Harold M. Mayer and Richard C. Wade, *Chicago: Growth of a Metropolis* (Chicago, 1969), 274.

39. Mayer and Wade 1969, 216–218.

40. Charles Zueblin, *American Municipal Progress* (New York, 1916), 303; City of Chicago, *Report of the Special Park Commission to the City Council of Chicago on the Subject of a Metropolitan Park Commission* (Chicago, 1905), 32.

41. Graham Romeyn Taylor, "Recreation Developments in Chicago Parks," *Annals of the American Academy of Political and Social Science* 35 (March 1910), 102, 105.

42. Carl W. Condit, *Chicago, 1910–1929: Building, Planning, and Urban Technology* (Chicago, 1973), 39.

43. Zueblin 1916.

44. "A List of American City Planning Reports," *The American City* 11 (December 1914), 490–497.

45. John Hancock, "John Nolen: The Background of a Pioneer Planner," *Journal of the American Institute of Planners* 26 (November 1960), 308–309.

46. Peterson 1967, 412–416.

47. The Commonwealth of Massachusetts, *Public Improvements for the Metropolitan District, Report of the Commission on Metropolitan Improvements,* (Boston, 1909).

48. "Notes and Comments," *Architectural Record* 26 (September 1909), 234–235.

49. Nolen 1916, 35–44, 76–83.

50. Olmsted, in Nolen 1916, 1–3.

General Plan
for the
Improvement
OF THE
U. S. CAPITOL GROUNDS.

DAVID C. STREATFIELD
University of Washington

The Olmsteds and the Landscape of the Mall

The landscape of the Mall proposed by the members of the Senate Park Commission in 1901–1902 was one of the most grandiloquent essays in civic space ever envisioned in America, or indeed in any Western country (pls. LX–LXXXII). The existing landscape is largely derived from this extraordinarily ambitious and noble vision, which was conceived as a restoration of the "spirit" of the plan for Washington made by Major Pierre Charles L'Enfant in 1791. The "Grand Avenue" in L'Enfant's plan ultimately became the Mall. The authors of the McMillan Plan and their principal supporters contended that it was not a departure, but represented a conscious attempt to recreate the "intentions" of L'Enfant, who a century before had created a plan in a longstanding landscape design tradition.

L'Enfant's plan was a bold essay in the mode of the French baroque garden tradition that attained its zenith in the second half of the seventeenth century. Yet the implementation of his vision, albeit in a reinterpreted form, was entrusted to Frederick Law Olmsted, Jr., who, like his father, was committed to the idea of a naturalistic landscape park as the central focus in the American city, symbolizing nature in a way that was civilizing, democratic, educative, and ultimately transcendental. The senior Olmsted's treatment of the Capitol grounds, begun in 1874, had been fully in this tradition. Despite the apparent paradox of a designer committed to this tradition being entrusted with the re-creation of a landscape

whose conceptual basis was its precise antithesis, the two Olmsteds were largely responsible for the design of the Mall as it developed until the late 1940s. This essay will explore that paradox and the related complexities of congressional opposition, indecision, and parsimony between 1874, when the senior Olmsted was hired to design the Capitol grounds, and 1948, when his son's influence ended.

LATE NINETEENTH-CENTURY LANDSCAPE DEVELOPMENT OF THE MALL

By the time that Frederick Law Olmsted, Sr. was commissioned by the Architect of the Capitol to prepare a design for the Capitol grounds on 26 March 1874, the area extending from that precinct to the Potomac bore no resemblance to the landscape that L'Enfant had visualized, but rather manifested what Glenn Brown later referred to as the "garden approach."[1] The Mall was in fact a series of gardens, each administered by a different congressional committee and professional staff and none particularly well maintained (pls. XLVIII–LVII). Lying directly to the west of the Capitol was the Botanic Garden, administered by the Joint Committee on the Library. Enclosed by a high wall and surmounted by a high fence, the garden separated the Mall from the Capitol grounds. The section of the Mall between Third Street and the grounds of the Smithsonian Institution was planted between 1872 and 1878 by Colonel Orville Babcock of the United States Army Corps of Engineers. The grounds of the Smithsonian Institution had been partially executed according to Andrew Jackson Downing's 1851 plan, but the remainder of his scheme was never realized (pls. XXVIII, XXIX, XXXVI). To the west, the grounds of the Agricultural Building were more formal in layout. To the east, Congress had granted in 1872 a right-of-way to the Baltimore and Potomac Railroad across the Mall on Sixth Street.[2]

The grounds around the Capitol had been enclosed and surrounded by a road a few years after President Washington's death. Between 1825 and 1830 John Foy, a gardener, laid out a simple design of flat rectangular plots bordered by trees and flowerbeds separated by gravel walks on the east side of the Capitol. According to Olmsted this scheme was "pretty and becoming" when it was properly maintained, but appropriations were irregular and inadequate. During Andrew Jackson's presidency, when it was obvious that the city was expanding on the west side of the Capitol, seven acres were added to the grounds on the western slope. This area was planted by John Maher with trees that later died because of the poor soil. By 1873 the Capitol grounds had been increased to about fifty acres.[3] Edward Clark, then Architect to the Capitol, had complained since 1871 about the necessity for a plan for the grounds. In his annual report of 1 November 1873, he wrote: "Not having a practice or potentials to skill as landscape gardener, I earnestly recommend that a first-class artist in this line may be employed to plan, plant, and lay out these grounds."[4]

Olmsted's approach to the design and planning of landscapes was comprehensive and rational. It was applied to a broad range of projects extending from small gardens to regional landscapes. It was democratic in nature and drew both from the natural and social sciences. Olmsted's vision was progressive and addressed issues of physical and psychological health, as well as questions of public open space, transportation, housing, recreation, and aesthetics. His approach was based on an organic theory that was derived from the idealism of German philosophers such as Friedrich Schelling; the work of Thomas Carlyle,

John Ruskin, and Ralph Waldo Emerson; and landscape theorists such as William Gilpin and Sir Uvedale Price.[5] With Calvert Vaux, his first partner, Olmsted founded the profession of landscape architecture in the United States. The sheer volume and diversity of Olmsted's landscape work is most impressive. But the true meaning of this legacy continues to attract divergent interpretations. Albert Fein believes that Olmsted was a progressive figure orchestrating the most avant-garde intellectual ideas of his time by using the role of the artist as a moral agent. Geoffrey Blodgett, on the other hand, views Olmsted as a member of a conservative and educated elite that advocated a genteel reform program to counter the vulgarities of a pluralistic society.[6]

In practice Olmsted's designs for gardens, parks, the grounds of public institutions, and subdivisions were dominated by a preference for naturalistic landscapes derived from that version of the picturesque style associated with Humphry Repton. Olmsted's pastoral designs reflected a fascination with the New England landscapes of his boyhood and a great admiration for English eighteenth-century parks. But his public landscape designs, which were derived from the forms of those aristocratic English parks, were created primarily for the urban poor and were intended to re-create images of rural landscapes that would have calming effects for people who led stressful lives in the cities.

Most of Olmsted's naturalistic landscapes contained minor formal elements, such as the malls in New York's Central Park and Boston's Franklin Park, which were largely subsumed within the surrounding informal imagery. But Olmsted was quite willing to develop more classically ordered plans. As an ardent advocate of regionalism, he had been forced to recognize the inappropriateness of lawns "west of Missouri and to hardly anything south of Pennsylvania," and the consequent suitability of formal, Mediterranean-inspired solutions to the peculiar problems of the California landscape at Stanford University.[7] At the same time, his willingness to adopt a formal solution at the 1893 World's Columbian Exposition in Chicago was not dictated by regional considerations, but rather by the obvious necessity of achieving architectural coherence within a monumental group of buildings.

1. Frederick Law Olmsted,
*General Plan for the
Improvement of the U.S.
Capitol Grounds*, 1875
From Glenn Brown, *History of the
United States Capitol*, vol. 2 (Washington, 1900–1903)

was fully in the picturesque tradition that he so much favored.

Olmsted believed that the design of not only the Capitol grounds but of the space designated by L'Enfant as the Mall was so important that a board of landscape architects be set up to develop a policy for designing the area between the Capitol and the Washington Monument "and a considerable area in process of reclamation from the Potomac flats." In a letter to William Hammond Hall, then superintendent of Golden Gate Park in San Francisco, he stated that, "The grounds were arranged in an absurd and wasteful way," since they were controlled by nearly a dozen independent congressional committees, assisted by a panoply of bureau heads, architects, surveyors, and gardeners. The preparation of a plan "to simplify and consolidate the present arrangement and bring all these grounds into subordination to a comprehensive scheme. . . ." was so important that he invited Hall to join him and H.W.S. Cleveland of Minneapolis to prepare such a design, "it being one, which, in my judgment, concerns the credit of the profession and the honor and dignity of the country." [9] Congress was not willing to fund such a board, and Olmsted was confined to designing the grounds of the Capitol by himself.

Olmsted hitherto had worked in collaboration with architects on the siting of new buildings within the landscape. This was the first scheme in which he had been involved where the landscape was subordinate to an existing building. The fifty-six pedestrian and carriage entrances to the Capitol and the large number of surrounding streets entering the grounds necessitated a landscape design of simple character that would enhance the nature of the building and be capable of absorbing large numbers of people. His solution was a layout of gently curving paths and roads with bold groups of trees to define a few large open spaces (fig. 1). Circulation of vehicles and pedestrians, climate, and the need to display the building, not only from within the grounds but from many parts of the city, dictated a planting arrangement of masses of "umbrageous trees" with shrubbery beneath. This was not a design in which individual plants were displayed. Rather the aim was to avoid the use of horticultural oddities or any plant that would itself attract attention. At the request

The problem Olmsted faced in redesigning the Capitol grounds also might have suggested a formal solution. Indeed, a brief note attached to an 1885 report that he wrote, listing the trees of the Capitol grounds, suggests he was by no means opposed to such a scheme, but that the general taste and prevailing sentiment did not support formal treatment. [8] Accordingly, the solution that Olmsted adopted

of Congress, Olmsted provided a list of the trees, which were to be labeled, so that the park, like Central Park and others he had designed, could fulfill an educational role.

Olmsted's massive and highly controversial terrace on the west side of the Capitol was designed to provide an appropriate visual base for the enormous building (fig. 2). For this reason he firmly rejected a proposal for a water cascade that Senator Justin Morrill had requested. Writing to Edward Clark on 15 July 1886, Olmsted pointed out that the proposed volume of water was insufficient. Even if this were not the case, "I am afraid that the result would be to lessen the impression of solidity and firm footing so desirable to be sustained at the base of so vast a pile." [11] The Capitol terrace also was conceived as an observation platform, commanding an impressive vista to the west and allowing the viewer to gain a sense of the regional landscape. Olmsted described his terrace as a place "from which an outlook is obtained between the northern and southern divisions of the city in which a slope of unbroken turf, seen over a strongly defined and darkly shadowed architectural base, will be the foreground; a wooded plain, extending a mile beyond the foot of the slope, the middle distance, and the partly overgrown, partly cultivated hills beyond the depression of the Potomac, the background; the latter so far removed that in summer conditions of light and atmosphere it is often blue, misty and ethereal. Because, perhaps, of the influence of the cool waters of the river passing between the dry hills from north to south across this field of vision, several effects are often to be enjoyed from the west face of the Capitol of a rare loveliness." [12]

In 1882, Congress passed an act for the regulation of the tidal flats of the Potomac. A park of 739 acres was created from material dredged from the main channel. It incorporated a tidal reservoir or basin with an automatic inlet and outlet gate which separated the East from the West Potomac Park (pls. XXXII–XXXV). This ambitious project had been largely completed by 1900, by which time numerous proposals for its detailed development had been made by members of the United States Army Corps of Engineers. [13]

Since 1867, the Office of Public Buildings and Grounds of the Army Engineers had controlled all federal lands within the District.

2. Western lawn, United States Capitol grounds, photograph c. 1900
From Brown 1900–1903

Its chief, Colonel Theodore Bingham, prepared plans dated 1 March and 1 April 1900 for the Centennial Avenue proposed by a Senate committee. These were so inept that Congress authorized the employment of Samuel Parsons, Jr., a landscape architect who had worked for Olmsted on Central Park. Parsons prepared the so-called "goose-egg" plan, which was strongly opposed by the American Institute of Architects (AIA), led by Glenn Brown.[14] Brown, who had written a monumental study of the Capitol, possessed an encyclopedic knowledge of the history of Washington and organized the annual conference of the AIA to be held in Washington that December. At this conference, a committee was formed to impress on Congress the need for a professional commission to study the improvement of the city. This committee played a major role in the formation of the Senate Park Commission.[15] The conference proceedings also included presentations by a number of architects who had been asked to address the issue of arranging monumental buildings about the Mall's central axis. All the architects accepted the desirability of reviving the L'Enfant plan. The most impressive scheme was that designed by Cass Gilbert, but like the others it treated the boulevard as a relatively narrow avenue.

The address given by Frederick Law Olmsted, Jr. was the most important conceptual contribution made at the AIA conference, since it addressed both the architectural and landscape dimensions of the problem.[16] Olmsted was the youngest speaker in attendance. There can be no doubt that his father would have been invited to deliver the address, but he had been admitted to the McLean Hospital at Waverly, Massachusetts, in 1898. It was assumed that the father's undisputed genius had passed to his son. Indeed, his father had assiduously tried to ensure that his own son would carry on both the name and the firm. Frederick Law Olmsted, Jr., born in 1870, had been christened Henry Perkins.[17] From his birth, his father intended that his only son should continue his own work in the profession of landscape architecture and should have those advantages of training that he lacked. So strong was his determination that Olmsted changed his son's name at the age of four to Frederick Law so that it might be identified with the firm and the profession. Since there were no schools of landscape architecture, the young Olmsted's professional education was supervised by his father to continue "a liberal general education" with work in the "post-graduate" school that he had established in his office.[18] In addition, the younger Olmsted accompanied his father on visits to work in progress and on a European tour. During several summers when he was a student at Harvard, the younger Olmsted worked for the United States Coast and Geodetic Survey, and on a number of his father's projects, including the Chicago fair and Biltmore, near Asheville, North Carolina. Such experience demonstrated the importance of collaboration in design. He later wrote about the time spent working on the Chicago fair: "the give and take, the fructification of new ideas to which none of the group had risen individually, or probably ever could have risen alone, and the ungrudging acceptance of the better ideas without regard to pride or personal authorship, offered an amazing indication of how human abilities can be multiplied when such a spirit of frank cooperation is once aroused."[19] In 1894 when Olmsted, Jr. was working at Biltmore, his father wrote a long letter urging him to take full advantage of the opportunity of working with Chauncey Beadle and Gifford Pinchot, who were developing what he believed would be the first exercise in scientific forestry in the country: "Beadle and Pinchot are your chief mines . . . for your life's work."[20]

Another major opportunity came in 1897 when, after the premature death of Charles Eliot, the brilliant son of President Charles Eliot of Harvard University, the younger Olmsted assumed his work on Boston's Metropolitan Park system. This regional network of large public parks and reservations linked by boulevards and parkways was the most ambitious of its kind to be created in the United States during the nineteenth century, and would serve as a conceptual model for the Washington park system.[21] Olmsted, Jr. was further propelled into prominence the following year when, with his older step-brother, John Charles, he founded Olmsted Brothers as the successor firm to that of his father, now incapacitated.[22]

The paper Olmsted delivered to the 1900 AIA conference was not only an important statement about the possible development of the Mall, it offered a superb definition of landscape architecture. He began by pointing out that landscape design was not limited to planned informality and the apparent imitation of nature; it should address the much broader subject of the relation of buildings to their surroundings and the design of those spaces. A scheme thus could be informal or formal depending on the architecture and the effect desired; the character of a landscape should be appropriate to that of related buildings and indeed to the plan of the city. In Washington, he asserted, "great public edifices must be strongly formal, whether they are perfectly symmetrical or not, and this formal quality ought to be recognized in the plan of their surroundings if the total effect is to be consistent." He discussed problems of scale and formal landscape treatment, pointing out that "where the scale of the general scheme is large, there should be a corresponding simplicity...." [23]

Olmsted commented favorably on his father's design for the Capitol grounds: "Although there is a great deal of informal detail, [the precinct] is massed in such a way as to give broad, simple openings that relate directly to the building. The main axis on the west below the terrace passes through a wide opening flanked by trees, but not cluttered with irrelevant detail of shrubs or trees in its midst." Yet the Mall was "a great opportunity thrown away through disregard of the large meaning of the original plan.... The original plan set [the Mall] apart not only to emphasize in a magnificent manner the axis of the Capitol and bring it into strong though indirect relation with the Executive Mansion, but as an open space to provide agreeable frontage for public buildings of minor importance. Not only would the Mall provide these buildings with the space needed to give them a good setting, but they would in turn strengthen its character, and while giving one another sufficient architectural support, would be brought into their proper places in the scheme of which the Capitol is the head." [24]

Olmsted accepted the presence of the railroad, which he proposed to roof over as a viewing terrace. This is somewhat surprising in view of his father's treatment of the crosstown traffic passing through the center of Central Park. [25] His proposals for treating the remainder of the Mall, however, were of far greater significance.

When I speak of the importance of treating the Mall in such a way as to relate strongly and visibly to the Capitol, I do not mean merely, or necessarily that a straight road should be slashed down the middle of it.... A different and more agreeable treatment would be a sort of compound 'boulevard,' marked by several parallel rows of trees with several pavements and turf strips. Such an avenue was that of the Champs Elysées.... The axis of the Capitol should neither be ignored by the use of a wiggling road and confused informal planning, nor should it be marked by a mere commonplace boulevard, but by an impressively broad and simple space of turf, with strong flanking masses of foliage and architecture and shaded driveways.

Olmsted also emphasized that the L'Enfant plan was formal up to the Washington Monument and natural beyond. [26]

THE McMILLAN PLAN

After the AIA convention, Senator James McMillan attempted to provide the means for the preparation of a comprehensive plan. On 17 December 1900, he introduced a joint resolution authorizing the president to appoint a commission of two architects and one landscape architect to study and prepare a report on the location and grouping of public buildings. According to Glenn Brown, this resolution failed because of the opposition of Representative Joseph Cannon. McMillan then secured the passage of a Senate resolution for the Committee on the District of Columbia to develop a park improvement plan for the entire district. The plan preparation expenses were to come from Senate contingency funds. Although the resolution referred specifically to parks, McMillan clearly intended that the plan should be broad in its scope. [27]

On the advice of Charles Moore, McMillan's secretary, Daniel Burnham and Olmsted were asked to serve on the commission that was formed to prepare the plan. Charles McKim was invited to join them, although J. M. Carrère had been Olmsted's tentative choice. Augustus Saint-Gaudens became the fourth member shortly before the three other commissioners journeyed to Europe. Of the four commissioners, Olmsted was the only member who had any previous association with Washington. The proposals made in his AIA paper were strikingly similar to the proposal that finally emerged. Furthermore, his early travels with his father, his student experience with the United States

Coast and Geodetic Survey, and his work at Chicago, Biltmore, and the Boston park system were excellent preparation for this ambitious landscape project.

While it might be tempting to give credit to Olmsted as the true author of the McMillan Plan, it is clear from the surviving evidence that Burnham and McKim were equally responsible for its conceptual basis, which was developed during their European trip. Subsequently, Burnham took overall responsibility for coordination, but most of his time was devoted to the design of the new Union Railroad Station. McKim designed the Mall, and the Olmsted Brothers were responsible for the planning and design of the outlying system of regional parks. This division of labors was partly a matter of convenience and partly a reflection of necessary professional skills.

The plan was conceived as a work of civic art in which the revival of L'Enfant's *intentions* was a central purpose. As Charles Moore wrote in 1917, this "was not a new plan, but merely a restoration and continuation of the original plan of the city."[28] L'Enfant's design was studied, but the vagueness of the nature of the "Grand Boulevard" and the changes that had occurred in the ensuing decades dictated the restoration of the spirit rather than the forms of this historic landscape.[29] The plan had to provide a grand boulevard, sites for major governmental structures, and deal with the problem of Washington's severe summer climate as well as provide appropriate facilities for recreation. By the turn of the century it had become apparent that public recreational needs could not easily be met by the provision of large, naturalistic parks. Such facilities addressed the psychological necessity for reducing stress, but were not well adapted to meeting the needs of the body. The playground movement emphasized the importance of also providing places for physical recreation. These places would have an underlying moral purpose, since, it was believed, supervised recreation produced potentially better citizens.[30] In practice, playgrounds were often provided as separate neighborhood parks.

The McMillan Plan tried to meet all these needs, but its most unusual aspect was the attempt made to recreate the intentions of a historic figure. Since the L'Enfant plan for the Mall had never been realized, the commissioners' understanding of his intentions was limited to early drawings and the historical interpretation provided by Glenn Brown. Brown had advanced the eminently plausible interpretation that the scheme was based on a conflation of the Wren plan for rebuilding London (1666) and the Le Nôtre plan for Versailles (1661–1687). This latter source led the commissioners to consider the Mall as a park or garden rather than an urban boulevard.[31]

To understand the original nature of L'Enfant's boulevard and the other elements of his plan, the commissioners attempted, in a remarkably short period of time, nothing less than what they believed would be a systematic exploration of the known American and European sources that *might* have guided the original plan, together with an examination of current European treatments of civic architecture in their relation to open space. The commissioners examined sites close to Washington that displayed the influence of baroque planning and design forms. Plantations on the James River were visited, as were Williamsburg and Annapolis, because those towns had been familiar to presidents Washington and Jefferson. But the major part of their historical analysis occurred during a five-week tour in France, Germany, Austria, Italy, and England, which Olmsted planned. Olmsted also recorded in photographs and meticulously detailed notes salient aspects of the places they visited. The central figure in their analysis of the baroque landscape was André Le Nôtre. They made no attempt to use any of the theoretical treatises that had informed Le Nôtre's work, such as Jacques Boyceau de la Barauderie's subtle discussion of the use of optical laws to create exquisite spatial illusions.[32] Instead, the commissioners relied on a thorough physical examination of sites that either might have been known to L'Enfant or were known to have been designed by Le Nôtre or to exhibit his influence.[33] At the same time they studied a number of other sites that were not particularly notable demonstrations of the principles of the baroque landscape tradition.

In Rome, the commissioners realized, "that the problems in Washington must be worked out along Roman rather than Parisian lines; that simplicity, directness and subordination of ornament to structural usage should prevail. . . ." Further it was determined, "that the fountain and not the man-on-horse-back is the proper ornament for Washington, and the heat

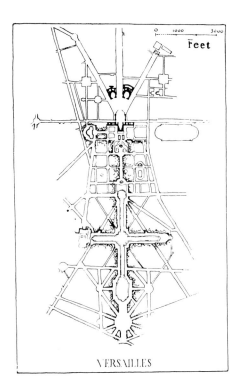

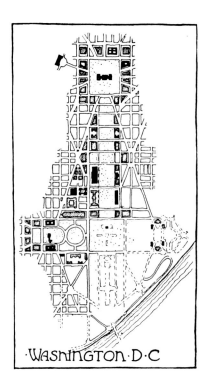

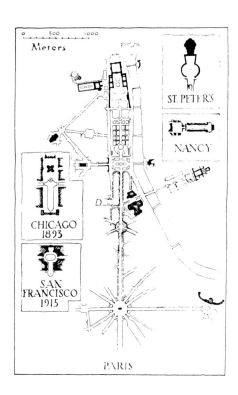

of our capital requires that the city should be filled with running water even as is Rome."[34] In any case, the resulting scheme owes more to Italy in the details, especially the use of water, than in the overall conception, which remains quintessentially French.

In the McMillan Plan the overall conception of the Mall is not unlike that of the *petit* and *grand parcs* at Versailles. Union Square corresponds to the water parterre, with a greatly extended *tapis vert* beyond. The Washington Monument garden corresponds to the fountain of Apollo with the cruciform canal beyond. The scheme also bears a marked similarity to the Tuileries Gardens and the Champs Elysées. As comparative diagrams made in 1922 by Elbert Peets show, however, there is a considerable disparity in the relative sizes of the parts (fig. 3).[35]

In cross-section the Mall was an inversion of the garden at Versailles and more closely resembled the distant part of the main vista at Vaux-le-Vicomte. At Versailles the *tapis vert* falls away from the building to the grand canal. The vista at Vaux-le-Vicomte rises from its canal to the statue of Hercules on the summit. The long eastern section of the Mall's *tapis vert* rises to culminate in the Washington Monument. The western section of the

Mall, a former swamp, lies below its base. Hegemann and Peets wrote that this section could not be considered an integral part of the Mall: "From the Capitol terrace it will be an effective continuation of the Mall, but from the floor of the Mall itself, the extension will not be visible, for the Mall rises to the south. It will be interesting to see how this will affect views from the Mall of the Lincoln Memorial, which is raised for this reason on a fifty-foot platform."[36]

At the eastern end of the Mall the proposed design for Union Square dealt rather brutally with the elder Olmsted's design for the Capitol grounds (pls. LXVIII–LXX). The gentle curve at the foot of Capitol Hill was replaced by a high retaining wall parallel to the west side of the Capitol, incorporating the gate piers designed by Charles Bulfinch, which had been removed. A cascade between the senior Olmsted's radial tree-lined paths fell into a large water basin in the center of this retaining wall. Union Square was conceived as a Beaux-Arts *place* centered on the Grant Memorial, which incorporated statues of Civil War heroes flanked by formal fountains and parterres. It was intended that it would "compare favorably in both extent and treatment with the Place de la Concorde in Paris,"[37] though

3. Elbert Peets, comparison sketches of the McMillan Plan, Versailles, and other public spaces
From Werner Hegemann and Elbert Peets, *The American Vitruvius: An Architect's Handbook of Civic Art* (New York, 1922)

4. Senate Park Commission, Plan of 1901–1902, *View of the Monument Seen from the Mall at Fourteenth Street, Looking West*
From Charles Moore, ed., *The Improvement of the Park System of the District of Columbia* (Washington, 1902)

5. Stansted, Sussex, engraving, seventeenth-century
From J. C. Shepherd and G. A. Jellicoe, *Gardens and Design* (London, 1927)

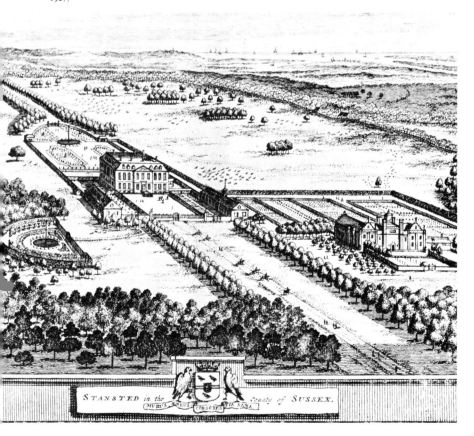

unlike its Parisian model, the cross-axis was terminated with buildings rather than axial vistas.

The eastern section of the Mall was compared in the report, written by Moore and Olmsted, to the "Mall in Central Park." However, it differed from this precedent in an extremely important respect, being much closer in spirit to the avenues created during the late seventeenth century as approaches to English country houses, here without a central road (figs. 4, 5).[38] The "green carpet" of the *tapis vert* was broken only by the cross-axes of the roads crossing the Mall and the block between Seventh and Ninth streets. No attempt was made to hide the traffic: "Indeed, the play of light and shade where the streets break through the columns of trees, and the passage of street cars and trams give needed life to the Mall . . . ."[39] But, as Elbert Peets later pointed out, the drawings and paintings prepared to illustrate this landscape were romantic in nature and largely devoid of life except for a "flock of sheep." Peets did not mention that these paintings also neglected to show the fountains on the axis in the center of the two most westerly blocks. The entire block between Seventh and Ninth streets was to be treated like Union Square with fountains and parterres. The cross-axis of this space on Eight Street was to be terminated by buildings, the northerly site eventually being occupied by the National Archives Building (1931–1935). This elimination of one of L'Enfant's major cross-axes particularly incensed Peets.[40] The cumulative effect of these adaptations of the tradition of the baroque *allée* was to create freestanding bosks with large, detached monumental buildings aligned behind them. This new conception of the treatment of monumental civic buildings had been first advanced in Olmsted's paper.

The commission took great care in determining the width of the *tapis vert*. Trials were made by placing flagpoles at 250, 300, and 400 feet apart. The final dimension of 300 feet was chosen for climatic as well as visual concerns. Equal attention was exercised in deciding how many rows of elm trees should form the groves on either side of the *tapis vert*. Burnham said: "Having examined every notable avenue in Europe, we found that no less than four trees constituted an avenue and three produced a bad effect. . . ." A number of fountains were proposed in the center of the *tapis vert* and within the bosks, expressing the central significance of water in this design. As Olmsted wrote in the report, "the original plans of Washington show the high appreciation that L'Enfant had for all forms of water decoration; and when the heats of our Washington summer are taken into consideration, further argument is unnecessary to prove that the first and greatest step in the matter of beautifying the District of Columbia is such an increase in the water supply as will make possible the copious and even lavish use of water in fountains."[41]

The eastern portion of the Mall was designed to terminate in a large paved viewing terrace around the base of the Washington Monument. The terrace, to be decorated with fountains, was contained within one arm of a Greek cross-shaped garden defined by bosks. The garden was to be approached from the Mall by a monumental flight of stairs slightly broader than the Mall itself (fig. 6; pls. LXVII–LXXVII). This garden, at the intersection of the main axis and the cross-axis through the White House, was described in the report as "the gem

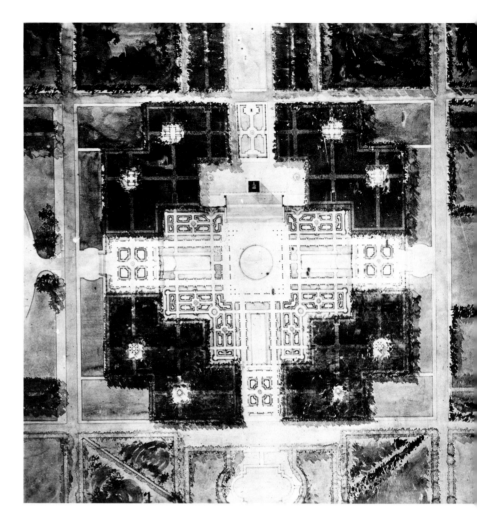

of the Mall system." It was a handsome, formal design reminiscent of large Italian Renaissance gardens. Indeed, the scheme was believed to owe its genesis to the inspiration of the Villa Medici in Rome.[42] In fact, its boxwood parterres, circular classical temples, large circular water basin, and formal clipped trees represented a conflation of ideas drawn from Italian Renaissance and French baroque examples.

The Mall's design was intended to resolve the visual awkwardness of the Washington Monument's lopsided location in relation to the intersection of the axes of the White House and the Capitol. The intersection occurs at the center of the circular basin in the middle of the garden. The garden was designed to be forty feet below the base of the monument, which would have served to enhance its grandeur when viewed from the west side. But this

6. Senate Park Commission, Plan of 1901–1902, *Plan Showing Proposed Treatment of the Monument Garden*, rendering by George de Gersdorff
From Moore 1902

arrangement also entailed placing the bosks on the north, west, and east sides on elevated masonry terraces, whose walls served to create a greater sense of enclosure within the garden. On the north and south sides the garden had to be entered by ascending to the terraces supporting the bosks, and then descending from the terraces into the garden. Only on the west side could the garden be entered by level paths.

The formal bosks on these terraces contained small structures in the manner of the *cabinets* of French baroque gardens. Their formality matched the formal planting of the east Mall and the adjoining areas on the north-south cross-axis. The splendid aerial view of the Mall scheme emphasizes the terminal nature of this section of the Mall with the more natural character of Potomac Park lying below it. (pl. LXV). It is surprising in view of the extensive engineering that this scheme necessitated, that the commissioners did not request more detailed engineering studies of the site, which occurred at the former east bank of the Potomac River.

To the north of the garden, the White Lot, the area between the Monument Garden and the grounds of the White House, was defined by parallel rows of linden trees planted outside the Oval, which remained a shape on the ground defined only by the forms of the path (fig. 7). The Washington Commons to the south was to be devoted to recreational use. At the end of a long, rectangular lawn flanked by rows of linden trees, an elevated terrace supported a circular pantheon-like structure in which it was proposed "shall be grouped the statues of the illustrious men, of the nation, or whether the memory of some individual shall be honored by a monument of the first rank may be left to the future. . . ." This structure was to be flanked by six larger ones containing baths, a theater, gymnasium, and athletic facilities (fig. 8). Because of the immense area occupied by this complex and the space to its north, the tidal basin was reduced to a relatively modest expanse of water designed to accommodate boating, wading, and swimming in the summer and skating in the winter. Boat pavilions, locker rooms, and public bathhouses were to be constructed on the model of Revere Beach near Boston.[43]

McKim's proposed design for the Lincoln Memorial was an open, belvedere-like structure on a circular mound in a *rond-point*. Its position recalled that of the Gloriette at

8. Senate Park Commission, Plan of 1901–1902, *View of the Washington Common and Public Playgrounds, Showing Proposed Memorial Building, Baths, Theater, Gymnasium, and Athletic Buildings*
From Moore 1902

9. Senate Park Commission, Plan of 1901–1902, *View Showing the Proposed Development of the Lincoln Memorial Site, Seen from the Canal*, rendering by Robert Blum
From Moore 1902

Schönbrunn, and its architecture the Greek revival buildings at Berlin's Thiergarten. Below, at the west end of the cruciform canal, was an arcaded terrace like the grotto at Vaux-le-Vicomte (fig. 9). The canal itself was to be decorated with large fountains clearly inspired by Vaux and Versailles. The circular space at the head of the canal, with the monument at its center, was conceived not only as the visual termination to the Mall axis but as a literal and symbolic gateway to the extensive regional park system designed by

Olmsted. From the Lincoln Memorial, the visitor could look back to the Washington Monument, out over the Potomac, and into the formal rides of Potomac Park and the regional park system.

The design of Potomac Park, recalling the character of the Bois de Boulogne, was proposed to include a national arboretum. In an appendix to the Senate Park Commission report, Olmsted pointed out the advantages for botanical science, horticulture, forestry, and landscape architecture of maintaining a systematic collection of living plants administered by the Department of Agriculture. The physical diversity of the country was so great, however, that it would be essential to establish several regional centers representing the major climatic and life zones of the country. Potomac Park would serve as a station representing the Middle Atlantic zone southward as far as the subtropical zone. The integrity of the design was not to be compromised by the visual disruption that a botanical collection could create. Olmsted pointed out that of the seventy or more species of oak that grow in the United States, only those that would thrive in Washington would be selected so that they would become "great and beautiful specimens of an aspect which will fit harmoniously with the proposed landscape of the park." Hawthorns would be represented by "a few of the commonest and most beautiful varieties, upon whose appearance when grown it is possible to count with reasonable certainty. . . ." In addition, a series of garden spaces could be created to contain special collections of lilacs, clematis, peonies, or poppies.[44]

The Senate Park Commission's design for the Mall was unusual in that it integrated monumental civic spaces into the overall fabric of the city; and it integrated formal and natural landscapes into a harmonious whole. The Boston Park plan had also attempted this, but without monumental structures, its spatial and symbolic character was completely different. No city hitherto had attempted the development of recreational structures at such a large scale, and it remained for Chicago to accomplish this with its ambitious Field House program.[45]

The McMillan Plan did not anticipate any of the problems of widespread automobile usage. The movement of pedestrians and vehicles across the Mall seems to have been envisioned as elements of liveliness in the same romantic way that Repton had enlivened his park designs with cattle and smoke from laborers' cottages.[46]

The process employed by the commissioners in re-creating the spirit of a historic plan introduced a new method into landscape design. Unlike the work of men such as Sir Charles Barry and Charles Adams Platt, who had adopted either a literal or painterly approach to interpreting past work of a single period, the new Mall plan drew on and synthesized a large number of sources from the Renaissance and baroque traditions.[47] Such a synthesis was not at all uncommon in architecture, but it had never been attempted before in landscape design. Hitherto, the creation of outdoor "rooms" in different styles within a naturalistic setting represented the most eclectic use of historic design sources. Furthermore, the scheme reveals a gradual transition in landscape character from the extreme formality of the area around Capitol Hill to the relatively ordered informality of Potomac Park. This is similar to the increasingly natural character that develops at Versailles as one moves away from the palace into the outer park.

As Elbert Peets later pointed out, the spatial character of the plan's axial vistas differed significantly from L'Enfant's plan and from the tradition of baroque landscape design.[48] In the baroque tradition the *allée* was used as a "shaft" of space leading the eye out toward an infinite exploration of space. A large, nontransparent structure placed within that "shaft" would impede this visual activity. In Le Nôtre's designs the *allée* is only punctuated by basins of water or statues, which are usually part of a complex symbolic program of meaning, and the eye is allowed to see a space that appears to be infinite. Late baroque designs, such as the palace of Schönbrunn, represent important departures from this tradition since the space of the *allée* is partially blocked. The McMillan Plan adopted this later convention. The great bulk of the Washington Monument does not interrupt the space of the Mall's eastern *allée*, but the Lincoln Memorial and the proposed shrine to the authors of the Constitution are terminal features which fill the "shaft" of space.

It took almost thirty-five years to bring into existence a landscape that bore any resemblance to that of the McMillan Plan. Because of his youth, Olmsted became an unofficial guardian of the plan through a series of individual commissions and membership in a number of bodies: the Commission of Fine Arts (1910–1918), the National Capital Park Commission (1924–1926), and the National Capital Park and Planning Commission (1926–1932). His role had been anticipated by the Senate Committee on the District, which stated in its report that it was a matter "for satisfaction that the fourth member of the commission enters upon the work at an age, when he might be expected to have a part in directing and shaping the development of the plans from the beginning to the end." [49] Indeed Olmsted, directly and indirectly, was involved from 1901 until the mid-1930s, by which time the main lines of the landscape of the Mall had been completed.

The McMillan Plan initially met with a cool reception because of the high costs involved in implementation, its monumental character, and the strong opposition of Speaker Cannon. These factors, combined with the death of Senator McMillan and the lack of an official group other than the AIA which could either lobby for the plan or pass judgment on specific projects, meant that between 1902 and 1910 the scheme was highly vulnerable. [50] From 1910, when the Commission of Fine Arts was established, until the mid-1930s when many crucial components were in place, Glenn Brown, Charles Moore, and Olmsted played different but critical roles in the plan's realization.

The first major decision to be made by the Commission of Fine Arts concerned the location of the Lincoln Memorial. After careful consideration of a number of sites, the commission recommended the Potomac Park site to the Lincoln Memorial Commission, primarily because its members believed that the memorial should stand on axis with the Capitol and the Washington Monument. The commission also recommended that Henry Bacon's design be accepted. His design differed from McKim's proposal in two significant ways. The structure was treated as a solid cella, housing the statue of Lincoln and surrounded

by a colonnade, and the arcaded grotto-like terrace below the memorial was replaced by a simple series of ramped terraces extending across the width of the mall. The main lines of this new design can be attributed to Burnham, who was the commission chairman. [51] The decision to build the Lincoln Memorial on the Potomac Park site was important since it irrevocably established the long spinal axis of the McMillan Plan from the Capitol to the Potomac (fig. 10).

No other landscape decisions were made during the period that Olmsted sat on the Commission of Fine Arts. Several buildings were constructed along the west side of the White Lot during the 1910s, and the Freer Gallery of Art (1913–1923) was built on the south side of the Mall in a position consistent with that of the original plan. No changes were made to what remained of Downing's arboretum on the central part of the Mall. A scheme published by the commission in 1921 still showed the proposed monumental garden below the base of the Washington Monument with a cruciform reflecting basin between it and the Lincoln Memorial. [52] The radial avenue connecting the Lincoln Memorial with the *rond-point* at the intersection of Virginia and New York avenues, however, now stopped at Constitution Avenue, thus changing the integrative nature of this part of the park. The corresponding avenue on the south side of the Mall was still proposed to terminate at the south end of the cross-axis through the canal.

THE MALL LANDSCAPE, 1927–1947

A major step in formalizing the process for the improvement of central Washington occurred in 1926 with the creation of the National Capital Park and Planning Commission. Its predecessor, the National Capital Park Commission, established in 1924, had accomplished very little. Now a strong federal commitment was finally made to realizing the objectives of the McMillan Plan. Following the commission's initial, fruitless search for a director, who would have served at a ridiculously low salary, Olmsted persuaded Charles Eliot II, the nephew of Charles Eliot, to take an appointment with the agency as a "city planner." Eliot later became the agency's di-

10. View of Reflecting Pool and Lincoln Memorial, looking west from Washington Monument, 1920s
Commission of Fine Arts

rector and remained on its staff until 1933. His previous work with Olmsted on several Massachusetts towns gave him "a strong sense of the popular interest in historic shrines, landmarks and scientific features." But his appointment at the age of twenty-seven startled Harlean James, executive secretary of the American Planning and Civic Association, who deprecatingly referred to him as "that kid."

Nevertheless, his educational background, strong historical orientation, and family roots enabled him to function effectively in this job, which he believed was one of "allowing for necessary municipal growth, yet preserving as much as . . . I can of the flavor of the past."[53]

Together with Olmsted and several other commissioners, Eliot developed guidelines for the Mall in 1927 according to their interpre-

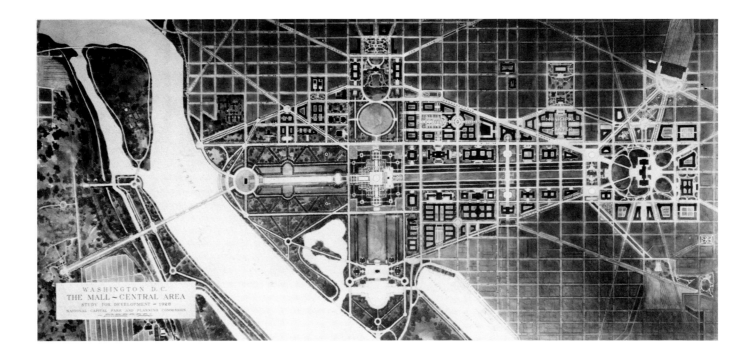

11. National Capital Park and Planning Commission, *The Mall, Central Area, Study for Development, 1928* Commission of Fine Arts

tations of what L'Enfant would have done, and what the Senate Park Commission had recommended. William Partridge, a consultant to the commission, had prepared an analysis of L'Enfant's report and letters. According to Eliot, these documents proved to be very difficult to interpret; Olmsted remarked that, "When you have tried reading some of L'Enfant's reports, it does not surprise you that those to whom they were addressed got impatient and were glad to get rid of him." [54] Eliot analyzed L'Enfant's intentions for the Mall as being an open vista "enframed by rows of elms." Olmsted built on this proposal by stating that to accomplish this geometric stretch of greenery, three major elements must first be coordinated. New buildings had to be designed to ensure the longitudinal boundaries and open vistas. The "intrusive trees" along the axis had to be removed. Finally, the Mall's entire length had to be graded and planted with formal rows of elms. Countering the opposition of many public officials, Olmsted argued that this plan promised "a very great permanent advantage" through the removal of trees from the area, "whatever their value as symbols of earlier landscapes." [55]

In 1928 the commission produced a beautifully rendered study of the Mall area (fig. 11). Subtle adjustments were made to the cross-axis through the White House. The shape of the Oval was emphasized by tree planting. The cruciform canal to the west of the Washington Monument was retained as a space but was filled by a long rectangular basin of water, the cross-axis taking the form of short apsidal recesses in the surrounding woods. The radial avenue from the *rond-point* in the southern cross-axis of the canal was extended toward the monument garden.

More important changes were proposed at the eastern end of the Mall. Bennett, Parsons, and Frost of Chicago had been commissioned to prepare plans for Union Square and the Union Station Plaza (fig. 12). The former was necessitated by the siting of the new Botanic Garden building to the south of the main axis. Olmsted, Sr.'s design for the Capitol grounds was retained with its fountains on the axes of Maryland and Pennsylvania avenues. The Grant Monument was placed on a new block between the avenues and First and Second streets, standing at the eastern end of a paved area flanked by wedge-shaped groves of trees. The island block to the west between Second and Third streets was somewhat similar in character to the McMillan Plan design with a large square basin of water flanked by par-

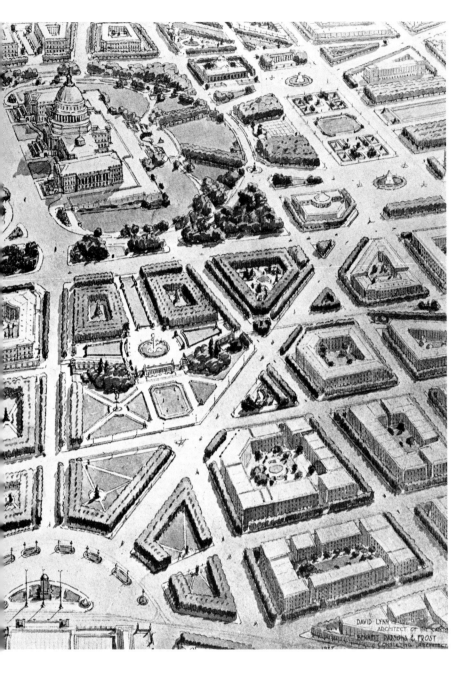

12. David Lynn and Bennett, Parsons, and Frost, *Proposed Enlargement for the Capitol Grounds – View Looking South toward the Capitol and the Mall*, 1928
From *The American Architect* 85 (20 May 1929), 651

terres and fountains. This feature of the cross-axis was emphasized by large, freestanding circular fountain basins on the axes of the two radial avenues. The scheme provided for a much more effective transition between the landscape of the Mall and the Capitol grounds.[56]

In the following year the commission published an even more ambitious plan. The design included the revisions of the 1928 plan, but also extended the Mall's axis along East Capitol Street (pls. LXXXIX–XCI). This new "Avenue of the States" continued across the Anacostia River to end in a large amphitheater. At the center of the new avenue was Colonial Square, a public space intended to be surrounded by buildings of the thirteen original states. At the west end of the Mall the *cabinets* within the bosks surrounding the monument garden were developed in a more complex fashion to receive the radial vistas of Virginia Avenue and the south-east radial vista from Potomac Park.[57]

The area of the Mall which remained controversial, however, was that surrounding the Washington Monument. Since the Lincoln Memorial grounds were completed and the Arlington Memorial Bridge under construction, the demand swelled to bring this central precinct into harmony with those lying to its east and west. Ferruccio Vitale, a prominent landscape architect, gave an address before the American Society of Landscape Architects in which he called for the implementation of McKim's design for the monument garden: "It has great merit, and the more it is studied the finer it becomes." He did believe that it needed modification because it would be costly to maintain as a public garden.[58] Soon thereafter a bill was introduced authorizing $5 million to execute McKim's design. In May 1930, an advisory committee was formed which examined the structure of the monument, studied old construction drawings, and had a number of test borings made to examine subsoil conditions. The engineers on this committee concluded that the Washington Monument was stable but that implementation of the McMillan Plan would necessitate fill that exceeded ten times the weight of the monument and its foundations.

To realize the garden design, two proposals were considered: underpinning the monument and complete dismantling and rebuilding. The cost of either plan was so prohibitive that Olmsted and architect William A. Delano each submitted proposals known as the "balustrade scheme" (Delano) and the "informal scheme" (Olmsted). Both plans were based on the elimination of a subway at Fifteenth Street, placing Fourteenth Street in a subway beneath the Mall, and reducing the extent of fill between the two streets. Olmsted's design, prepared in association with Henry Hubbard, was intended to reduce the cutting and filling to an absolute minimum. The plan of the oval island was simple, with two oval spaces defined by roads leading to the monument. It was particularly notable for its recognition of the automobile (fig. 13, pl. XCIV). Olmsted and Hubbard believed that "the Monument should be visible from numerous different enframement points within the grounds. All these views should be offered from appropriate points not only by pedestrians but to persons in automobiles." They continued, "We believe it essential that circulation of automobile pleasure traffic be provided around the Monument at a sufficient distance from it, and views of the Monument be presented to this traffic, and that the traffic be separated entirely through its circuit from business traffic." Despite the fact that the Commission of Fine Arts had given cautious approval to the Olmsted proposal, the committee's chairman stated, "It appears wisest at this time to do the minimum necessary to bring the roads and planting into the Mall and the Lincoln Memorial Grounds, following the horizontal layout of the informal plan herewith submitted, but without the grading operations necessary to carry the Mall plateau across Fourteenth Street. . . ." [59] Nothing came of the initiative, and significant improvements to this area have yet to be made.

An equally controversial aspect of developing the Washington Monument grounds was the extensive filling of the northern section of the Tidal Basin that the expansion of this precinct would have necessitated. A plan showing proposals and existing conditions, published in 1931 by the National Capital Park and Planning Commission, surprisingly still shows the monument garden with the waters of the Tidal Basin lapping at its southern edge,[60] though it does not show a southern termination to the White House cross-axis (pl. XCII). Five years earlier a competition had been held for a memorial to President Theodore Roosevelt situated at this axial terminus. The winning entry by James Russell Pope proposed to replace the rectangular platform advocated by the Senate Park Commission with what Glenn Brown called "a white granite island," consisting of a circular platform, 280 feet in diameter, defined on the east and west by hemispherical colonnades.[61] Within the colonnades was a large circular basin with a single jet of water. This was to be the only proposal made for any part of the Mall landscape

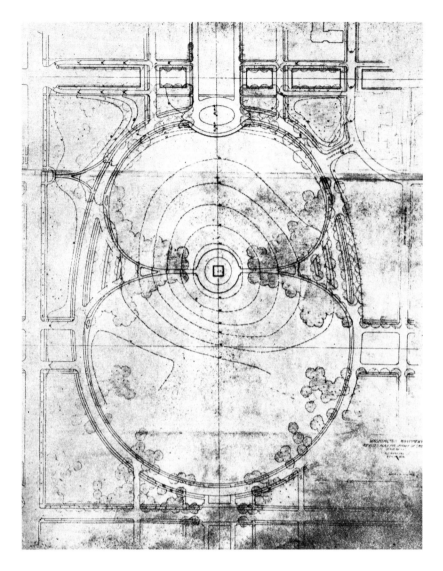

which respected the baroque landscape tradition of the "vista into space."[62] Pope's executed design for the Jefferson Memorial, completed in 1938, accepted the spirit of the McMillan Plan by providing a terminal structure on this axis and was not unlike the 1926 design.

Olmsted participated in this equally controversial endeavor by providing a study for the Jefferson Memorial Commission. He was skeptical about the whole enterprise: without any foreseeable improvement of the Washington Monument grounds, the proposed plans "involve far too great a risk of leaving the Jefferson Memorial stranded in an isolated location in Potomac Park, forever shut off from the central congestion of the Washington Plan

13. Frederick Law Olmsted, Jr. and Henry V. Hubbard, plan of "Informal Scheme" for Washington Monument Grounds, 1932
From *Landscape Architecture* 39 (July 1949)

by the 'cold shoulder' of the slanting wooded ridge which now intervenes." Nonetheless the Commission of Fine Arts, under the chairmanship of landscape architect Gilmore D. Clarke, concluded that the Tidal Basin was the most favorable site for it "completed the framework of the 'Central Area' as laid down by the McMillan Commission" and was no more isolated than the Lincoln Memorial once had been.[63]

The eastern section of the Mall was finally executed in the mid-1930s. The Mall Development Plan had been passed in 1929, but was not funded until 1933. This appropriation by the Public Works Administration included funds for the east Mall proper, Union Square, and general grading, landscaping, and tree planting (pls. CI–CV). The act instructed that the modernization of the Mall be in accordance with the L'Enfant and McMillan plans, with any modifications that might be recommended by the National Capital Park and Planning Commission and approved by the Commission for the Enlarging of the Capitol Grounds.[64]

The plan prepared by Olmsted for the eastern section represented an important reassessment of the McMillan Plan, which had proposed extending Second Street from Constitution Avenue to Independence Avenue. Olmsted conferred with W.L. Parsons of Bennett, Parsons, and Frost about their Union Square proposal and developed another scheme which subsequently was executed. Olmsted expressed reservations about the McMillan Plan, which would have curtailed the extent of the Capitol grounds by straightening First Street, with the consequent introduction of a high retaining wall and a water basin on the axis of the Capitol. He justified this assessment on the basis of an analysis that he had made of plans by L'Enfant, Latrobe (1803), and Thomas U. Walter (1864). Olmsted stated that the Union Square unit of the McMillan Plan had "received less mature and deliberate study by the Commission as a whole than the portions of the central composition further west, and was embodied in the report under pressures of time as a tentative solution in spite of expressed doubts within the Commission as to some of its features." He believed that the report's reference to the agreeable simplicity of outline of the Capitol grounds ending on a straight line on Latrobe's plan was a

misinterpretation of L'Enfant's intentions. He demonstrated that L'Enfant's plan showed a pair of "pylons or other monumental structures" flanking Pennsylvania and Maryland avenues on a curved line at First Street. His father's plan of 1875 had been based on this concept.[65]

An additional consideration of Olmsted's new scheme was the vista toward the Washington Monument. He believed that the "length of the unbroken foreground unit of that vista within the present Capitol Grounds and free from the interrupting cross lines of any roadway is even now none too long, and that any shortening of it as in the studies of 1901 would be distinctly unfortunate."[66] Olmsted's scheme therefore placed the Grant Memorial in a simple oval traffic island flanked by grass panels. The area between First and Third streets, Pennsylvania and Constitution avenues was amalgamated into a single block (fig. 14). The vista from the Capitol was enhanced by additional planting at the foot of Capitol Hill. One striking omission from this design, as well as in the reestablishment of the eastern area of the Mall itself, was any water feature. Olmsted evidently shared his father's dislike of water in this part of the Mall landscape.

Olmsted's elimination of the grand, Beaux-Arts design for Union Square married his father's design for the Capitol grounds to the simple boulevard treatment of the Mall and thereby virtually eliminated a cross-axis at the base of Capitol Hill. The new design for Union Square and the completion of the eastern part of the Mall marked the end of his direct involvement with realizing the McMillan Plan's vision.

In 1941, the National Capital Park and Planning Commission unveiled a design prepared by Gilmore Clarke and partly based on the 1929 proposal for the whole of central Washington (pl. XCV).[67] This scheme is extremely valuable in summarizing the changes to the McMillan Plan that had been made since the beginning of the century. The most significant of these alterations concerned the western section of the Mall, including the area around the Washington Monument and the Oval. The cruciform canal had disappeared and had been replaced by a single long rectangular body of water, the cross-axis of this canal having disappeared completely. The area on both sides of the canal was now formed of naturalistic planting recalling the character of the English forest parks of the early eighteenth century such as Cirencester Park. The western section of the Mall was now distinctly different in character from the eastern part. The design of the area around the Washington Monument was derived from Olmsted's 1932 proposal.

Olmsted had been responsible for most of the changes made to the McMillan Plan. These changes acknowledged ecological conditions, but had always been conceived with respect to the general spirit of the L'Enfant plan as well as that of its twentieth-century successor. Olmsted's approach was completely unaffected by the so-called "Harvard Revolution" initiated in the 1930s by Garrett Eckbo, James Rose, and Dan Kiley or by the contemporaneous work of Thomas Church in the San Francisco Bay area.[68] The establishment of modernist landscape design in the United States by the coincidental efforts of the Harvard group and Church did not affect the work of the Olmsted Brothers, which was by now the largest and most prestigious firm in the country.

The grandiloquent monumentality of Washington was antithetical to the aims of the modernist movement; but as early as 1935 the possibility of injecting new ideas into this public landscape was raised by Elbert Peets, who previously had championed a more tradition-oriented approach. Peets' critique emphasized the conceptual basis of the Mall in L'Enfant's plan as a fashionable Parisian avenue rather than as a romantic and rustic grassy park. With great perception he emphasized how the overgrown formal groves that the Senate Park Commission had visited in Europe must have appealed to Olmsted, Jr. in that they appeared to be "a happy reconciliation of American garden tradition with the L'Enfant architectural framework." The handsome paintings ordered by the commission to illustrate its report portrayed an almost empty and highly bucolic pastroal landscape. Yet as Peets sagely observed, the "sheep have gone, but their aesthetic preferences still prevail." Peets proposed a broad paved walk on the axis of the Mall, to be lined with benches, lamp-standards, and poles flying the flags of every country in the world. This promenade was intended to be a lively place which also would be appropriate for ceremonial parades: "City planning is art, engineering, and social

morals, but it must also be showmanship. In planning a city, we plan the movements of people," Peets believed. The broad walk was intended to restore the true spirit of L'Enfant's "grand and majestic avenue" as a place where Washington's citizens and visitors could hear "the fife and drum and see the gay flags of peace."[69]

Peets' proposal was not adopted, and the

14. Frederick Law Olmsted, Jr., general plan for Union Square, 1934
From *Landscape Architecture* 39

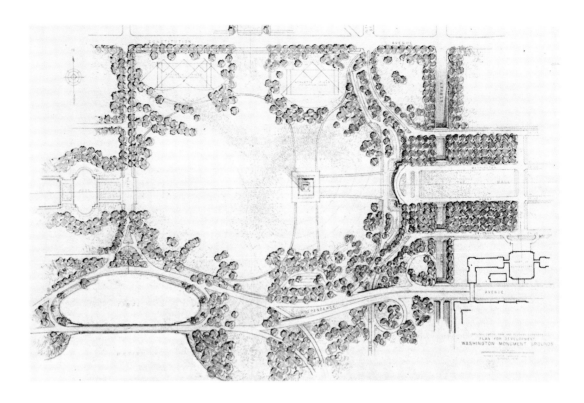

15. Thomas C. Jeffers, *Plan for Development, Washington Monument Grounds,* 1948
From *Landscape Architecture* 39

next development of the Mall landscape continued in the tradition of bucolic pastoralism that he deplored. In 1943 Independence Avenue was extended through the south end of the Washington Monument grounds as a dual parkway on the exact place where the southern part of Olmsted's circumferential road had been proposed. Mounds placed on the edge of this road had to be balanced on the north side of the Monument. This project initiated a further study of the area by Thomas Jeffers in 1948 (fig. 15).[70] The Jeffers plan eliminated the circumferential road which was now superfluous. He proposed a plaza just west of Fourteenth Street which was intended to serve as a terminus for the Mall roads and act as an interchange for traffic between them, Constitution and Independence avenues, and Fifteenth Street. Since the plaza was proposed at the level of the Mall roads, it was designed to terminate at an overlook providing a view of the monument. Roads around the monument were eliminated, and ample parking was provided at several places around the base of the hill. Jeffers' plan had less spatial clarity than the Olmsted scheme of 1932; nevertheless, it was conceived as a continuation of the spirit of the "informal scheme," and was approved by the National Capital Park and Planning Commission and the Commission of Fine Arts.

THE SKIDMORE, OWINGS, AND MERRILL PLAN OF 1965

Olmsted's naturalistic forest in Potomac Park at the west end of the Mall was not executed. From World War II until 1969, the area around the Washington Monument and the areas flanking the *allée* on the western section of the Mall were occupied by a series of temporary structures which interrupted the view toward the Potomac and prohibited the completion of this forest landscape. Up to this time, the execution of the McMillan Plan had been one of progressive simplification that was a pragmatic response to low budgets and more detailed ecological information. In this process the picturesque nature of the Capitol grounds had been married to a simple formal treatment on the Mall. New plans, proposed in 1964 and 1965, represented more a return to the formality of the McMillan Plan than an evolving interpretation of that plan's principles and those of L'Enfant's design, which Olmsted had sought to practice.

In 1964, the Presidential Council on Pennsylvania Avenue recommended a new design for Union Square. Beyond the senior Olmsted's fountains at the head of Pennsylvania and Maryland avenues, the island designed by Olmsted, Jr. was to be replaced by a large, wedge-shaped water basin.[71] That same year, Skidmore, Owings, and Merrill, with Dan Kiley as a landscape consultant, undertook to design a redevelopment of the Mall for the National Park Service. Unveiled on 14 December 1965, the scheme retained most of the basic elements of the 1964 design but included additional proposals and refinements (pls. CXIV–CXVI).[72] The senior Olmsted's fountains and the trees at the base of Capitol Hill between the diagonal walks were eliminated to encompass the view of the new Union Square, the new water basin, and views down Pennsylvania and Maryland avenues. The Grant Memorial extended into the six-acre water basin, so that it almost became an island. This new design captured something of the spirit of the water parterre at Versailles. In addition, the proposal suggested a modification of the Capitol forecourt by the introduction of freestanding bosks of pollarded trees. Both proposals thereby reasserted a strong sense of formality between the Capitol grounds and the Mall itself, although no attempt was made to reestablish a cross-axis.

In the eastern section of the Mall, the new plan recommended that the rows of trees on either side of the *tapis vert* be doubled to provide deeply-shaded walkways along graveled paths, similar to those of the Tuileries Gardens in Paris. An inner row of magnolia trees was proposed on the outside edges of the *tapis vert* to narrow this space. The cross-axes of the major buildings on the Mall were marked by fountains and paved courts, placed in the center of the *tapis vert*, and the axis of the National Archives Building was marked by a square pool in a paved court. Pavilions, kiosks, and bandstands were proposed within the bosks of trees at the side of the Mall to provide refreshment and recreation facilities. It was hoped that all these features would establish a livelier atmosphere. A viewing platform at the head of the eastern section was designed to provide the public a vista of the Washington Monument. Regrading the ground around the monument enabled ramps to descend from this platform to a new ground plane. This space

was treated as a single loosely naturalistic oval graded up to the monument. The cross-axis to the Jefferson Memorial was also treated in a naturalistic fashion.

The design of the western end of the Mall involved a slight lengthening of the reflection pool below the Lincoln Memorial to terminate in an island lookout platform at Seventeeth Street. Its cross-axis continued across the Mall to a viewing platform at the edge of the Tidal Basin. The traffic circle around the Lincoln Memorial was eliminated so that there would be direct pedestrian access between the memorial and the Mall. The area on the north side of the Mall that had been occupied for several decades by temporary structures was redesigned with a varied series of formal bosks evoking the character of baroque woodlands.

The Skidmore, Owings, and Merrill design reestablished, in a somewhat simplified fashion, many features of the McMillan Plan. It thereby reflects one of the tendencies in landscape design of the 1960s toward an abstract monumentality in the design of large-scale public open spaces, such as the design of Independence Mall in Philadelphia. The planned infusion of the pavilions, kiosks, and bandstands into the eastern section of the Mall was the first reaffirmation of the recreational component of the McMillan Plan. The introduction of fountains also recaptured an important intent of the McMillan Plan.

CONCLUSION

By the late 1940s, the landscape of the Mall and Capitol grounds had been developed almost entirely by the two Frederick Law Olmsteds, although the younger Olmsted had played the more significant role. His remarkable paper, delivered to the American Institute of Architects in 1900, had formed the basis for the McMillan Plan. After the plan's completion, he was involved directly and indirectly with its implementation, both because of his role as one of the authors and as one of the country's foremost landscape architects. Yet the changes for which he was responsible over a period of almost four decades gradually came to reveal an important reciprocal relationship to the picturesque character of his father's design at the Capitol grounds.

The McMillan Plan repudiated this tradition, since it purportedly was based on baroque landscape principles and was designed to restore the *spirit* of the L'Enfant plan. The attempt represented a new process of landscape design in which a somewhat scholarly effort was made to conflate an assembly of almost all that was known about a particular design tradition from a wide range of sources. The McMillan Plan also attempted to marry civic and recreational space so that civic space, with its symbolic gathering spaces and shrines for national figures, was integrated with facilities for physical recreation. This latter objective, proposed with conspicuous generosity in the plan, was never executed. An educational role was proposed for part of Potomac Park, in a way that continued the tradition of the nineteenth-century naturalistic park.

The subsequent development of the plan is a clear reflection of congressional indecision and parsimoniousness, as well as a reflection on the L'Enfant plan and the intentions of the Senate Park Commission. Olmsted's design of 1934 was a serious attempt to reconcile a meager budget, the concerns of historic authenticity to the L'Enfant plan, and the spirit of his father's design for the Capitol grounds. His designs for the Washington Monument grounds, however, reflect only budgetary concerns.

16. Untitled view of the Mall and Washington Monument, oil by unknown artist, c. 1855
Private collection. Photograph by Steve Burns

The character of these later designs may also confirm that Elbert Peets was correct in criticizing Olmsted's romantic delight in the pastoral qualities of seventeenth-century avenues as a fusion of geometric order and nature. The lack of architectural detail in these schemes is striking. It conforms well with his father's design and may suggest that Olmsted had rediscovered his father's romantic fascination with an idyllic western view from the Capitol that linked the picturesque foreground to the picturesque distance. Olmsted's increasing involvement in the late 1920s and 1930s with conservation projects in the West would certainly support this contention.

The third phase of reevaluation, introduced by the Skidmore, Owings, and Merrill plan of 1965, confirms that when compared with the McMillan Plan and the later Olmsted schemes, the attempt to revive historical ideas will ultimately say as much about present values as those of the past. The McMillan Plan was a selective view of the baroque landscape tradition tempered by and adjusted to contemporary exigencies. Olmsted's reevaluation of Union Square was undertaken in a more serious and scholarly way, but it was also determined by later changes to that area. However, the Skidmore, Owings, and Merrill plan was contemporary in nature, and the past that it revered was the Beaux-Arts spirit of the McMillan Plan.

All three of these periods show an extraordinary fidelity to the ideal of preserving a historic vision; however, work in each of these periods was also subject to the decisions of Congress. A recently discovered painting suggests the arbitrariness that can ensue in such a relationship (fig. 16). Without a strongly defined and defended vision of what a landscape ought to become, it is doubtful if the vision will be realized. Between 1900 and 1948 Olmsted, as unofficial guardian of a vision, played a major role in the development of the Mall. It was a role whose significance he had anticipated in his remarkable 1900 paper to the American Institute of Architects when he said: "In any great plan, time must develop features which seem under the conditions of the present moment capable of improvement, but unless the plan appears upon thoughtful or conservative judgement distinctly bad, the one safe course is to adhere steadfastly to its fundamental features. Once open the plan to a radical change, once establish the precedent of seriously altering it to meet the ideas of the moment, the bars are thrown down for caprice and confusion."[73]

NOTES

1. Glenn Brown, comp., *Papers Relating to the Improvement of the City of Washington, District of Columbia*, 56th Cong., 2d sess., 1901, S. Doc. 94, 192.

2. Charles Moore, "Notes on the Parks and Their Connections," Park Improvement Papers 6; and Frederick Law Olmsted, Sr., "A Paper Relating to the Trees, Shrubs, and Plants in the United States Capitol Ground, and an Index of the Same, Together With Some Observations Upon the Planting and Care of Trees in the District of Columbia," Park Improvement Papers 15, Glenn Brown, comp., in *Park Improvement Papers*, a series of papers relating to the improvement of the park system of the District of Columbia: printed for the use of the Senate Committee on the District of Columbia (Washington, 1901), 79–97, 201–221.

3. Olmsted, Sr. 1903, 202–204.

4. *Annual Report of the Architect to the Extension to the Capitol*, 1 November 1873, (Washington, 1873).

5. Irving D. Fisher, *Frederick Law Olmsted and the City Planning Movement in the United States* (Ann Arbor, 1986), 27–50; Laura Wood Roper, *FLO: A Biography of Frederick Law Olmsted* (Baltimore and London, 1973), 11.

6. See Bruce Kelly, Gail Travis Guillet, and Mary Ellen W. Hern, *Art of the Olmsted Landscape* (New York, 1981), 99–109, 111–122. See also: Albert Fein, *Frederick Law Olmsted and the Environmental Tradition* (New York, 1972); and Geoffrey Blodgett, *The Gentle Reformers; Democrats in the Cleveland Era* (Cambridge, 1966).

7. Frederick Law Olmsted (Senior) to Frederick Law Olmsted (Junior), 1 August 1892, Frederick Law Olmsted Papers, Library of Congress (hereafter Olmsted Papers). See also Paul V. Turner, Marcia E. Vetrocq, and Karen Weitze, *The Founders and the Architects: The Design of Stanford University* (Stanford, 1976).

8. Olmsted, Sr. 1903, 206.

9. Olmsted to William Hammond Hall, 28 March 1874 (draft), Olmsted Papers.

10. Olmsted, Sr. 1903, 207.

11. Olmsted to Edward Clark, 15 July 1886 (draft), Olmsted Papers.

12. Olmsted, Sr. 1903, 210.

13. John W. Reps, *Monumental Washington: The Planning and Development of the Capital Center* (Princeton, 1967), 66–69.

14. Reps 1967, 78–81.

15. Glenn Brown, *Memories, 1860–1930* (Washington, 1931), 259–264.

16. Brown 1901, 25–34.

17. Roper 1973, 338.

18. Olmsted (Senior) to Olmsted (Junior), 1 August 1894, Olmsted Papers.

19. Edward Clark Whiting and William Lyman Phillips, "Frederick Law Olmsted 1870–1957: An Appreciation of the Man and His Achievement," *Landscape Architecture* 48 (April 1958), 145.

20. Olmsted (Senior) to Olmsted (Junior), 23 December 1894, (draft), Olmsted Papers.

21. Cynthia Zaitzevsky, *Frederick Law Olmsted and the Boston Park System*, (Cambridge and London, 1982).

22. No comprehensive study has been written of the work of the Olmsted Brothers. See John Taylor Boyd, Jr., "The Work of Olmsted Brothers, Parts 1 and 2," *Architectural Record* 44 (November-December, 1918), 456–464, 502–521.

23. Brown 1901, 26.

24. Brown 1901, 27, 29–30.

25. Roper 1973, 138–139.

26. Brown 1901, 29–30; 32.

27. Reps 1967, 92–93.

28. United States Public Buildings Commission, *Public Buildings of the District of Columbia. Report of the Public Buildings Commission. Pursuant to Certain Provisions of the Sundry Civil Appropriations Act. Appropriated July 1st, 1916. Authorizing the Appointment of a Commission to Investigate and Ascertain What Public Buildings are needed to provide permanent quarters for All the Government Activities in the District of Columbia* (Washington, 1918), 48.

29. Frederick Law Olmsted, "Beautifying a City," *The Independent* 54 (7 August 1902), 1870–1877.

30. The earliest scientifically designed playground in the United States was Charlesbank in Boston, designed in 1892 by John Charles Olmsted; see Zaitzevsky 1982, 97–99.

31. Moore 1903, 193.

32. F. Hamilton Hazlehurst, *Jacques Boyceau and the French Formal Garden* (Nashville, 1966).

33. Charles Moore, *The Life and Times of Charles Follen McKim* (Boston, 1929); J. L. Sibley Jennings, Jr. and Susan Rademacher Frey, "The Garden in Black and White: Turn of the Century in Europe," *Garden Design* 1 (Autumn 1982), 72–75.

34. Moore 1929, 192.

35. Werner Hegemann and Elbert Peets, *The American Vitruvius: An Architect's Handbook of Civic Art* (New York, 1922), 285.

36. Hegemann and Peets, 1922, 290.

37. Charles Moore, ed., *The Improvement of the Park System of the District of Columbia*, 57th

Cong., 1st sess., 1902, S. Rept. 166 (hereafter Moore 1902), 42.

38. Moore 1902, 45; Moore 1929, 199.

39. Moore 1902, 45.

40. Paul Spreiregen, ed., *On the Art of Designing Cities: Selected Essays of Elbert Peets* (Cambridge and London, 1968), 93–94, 67–87. The book contains a number of articles Peets wrote about planning in Washington from 1922 to 1937.

41. Charles Moore, *Daniel H. Burnham*, 2 vols. (Boston, 1921), 1:224; Moore 1902, 28.

42. Moore 1902, 47; Brown 1931, 269. The Villa Medici is the only garden in Rome visited by the commissioners that contains an obelisk.

43. Moore 1902, 24, 28, 47, 127–129.

44. Moore 1902, 144–145; memorandum by F. L. Olmsted, Jr.

45. Playground Association of America, *Proceedings of the 1st and 3rd Playground Conference, New York City, September 8–12, 1908; and Year Book, 1908* (New York, 1909), 148–154, 255–262; Arthur Leland and Lorna Higbee Leland, *Playground Technique and Playcraft*, 1 (Springfield, 1909), 70–78.

46. David C. Streatfield, "Art and Nature in the English Landscape Garden: Design Theory and Practice, 1700–1818," *Landscape of Eighteenth Century England* (Los Angeles, 1981), 67–69.

47. There is no comprehensive study of Sir Charles Barry's garden designs; see George F. Chadwick, *The Park and the Town* (New York and Washington, 1966), 141–146. For Charles Adams Platt, see Keith N. Morgan, *Charles A. Platt, the Artist as Architect* (New York and Cambridge, 1985).

48. Hegemann and Peets 1922, 48; Spreiregen 1968, 106.

49. Moore 1902, 10.

50. Reps 1967, chap. 6. A detailed analysis of this period is given in William Bushong, "Glenn Brown, the American Institute of Architects, and the Development of the Civic Core of Washington, D.C." (Ph.D. diss., George Washington University, 1988).

51. Moore 1921, 2:132–136.

52. Reps 1967, 167.

53. National Capitol Planning Commission and Frederick Gutheim, *Worthy of the Nation, the History of Planning for the National Capitol* (Washington, 1977) (hereafter NCPC 1977), 186.

54. William T. Partridge, "L'Enfant's Methods and Features of His Plan for the Federal City," in National Capital Park and Planning Commission, *Reports and Plans, Washington Region*, Supplementary Technical Data to Accompany Annual Report (Washington, 1930), 21–38; Charles W. Eliot II, "L'Enfant as a Landscape Architect," *Landscape Architecture* 30 (April, 1930), 236.

55. NCPC 1977, 218.

56. *American Architect* 136 (20 May 1929), 651.

57. *American Architect* 1929, 662.

58. Ferruccio Vitale, "The Washington Monument Gardens," *Landscape Architecture* 30 (April, 1930), 234–235.

59. United States Director of Public Buildings and Public Parks, *Improvement of the Washington Monument Grounds: Instructions from the President of the United States Concerning a Report on the Improvement of the Washington Grounds Authorized by the Independent Offices Act of 1931, Approved April 19, 1930, together with Several Plans and Estimates, Therefor*, 72d Cong., 2d sess., 1934, H. Doc. 528, 12, 20, 33, 41.

60. Reps 1967, 170.

61. Glenn Brown, "The Artistic Growth of the Washington Plan," *Architectural Record* 59 (April 1926), 324.

62. Spreiregen 1968, 106.

63. NCPC 1977, 219, 220.

64. NCPC 1977, 216, 218.

65. Frederick Law Olmsted, "Union Square in Washington: A Report on the Redesign of This Area in 1934," *Landscape Architecture* 35 (July 1945), 130–136.

66. Olmsted 1944, 133.

67. Reps 1973, 176–177.

68. "The Harvard Revolution" was an attempt by Garrett Eckbo, James Rose, and Dan Kiley to overthrow the Beaux-Arts system of design which had largely dominated education in landscape architecture. Some of its products can be seen in Garrett Eckbo, "Sculpture and Landscape Design," *Magazine of Art* 31 (April 1938), 202–208; Garrett Eckbo, "Small Gardens in the City," *Pencil Points* 18 (September 1937), 573–586; and James C. Rose, "Freedom in the Garden: A Contemporary Approach in Landscape Design," *Pencil Points* 19 (October 1938), 639–643. For Thomas Church's work, see David C. Streatfield, "Thomas Church and the California Garden, 1929–1950," in *Festschrift: A Collection of Essays in Architectural History Prepared by the Northern Pacific Coast Chapter Society of Architectural Historians; Dedicated to Professor Marion Dean Ross, Chapter Founder on the Occasion of His 65th Birthday*, ed. Elisabeth Walton Potter (Salem, Ore., 1978), 68–75.

69. Spreiregen 1968, 94, 96–97.

70. Thomas C. Jeffers, "The Washington Monument: Various Plans for the Improvement of Its Surroundings," *Landscape Architecture* 39 (July 1949), 158–163.

71. United States President's Council on Pennsylvania Avenue, *Pennsylvania Avenue* (Washington, 1964).

72. *The Grand Design* [exh. cat., Library of Congress] (Washington, 1967), 20–23.

73. Brown 1901, 34.

RICHARD GUY WILSON
University of Virginia

High Noon on the Mall:

Modernism versus Traditionalism, 1910–1970

Western movie and the Mall may seem anachronistic, yet in many ways the history of the Mall's development since the 1901–1902 McMillan Plan has been a battle royal. Out of what seemed an unkempt gardenesque park with little particular symbolic value, the Mall emerged to become the locus of American secular religion. In the creation of this ensemble, equivalents of Western shootouts have taken place which include strenuous opposition to the location of such buildings as the Lincoln Memorial; Bertram Goodhue jabbing at Charles Moore after the Commission of Fine Arts rejected Goodhue's design for the National Academy of Sciences; and face-offs such as occurred in the late 1930s with the classical National Gallery of Art by John Russell Pope arising unimpeded, while across the way lay the empty site of a modernist dream, the unrealized Smithsonian Gallery of Art by Eliel and Eero Saarinen and Robert Swanson (figs. 1, 2).

In each of these cases, and in many others, the fundamental issue concerned what the Mall represented and how the various constituencies involved interpreted its meaning. The Smithsonian conflict involved the well-known twentieth-century battle of modernism versus traditionalism in the arena of image and style. Such a stylistic war, however, hid a more subtle and profound confrontation concerning the meaning of history and culture and how Americans defined and redefined, or revised, themselves with regard to the past.

HISTORY AND THE MODERN CONSCIOUSNESS

Modernism and its sense of history are crucial to understanding the Mall. Modern consciousness does not mean irrationalism or alienation; those are aspects of bohemianism and the avant-garde.[1] Nor is it Karl Popper's "historicism," though certainly many individuals – especially those involved with the Mall – have subscribed to the "historicist" assumption.[2] People define themselves by history; they locate themselves in a particular system of beliefs and values which are historic. A modernist myth was the escape from history, though proponents of such an escape usually based their arguments on a historical imperative or necessity. The core of modern consciousness had been not escape, but a recognition of the many historical alternatives. Historical knowledge began exponentially to multiply in the eighteenth century. As the German architect-theorist, Gottfried Semper, later complained, with the abundance of knowledge, direction was lost.[3] For the traditional or premodern imagination, only one history existed, and many people in the modern era continued to try to recapture the safety of the traditional mind by claiming only one history. But the modern consciousness knows that what is history is imprecise; the past is quicksand, constantly revised and capable of being manufactured. Washington politics exemplifies this shifting history, for the past can

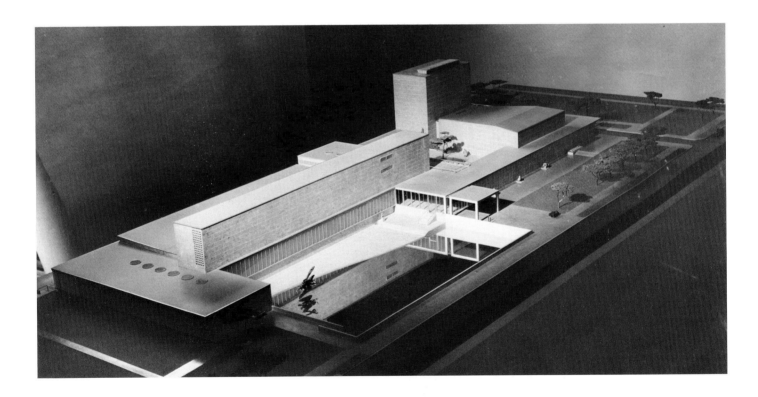

be shredded, elaborated, forgotten, or declared inoperative.

Charles Moore once claimed: "In the monuments of the National Capital you shall read the history of America."[4] Moore's history is selected, ideal, fabricated. History in the modern sense is polemical and ideological. This is not to suggest the crudity of the Marxian interpretations in which classicism frequently equates with fascism. The classicism

advocated by Franklin Roosevelt's administration conveyed authority, security, and liberal hope. Similarly, Chicago architect and
planner Daniel Burnham's classicism was in-
timately tied to progressive urban reform. Style
as a symbol is never constant; the meanings
of styles change or are revised. The Mall's
buildings, sculpture, landscaping, and space
represent attempts to convey meanings about
America—its history, culture, and civilization; some of its buildings are easily understood, others more difficult. Displayed on the
Mall is history as symbol, a carefully chosen
ensemble that has been revised many times
and will be revised again.

The Mall as historical symbol must be seen
against the background of the explosion of
American historiography and notions of culture and civilization in the twentieth century.
Raymond Williams labels history, culture, and
civilization keywords, that is, crucial to dis-
course and controversial in meaning.
Throughout the twentieth century in America, as Warren Susman explains, our view of
what constitutes history and culture has expanded. Matthew Arnold's concept of culture
as only the best was challenged in the 1920s;
by the 1930s even a mandarin such as T. S.
Eliot would accept an anthropological interpretation of culture.[5] As the constituents of
culture and history have expanded, their uses
have changed. From being simply a validation
by politicians or something taught in schools
and an activity of historians, history became
popularized. Movies, television, and novels
trivialize history but make it omnipresent, an
indelible aspect of the daily life of nearly all
Americans and far more immediate than any
statue of the "Yank" or "Johnny Reb" on the
town square ever was. Perhaps even more
crucial has been history as "edutainment" (education and entertainment): the historical
recreation of Henry Ford at Greenfield Village
or of John D. Rockefeller at Williamsburg,
which entered the national consciousness in
the 1930s and combined in one tidy package
tourism, patriotic duty, vacation, education,
and fun.[6]

Americans in the nineteenth century evolved
the myth of the American Adam, the idea of
the uniqueness of the American experience
and an escape from history.[7] This became, in
the hands of D. H. Lawrence, the Americans
with no past against those who sought the
safety of tradition and paid homage to Europe;
and with Philip Rahv, "redskins" against
"palefaces." George Santayana in "The Genteel Tradition" elucidated an opposing view
while indicating architectural preferences:
"The American Will inhabits the sky-scraper;
the American Intellect inhabits the colonial
mansion."[8] The question of America as unique
or as the heir of Europe remained at the bot-
tom of many cultural debates but with the
important difference that now the positions
would be validated by history. On the Mall in
the twentieth century, battles raged over the
appropriate images: Wasn't classicism too old-
fashioned or too European? But the modernist
answer contained perplexing problems in that
it revealed a colonial mentality; in place of
paying homage to Beaux-Arts ideals and Rome,
the modernist colonials imported the International style.[9]

For Americans in the twentieth century,
history became a retreat, a cultural therapeu-
tic from the neurasthenia of the Machine Age,
the hard times of the Depression, and the sus-
picion of the McCarthy years. It provided validity for the imperialism of the Spanish-American War and for the euphoria of a super power.[10]
History has become ubiquitous and domes-
ticated; it is invoked as a cause for "white
sales," to promote service stations, and to guide
political decisions. In the twentieth century
the countryside has been plagued: the locations of minor engagements of the Revolutionary and Civil wars have been labeled, while
houses built before 1800, and in some cases
before 1900, are indiscriminately deemed
"historic."[11] Anniversaries, no matter how
insignificant, become celebrations of patriotism and consumption and calls to action.
One way to view the Mall's development in
the twentieth century is through the celebration of anniversaries, including: the bicentennial of 1976, the sesquicentennial of 1926, the
bicentennials of Washington's birth in 1932
and Jefferson's birth in 1943, and the centennial of Lincoln's birth in 1909. These dates
spurred action: chronology became an actor.

The Mall in the twentieth century becomes
the physical representative of American history as an ideal. Most of the structures, statues, and indeed the landscaping and space,
carry this message, even though other causes
originally may have brought them into being.
Memorial Bridge, projected in the McMillan

Plan, was not built until the 1920s, for political and commercial interests wanted it placed elsewhere. Henry Bacon fought for the bridge, claiming it would link his Lincoln Memorial with Arlington Cemetery, which contained "the dust of those who gave 'the last full measure of devotion' to their country."[12] Patriotic in intent, Memorial Bridge was commissioned in 1923 only after an extraordinary traffic jam in 1921 for the dedication of the Tomb of the Unknown Soldier delayed the president by over an hour. Memorial Bridge and Avenue B North — which was widened and renamed Constitution Avenue in 1931 — were specifically intended to be processional ways for funerals. The congressional resolution for Constitution Avenue stated its purpose was to hold "countless processions of American patriots and millions of liberty-loving men, women, and children, wending their way to Arlington and the Tomb of the Unknown Soldier" (pls. LXXXIII, LXXXIV, CXXXV, CXXXVI).[13]

The Mall as it now stands is a recent creation. Not until 1929 did Congress accept and direct that the L'Enfant and McMillan plans be the official ones for the Mall.[14] And even with this act, both plans were general guides to the future, subject to frequent revisions (fig. 3; pls. LXXXVI–XCV, CI–CXIII). The Capitol, White House, and Washington Monument provided existing anchor points, but the terminuses formed by the Lincoln and Jefferson memorials were not finished until 1922 and 1943, respectively. A few other buildings on or peripheral to the Mall — the Smithsonian Institution's (1847–1855) and Arts and Industries (1879–1881) buildings, the Bureau of Engraving (1880), the Treasury (1836–1869), and the Executive Office Building (formerly State, War and Navy) (1871–1888) — remain, but many others have been destroyed in a concerted program to provide a monumental background and revise American history. The "tempos," or temporary buildings erected during World

3. View of Mall, looking east from Washington Monument, 1938
Commission of Fine Arts

War I, covered great portions of the Mall into the post-World War II years, and the last ones were not removed until 1970 under the prodding of President Richard M. Nixon (fig. 4; pls. XCVI–CI, CVI–CXIII). New plans for landscaping dating from 1964–1965 (pls. CXIV–CXVI), and 1972–1974 by Skidmore, Owings, and Merrill teams were carried out in part during the late 1970s and early 1980s.

The twentieth-century Mall resembles a geological fault line in all its movements and shifts, with layers of different thicknesses representing competing interests or constituencies stacked in their order of impact: first, politicians; second, protectors; third, users, the occupants of the buildings; next, architects and other designers; and finally the City of Washington, D.C. While these constituencies are intertwined, each has viewed the Mall differently in terms of history, symbolic value, and purpose, and will be treated separately.

WASHINGTON

Washington ranks last in impact, yet it must be discussed first to put into perspective the power of the other constituencies and to provide a context. Noticeably lacking as a constituency for the Mall are commercial interests, which are confined to other parts of the city. Washington has never been a large commercial center in comparison to other American metropolises. Until home rule was granted in 1973 Washington was governed by a board of three commissioners appointed by the president and by committees of the House and Senate, which passed all legislation. In contrast to most major American cities, Washington, D.C., has lacked a manufacturing base, and it never experienced firsthand the harsher aspects of the industrial revolution. Washington's principal industry was government, which afforded an unusual degree of economic security in spite of depressions and recessions.

Moreover, the federal government and the services related to it have undergone more or less continual, sometimes dramatic, increases in size during the twentieth century. Washington's population rose from 331,069 in 1910 to 802,172 in 1950, by which time many additional people were residing in the adjacent counties as well. Washington has long attracted persons of talent in fields related to government. Yet up through the 1970s, the prevailing image of official Washington, including the Mall, was as the center of a white, Anglo-Saxon, Protestant city. Washington until recently was unusual among major American cities in its low percentage of foreign-born residents. On the other hand, nearly 95,000 residents, 28.5 percent of the total populace, were African American by 1910, then the greatest number of these people concentrated in one city anywhere on the globe. By 1970 the African American population was 71 percent of the total. Although seldom recognized outside the city, African American Washington has long been a place of extraordinary cultural and intellectual contributions, making the city a center of African American achievement.[15] But until recently, the national and local ruling class has been white, male, generally Protestant, and Western European in origin. The elite has represented itself on the Mall: minority populations lack a presence there. The Mall exists as a self-contained entity, largely independent of its city.

POLITICS

Politics and power are frequently seen as synonymous; however, some distinctions are in order. On the Mall, politics is central: nothing gets done without the involvement of at least one branch of government, Congress, and generally the executive branch as well. No building is placed on the Mall, and few have been placed adjacent to the Mall, without legislative approval and, in most cases, appropriations. Seldom is Aristotle openly invoked, yet his concept that man is a political animal and that it is natural and good for man to form the polis has been at the heart, consciously or otherwise, of many decisions made in Washington concerning the Mall. For most politicians the Mall has been a symbol of the virtuous life, a view that can be seen in their

language. President Calvin Coolidge said in a 1926 speech central to advancing the Mall's development, "If our country wishes to compete with others, let it not be in the support of armaments but in the making of a beautiful Capital City. Let it express the soul of America." [16] Thirty-seven years later President John F. Kennedy presented a similar message: "Washington today is the capital of an urban nation. As a city it should express our highest aspirations for urban life . . . providing . . . a setting in which men and women can fully live up to their responsibilities as free citizens." Daniel Patrick Moynihan openly invoked Aristotle in 1967: "The American polity – both the experience and the awareness of community and shared conviction – has been impaired, has atrophied in our time because of the retreat from architecture and public buildings as a conscious element of public policy and a purposeful instrument for the expression of public purposes." [17]

In twentieth-century America, politics also means power, and political power is represented on the Mall in two very different ways. The concentration on making Washington a city beautiful in the twentieth century is related to the growth and dominance of a central government. This development resulted in massive building programs such as the Federal Triangle and various buildings on Independence Avenue, and in a change in dominant symbols. From the various longstanding fictional symbols such as Columbia, Liberty, and Uncle Sam, the persistent, new emblems of America became the White House, the Capitol, and the broad expense of the Mall.

Political power also resulted in dictatorial control by some politicians, especially those in Congress. House Speaker "Uncle" Joseph Cannon of Illinois strongly opposed the McMillan Plan (primarily because the Senate took the lead without consulting him), and hence delayed for nearly a decade the establishment of a Commission of Fine Arts. Cannon also wanted the Lincoln Memorial placed anywhere except the present Potomac Park location, and because of this John Russell Pope made a series of studies for Meridian Hill and Soldier's Home sites. Cannon represents that strain of autocratic American politician proud of his aesthetic philistinism. As he once said in an address to the American Institute of Architects: "For what I don't know about ar-

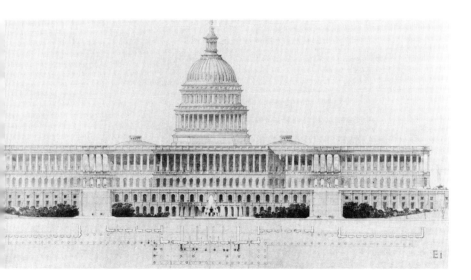

5. J. George Stewart (Architect of the Capitol) and Harbeson, Hough, Livingston, and Larson, associated architects, Rayburn House Office Building (1955–1965), view from southwest
Office of the Architect of the Capitol

6. J. George Stewart, United States Capitol, proposed west front extension, 1963
Office of the Architect of the Capitol

chitecture, Mr. [J.P.] Morgan would make a library larger than all your wealth could buy." Cannon was finally brought to bay by President William Howard Taft, who served as chairman of the Lincoln Memorial Commission and made the final decision on the Mall site.[18]

Autocratic congressional power also projects from the office of the Architect of the Capitol. Although appointed by the president, the Architect of the Capitol serves exclusively at the pleasure of Congress and particularly of its leaders. The architect is not bound by *any* regulatory agency. The reign of House Speaker Sam Rayburn of Texas and his protégé, J. George Stewart (1954–1970), indicates the possibilities of the position. Stewart was not an architect at all, but an engineer who had worked as a building contractor and served briefly as Republican congressional representative from Delaware from 1935 to 1937. Appointed Architect of the Capitol by President Eisenhower, Stewart served the Democratic congressional leadership, principally Rayburn and Lyndon B. Johnson, with aplomb, overseeing the design and erection of several congressional office buildings. His work, such as the Rayburn House Office Building facing the Mall at Independence Avenue and First Street, was roasted by the architectural and popular press as banal and outmoded: "A Monument to Power," "Texas penitentiary," and "King Hottentot's Temple" (fig. 5). Many of the architectural decisions on the $135 million pile were made by Rayburn himself with the assistance of Stewart. The associated architect, William Livingston of Harbeson, Hough, Livingston, and Larson (now H2L2) of Philadelphia, died a broken man from the experience.[19] The dress of the Rayburn is classical, but it is crudely handled: great flights of stairs lead nowhere, moldings are treated as thick clumps. Stewart also shepherded the thirty-two-foot extension of the east front of the Capitol (1955–1962), popularly known as the "Texas Front," because both Rayburn and Johnson viewed its completion as a sign of their personal power and prestige. Similarly, the controversial and ultimately ill-fated west front extension, which would have changed the relation of the Capitol to the Mall and which was heavily promoted by Stewart from 1962 onward, was regarded by Rayburn's successor, House Speaker John McCormick as a sign of his prestige (fig. 6).[20] *Sic transit gloria mundi!*

That the exercise of political power need not result in such trivial arrogance can be seen in the leadership of Andrew W. Mellon, the Pittsburgh financier and secretary of the Treasury under Harding, Coolidge, and Hoover. As Treasury secretary, Mellon directed most federal building activities, and he personally chose and inspired the board of architectural consultants for the Federal Triangle. Much of the quality of that complex must be attributed to Mellon, who had the good sense to follow advice and engage for the board Edward H. Bennett (chairman), Arthur Brown, Williams Adams Delano, John Russell Pope, Louis Ayres, Milton Medary, and Clarence Zantzinger — certainly among the leading architects in the country. Mellon did more than listen; he directed, instructing Bennett that the appropriate models should include "large interior courts or plazas" such as those of "the Louvre in Paris" (fig. 7).[21] Mellon was the architectural czar of Washington in the 1920s, and with Bennett as his personal consultant, he followed the general spirit of McMillan Plan in locating buildings such as the Supreme Court.[22]

Building at such a scale becomes a narcotic. Even after the Republicans were swept out of office in 1933, Mellon remained addicted, though he was under a politically motivated investigation for tax fraud through the mid-1930s. Certainly the National Gallery of Art is in part a reflection of Lord Duveen's careful orchestration of Mellon's collecting and Mellon's patriotic wish for the United States to have a national museum similar to those of other nations. But it seems Mellon also liked building. He personally commissioned and paid for the design by John Russell Pope. Until his death in 1937 Mellon oversaw the plans and their revisions. In many ways the National Gallery was a capstone to the Federal Triangle. Andrew Mellon apparently just had to have one more big building![23]

PROTECTORS

Officially legislated bodies such as the Commission of Fine Arts and the National Capital Planning Commission, along with some self-appointed individuals such as Glenn Brown, have seen a duty in protecting the visions of the Senate Park Commission and L'Enfant. The protectors' role has been not only defense but aggressive pursuit of goals. Founded in 1910, the Commission of Fine Arts is the most direct outcome of the Senate Park Commission. It oversees and advises on the placement of monuments, statuary, and buildings on the Mall. Additional legislation, such as the Shipstead-Luce Act of 1930, has extended its role to approving structures that face on govern-

7. Federal Triangle, model on exhibit at Corcoran Gallery of Art, 1929, with Secretary of the Treasury, Andrew W. Mellon
National Archives

ment property in the District.[24] The Commission of Fine Arts advises and approves, it does not design. Concerned that the planning of Washington, and the development of the Mall in particular, was not proceeding smoothly, a number of public-spirited citizens such as Frederick A. Delano and Frederick Law Olmsted, Jr. established the Committee of One Hundred. This group, in turn, persuaded Congress and the president to establish the National Capital Park Commission in 1924, which became the National Capital Park and Planning Commission two years later and then the National Capital Planning Commission in 1952 (hereafter, Planning Commission). Fueled by post-World War I hubris and the sesquicentennial of 1926, the Planning Commission initiated the Mall's development.[25] Among other key protector groups have been the Army Corps of Engineers, which physically carried out the work and provided advice, and the National Park Service, which assumed these responsibilities in 1933.[26] Protectors can be actors. Secretary of the Interior Stewart Udall, under whom the National Park Service operated, personally hired Skidmore, Owings, and Merrill in 1964 to provide a new master plan for the Mall.[27] Temporary and not-so-temporary commissions, such as that for Pennsyl-

8. Henry Bacon, Lincoln
Memorial (1911–1922), east
elevation, photograph 1923
Commission of Fine Arts

vania Avenue, also play important roles in this arena. This protective maze is distinguished by three features: the homage always paid to the precedents of the McMillan and L'Enfant plans, the importance of the counsels of elders or advisors, and the role of chairmen.

The McMillan Plan has been the holy talisman for almost everyone concerned with the Mall; but, like the Bible, it is open to interpretation. Those who question its wisdom resurrect L'Enfant as the true touchstone. During the 1930s, Elbert Peets, a landscape architect and self-appointed protector, advocated L'Enfant's plan as more appropriate than the grand formality and Beaux-Arts pomp of the 1901-1902 scheme.[28] Modernist critics such as Joseph Hudnut, dean at Harvard in the late 1930s, also evoked L'Enfant, claiming that he envisioned a garden at the center, not an imperial mall. Hudnut's compatriot, Alfred Kastner, was even more heretical, claiming that " 'The Grand Plan' need not be symmetrical," and he believed Rockefeller Center to be a more appropriate symbol of a modern democracy than the Federal Triangle.[29]

The Skidmore team of 1964 felt, at least privately, that they also were returning to L'Enfant rather than the McMillan Plan; yet what they meant was not so much the French-

man's plan itself as the French eighteenth-century formality and dense tree planting similar to forests at Compiègne or Versailles. The results were certainly not informal; and indeed closer to the McMillan Plan than to L'Enfant's (pls. CXIV-CXVI).

The staying power of the McMillan Plan lay with its open invocation of imperial grandeur and the placement of one key building, the Lincoln Memorial, without which the Mall undoubtedly would not have been realized.[30] For those who believed in an "American Renaissance," such as McKim, Burnham, Saint-Gaudens, and Olmsted did, the function of the memorial was to serve as a noble backdrop for ritualistic acts of citizenship and patriotism.[30] The Lincoln Memorial fulfilled these criteria and more; in the McMillan Plan it becomes the "Arc de Triomphe" of America, and in similar, evocative language it was described for years afterward.[31] The outcome of the fierce battle over the site in Potomac Park was never really in jeopardy since both the Lincoln Memorial Commission and the Commission of Fine Arts, which had to approve the scheme, were stacked with former Senate Park Commission members or supporters. McKim had designed the memorial in the McMillan Plan; Henry Bacon, his protégé, be-

9. John Russell Pope,
Thomas Jefferson Memorial,
proposal for Mall site, 1936
rendering
University of Virginia Archives

came the architect despite the sentiment in some quarters to hire John Russell Pope. Bacon took McKim's rectangular form of an open colonnade, eliminated the wings and the attic heraldic group, and tightened the general composition into an enclosed cella-type structure (fig. 8). The design, with its thirty-six exterior columns and frieze, symbolizes the reunited states of the Union at Lincoln's death. Within this Greek peripteral temple, severely rectangular, lacking the traditional pediments, and placed with the long sides perpendicular to the Mall's axis, sits the giant figure of Lincoln by Daniel Chester French. From a homespun Midwestern heritage to enshrinement in a grand, classical pile, the memory of the Great Emancipator was compressed and apotheosized.

Other features of the McMillan Plan were found more open to reinterpretation. The scheme delineated a reflecting pool with cross-axial arms in front of the Lincoln Memorial. In 1919–1920 this design was debated among Fine Arts commission members. Thomas Hastings and Cass Gilbert argued strongly in favor of McKim's scheme. Olmsted and Bacon favored straight sides.[32] A far bigger controversy broke out concerning the buildings on the main cross-axis south from the White House, which the McMillan Plan reserved for recreation and a pantheon honoring either an individual or a group. This area, which Olmsted

noted in 1923 "was less carefully studied than any other major part of the 'Mall area,' " had been discussed as the site for a Theodore Roosevelt Memorial. A competition was held in 1926 and won by John Russell Pope; however, the project never received funds and the site soon fell prey to the politicians advancing the proposal to erect the Jefferson Memorial.[33]

Beginning in 1934 the scheme to place a memorial to Thomas Jefferson on the Tidal Basin or White House south axis was fought bitterly by both the Commission of Fine Arts and the Planning Commission (figs. 9, 10). The Thomas Jefferson Memorial Commission had investigated other sites: East Capitol Street on the axis with the Capitol, a site south of the Capitol in Anacostia Park, and on the Mall across from the National Archives. John Russell Pope did studies for all these locations; however, both he and the majority of the Memorial Commission members preferred the Tidal Basin site from the start.[34] A battle against that site erupted in the popular and architectural presses. Some critics argued that the Japanese cherry trees, planted between 1911 and 1915, would be irremediably damaged. The Commission of Fine Arts went to the extraordinary length of publishing a pamphlet attacking the location.[35] In spite of such opposition, the Jefferson Memorial was built, in part because the Memorial Commission gathered the support of President Roosevelt. Fur-

thermore, this body was a creature of Congress, with Johnny Boylan, a powerful Tammany Hall politician and representative from New York's Fifteenth Congressional District serving as its chairman. Congress had the final say.[36]

The story is a bittersweet one, for many of the most vocal opponents to Pope's pantheon were modernists such as Frank Lloyd Wright and Joseph Hudnut.[37] Pope had been chosen by Fiske Kimball, the historian on the Memorial Commission and director of the Philadelphia Museum of Art. Kimball, an architect trained in the Beaux-Arts manner, an eminent architectural historian, and an authority on Jefferson, told the commission: "the old form of classical architecture is dying out . . . McKim is dead. . . . Pope is the last of those men." Kimball wrote an open letter in which he said, "the day of the classic in American architecture is over," modernism is here, and he implied, just give us, the old guard, one more building and we will fade away.[38] The Pope design is brilliant, the temple portico terminates the Mall's north-south axis, while the open, circular colonnade absorbs the other view lines that converge on the site. The structure is at once a terminus and an open, midspace focal point.

Nearly every building's location on the Mall has been disputed. The Senate Park Commission located museums and scientific institutions on the north and south sides of the Mall between the Capitol and the Washington Monument.[39] Their report favorably noted that a new Department of Agriculture would be built on the Mall west of the Smithsonian to replace a much despised Second Empire structure of 1868 (pl. LIII). Almost immediately thereafter, in 1903–1904, a fight broke out over the proper setback of the new building. The Agriculture Department wanted to invade the Mall; McKim, Burnham, and others testified on the proper setback and won the shootout with the help of President Theodore Roosevelt and Secretary of War Taft.[40] Out of spite, though under the veil of inadequate funds, the Secretary of Agriculture, James Wilson, directed the architects, Rankin, Kellogg, and Crane to design only the wings, which were built in 1904–1908. The old mansarded structure, resembling a decayed tooth amid limestone grandeur, remained until 1926, when construction on a newly designed central section began (pls. XCVI, CV).

A proposal came forth in the late 1920s to line the Mall from the Capitol to the Washington Monument with forty-eight state "temples," "symbolic of the Union." Ulysses S. Grant III, a member of the Planning Commission and director of Public Buildings, found merit in the proposal but noted the lack of space and suggested East Capitol Street as an alternative (pls. LXXXIX–XCI, XCV).[41] Not until

1938 did the Planning Commission formally give the Smithsonian rights to most of the remaining sites on the Mall between the Capitol and the Washington Monument.[42] The assignment of other areas has been more haphazard and fraught with the usual political problems.

The protectors have frequently tried to expand the Mall beyond the limits delineated in the McMillan and L'Enfant plans. The state temple proposal found serious support in 1929 with an East Capitol Street study, which suggested a boulevard lined with these temples extending eastward to a stadium at Anacostia Park.[43] Another serious proposal of the 1930s was to balance the Federal Triangle extension with a Southwest rectangle containing the War and State departments. In the 1950s a plan by William Zeckindorf, with I. M. Pei as his designer, put forth what has come to be called L'Enfant Plaza, an extension south from the Smithsonian Institution Building on Tenth Street.[44] On the other hand, the study and re-

development of Pennsylvania Avenue beginning in 1963 has shifted some focus away from the Mall to that great boulevard between the White House and the Capitol. What the character of Pennsylvania Avenue should be — a working street or a monumental corridor — has been no less controversial than matters pertaining to the Mall. Early schemes by Nathaniel Owings' team showed monumental squares and plazas very formal in character (pl. CXIV).[45] Another proposed expansion was Paul Cret's Peace Memorial and Northwest Rectangle of the late 1930s which, in spite of President Franklin Roosevelt's support, came to naught owing to the exigencies of World War II.[46] While the Mall acts as a self-contained entity separate from the city surrounding it, the protectors have tried to expand it outward.

The members on the two principal protection agencies, the Commission of Fine Arts and the National Capital Planning Commission, have been important to the development

11. Commission of Fine Arts, photograph of: (left to right) William Mitchell Kendall, Charles Moore (chairman), John Russell Pope, Charles Adams Platt, Herbert Adams, James L. Greenleaf, H.P. Caemmerer (clerk), Major C.S. Ridley (secretary), 1919
Commission of Fine Arts

12. *Charles Moore*, oil
by Eugene F. Savage, 1937
Commission of Fine Arts

of the Mall (fig. 11). Equivalent to Aristotle's council of wise men who should lead the state, both groups were intended to be composed of eminent figures in art and architecture. This generally has meant the "old guard" of the period in question: Henry Bacon, Milton Medary, Frederick Law Olmsted, Jr., Daniel Burnham, John Russell Pope, William Adams Delano, William Mitchell Kendall, Charles Platt, and Cass Gilbert on the Fine Arts Commission during the 1910s and 1920s; and Gordon Bunshaft, John Carl Warnecke, Burnham Kelly, and Kevin Roche during the 1960s and 1970s. The Planning Commission originally had as members Olmsted, Medary, Frederick A. Delano, and J. C. Nichols. In many cases these individuals or their firms received commissions on the Mall or in tangential areas. This connection was neither underhanded nor covert, but intended: the major American architects should be designing in the nation's capital. The ties between public service and private practice could extend over a considerable period of time. Charles McKim, as a member of the original Senate Park Commission, provided secret designs for the Smithsonian's Museum of Natural History, even though the architects of record are Hornblower and Marshall.[47] McKim's protégé, Henry Bacon, received the Lincoln Memorial commission, and all the working drawings for it were prepared in the McKim office.[48] Memorial Bridge was designed by McKim, Mead, and White with William Mitchell Kendall as the chief designer. The McKim firm lingered in the capital well into the post-World War II years, providing plans in 1953 for the Smithsonian's Air and Space Museum, and two years later the firm was selected to design the Smithsonian's Museum of History and Technology (now the National Museum of American History).[49]

The chairmen of the different protective agencies frequently became the key players. Their status and relationship to politicians, especially the president and leaders of Congress, has been crucial. William Walton, a painter and journalist, was chosen by his close friend, President Kennedy, to be chairman of the Commission of Fine Arts, though much to the president's surprise, he discovered that it was not his prerogative to make this appointment. The commission members elected Walton chairman in any event. Thereafter, he proved essential to bringing a "New Frontier" to Washington architecture, and to having Gordon Bunshaft and Aline Saarinen appointed members as well as suggesting Nathaniel Owings as chairman of the Pennsylvania Avenue Commission.[50] With the right contacts decisions could be made informally; Ulysses S. Grant III, the head of the Army Corps of Engineers for Washington and a prominent member of the Planning Commission, would drop by the White House for afternoon tea and present his views.[51] Frederick A. Delano, a railroad executive and financier from Chicago who moved to Washington to become the kingpin of the Planning Commission in the 1920s, had the ear of every president as well as being the uncle of Franklin D. Roosevelt.[52] Lacking contacts, the chairman could be ineffective. Even though he headed the Commission of Fine Arts, Gilmore Clarke could not prevent the Jefferson Memorial's location by the Tidal Basin.

Charles Moore stands apart as the most persuasive of all the chairmen for his longevity both as a member of the Commission of Fine Arts from its inception in 1910 to 1940, and as chairman from 1915 to 1937 (fig. 12). Beforehand, Moore had served as secretary to the Senate Park Commission, edited its report, wrote and edited most of Burnham and Bennett's *Plan of Chicago* (1909), and later wrote the biographies of Burnham and McKim. The origins of his belief in the importance of architecture and the other arts lay, he claimed, with undergraduate courses he had taken under Charles Eliot Norton at Harvard. Norton argued in a Ruskinian vein that art not only gave evidence of sentiments, beliefs, and opinions of men, but more than literature, architecture revealed "the moral temper and intellectual culture of the various races." [53] Moore worked tirelessly, writing letters, speeches, articles, and his biographies—all essentially pleas for the McMillan Plan—and lobbying behind every scene to promote the ideal of the Mall as a classic center of Western civilization. [54] A "family dinner at the White House" with Coolidge early during his administration and the president's puzzlement over new government office buildings led Moore to suggest the Federal Triangle. [55] Through Moore came the gift for a museum from his former business partner in Detroit, Charles Freer. The Freer Gallery (1913–1923) by Charles Adams Platt is quintessential Moore with a purpose that far transcends its function to house oriental art. [56] Inspired by the Palazzo del Te, the Freer's facade not only hides the Orient while paying homage to the Renaissance, it confronts the rambling, picturesque Smithsonian Institution Building which the Senate Park Commission had slated for destruction in their laundering of the American past. Moore controlled official Washington's aesthetics: he picked jurors and competitors. Moore disallowed Eliel Saarinen to participate in the 1935 Federal Reserve competition because he was an "alien." [57] Moore frequently claimed Washington, and the Mall, would never be completed, for if this occurred, the nation would be finished, destined only for "stagnation and decay." [58] However, his version of America's future and past encompassed only a classical perspective.

USERS

Buildings on the Mall must serve functional purposes. In most cases the perceived requirements of a particular facility and the broader issues of planning have led to dramatic confrontations over interpreting what is and is not appropriate to this precinct. The National Academy of Sciences and National Research Council building on Constitution Avenue symbolizes the central role scientific research played in World War I—and would play in the future of America—as well as the eclipse of the Smithsonian as the leader in American science. The academy's leaders had long desired a permanent home in Washington. In 1914 they engaged Shepley, Rutan, and Coolidge to prepare schematic floor plans for an office structure in a classical idiom. [59] Two years later, George Ellery Hale, a noted solar physicist, head of the Academy Building Committee, and founder of Mount Wilson Observatory, asked Bertram Grosvenor Goodhue, who had done work for him in Pasadena, to develop a new proposal. Goodhue selected a site on Meridian Hill and designed a Byzantine, vaguely Austrian Secessionist building (fig. 13). The National Academy rejected so removed a site and acquired one on Constitution Avenue adjacent to the Lincoln Memorial in 1919. Earlier, Hale had submitted Goodhue's scheme for informal review by the Commission of Fine Arts, and it was rejected. Goodhue felt "distinctly discouraged" about the new Mall site, for it opposed his medievalist Arts and Crafts aesthetic with the classical lines of the Lincoln Memorial. He offered to resign, but Hale and Charles Moore, who wanted leading American architects to work in Washington, convinced him to stay.

Subsequently, Goodhue proposed a semiclassical rectangular block surrounding a dome or rotunda. He planned for construction to begin at the rear and hoped that building funds would be expended before the rotunda's base was obscured. This idea failed to win the Academy Building Committee's approval, and Goodhue revised his approach: a semiclassical block-like front and dome would be constructed first. In March 1920 the Commission of Fine Arts rejected this design as "not working in the spirit of the city"; Goodhue needed to subordinate his imagination to the "Washington ideal." [60] The objections were not to the rotunda itself but to the ostensibly bland character of the front. Personal animosity played a role in the rejection. Goodhue minced no words in his antagonism to the Beaux-Arts approach, and on the Commission of Fine Arts William Mitchell Kendall and Charles Adams Platt personally disliked the architect.

Goodhue's Academy of Sciences design only received the commission's approval in May

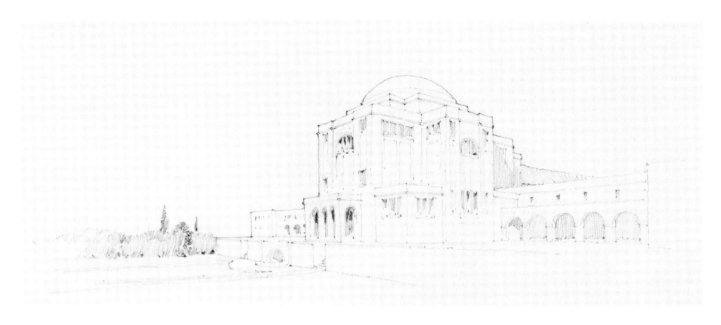

13. Bertram Grosvenor
Goodhue, National Academy
of Sciences and National
Research Council Building,
proposal for Meridian Hill
site, c. 1917
National Academy of Sciences

14. Bertram Grosvenor
Goodhue, National Academy
of Sciences and National
Research Council Building
(1920–1924), 1921 rendering of
design as executed on
Constitution Avenue site
National Academy of Sciences

1921, by which time Charles Moore had replaced Kendall and Platt with Henry Bacon, Milton Medary, and Louis Ayres, who were more supportive of Goodhue himself and of the idea that buildings should be designed by architects, and not committees. For his part Goodhue modified the design slightly, presented more elegant renderings, and noted that landscaping would mask the facade (fig. 14). When asked to describe the style of the academy, Goodhue satirized the conservative classicists, claiming—through his employee, Wallace K. Harrison—that it could not be dated, it was "Alexandrian" and "imprecise." [61] The design avoided the traditional orders; elongated pilasters at once frame the openings and merge with adjacent wall surfaces; decoration is recondite and unorthodox. The building established a precedent for the introduction of "conservative" or "stripped" classicism in Washington, D.C., of which the Folger Shakespeare Library (1928–1932) by Paul Cret and Alexander Trowbridge ranks among the finest examples. By this time, the Commission of Fine Arts enthusiastically accepted the proposal, characterizing it as "somewhat modern [-*istic* is crossed out in the minutes] but . . . designed as a building which should be considered of the classical order" (fig. 15).[62]

The issue of institutional goals and the perceived "classical spirit" of Washington as antagonistic to the architect's personal aims can be examined with two Mall buildings for the Smithsonian. In 1936 Edward C. Bruce, chief of the Department of the Treasury's Section of Fine Arts and founder of the Works Progress Administration's Treasury Relief Art Project (TRAP), conceived of a museum "dedicated to living artists."[63] Bruce thought the facility would complement Pope's "mausoleum for dead masters" that would shortly rise across the Mall from his proposed site. The project gained the support of Massachusetts Senator David Walsh, who convinced the secretary of the Smithsonian, C. G. Abbot, to take it under his institutional wing. After a year of lobbying and one defeat, a bill passed Congress in May 1938 for $40,000 to hold a national design competition. Since 1937 numerous modernists and their few supporters in Congress had pressed for competitions as a way to break the "old boy" stranglehold on Washington, D.C.[64] Openly seeking to have a "modern" design realized, the program called for a "flexible" solution, one not "requiring a formal or balanced relationship to other buildings."[65] Thomas Marby, Jr., formerly of the Museum of Modern Art, was the technical advisor and Harvard's Joseph Hudnut the professional advisor. Hudnut chose a jury weighted in favor of a modernist outcome with George Howe, Walter Gropius, Henry Shepley, Frederick A. Delano, and John A. Holabird as members. A caveat in the competition program noted that no funds for construction were provided and that the advice and approval of the Commission of Fine Arts were necessary before working drawings could begin. In the two-stage

competition, Saarinen, Saarinen, and Swanson were awarded first prize, Percival Goodman, second place. Aggressively modern, the Saarinen design eschewed not only classical trim and decoration, but also symmetry and balance for a dynamic tension between rectangular blocks of differing functions. Large walls of glass, horizontal strip windows, and flat, blank, and "weightless" marble surfaces pervaded the major elevations. While modernist architectural critics strenuously promoted the scheme for a number of years, it never stood a chance of being erected.[66] The members of the Commission of Fine Arts, and especially its new chairman, Gilmore D. Clarke stood unalterably opposed. If there had to be a gallery Clarke wanted Paul Cret's entry, an amalgamation of his Folger Library front elevation with the entrance porticoes of the Federal Reserve (figs. 16, 17). Clarke noted in 1940: "The sketch for the proposed Smithsonian Gallery of Art is frankly radical, conspicuously defiant of the existing patterns of Washington. If executed, it doubtless would set a fashion for further adventures in a futuristic direction."[67] Moreover, funding from private

15. Paul Cret and Alexander Trowbridge, Folger Shakespeare Library (1928–1932), north elevation, photograph 1982
Folger Shakespeare Library

16. Paul Cret, Federal Reserve
Board Building (1935–1937),
south elevation
Author photograph

17. Paul Cret, Smithsonian
Gallery of Art, competition
entry, 1939, detail of north
elevation
Paul Cret Harbeson

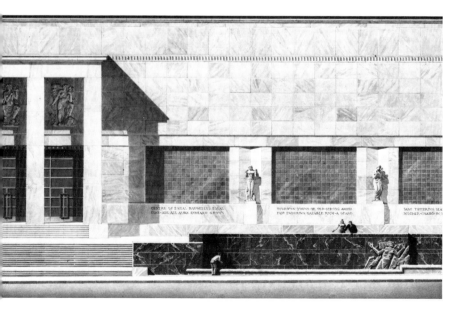

sources—Bruce had hoped Andrew Mellon
might foot the bill—or from Congress never
materialized. Finally, in the scheme of the
Smithsonian's development such a gallery did
not rank high.

In the mid-1950s the Smithsonian did receive an appropriation for a new building, the
Museum of History and Technology (now the
National Museum of American History) (1955–
1964). While Robert Swanson and others tried
to claim the Smithsonian had a "moral obli-
gation" to construct the 1939 prize winner,
this was never considered seriously. From the
outset, McKim, Mead, and White were favored to design an entirely different kind of
facility.[68] Their long association with the Mall
stood in their favor; so did their work, with
Walker O. Cain as chief designer, for the
Smithsonian secretary, Leonard Carmichael,
while he was president of Tufts University.
And finally, the political climate of Washington towards modernism in the 1950s remained openly hostile. A very important figure in this regard was Michigan Representative
George A. Dondero, chairman of the House
Committee on Public Buildings and a member
of the Smithsonian Board of Regents, who
helped shepherd the $36 million appropria-
tion through Congress. Dondero's 1952 talk,
"Communist Conspiracy in Art Threatens
American Museums," clearly revealed his position. He charged that the " 'isms' (cubism,
expressionism, surrealism, dadaism. . .)" had
been "transplanted" and "infiltrated" America. "So-called modern or contemporary art in
our own beloved country contains all the 'isms'
of depravity and destruction." Needless to say
the congressman felt modern art deserved no
place in America, especially on the Mall, and
under the circumstances no secretary of the
Smithsonian would have dared to suggest an
outwardly radical modern building.[69] While
the Smithsonian and the General Services Administration went through the motions of an
elaborate search, considering sixteen firms such
as Saarinen and Saarinen; Holabird, Root, and
Burgee; Harrison and Abramovitz; and Eggers
and Higgins, the decision was foreordained:
Carmichael wanted McKim, Mead, and
White.[70]

Over twenty alternative designs were submitted by McKim, Mead, and White to the
congressional oversight committee, the
Smithsonian, and the Public Buildings Ser-

vice. The scheme selected had a platform or podium plan with a large basement hidden from the Mall elevation, which allowed expansion on Constitution Avenue while reducing the overall bulk and mass. The Commission of Fine Arts "agreed that the proposed structure conformed nicely to the accepted planning of the area."[71] Called "Contemporary Classic" by the Smithsonian, the exterior, clad in smooth pink Tennessee marble, was intended to become an exhibit unto itself, with colored lights punctuating the huge vertical recesses (fig. 18). The overall massing, with the setback attic, cornice outrigging, and heavy moldings, is derived from nearby work such as the Lincoln Memorial. The scheme's elevations also owed a debt to published studies of Cret's Folger Library.[72] Highly regarded among traditionalists as a building that reconciled the conflicting claims of modernism and eclecticism, the Folger ranked as the most admired building in the United States in a 1948 poll of architects.[73] No such approbation attached itself to the Museum of History and Technology; the press roasted it, and together with the machinations of George Stewart, it became a major reason President John Kennedy took such an interest in bringing prominent modernist architects to Washington.[74]

ARCHITECTS

A primary challenge facing architects in the twentieth century, as in earlier periods, has been the need to interpret salient cultural forces and create meaningful symbols for them. Faced with an institutionalized system such as that regulating design on the Mall, with its various and often conflicting constituencies, how much could architects subvert that system before losing their commissions? Most architects working on the Mall prior to 1950 agreed, or appeared to agree, with the classical ideal and its perceived historical symbols upheld by the system. Men who did not, such as Goodhue, were forced to conform. A major reason Paul Cret won the 1935 Federal Reserve Building competition, according to a juror, was that his stripped or modernized classicism recalled the work of Robert Mills.[75] By the later 1920s, however, some American architects began to argue that these ties to the past lacked conviction. By 1944 even Gilmore D. Clarke, the

18. McKim, Mead, and White (Walker O. Cain, designer), Museum of History and Technology (now National Museum of American History), Smithsonian Institution (1955–1964), north elevation, rendering by Hugh Ferriss
Smithsonian Institution

19. Skidmore, Owings, and Merrill (Gordon Bunshaft, designer), Hirshhorn Museum and Sculpture Garden, Smithsonian Institution (1965–1974), rendering 1967
Skidmore, Owings, and Merrill

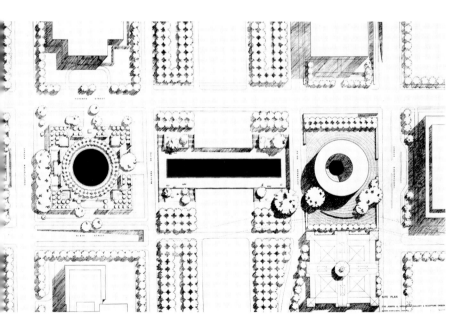

20. Skidmore, Owings, and Merrill, Hirshhorn Museum, site plan showing proposed sculpture garden across Mall, c. 1967
Skidmore, Owings, and Merrill

eminent landscape and parkway designer and chairman of the Commission of Fine Arts, acknowledged changes in the aesthetic climate; no longer were details of Greek or Roman derivation demanded; nevertheless, work on the Mall should remain fundamentally classical in character.[76]

In spite of mounting criticism, the Mall never experienced radical modernist or abstract ahistorical design until the 1960s. By the time that its proponents gained a foothold, they had also risen to positions of power in the commercial and architectural worlds; they were no longer the avant-garde, but the old guard. Significantly, radical modernism had passed out of its "factory" or "proletariat" stage, with its disavowal of monumentalism; from the late 1940s on, the issue of modern monumentality became a topic of concern.[77] Opinions varied as to how this characteristic should be pursued. A 1956 discussion of the subject as it pertained to Washington found I.M. Pei avowing, "I cannot possibly imagine the neoclassic approach"; Joseph Hudnut suggesting that Le Corbusier's 1927 League of Nations competition entry might be a model; and Eero Saarinen advocating Edward Durrell Stone's American Embassy at New Delhi (1957–1959) as appropriate.[78]

The emerging preeminence of radical modernism was accompanied by the changing perception of Washington as an international center. Instead of the turn-of-the-century commitment to making the federal city "worthy of the nation," creating a place "worthy of the world," now seemed a more appropriate aim, given America's global leadership responsibilities. As the self-anointed hope of the future and the savior of the free world, America also was setting an international modernist standard for office buildings, factories, and other building types, not the least of which were its own embassies abroad. The need for comparable work on the Mall seemed imperative.[79]

The Hirshhorn Museum and Sculpture Garden was the principal emblem on the Mall of radical modernism's cause during the 1960s, though its actual construction dates were from 1970 to 1974 (figs. 19, 20). In contrast to his predecessors, Smithsonian Secretary S. Dillon Ripley wanted a major collection of modern art for the institution and aggressively pursued that of Joseph H. Hirshhorn, a uranium and gold speculator. An agreement was reached by early 1965; President Lyndon Johnson announced the gift on 17 May 1966; Congress officially accepted it on 7 November 1966. Ripley, who served ex-officio on the Pennsylvania Avenue Commission, turned to its chairman, Nathaniel Owings, for assistance in securing an appropriate design for the museum building. Charles Bassett, one of Owings' lieutenants in the Skidmore, Owings, and Merrill San Francisco office, who was then working on the new plan for the Mall, developed a scheme for the Hirshhorn during the spring of 1965. Bassett's solution called for an underground, earth-covered building and sculpture garden located on Constitution Avenue in front of the National Archives. An open, cross-axial treatment at this point had appeared on both the L'Enfant and McMillan plans; Pope's Archives Building, lying directly to the north, and the new Skidmore, Owings, and Merrill Mall plan reemphasized this feature. Consequently any structure on the site needed to be low. Ripley tried to sell the idea to Hirshhorn, claiming a large plaza and plaques with Hirshhorn's name would be erected. "Rembrandt belongs in a marble hall," he argued. "Contemporary art belongs in an area of understatement." Hirshhorn "blew up": he could be buried but not his collection. Owings was wily, not about to lose such an important commission, and as David Childs recalled, he replied that, "If you want a monument, if you want travertine, I have the man for you!" An involved courtship ensued. Owings and Ripley explained the situation to Gordon Bunshaft, head of Skidmore, Owings, and Merrill's New York office, and then drove him up to Hirshhorn's Connecticut estate. Recently Bunshaft recalled: "Joe and I hit it off right away. . . . It was all settled in five minutes." [80]

Ripley abandoned hopes for the Constitution Avenue-Archives site and gave Bunshaft one across the Mall on Independence Avenue. The land contained a National Historic Landmark, the Armed Forces Medical Museum, which was destroyed. The staff of the National Capital Planning Commission encouraged Bunshaft to design a circular structure since this was a cross-axis and a round form would be less disruptive. [81] Bunshaft analyzed the Mall as marked by a thousand-foot module and believed that a "small rectangular building would have looked silly there." As a result, he designed a massive, elevated cylinder to emphasize sculptural qualities and to allow the site "to be seen through." Early drawings show comparatively thin piers holding the circular block aloft, but loading requirements significantly increased their bulk in the final scheme. [82] The circular design reflects Bun-

shaft's interests as a collector of contemporary art and a self-described "nut about modern sculpture." While Bunshaft rejects the idea that this building parallels the minimalist movement of the 1960s, he has always explained it as a "piece of sculpture on the Mall." In presentations to the Commission of Fine Arts, the Skidmore, Owings, and Merrill team described the design as "a very strong sculptural shape." [83] A possible source for the concept, though one never acknowledged, was the neoclassical visions of Etienne Louis Boullée, Jean-Jacques Lequeu, and Claude Nicolais Ledoux, who were then attracting considerable attention as lineal predecessors to the radical modernists. [84]

As part of the design, Bunshaft projected a sculpture garden, sunken eighteen feet deep as a trench running across the Mall to Constitution Avenue. This element was to link the Hirshhorn sculpture collection with a proposed outdoor sculpture collection of the National Gallery. The entire package passed both the Commission of Fine Arts and the National Capital Planning Commission in 1967, though murmurs were made about the sculpture garden's interruption of the Mall. Even Owings was concerned with the aggressiveness of the Bunshaft proposal. [85] In 1970 a battle erupted over the scheme. Charges were raised about unsavory aspects of Hirshhorn's business dealings, whether a museum with his name should be on the Mall when the Mellons had kept theirs off the National Gallery, and the highhanded methods of Ripley and others. Part of the concern involved Hirshhorn's demand that the Smithsonian eliminate the modern art component of the newly established National Collection of Fine Arts. This stipulation was not accepted, but the rumors of scandal were not easily squelched. [86] Attention ultimately focused on the sunken garden; opponents called it "disgraceful" in disturbing the "hallowed sanctity of the Mall's 'gamboling greensward.'" [87] In March 1971, Ripley and Bunshaft bowed, the sculpture garden was reduced to its present site. During the battle some budget cuts were made and the intended travertine sheathing for the Hirshhorn was replaced with Swanson pink granite aggregate. The building opened in 1974 to mixed reviews. Critics noted its conflict with the picturesque, red brick and tiled Arts and Industries Building next door, since by now contextual issues had gained a foothold in American architectural criticism.[88] The Hirshhorn is radically modern; it eschews historical reference. Yet the building relates well to most others on the Mall through its geometrical purity and bold, simple treatment, becoming almost classical in character.

CONCLUSION

The approval granted the Hirshhorn in 1967, fifteen years after modern art had been condemned as communistic, indicates basic shifts in official practice and even in public acceptance. Yet George Stewart's Rayburn House Office Building, which was completed two years earlier, suggests a conflict as to what were appropriate national symbols. The Hirshhorn was only possible when enough of the Mall's constituencies had changed their perspective. The Hirshhorn represented modern history in the making; its abstract qualities manifested the attempt to reject explicit ties to the past. Sited across from Pope's National Archives, the Hirshhorn is a redskin confronting a paleface. One view of America and its history replaced another.[89]

Criticisms can be directed at the Mall's functional relationships and what the whole represents. While the Supreme Court is balanced by knowledge in the form of the Library of Congress, a more symbolic placement would be, as had been suggested in the 1920s and as Paul Rudolph suggested again in 1963, to place the court near the Jefferson Memorial.[90] The Mall is populated by museums and memorials to the dead; muted and pushed into the background are indications of the workings of government. Yet when one looks at the Mall many of the buildings fade; trees block them and the space appears very large.

The space of the Mall as an American space, or an urban space, is unique. Americans, it is frequently charged, have not appreciated urban space, especially in the twentieth century. Yet from a cultural perspective, Americans have long had a penchant for celebrating great spaces, especially those of nature such as those depicted by Hudson River School painters or writers describing the Western prairie. Many of our city parks attempt to emulate nature. The Mall has some aspects of this vastness, the space does "leak," and yet fundamentally it is different: it is limited, has boundaries, emphasizes direction, and does not imitate nature. Yet it certainly is not an urban space; its connection with the city is not stressed; it sits as a self-contained entity.

What did the Senate Park Commission members or, later, politicians, protectors, users, and architects envision as the purpose for the Mall? Their renderings show the Mall populated with well dressed, white citizens, properly subservient to the memorials and spaces. By visiting this place some ritual of patriotism ostensibly would be accomplished. Could those responsible for the Mall have imagined demonstrations there by the Ku Klux Klan, impoverished farmers, civil rights activists, or gay rights groups? That the Mall has been the setting for their concerns indicates its multidimensional nature. The Mall is a setting for peculiar American rituals, from picnics and fireworks to funerals, and from rallies and education to recreation.[91] That the Mall can accept such diversity and also accept stylistically different buildings, landscapes, statues, and memorials indicates the varying views of American history and the polymorphous nature of American culture. The Mall is the *axis mundi*, the great stage for American secular worship.

The Mall is a powerful symbol, and as all great symbols it is ambiguous in interpretation and meaning. And it is physical, visual, and spatial. Historians try to reduce all experience to words, but in the end words cannot adequately represent the passions, the beliefs, and the experience of the Mall. In spite of the battles or showdowns by politicians, protectors, users, and architects, the Mall escapes exact definition. Great symbols defy exactness; the Mall succeeds and endures.

NOTES

A debt of gratitude is owed to many people who over the years have assisted with research. In addition to those cited in notes below I would like to acknowledge: Sue A. Kohler and Charles H. Atherton, Commission of Fine Arts; Roger Kennedy, National Museum of American History, Cynthia Field, Office of Architectural History and Historic Preservation, and William Massa, Archives, Smithsonian Institution; Tony Wrenn, archives, American Institute of Architects; Donald Jackson, National Capital Planning Commission; Barbara A. Wolanin, Curator, Office of the Architect of the Capitol; JoAnne Lehrfeld, Skidmore, Owings, and Merrill; and Steve Bedford, historian of John Russell Pope.

1. For treatments of this problem, see William Barrett, *Irrational Man: A Study of Existential Philosophy* (New York, 1958); and Renato Poggioli, *The Theory of the Avant-Garde* (Cambridge, 1968).

2. Karl Popper, *The Poverty of Historicism* (London, 1961).

3. Gottfried Semper, "A Critical Analysis and Prognosis of Present-Day Artistic Production," written in 1856–1859, reprinted in Wolfgang Herrmann, *Gottfried Semper: In Search of Architecture* (Cambridge, 1984), 249, 251, 253.

4. H. Paul Caemmerer, "Charles Moore and the Plan of Washington," *Records of the Columbia Historical Society of Washington, D. C.* 46–47 (1947), 252.

5. Raymond Williams, *Keywords: A Vocabulary of Culture and Society* (New York, 1976); Warren I. Susman, *Culture as History: The Transformation of American Society in the Twentieth Century* (New York, 1984); T. S. Eliot expressed this in the Page-Barbour lecture at the University of Virginia, 1933, published as *After Strange Gods* (New York, 1934).

6. Charles B. Hosmer, Jr., *Preservation Comes of Age: From Williamsburg to the National Trust, 1926–1949*, 2 vols. (Charlottesville, 1981).

7. R. W. B. Lewis, *The American Adam* (Chicago, 1955).

8. D. H. Lawrence, *Studies in Classic American Literature* (New York, 1923), first elucidated the dichotomy. Philip Rahv gave it the name: "Paleface and Redskin," *Kenyon Review* (1939), reprinted in Rahv, *Essays on Literature and Politics, 1932–1972* (Boston, 1978), 3–7. George Santayana, "The Genteel Tradition in American Philosophy," in his *Winds of Doctrine* (New York, 1913).

9. Henry-Russell Hitchcock and Philip Johnson, *The International Style; Architecture since 1922* (New York, 1932); see also, Richard Guy Wilson, "International Style: the MoMA exhibition," *Progressive Architecture* 58 (February 1982), 92–105.

10. Some of this terminology comes from T. J. Jackson Lears, *No Place of Grace: Antimodernism and the Transformation of American Culture, 1880–1920* (New York, 1981), yet I find his treatment too narrow.

11. William B. Rhoads, "Roadside Colonial," *Winterthur Portfolio* 21 (Summer/Autumn 1986), 133–152; Reuben Rainey, "The Memory of War: Reflections of Battlefield Preservation," and Kenneth I. Helphand, " 'Magic Markers,' " in *The Yearbook of Landscape Architecture* (New York, 1983), 69–89, 95–102; and Hosmer 1981.

12. Office of Public Buildings and Public Parks of the Nation's Capital, *The Lincoln Memorial, Washington* (Washington, 1927), 40–41. See also Sue A. Kohler, *The Commission of Fine Arts, A Brief History, 1910–1976* (Washington, 1985), 24.

13. Joint Resolution 71–123, *The Statutes at Large of the United States*, 71st Cong., 2d sess., 25 February 1931, 1419–1420. See also Milton Medary, "Making a Capital City," *American Architect* 135 (20 May 1929), 630. Avenue B South was renamed Independence Avenue in 1934: see Public Law 73–150, *The Statutes at Large of the United States*, 73d Cong., 2d sess., 13 April 1934, 574.

14. Public Law 70–1036, *The Statutes at Large of the United States*, 70th Cong. 2d sess., 4 March 1929, 1694–1696.

15. Constance McLaughlin Green, *Washington: Capital City, 1879–1950* (Princeton, 1963), vii–viii, 89, 132; I am indebted to this book for much of the background on Washington.

16. Coolidge's address to Congress, 7 December 1926, quoted in Charles W. Eliot II, "Planning Washington and Its Environs," *City Planning* 3 (July 1927), 177; and Kenneth L. Roberts, "Nobody's Capital," *Saturday Evening Post* 199 (9 April 1927), 20.

17. John F. Kennedy, "A Message from the President," *AIA Journal* 39 (January 1963), 25. Daniel Patrick Moynihan, "Civic Architecture," *Architectural Record* 142 (December 1967), 107, excerpted from a longer paper. Moynihan was Secretary of Labor Arthur Goldberg's executive assistant and in 1961 suggested the redevelopment of Pennsylvania Avenue.

18. Quoted in Glenn Brown, *Memories, 1860–1930*, (Washington, 1931), 96, 183. See also Charles Moore, *Daniel H. Burnham, Architect, Planner of Cities*, 2 vols. (New York, 1921), 2:151–153; and *The Lincoln Memorial*.

19. Paul Cret Harbeson and Charles Ward of the H2L2 Office, interview, 6 January 1984. Harold B. Meyers, "A Monument to Power," *Fortune* 71 (March, 1965), 122–125, 174, 176, 178; and Rasa Gustaitis, " 'The Emperor of Capitol Hill,' " *Architectural Forum* 129 (September 1965), 80–85. See also my entry on Stewart in *The Dictionary of American Biography*, supp. 8 (New York, 1988), 629–631. H2L2 is the successor firm to that of Paul Cret, who designed the Pan American Union, Folger Library, and Federal Reserve Building, among others, in Washington.

20. Hunter Lewis, "Capitol Hill's Ugliness Club," *Atlantic Monthly* 219 (February 1967), 64.

21. Mellon quoted in Edward H. Bennett, "The Architecture of the Capital," *Development of the United States Capital*, 71st Cong., 1st sess., 1930, H. Doc. 35, 66. On the Federal Triangle, see Harry Weese and Associates, *The Master Plan for the Federal Triangle, Historic Report: "What Is Past Is Prologue"* (Washington, 1981); and George Gurney, *Sculpture and the Federal Triangle* (Washington, 1985).

22. No good study of Mellon exists. Concerning Bennett, see Joan E. Draper, *Edward H. Bennett: Architect and City Planner, 1874–1954* (Chicago, 1982).

23. J. B. Eggen, "The National Gallery of Art, Washington," *Mouseion* 57–58 (1946), nos. 3–4, corrected English language copy, National Gallery of Art, Washington; David Edward Finley, *A Standard of Excellence: Andrew W. Mellon Founds the National Gallery of Art at Washington* (Washington, 1973); John Walker, *The National Gallery of Art, Washington, D. C.* (New York, 1976); *Acceptance of Gift from Andrew Mellon*, 75th Cong., 1st sess., Doc. 139 (Washington, 1937).

24. Kohler 1985; see also, *Commemorating the Fortieth Anniversary of the Establishment of the National Commission of Fine Arts* (Washington, 1950).

25. Public Law 158–69. *The Statutes At Large of the United States* 69th Cong., 1st sess., 30 April 1926, 374–376; "National Capitol Park and Planning Commission Appointed," *American City* 35 (July 1926), 103; "The Federal City Committees of the American Civic Association," and Lieut. Col. U. S. Grant III, "Washington Looks Ahead," *American Civic Annual* 1 (1929), 66–68, 69–76.

26. Albert E. Cowdrey, *A City for the Nation: The Army Engineers and the Building of Washington, D. C., 1790–1967* (Washington, 1979).

27. David Childs [of Skidmore, Owings, and Merrill], interview, 14 October 1987.

28. Initially Peets expressed qualified approval for the McMillan Plan; see Werner Hegemann and Elbert Peets, *The American Vitruvius: An Architect's Handbook of Civic Art* (New York, 1922), chap. 7; but he later championed the L'Enfant plan and disapproved the McMillan; see Peets in "Washington, Williamsburg, the Century of Progress and Greendale," in Werner Hegemann, *City Planning, Housing*, 3 vols. (New York, 1936), 2: chap. 27; Peets, "The New Washington," *The American Mercury* 8 (August 1926), 449–452; and Peets, "Original Plan of Washington," *House and Garden* 78 (July 1940), 16–18.

29. Joseph Hudnut, "Recent Buildings," and Alfred Kastner, "The Plan," *House and Garden* 78 (July 1940), 39, 41.

30. ". . . here is a shrine at which all can worship. Here an altar upon which the sacrifice was made in the cause of liberty. Here a sacred religious refuge in which those who love country and love God can find inspiration and repose": William Howard Taft, "The Lincoln Memorial," *National Geographic Magazine* 43 (June 1923), 602. See also Taft's dedication speech in *The Lincoln Memorial*, 83–86.

31. Charles Moore, ed., *The Improvement of the Park System of the District of Columbia*, 57th Cong., 1st sess., 1902, S. Rept. 166 (hereafter Moore 1902), 51; see also Charles Moore, "The Transformation of Washington," and Taft 1923, 591, 597.

32. Kohler 1985, 13–15.

33. Commission of Fine Arts, *Minutes*, 15 November 1923, Exhibit E.; and Kohler 1985, 69. Pope's design for the Theodore Roosevelt Memorial is illustrated in *American Architect* 129 (20 May 1926), pl. 106–108. This site was also suggested for the Supreme Court; see Allan Greenberg and Stephan Kieran, "The United States Supreme Court Building, Washington, D. C.," *Antiques* 128 (October 1985), 760–769; Robert Shnayerson, *The Illustrated History of the Supreme Court of the United States* (New York, 1986); Moore 1902, 38.

34. Thomas Jefferson Memorial Commission, "Minutes," typescript, 5 June 1935, 18 February 1937, Judge Howard Smith Papers, University of Virginia, Charlottesville. Pope's alternative designs are in this collection as well.

35. Commission of Fine Arts, *Report to the Senate and the House of Representatives concerning the Thomas Jefferson Memorial* (Washington, 1939); *Report of the Thomas Jefferson Memorial Commission* (Washington, 1939).

36. Marquis W. Childs, "Mr. Pope's Memorial," *Magazine of Art* 30 (April 1937), 200–203; "Facts from the Fine Arts Commission," *Magazine of Art* 31 (June 1938), 348–349, 372–375.

37. Joseph Hudnut, Frank Lloyd Wright, letters, *Magazine of Art* 31 (June 1938), 36. See also "Thomas Jefferson Memorial Absurdities," *Planning and Civic Comment* 4 (October-December 1938), 6–8.

38. Thomas Jefferson Memorial Commission, "Minutes," typescript, 24 March 1936, 234. Fiske Kimball, letter, *Magazine of Art* 31 (May 1938), 315; a shorter form of the letter appeared in the *New York Times*, 17 April 1937. See also Fiske Kimball, "John Russell Pope, 1874–1937," *American Architect* 151 (October 1937), 87, in which he notes the value of classicism is in question. Especially poignant is that the *American Architect*, founded in 1876, one of the first, and oldest, of American architectural periodicals, would cease publication early in 1938.

39. Moore 1902, 40.

40. General Services Administration, *Historical Study No. 2: Agriculture Administration Building* (Washington, 1964), 9–11; and H. P. Caemmerer, *Washington: The National Capital* (Washington, 1932), 91.

41. John Leo Coontz, "L'Enfant's Dream of Washington Coming True," *The American City* 38 (February 1928), 79–82.

42. Letter, Frederick A. Delano to C. G. Abbott, Secretary of the Smithsonian, 21 April 1938, Office of

the Director, Records, Smithsonian Institution Archives, Washington.

43. National Capital Planning Commission and Frederick Gutheim, *Worthy of the Nation: The History of Planning for the Nation's Capital* (Washington, 1977), 201–203.

44. "From Module to Mall," *Progressive Architecture* 49 (November 1968), 94–101; Jane Jacobs, "Washington," *Architectural Forum* 104 (January 1956), 95–97.

45. Illustrated in *The Grand Design* [exh. cat., Library of Congress] (Washington, 1967); Richard Guy Wilson, *Honor and Intimacy: Architectural Drawings by AIA Gold Medalists* [exh. cat., The Octagon, AIA Foundation] (Washington, 1984), 23; and Nathaniel Alexander Owings, *The American Aesthetic* (New York, 1969), 133–137.

46. Travis C. McDonald, Jr., "Modernized Classicism: The Architecture of Paul Philippe Cret in Washington, D.C." (M.A. thesis, University of Virginia, 1980), chap. 6.

47. Cynthia Field, "A Case of Hidden Authorship: The Role of Charles Follen McKim in the Design of the Natural History Museum of the Smithsonian" (unpublished article). Also it should be noted that Arthur Brown, Jr., fresh from the Ecole des Beaux-Arts was in the Hornblower and Marshall office in 1904 and certainly contributed to whatever distinguishing features the Natural History building contains; see Richard Guy Wilson, "Precursor: Arthur Brown, Jr.," *Progressive Architecture* 56 (December 1983), 64–71.

48. Wallace K. Harrison, interview, 8 January 1981; Harrison was in the McKim firm in 1916–1917 and saw the drawings under preparation.

49. "For the Air Age, a National Museum," *Architectural Record* 118 (September 1955), 163–170; Walker O. Cain, interview, 21 September 1987.

50. William Walton, interview, 15 September 1987. Owings, however, claimed the contact came through Secretary of Labor Arthur Goldberg; see Nathaniel Alexander Owings, *The Spaces in Between: An Architect's Journey* (Boston, 1973), 230.

51. Donald Jackson, interview, 29 September 1987; U. S. Grant III, "The L'Enfant Plan and Its Evolution," *Records of the Columbia Historical Society* 33–34 (1932), 1–23; and Grant, "The New City of Washington," *Review of Reviews and World's Work* 86 (November 1932), 33–35.

52. Green 1963, 288–289; Frederick A. Delano, "Progress Report," *American Civic Annual* 2 (1930), 83; and "Frederick Adrian Delano," *National Cyclopedia of American Biography* (New York, 1955), 40, 564–565.

53. Norton quoted in Charles Moore, "Personalities in Washington Architecture," *Records of the Columbia Historical Society* 37–38 (1937), 1.

54. In addition to those cited, other important writings by Moore include: *Washington, Past and Present* (New York, 1929); "The Government's Architectural Tradition," *Federal Architect* 6 (January 1934),

8–11; "The Washington Monument Gardens," *Journal of the American Institute of Architects* 16 (January 1928), 11–13; and "Standards of Taste," *American Magazine of Art* 21 (July 1930), 363–367.

55. Moore, "Personalities," 12–13; and Moore, "Washington, City of Splendor," *Current History* 32 (May 1930), 251.

56. Keith Morgan, *Charles A. Platt: The Artist as Architect* (New York and Cambridge, 1985), 162–170.

57. Federal Reserve Board, memorandum, 25 January 1935, Files, Architect, Federal Reserve Board Building, Washington, D.C.

58. Moore, "Washington—City of Splendor," 249. For background on Moore, see Kohler 1985, 51–52; and H. Paul Caemmerer, "Charles Moore and the Plan of Washington," *Records of the Columbia Historical Society* 46–47 (1947), 237–258.

59. George E. Hale, "National Academies and the Progress of Research," *Science* 41 (1 January 1915), 12–21.

60. Richard Oliver, *Bertram Grosvenor Goodhue* (Cambridge and New York, 1983), 180–181.

61. W[allace] K. Harrison, "The Building of the National Academy of Sciences and National Research Council," *Architecture* 50 (October 1924), 330.

62. Commission of Fine Arts, *Minutes*, 25 April 1932, 16. A full account of both the Folger and the National Academy appears in Richard Guy Wilson, "Modernized Classicism and Washington, D.C." in *American Public Architecture: European Roots and Native Expressions*, ed. Craig Zabel and Susan Scott Munshower, *Papers in Art History from The Pennsylvania State University* 5 (1989), 272–303.

63. Richard D. McKinzie, *The New Deal for Artists* (Princeton, 1973), 43.

64. Othad Wearin, "Wanted: Competitions for Federal Buildings," *Magazine of Art* 31 (May 1938), 266–267, 314; and Henry S. Churchill, letter to editor, *Shelter* 3 (April 1938), 3, 55.

65. "Smithsonian Institution Gallery of Art Competition," 3, no. 16, Smithsonian Archives, Washington, reprinted in Travis C. McDonald, "Smithsonian Institution, Competition for a Gallery of Art, January 1939–June 1939," in *Modernism in America, 1937–1941* [exh. cat. Muscarelle Museum of Art, College of William and Mary] (Williamsburg, 1985), 238.

66. The most recent advocacy of the project's realization appears to be Roy F. Larson, "Federal Architecture," *AIA Journal* 39 (January 1963), 94.

67. *Washington Star*, 25 April 1940, clipping, Files, Commission of Fine Arts, Washington.

68. Robert F. Swanson, letter to Leonard Carmichael, 27 September 1955; Swanson, letter to Jerome C. Hunsaker, 8 December 1955; Office of the Secretary, Records, 1949–1964, Smithsonian Institution Archives. For an overview history, see Marilyn Sara Cohen, "American Civilization in Three Dimensions: Evolution of the Museum of History and

Technology of the Smithsonian Institution" (Ph.D. diss., George Washington University, 1980). The firm of McKim, Mead, and White, it should be noted, changed its name in February 1961 to Steinmann, Cain, and White.

69. George A. Dondero, "Communist Conspiracy in Art Threatens American Museums," *Congressional Record*, 82d Cong. 2d sess., 17 March 1952, 2423–2427.

70. "Statement Relating to Selection of Architectural Services," 24 October 1955; and other copies of correspondence, Office of the Secretary, Record, 1949–1964, Smithsonian Institution Archives.

71. Commission of Fine Arts, *Minutes*, 14 June 1956, 11, 13–14.

72. Walker Cain, interview, 21 September 1987. Lancelot Sukert, "Folger Shakespeare Library," *American Architect* 142 (September 1932), 42–43.

73. "What Buildings Give You a Thrill?," *Journal of the American Institute of Architects* 10 (December 1948), 272–277.

74. William Walton, interview, 15 September 1987. For reviews of the History and Technology building, see "The Monumental City: Symbolism, Banality, and a New Direction," *Architectural Forum* 118 (January 1963), 59–60; Wolf Von Eckardt, "New Smithsonian Cries for a Spark of Life," *Washington Post*, 31 March 1963, E2; and Von Eckardt, "Architects Goofed on Interior of Museum," *Washington Post*, 26 January 1964, G6.

75. John Mead Howells, Memorandum to Federal Reserve Board, 20 May 1935, Files, Architect, Federal Reserve Board, Washington.

76. Gilmore D. Clarke, "Aesthetic Standards for the National Capital," Address to the Joint Committee of the National Capital, 18 February 1944, copy in file, Commission of Fine Arts; reprinted in *Landscape Architecture* 34 (July 1944), 145–146.

77. "In Search of a New Monumentality," *Architectural Review* 104 (September 1948), 117–128.

78. "Washington Monumental," *Architectural Forum* 104 (January 1956), 104–112.

79. Frederick Gutheim, "The Mess in Washington," *AIA Journal* 19 (January 1953), 17. Green 1963, 466, uses the term "Capital of the Free World, 1940–1945," as an indication of the changing perceptions. Richard Guy Wilson, *The AIA Gold Medal* (New York, 1984), 114–115.

80. S. Dillon Ripley, letter to Nathaniel A. Owings, 27 May 1965, Records, Under Secretary, Smithsonian Institution Archives. See also Barry Hyams, *Hirshhorn, Medici from Brooklyn* (New York, 1979). Gordon Bunshaft, interview, 22 October 1987; Childs, interview, 14 October 1987. Nathaniel A. Owings, letter to S. Dillon Ripley, 13 September 1965; Ripley, letter to Joseph H. Hirshhorn, 16 September 1965, Records, Under Secretary, Smithsonian Institution Archives. See also Carol Herselle Krinsky, *Gordon Bunshaft of Skidmore, Owings, and Merrill* (New York, 1988), 251–257.

81. Donald Jackson, interview, 30 October 1987.

82. Bunshaft interview; he explained that the reinforcing was so thick in the piers that the concrete "practically had to be put in with a spoon."

83. Bunshaft interview; see also David Jacobs, "The Establishment's Architect-plus," *New York Times Magazine*, 23 July 1972, 12–14, 16, 18, 21, 23. Charles Atherton, interview, 30 October 1987, recalls visiting Bunshaft in his New York office in 1965 and noting that he was in a "circular phase" with numerous projects for circular buildings under design. Commission of Fine Arts, *Minutes*, 20 June 1967, 78.

84. Emil Kaufmann, *Architecture in the Age of Reason*, (Cambridge, 1955); Henry-Russell Hitchcock, *Architecture: Nineteenth and Twentieth Centuries* (London, 1958); and Jean-Claude Lemagny, *Visionary Architects: Boullee, Ledoux, Lequeu* [exh. cat., University of Saint Thomas] (Houston, 1968).

85. Childs, interview. William Walton, letter to Lawson B. Knott, 13 July 1967; and Commission of Fine Arts, *Minutes*, 20 June 1967, 77–89.

86. Robert Simmons, interview, 31 October 1987. Simmons was working as a consultant for the National Collection of American Art at that time and helped to make the matter public.

87. Gilmore D. Clarke, letter, *New York Times*, 7 August 1970; Conrad L. Wirth quoted in Benjamin Forgey, "Hirshhorn Garden Plan Is Vastly Improved," [Washington] *Evening Star*, 1 April 1971, b–9. See also Wolf Von Eckardt, "Trench Warfare," *Washington Post*, 6 February 1971, E1.

88. Paul Goldberger, "A Fortress of a Building That Works as a Museum," *New York Times*, 2 October 1974; and Suzanne Stephens, "Museum as Monument," *Progressive Architecture* 56 (March 1975), 42–47.

89. Walter L. Creese, "The Evolution of Images in Washington," abstract, *Journal of the Society of Architectural Historians* 29 (October 1970), 267–268, seems to imply what I have been arguing.

90. Paul Rudolph, "A View of Washington as a Capital—or What Is Civic Design?," *Architectural Forum* 118 (January 1963), 64–70.

91. Richard Longstreth, "Make No Little Plans . . . I Have a Dream," in *Historial Perspectives on Urban Design: Washington, D.C., 1890–1910*, ed. Antoinette J. Lee, Occasional Paper No. 1, Center for Washington Area Studies, George Washington University (Washington, 1984), 27–29.

National Gallery   War Department White House.   Treasury Department.   Patent Office.   Post Offi

Plates – The Mall in Washington

ton. Mon.^nt Ent.^ce to Long Br'^s City Hall.   Smithsonian Institute. Armory   U S Capitol.

EDITOR'S NOTE

In addition to illustrating the essays in this volume, the plates are intended as a pictorial reference in their own right, a need especially felt since John W. Reps' *Monumental Washington: The Planning and Development of the Capital Center* (Princeton, 1967) has been out of print.

While assembling a truly comprehensive range of images exceeded the scope of this project, the selection is meant to be reasonably complete for those periods and aspects of the Mall's development addressed in the essays. Efforts have been made to secure reproductions of all key maps, plans, and views. Images were chosen for their documentary and historical value; most date from prior to 1950. A few photographs, however, have been included to depict events and activities that have taken place on the Mall in recent years and to afford a sense of the Mall's contemporary physical qualities.

The plates for the most part are arranged chronologically by period and subject matter within five divisions: late eighteenth and nineteenth century plans and maps; nineteenth century views; twentieth century plans and maps; twentieth century views to 1950; and contemporary plans, views, and scenes of events. Duplicate illustrations appear in those essays warranting reference close at hand.

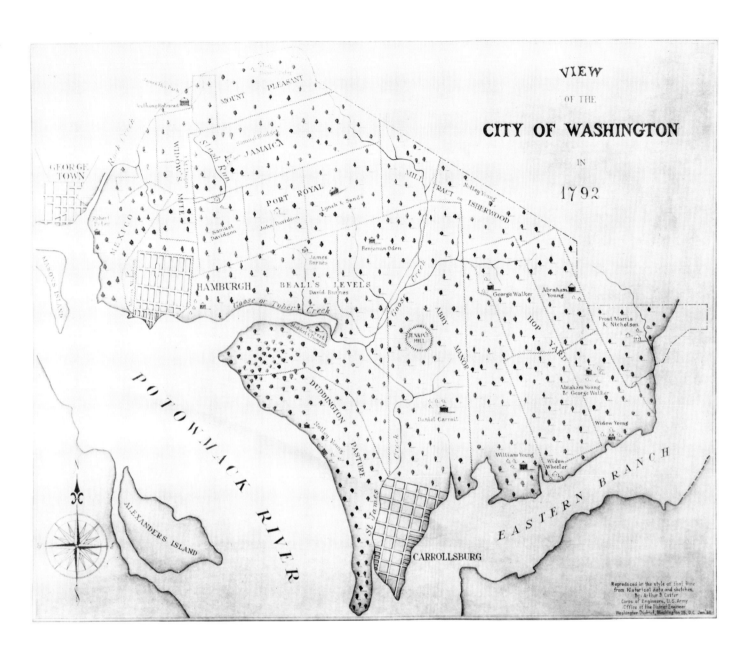

I. *View of the City of Washington in 1792*, reproduced in the style of that time by Arthur B. Cutter, United States Army Corps of Engineers, 1952
National Archives

II. *Territory of Columbia*, topographical map drawn by Andrew Ellicott, 1793, engraving by Thackara and Vallance, c. 1793–1794
Library of Congress

III. Thomas Jefferson, sketch plan for Washington, March 1791
Library of Congress

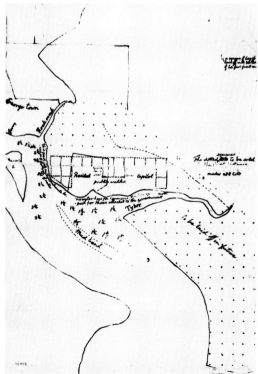

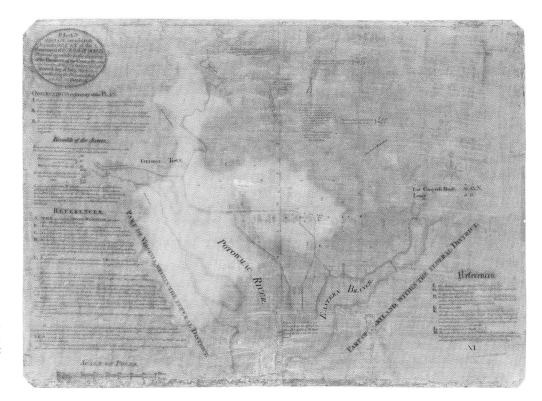

IV. Attributed to Pierre Charles L'Enfant, *Plan of the City intended for the Permanent Seat of the Government of the United States . . . ,* August (?) 1791
Library of Congress

V. Detail pl. IV

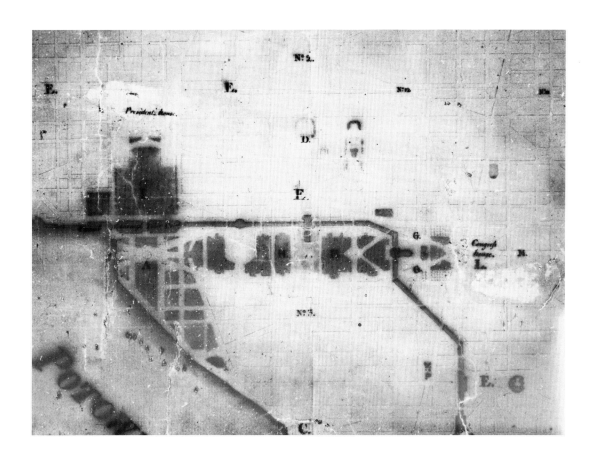

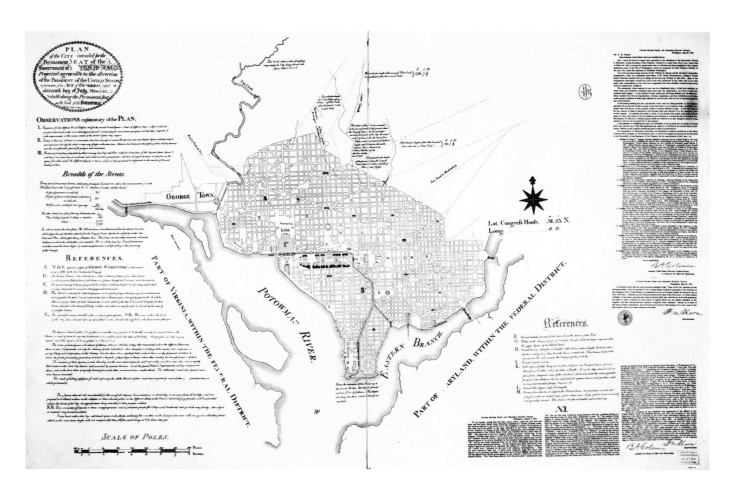

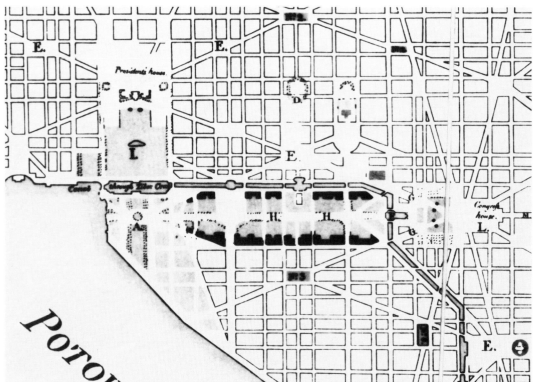

VI. Attributed to Pierre
Charles L'Enfant, *Plan of the
City intended for the Perma-
nent Seat of the United States
...*, facsimile reproduction of
August (?) 1791 map by the
United States Coast and
Geodetic Survey, 1887
Library of Congress

VII. Detail pl. VI

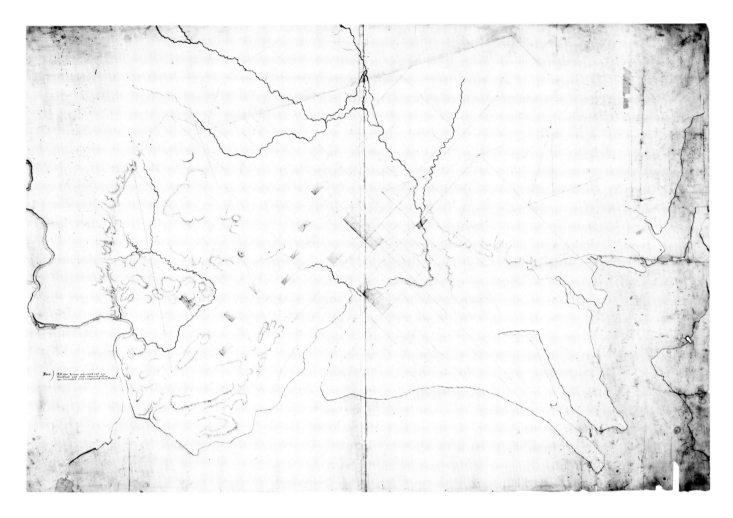

VIII. Attributed to Pierre
Charles L'Enfant, "Map of
Dotted Lines," 1791
Library of Congress

IX. Detail pl. VIII

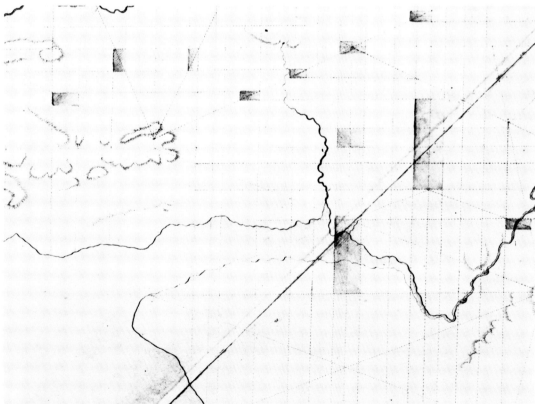

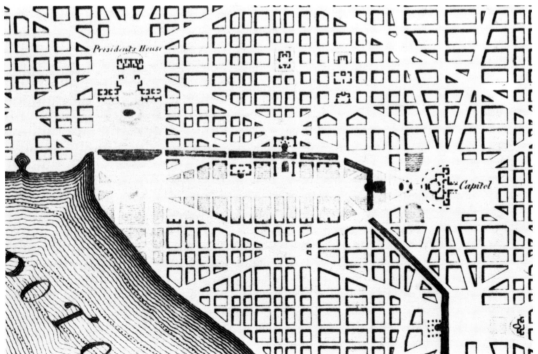

X. *Plan of the City of Washington* . . . , drawn by Andrew Ellicott, engraving by Thackara and Vallance, March 1792, showing changes recommended by George Washington and Thomas Jefferson to L'Enfant plan
Library of Congress

XI. Detail pl. X

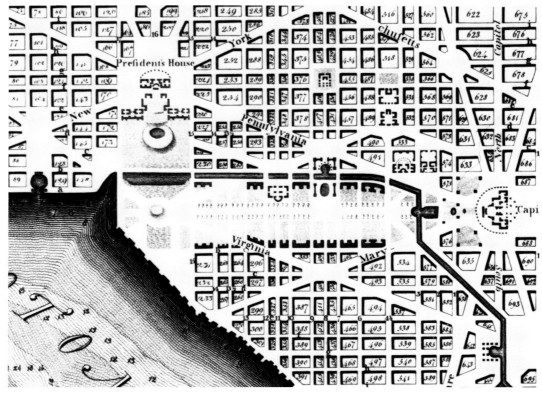

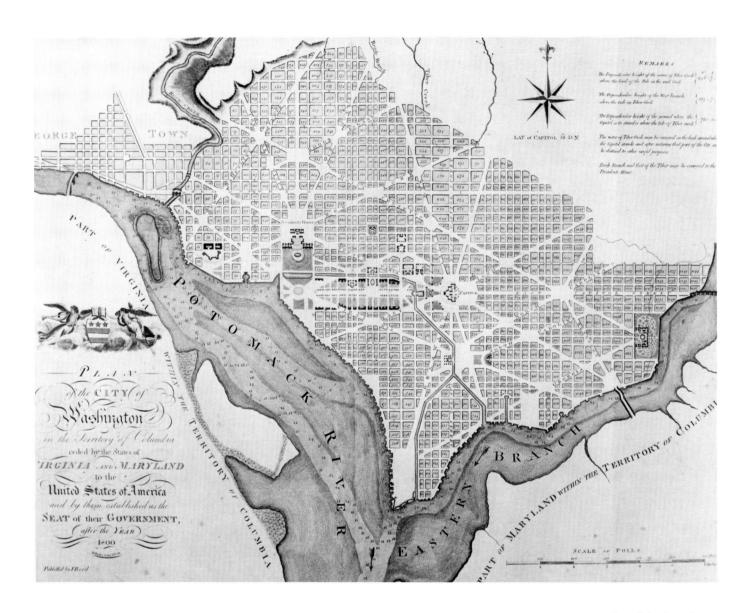

xiv. *Plan of the City of Washington . . .* , based on March 1792 plan (pl. x), engraving by William Rollinson, 1795
White House Collection

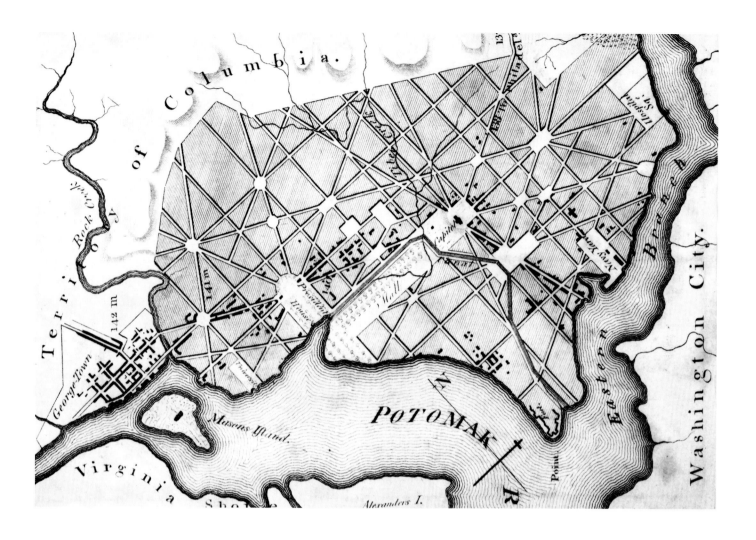

xv. *District of Columbia and Vicinity*, engraving by Moore and Jones, c. 1804, map showing extant buildings
Library of Congress

xvi. Detail pl. xv

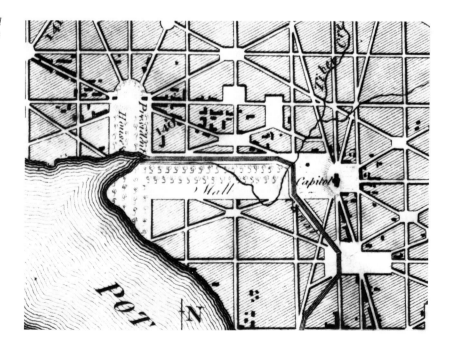

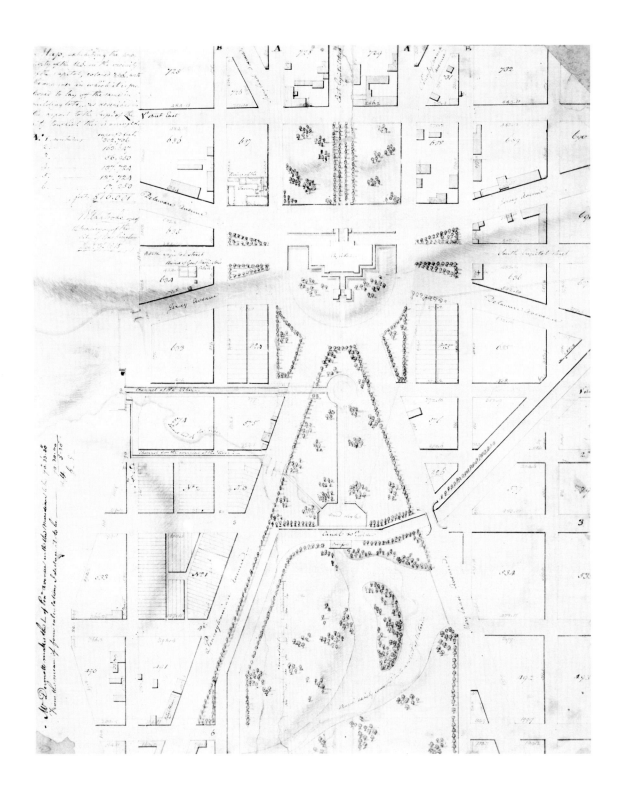

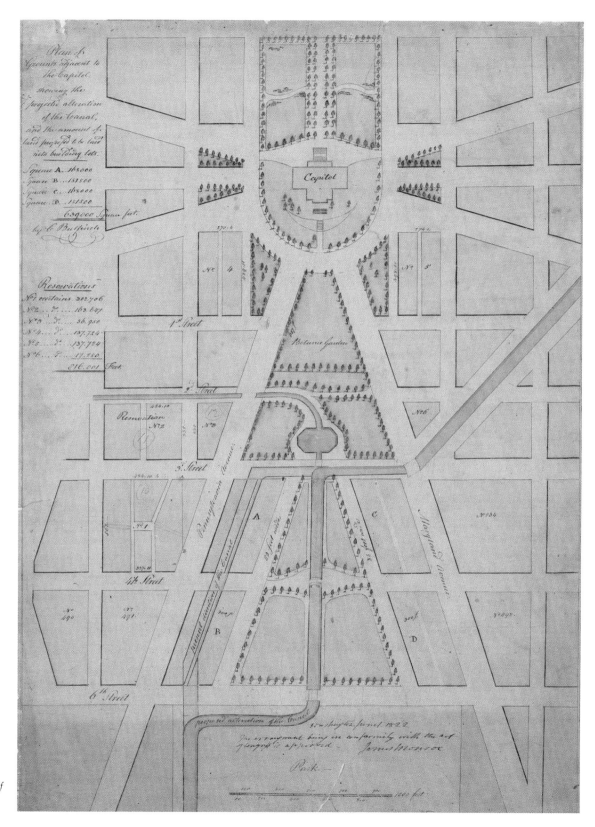

XVIII. Charles Bulfinch, *Plan of the Capitol Grounds*, 1822
National Archives

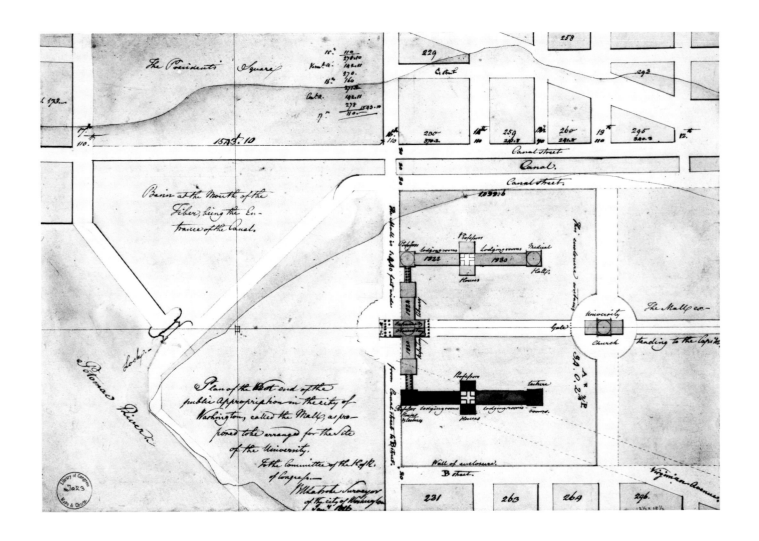

XIX. Benjamin Henry Latrobe,
*Design for the National
University*, 1816, located just
east of later Washington
Monument site
Library of Congress

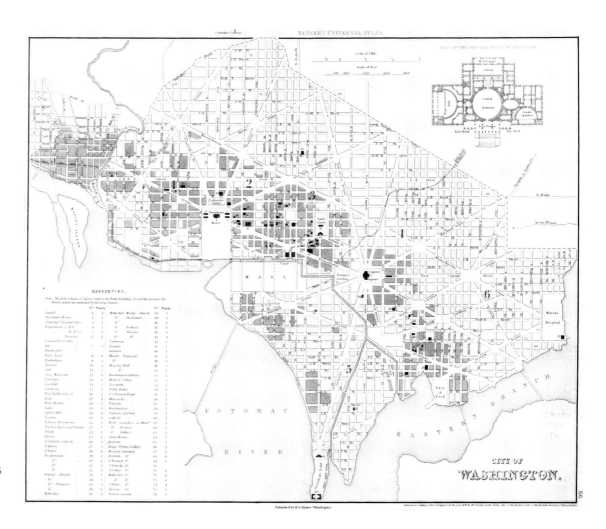

xx. *City of Washington*, 1836
From *Tanner's Universal Atlas* (Philadelphia, 1846)
Library of Congress

xxi. Detail pl. xx

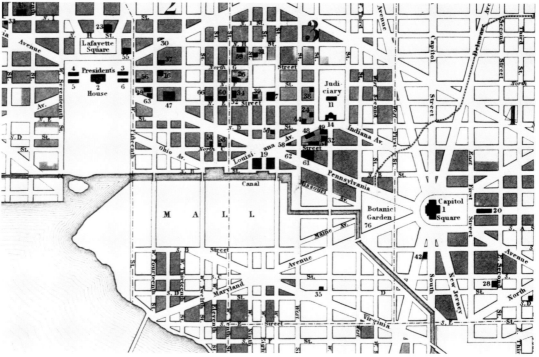

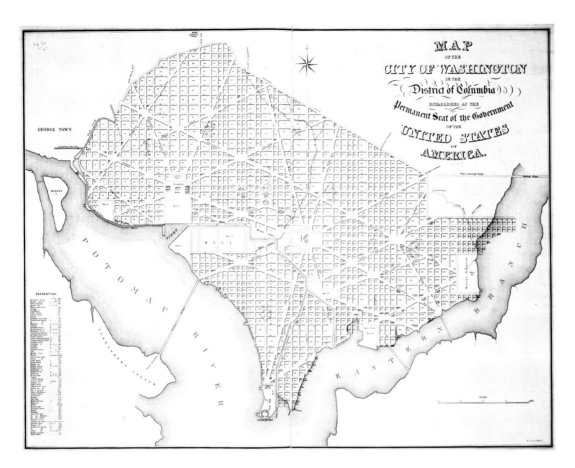

XXII. *Map of the City of Washington . . .*, drawn by William J. Stone, 1839
Library of Congress

XXIII. Detail pl. XXII

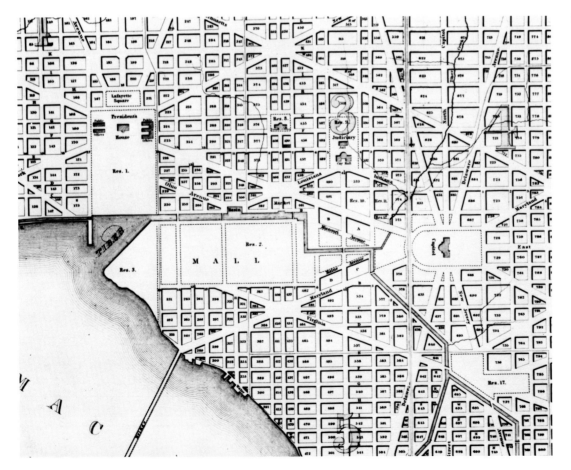

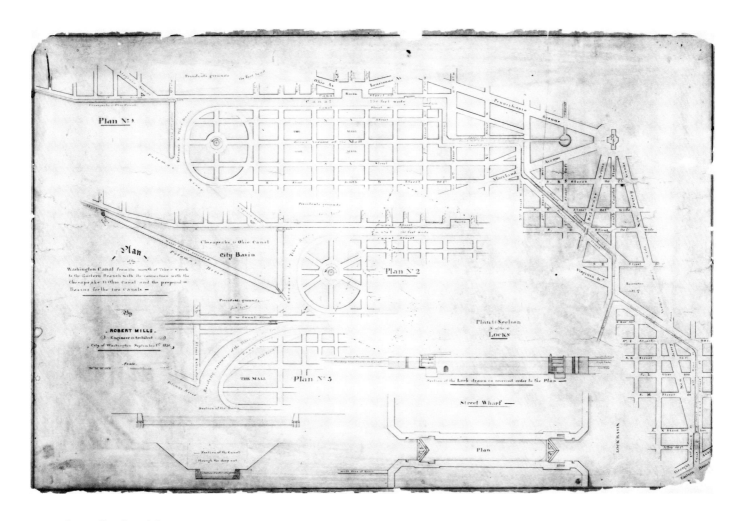

xxiv. Robert Mills, *Plan of the Washington Canal*, 1831
National Archives

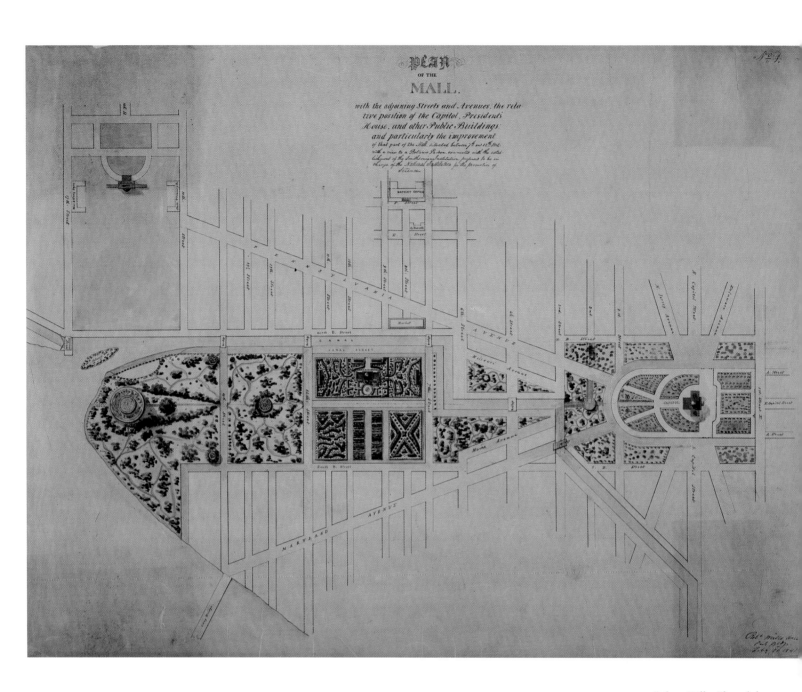

XXVI. Robert Mills, proposal
for Smithsonian Institution,
1841, plan of grounds
National Archives

XXVII. Robert Mills, proposal
for Smithsonian Institution,
1841, general view
National Archives

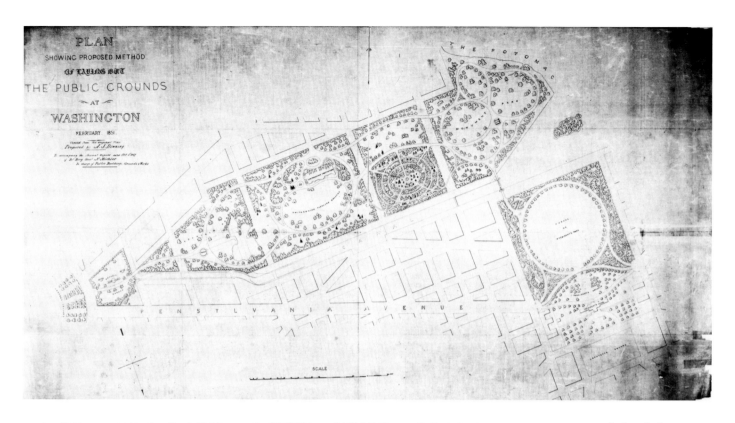

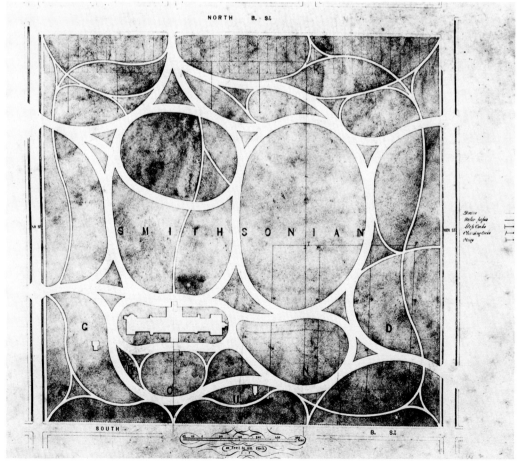

XXVIII. Andrew Jackson
Downing, *Plan Showing
Proposed Method of Laying
Out the Public Grounds at
Washington*, 1851, copy
by N. Michler, 1867
National Archives

XXIX. Smithsonian Institution,
plan of grounds, c. 1861
Smithsonian Institution

xxx. *Plan of the City of Washington . . .*, drawn by William Forsyth, 1870
Library of Congress

xxxi. Detail pl. xxx

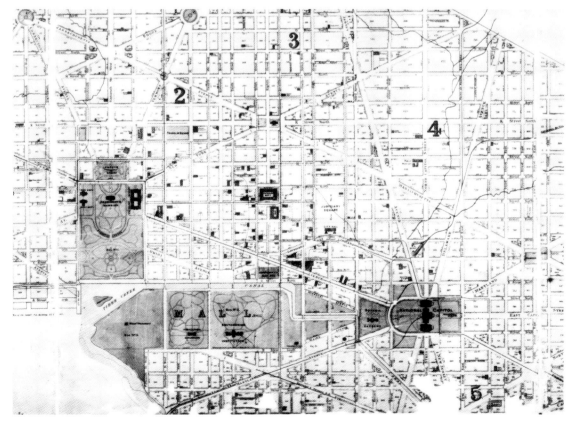

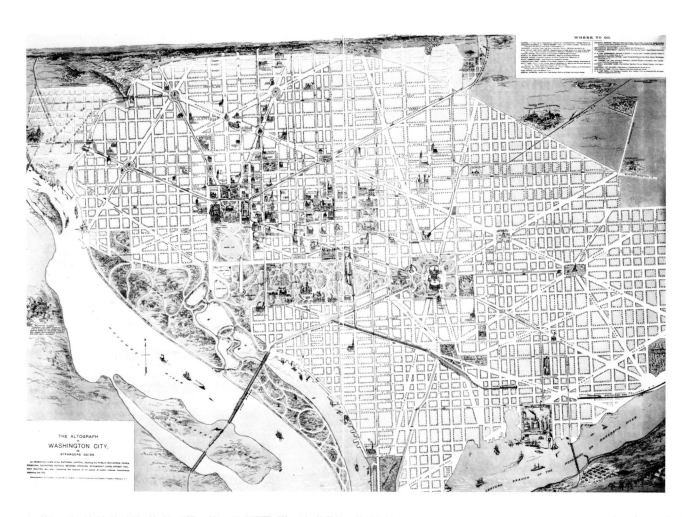

XXXII. *The Altograph of
Washington City, or
Strangers' Guide*, printed by
Norris Peters Company, 1892
Library of Congress

XXXIII. Detail pl. XXXII

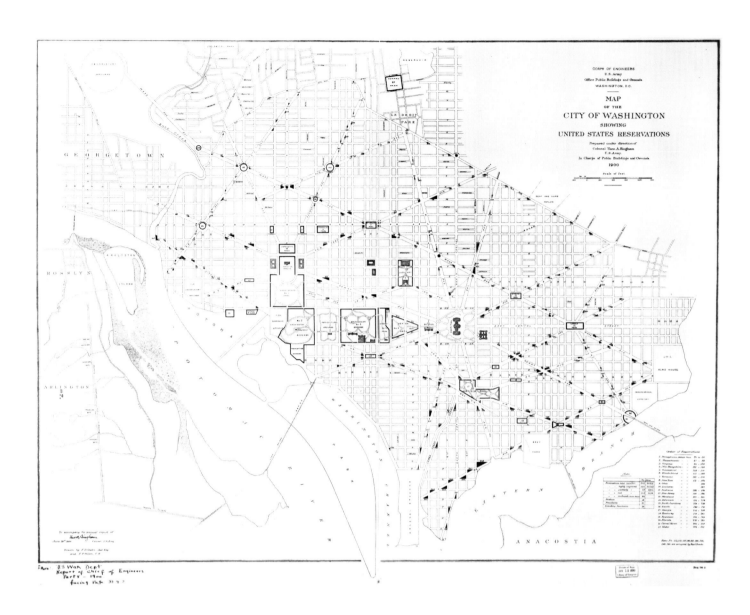

xxxiv. *Map of the City of Washington Showing United States Reservations*, drawn by United States Army Corps of Engineers, 1900
Library of Congress

xxxv. Detail pl. xxxiv

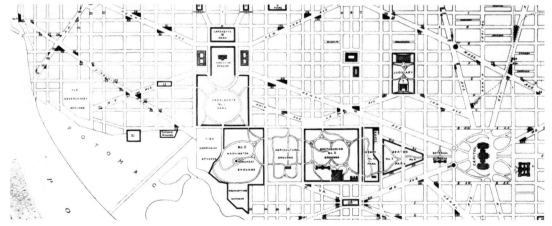

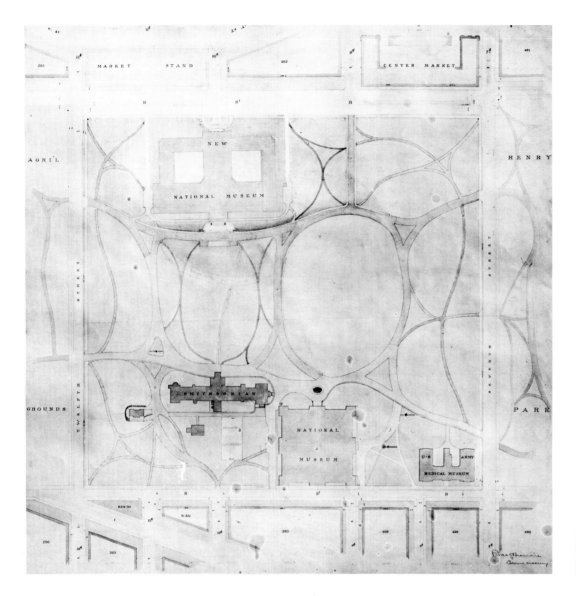

XXXVI. Smithsonian
Institution, plan of existing
grounds, c. 1911–1919
Smithsonian Institution

XXXVII. *George Town and
Federal City, or City of
Washington*, lithograph
by J. Cartwright, c. 1800,
after painting by George
Jacob Beck, c. 1795, view
looking southeast
Library of Congress

XXXVIII. William McLeod,
A Glimpse of the Capitol,
1844, view looking southwest
United States Department of State

XXXIX. *Elements of National Thrift and Empire*, lithograph by E. Weber, 1847, after drawing by J.G. Bruff
Library of Congress

XL. *Washington's Monument*, sketch by Seth Eastman, 1851, looking east from Tiber Creek toward Capitol
Museum of Fine Arts, Boston

XLI. *View of the Washington, D.C., Canal*, sketch by Seth Eastman, 1850, looking west on Tiber Creek
Museum of Fine Arts, Boston

Washington's monument   16 Nov. 1851   102 feet high

XLII. *Panoramic View of Washington from the Potomac,* lithograph by L.N. Rosenthal, 1862
Library of Congress

XLIII. *Washington, D.C., with Projected Improvements,* lithograph by B.S. Smith, Jr., 1852, showing Robert Mills' design for the Washington Monument and Andrew Jackson Downing's plan for the Mall
Library of Congress

Mont Ent to Long Br City Hall   Smithsonian Institute. Armory   U.S Capitol   Navy Yard   Arsenal   Insane Asylum

XLIV. *View of Washington
City and George Town*,
lithograph by E. Weber, 1849,
detail, looking west from
Capitol
New York Public Library

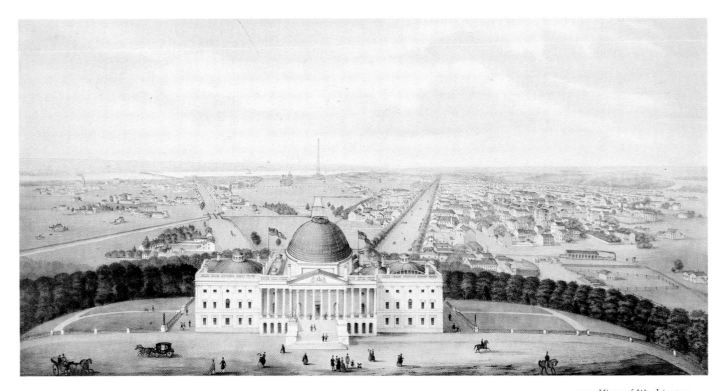

XLV. *View of Washington*,
lithograph by Robert P. Smith,
1850, looking west from
Capitol Hill
Library of Congress

XLVI. *View of Washington*,
lithograph by E. Sachse, 1852,
looking west from
Capitol Hill
Library of Congress

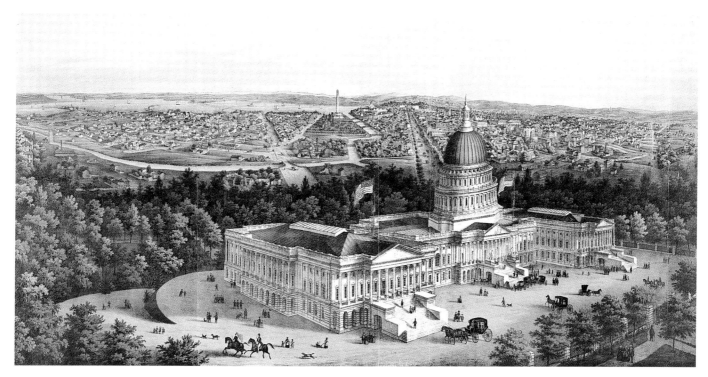

XLVII. *Panoramic View of
Washington City*, lithograph
by E. Sachse, 1856, looking
west from Capitol Hill
Library of Congress

XLVIII. *View of Washington
City*, lithograph by E. Sachse,
1871, looking west from
Capitol Hill
Library of Congress

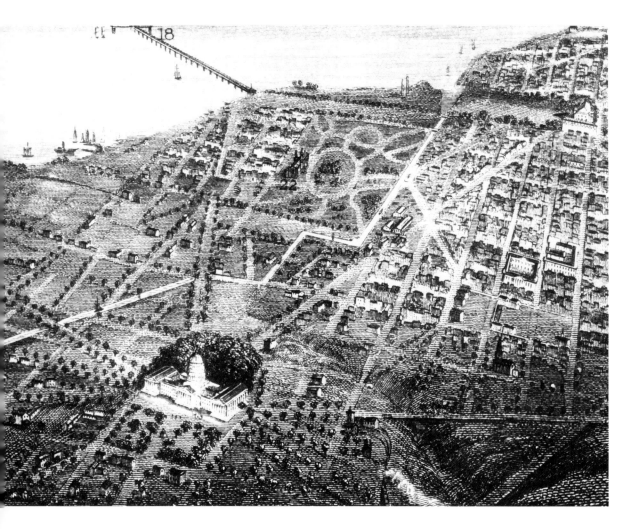

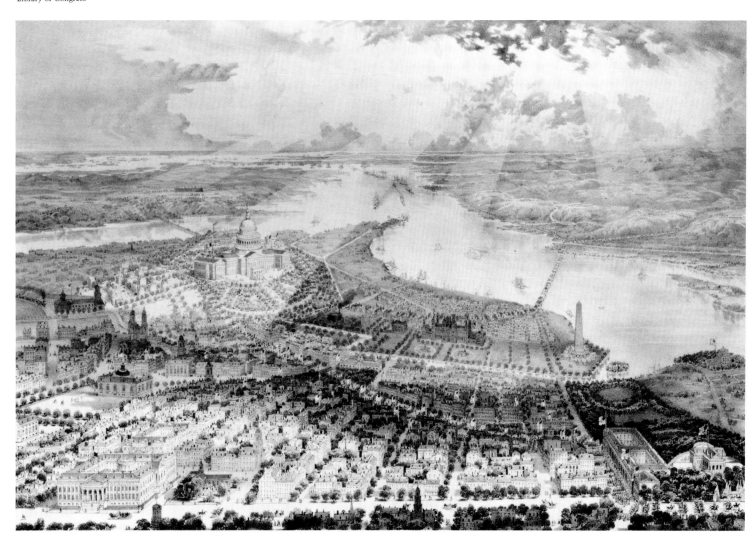

LIII. View of Mall looking west
from Smithsonian Institution
Building, Department of
Agriculture Building and
grounds in foreground, 1870s
Library of Congress

LIV. View of Department of
Agriculture grounds, looking
east toward Smithsonian
Institution Building, late
nineteenth century
Library of Congress

LV. View of Mall, looking east
toward Capitol from Third
Street vicinity, 1860
National Archives

LVI. View of Mall, looking east from Smithsonian Institution Building, photograph by Titian R. Peale, c. 1863
Library of Congress

LVII. View of Mall looking east from Washington Monument, 1901
Smithsonian Institution

LVIII. Senate Park Commission,
Plan of 1901–1902, *Model of
the Mall, Showing Present
Conditions, Looking East*
From Charles Moore, ed., *The
Improvement of the Park System of
the District of Columbia* (Washington, 1902)

LIX. Senate Park Commission,
Plan of 1901–1902, *Model of
the Mall, Showing Present
Conditions, Looking West*
From Moore 1902

LX. Senate Park Commission,
Plan of 1901–1902, *Model of
the Mall, Showing Treatment
Proposed, Looking East*
From Moore 1902

LXI. Senate Park Commission,
Plan of 1901–1902, *Model of
the Mall, Showing Treatment
Proposed, Looking West*
From Moore 1902

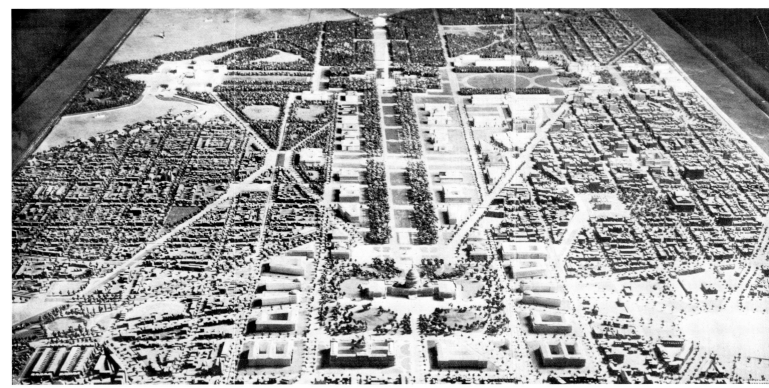

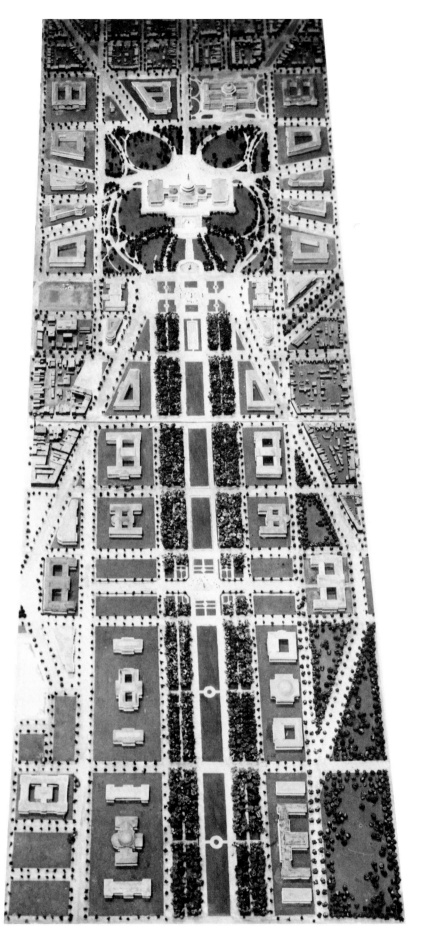

LXIII. Senate Park Commission,
Plan of 1901–1902, map of
Washington, showing
proposed park system
From Daniel H. Burnham and Edward
H. Bennett, *Plan of Chicago* (Chicago,
1909)

LXII. Senate Park Commission,
Plan of 1901–1902, models
showing present conditions
and treatment proposed,
comparative details of the
Mall
Commission of Fine Arts

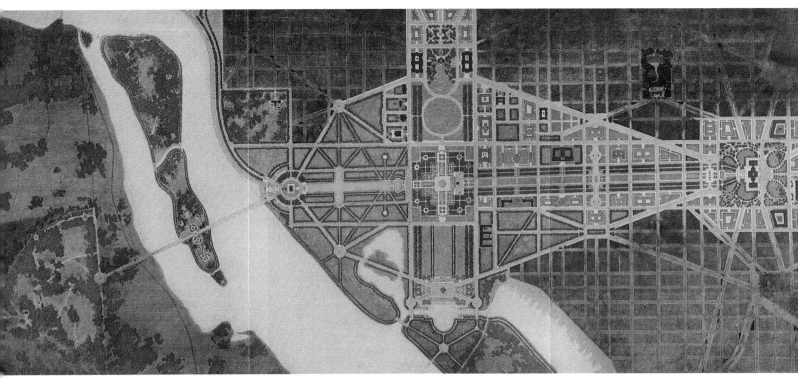

LXIV. Senate Park Commission,
Plan of 1901–1902, *General
Plan of the Mall System*
From *National Geographic*,
March 1915

LXV. Senate Park Commission,
Plan of 1901–1902, *Bird's-Eye
View of General Plan, from
Point Taken 4,000 Feet above
Arlington*, rendering by F.L.V.
Hoppin
From *National Geographic*,
March 1915

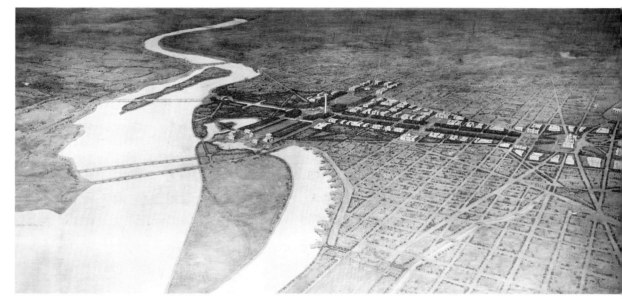

LXVI. Senate Park Commission,
Plan of 1901–1902, *Bird's-Eye
View of General Plan, from a
Point Taken 4,000 Feet Above
the Government Hospital for
the Insane* (Saint Elizabeths)
Commission of Fine Arts

LXVII. Senate Park Commission,
Plan of 1901–1902, *General
View of the Monument
Garden and Mall, Looking
toward the Capitol,* rendering
by C. Graham
From *National Geographic*,
March 1915

LXVIII. Senate Park Commission, Plan of 1901–1902, *View Showing the Proposed Treatment of Union Square, at the Head of the Mall*, rendering by C. Graham
From *National Geographic*, March 1915

LXIX. Senate Park Commission, Plan of 1901–1902, *View of the Capitol, as seen from the Mall*, rendering by Robert Blum
Commission of Fine Arts

LXX. Senate Park Commission,
Plan of 1901–1902, *View
Showing Proposed Treatment
of Basin, Terraces, and
Capitol Approaches, Head of
Mall*, rendering by
Henry McCarter
Commission of Fine Arts

LXXI. Senate Park Commission,
Plan of 1901–1902, *View of
the Mall from Sixth Street*,
rendering by Jules Guerin
Commission of Fine Arts

LXXII. Senate Park Commission,
Plan of 1901–1902, *View of
the Monument Seen from the
Mall at Fourteenth Street,
Looking West,* rendering by
Jules Guerin
Commission of Fine Arts

LXXIII. Senate Park Commission,
Plan of 1901–1902, *View in
the Monument Garden, Main
Axis, Showing Proposed
Treatment of Approaches and
Terraces, Forming a Setting
for the Washington
Monument, Looking East,*
rendering by Jules Guerin
From *National Geographic,*
March 1915

LXXIV. Senate Park Commission, Plan of 1901–1902, *Plan Showing Proposed Treatment of the Monument Garden*, rendering by George de Gersdorff
Commission of Fine Arts

LXXV. Senate Park Commission, Plan of 1901–1902, *View in Monument Garden, Main Axis, Showing Proposed Treatment of Approaches and Terraces, Forming a Setting for the Washington Monument*, looking north, rendering by Jules Guerin
Commission of Fine Arts

LXXVI. Senate Park Commission, Plan of 1901–1902, *View in the Monument Garden, Looking toward the White House,* rendering by O. H. Bacher
Commission of Fine Arts

LXXVII. Senate Park Commission, Plan of 1901–1902, *View from the Monument Terrace, Looking toward Arlington,* rendering by Jules Guerin
Commission of Fine Arts

LXXVIII. Senate Park Commission, Plan of 1901–1902, *View of the Monument and Terraces from the White House*
Commission of Fine Arts

LXXIX. Senate Park Commission, Plan of 1901–1902, *View of the Washington Common and Public Grounds Playgrounds, Showing Proposed Memorial Building, Baths, Theater, Gymnasium, and Athletic Buildings*, rendering by Jules Guerin
Commission of Fine Arts

LXXX. Senate Park Commission, Plan of 1901–1902, *View Showing the Proposed Development of the Site for the Lincoln Memorial, Seen from the Washington Monument*, rendering by O. H. Bacher
Commission of Fine Arts

LXXXI. Senate Park Commission, Plan of 1901–1902, *View of the Lincoln Memorial Site from the Old Naval Observatory*, rendering by Jules Guerin
Commission of Fine Arts

LXXXII. Senate Park Commission, Plan of 1901–1902, *View Showing the Proposed Development of the Lincoln Memorial Site, Seen from the Canal*, rendering by Robert Blum
Commission of Fine Arts

LXXXIII. Senate Park Commission, Plan of 1901–1902, *Proposed Development of Lincoln Memorial Site, Seen from Riverside Drive*, rendering by Carlton T. Chapman, subsequently altered to depict Henry Bacon's design (1912) for the Lincoln Memorial
From *National Geographic*, March 1915

LXXXIV. Lincoln Memorial site and Memorial Bridge, rendering of aerial view looking northwest, c. 1923
Commission of Fine Arts

LXXXV. Federal precinct, looking northeast from National Cemetery, Arlington, L'Enfant's tomb (1911) in foreground, rendering by Jules Guerin, c. 1911
From *National Geographic*, March 1915

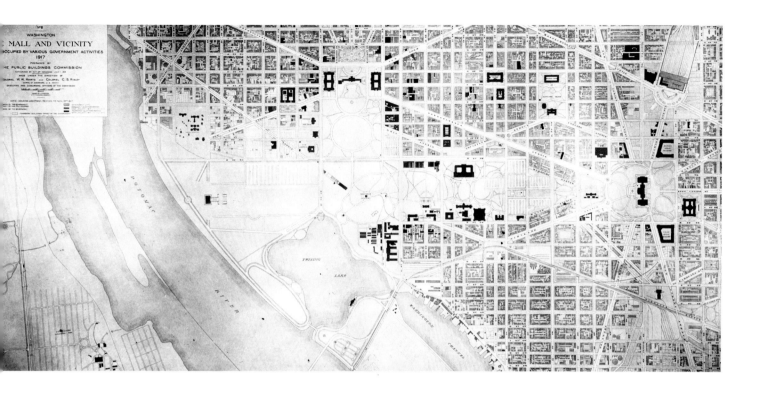

LXXXVI. *The Mall and Vicinity, Buildings Occupied by Various Government Activities*, map prepared by Public Buildings Commission, 1917
Commission of Fine Arts

LXXXVII. *Map Showing Progress on Commission Plan for Public Buildings and the Mall*, map prepared for Commission of Fine Arts, 1921
Commission of Fine Arts

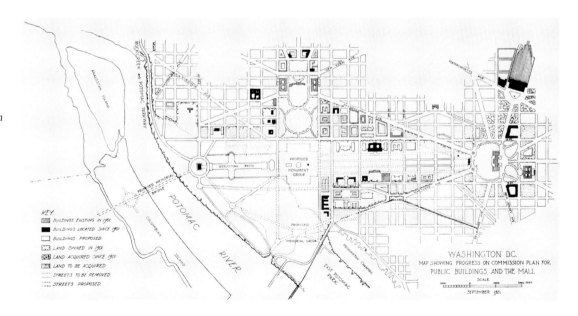

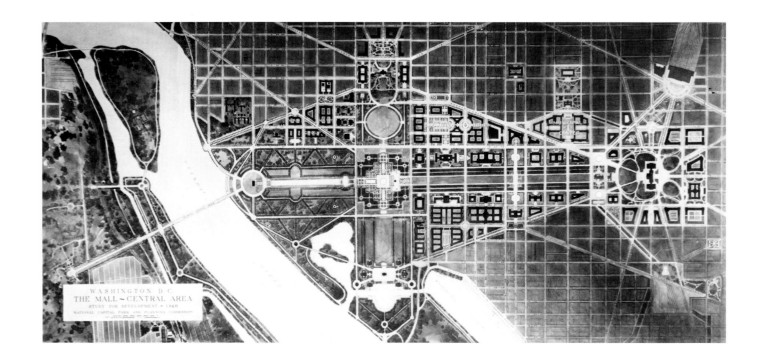

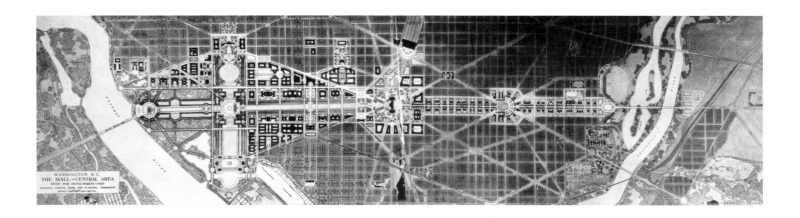

LXXXVIII. National Capital
Park and Planning Commis-
sion, *The Mall, Central Area,
Study for Development, 1928*
Commission of Fine Arts

LXXXIX. National Capital Park
and Planning Commission,
*The Mall, Central Area, Study
for Development, 1929*
Commission of Fine Arts

XC. National Capital Park and Planning Commission, plan for eastern extension of Mall, 1929, aerial view looking northeast
National Capital Planning Commission

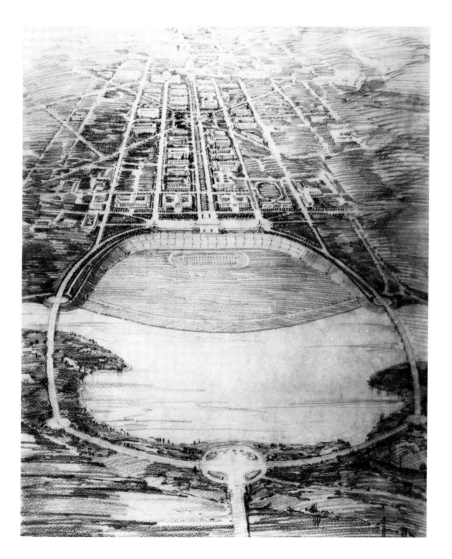

XCI. National Capital Park and Planning Commission, plan for eastern extension of Mall, 1929, aerial view looking west
National Capital Planning Commission

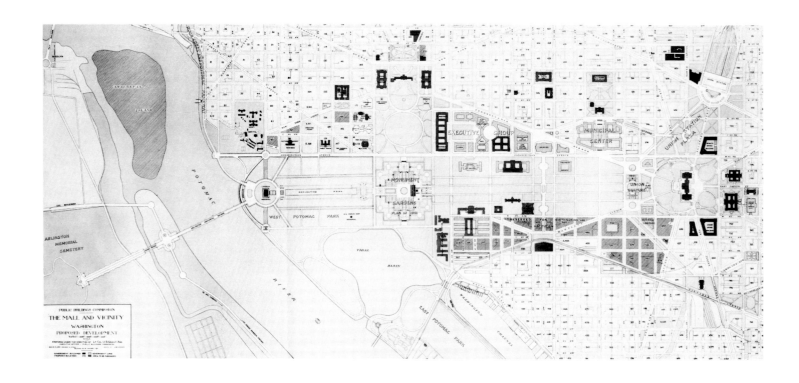

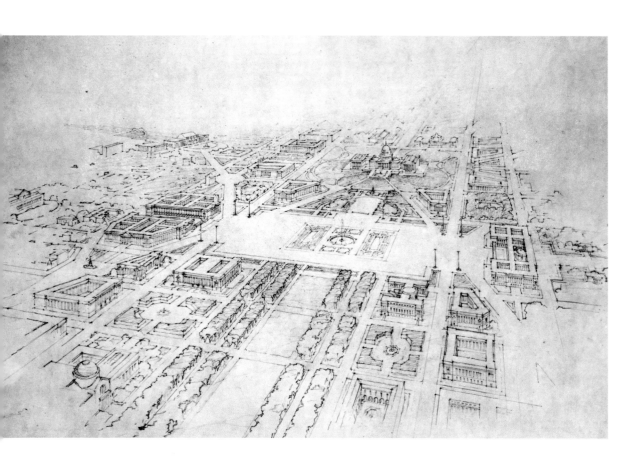

XCII. Public Buildings
Commission, *The Mall and
Vicinity, Washington,
Proposed Development*,
1931
Library of Congress

XCIII. Study for development
of east end of Mall and
Capitol environs, based on
plan of 1901–1902 with subsequent modifications, probably
early 1930s
Commission of Fine Arts

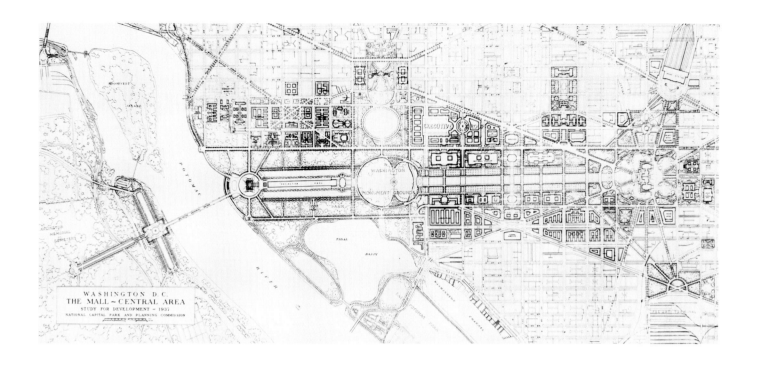

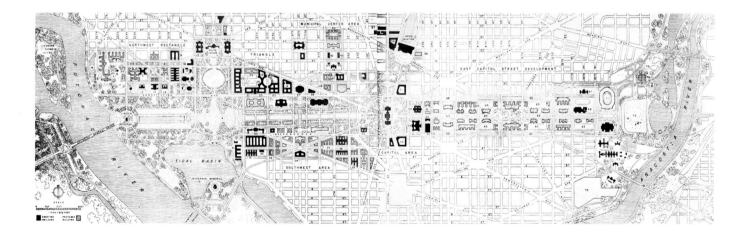

xciv. National Capital Park
and Planning Commission,
*The Mall, Central Area, Study
for Development, 1937*
Commission of Fine Arts

xcv. National Capital Park
and Planning Commission,
Gilmore D. Clarke, consul-
tant, *Development of the
Central Area West and East
of the Capitol, Washington,
D.C., 1941*
Library of Congress

XCVI. Aerial view of Mall, looking east, c. 1915
Commission of Fine Arts

XCVII. Aerial view of Capitol Hill and Mall, looking west, c. 1920
National Archives

XCVIII. Aerial view of Mall and Southwest district, c. 1920
National Archives

XCIX. Temporary government buildings on Mall, looking west, photograph before 1926
Commission of Fine Arts

C. View of Mall, looking northeast, Internal Revenue Service Building on left, 1930s
Commission of Fine Arts

CI. Aerial view of Mall, looking west, 1937
Library of Congress

CII. View of Mall, looking west from Capitol dome, 1936
Commission of Fine Arts

CIII. View of Mall, looking
west from Capitol terrace,
1939
Commission of Fine Arts

CIV. View of Mall, looking
west from Capitol dome, 1940
Commission of Fine Arts

CV. View of Mall, looking east from Washington Monument, 1941
Commission of Fine Arts

CVI. View of Washington Monument and Lincoln Memorial grounds, looking west, with temporary government buildings constructed during World War I at right, 1921
Library of Congress

CVII. View of Reflecting Pool and Lincoln Memorial, looking west from Washington Monument, 1920s
Commission of Fine Arts

CVIII. View of Reflecting Pool, Lincoln Memorial, and temporary government buildings, looking west from Washington Monument, c. 1930s
National Archives

CIX. View of Reflecting Pool, Lincoln Memorial, and temporary government buildings, including those constructed during World War II (left), 1943
National Capital Planning Commission

CX. View of Reflecting Pool, looking east from Lincoln Memorial, c. 1918
Commission of Fine Arts

CXI. View of Reflecting Pool, looking east from Lincoln Memorial, 1926
Commission of Fine Arts

CXII. Aerial view of Mall, looking east, early 1920s
National Capital Planning Commission

CXIII. Aerial view of Mall, looking east, 1946
National Archives

CXIV. Skidmore, Owings, and Merrill; Mall Master Plan, 1965–1966, prepared for National Park Service, site plan
Skidmore, Owings, and Merrill

CXV. Skidmore, Owings, and
Merrill; Mall Master Plan,
1965–1966, model c. 1970
Skidmore, Owings, and Merrill

CXVI. Skidmore, Owings, and
Merrill; Mall Master Plan,
1965–1966, model c. 1970
Skidmore, Owings, and Merrill

CXVII. Aerial view of Capitol
Hill and Mall, looking west,
1985
Photograph by Dennis Brack

CXVIII. Aerial view of Mall,
looking east from Potomac
River, 1990
Photograph by Dennis Brack

CXIX. View of Mall, looking
west from Union Square, 1984
Photograph by Richard Longstreth

CXX. View of Mall, looking
west from Third Street
vicinity, 1979
Photograph by Richard Longstreth

CXXI. View of Mall, looking
southwest from Fourth Street
vicinity, 1979
Photograph by Richard Longstreth

CXXII. View of Washington Monument, looking west from Fourteenth Street, 1989
Photograph by Richard Longstreth

CXXIII. View of Reflecting Pool and Lincoln Memorial, looking west from Washington Monument grounds, 1970
Photograph by Richard Longstreth

CXXIV. View of fountain at east end of Reflecting Pool, looking south, 1987
Photograph by Richard Longstreth

CXXV. View of Memorial
Bridge axis, looking southwest
toward Arlington National
Cemetery, 1971
Photograph by Richard Longstreth

CXXVI. View of Memorial
Bridge axis, looking northeast
toward Lincoln Memorial,
1970
Photograph by Richard Longstreth

CXXVII. View of Memorial
Bridge, looking west from
West Potomac Park, 1987
Photograph by Richard Longstreth

CXXXI. Grand Army of the
Republic encampment on
Mall, photograph by W. C.
Babcock (?), c. 1892
Library of Congress

CXXXII. Marian Anderson at
memorial service for Harold
Ickes, at Lincoln Memorial,
1952
Library of Congress

CXXVIII. View of West
Potomac Park, looking west
along Independence Avenue,
1987
Photograph by Richard Longstreth

CXXIX. View of Tidal Basin
and Jefferson Memorial, looking southeast toward Jefferson
Memorial, 1987
Photograph by Richard Longstreth

CXXX. View of Constitution
Gardens, looking east toward
Washington Monument, 1987
Photograph by Richard Longstreth

CXXXIII. Civil Rights March on Washington, aerial view looking northeast from above Lincoln Memorial, 1963
Library of Congress

CXXXIV. Twenty-fifth Anniversary Civil Rights March on Washington, view looking east from Lincoln Memorial, 1988
Smithsonian Institution

CXXXV. Veterans Day visitors
at Vietnam Veterans
Memorial, 1988
Smithsonian Institution

CXXXVI. Presidential inauguration of George Bush, looking
west from Capitol, 1989
Smithsonian Institution

CXXXVII. View of Mall, looking
east from Twelfth Street
vicinity, 1989
Photograph by Richard Longstreth

CXXXVIII. View of Mall looking
west from Seventh Street
vicinity, 1989
Photograph by Richard Longstreth

CXXXIX. View of walk adjacent
to Reflecting Pool, looking
west, 1987
Photograph by Richard Longstreth

CXL. Hands Across America,
view looking east from
Lincoln Memorial, 1986
Photograph by Dennis Brack

J. CARTER BROWN
National Gallery of Art

The Mall and the Commission of Fine Arts

No aspect of the Commission of Fine Arts' work has been more important than that of the Mall. This essay focuses on efforts there after the Skidmore, Owings, and Merrill Master Plan for the Mall of 1965, with particular emphasis on the last twenty years, since I joined the Commission.

The Reflecting Pool at the foot of the Capitol is one of the great success stories of recent years (pl. CXIX). In this case, the money was provided by the proposed construction of an eight-lane freeway to cut across the surface of the Mall right in front of Capitol Hill! Luckily, the Commission stopped that project in the 1960s, and then with others suggested that since the redesigned freeway was to be underground in a cut-and-cover tunnel, it be covered with a great reflecting pool. This design solution was executed and has worked extremely well. Placing a water display there was an idea that had appeared in the L'Enfant plan.

We have been delighted to see that the solution has drawn people to this space. A high point in the Mall's history occurred in June 1976, when the *Eye of Thomas Jefferson* exhibition was opening at the National Gallery. We decided to re-create the kind of fireworks that had been known to Jefferson when he was in Paris, splendid displays documented in his letters. Fortunately, Ruggieri Brothers, the successor firm to the producer of those spectacles, was still in business there, and we requested that they use only chemicals available in the eighteenth century (fig. 1). The crowds stretched all the way back to the Washington Monument.

The Skidmore, Owings, and Merrill plan, which had been brought to the Commission in the fall of 1965, incorporated the Reflecting Pool. The scheme also called for planting additional trees to reduce the Mall's greensward from the proportions established by the McMillan Plan at the start of the century. Since there was no hope of matching the existing elms, the idea was to place a row of trees along the inner border. The idea has a checkered history, for the Commission kept changing its mind. The idea of adding trees was turned down in 1966 and 1972, and the architects removed it from the plan. Then in June 1973 Owings really pleaded for this feature. Finally, the Commission agreed. But it was soon discovered that no one else in town seemed partial to adding trees. The National Capital Planning Commission and the Joint Committee on Landmarks turned it down. So the Commission of Fine Arts conducted a site inspection in April 1974 to make a final decision. We concluded that although there was an obvious argument for new trees, they would narrow the vista tremendously and that the effect of greensward would become much too linear approaching an axial street: the fate of the mall emanating from the hill of the seat of government in New Delhi, which fails, I believe, because of its tremendous length in relation to its width. The Commission re-

solved that the width of the open space on the Mall is about right.

Another reason for new rows of trees in the Skidmore, Owings, and Merrill plan was to eliminate the double row of parking that existed along the Mall's inner drives — a concept we applauded. None of the Commission thought that cars contributed to the character of the Mall (fig. 2). The glory is that the cars are now gone, and one of the greatest achievements of the 1970s was to persuade the National Park Service to replace the drives with walks (fig. 3; pl. CXX). We worked hard with them on the exact composition of the aggregate, to approximate that in the Tuileries Gardens as closely as possible. There was tremendous opposition with on-site protests from the handicapped community over the material suggested. After site visits, we won the approval of those testing it in wheelchairs; and in the end our belief that the walks should not be a hard, paved surface prevailed. The aggregate is a natural material and has enlivened the Mall's visual impact.

The trees along the Mall, of course, are now quite mature. They were envisioned to pro-

duce an arching, cathedrallike effect (pl. CXXI). The fragility of elms is well known; however, it is not widely known that the Park Service has made strides to preserve them as long as possible. The rate of loss is down to three percent, which is extraordinary considering normal losses to any trees due to old age, lightning, and other natural causes. The Park Service operates a nursery on Daingerfield Island where two hundred elms of a new, disease-resistant strain are being nurtured. This achievement is all the more remarkable in that commercial nurseries have virtually given up elms, because of the conventional wisdom that one cannot grow them satisfactorily. The Park Service still faces a considerable challenge. It has had to direct its efforts primarily to the Mall area and will not spread its resources trying to save every elm in the District of Columbia, sadly. But this focus is essential because the elms are a major contributor to the experience of the Mall.

Another great change since the early 1970s has been Constitution Gardens, designed by Skidmore, Owings, and Merrill. Legend has it that the idea originated with President Rich-ard Nixon's remark to John Ehrlichman, while on the presidential helicopter, that the site's temporary buildings, in which he had worked during World War II, ought to go (pls. CVI–CXIII). Supposedly, every time he flew over them Nixon would fire off memos asking why they had not been demolished. The Navy Department, rather accustomed to being three blocks from the White House, saw no reason to move. Luckily, the president of the United States, as commander-in-chief, was able to realize his objective, an accomplishment of great consequence. However, Nixon's idea was to replace the "tempos" with what he called Tivoli Gardens, an amusement park, with two levels of parking underneath and a high density of excitement above (fig. 4).

Skidmore, Owings, and Merrill's initial scheme created a new precinct in response to the president's wishes, but the Commission rejected the scheme as being far too busy and functionally inappropriate. Our idea was quite different. Tastes were changing: people were rediscovering Victorian architecture and the naturalistic landscape plans of Andrew Jackson Downing and Frederick Law Olmsted.

1. Re-creation of Jeffersonian fireworks opening national bicentennial exhibition, *The Eye of Thomas Jefferson*, at the National Gallery of Art, 1976

2. View of Mall looking east from Ninth Street vicinity, showing inner drives, c. 1973 Skidmore, Owings, and Merrill

3. View of Mall looking east from Fourth Street vicinity, showing inner drives replaced with gravel paths, c. 1976 Skidmore, Owings, and Merrill

4. Skidmore, Owings, and
Merrill, rejected design for
Constitution Gardens, 1972
Skidmore, Owings, and Merrill

Moreover, we believed that the structure of the Mall was now so established that something of a much more relaxed nature was warranted for this space. Kevin Roche, then a member of the Commission, helped tremendously, working in an unofficial capacity with David Childs of Skidmore, Owings, and Merrill to revise the scheme completely (fig. 5; pl. CXXX). Childs drew inspiration from the work of André Le Nôtre; I confess I had Saint James's Park in London much more in mind. Now that the work is completed and the plants are maturing, Constitution Gardens is becoming an inviting place for people. We are particularly pleased not only with the lake as a central feature, but with the lovely open meadow, which we hope will stay that way. From the air, the juxtaposition of the gardens' free form with the sharp geometry of the Reflecting Pool may seem odd, but at ground level the two are never seen together. Moreover, the geometric form of the Lincoln Memorial is assertive enough to allow for successful cohabitation with the organic outlines of lake and meadow.

The other major planning issue that the Commission faced was the question of the Eighth Street cross-axis, which is strongly ex-

pressed on the 1965 Skidmore, Owings, and Merrill plan. Punctuated by John Russell Pope's National Archives Building (1931–1937), the axis extends north to the Patent Office (1836–1867), now the National Portrait Gallery and National Museum of American Art. No appropriate southern terminus existed however. In L'Enfant's plan, the axis was primarily defined by water on the north side of the Mall. We have respected the idea of this axis, and so has the National Capital Planning Commission. Not allowing a building there was a great disappointment to Joseph Hirshhorn, who wanted to nestle his collection next to the National Gallery of Art. Thus, in first designing the Hirshhorn Museum on the Eighth Street axis, but on the north side of the Mall, the objective became to develop an appropriate garden setting and perhaps construct an underground building. The success of Kevin Roche's Oakland Museum in California (1961–1968) was in many minds. But Hirshhorn himself did not find this suitable.

The next design solution for the museum placed its sculpture garden below grade crossing the Mall, a scheme approved by the Commission before my time on it. Such a sunken garden could have been incorporated from an

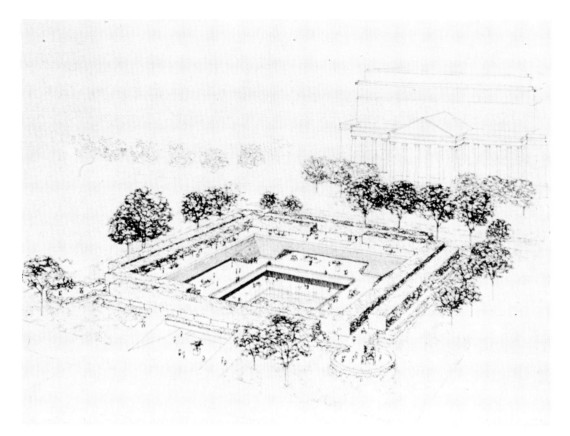

6. Skidmore, Owings, and Merrill, National Sculpture Garden, original plan, 1966
Skidmore, Owings, and Merrill

7. Skidmore, Owings, and Merrill, National Sculpture Garden, intermediate plan, c. 1971
Skidmore, Owings, and Merrill

urban-design point of view, but it never would have worked as a place to display sculpture. If the base level were low enough for the sculpture not to protrude above the edge of the wall, it would have been a deep pit. And if it were not, upper portions of the sculpture would have been quite visible when one looked down the axis of the Mall, creating a very odd visual effect indeed.

It is for the best that the Hirshhorn garden was redesigned. Meanwhile, the space on the Mall's north side, south of the Archives building and west of the National Gallery, remained undeveloped. A building cannot occupy the site. In 1966, Paul Mellon, as president of the National Gallery, and Stewart Udall, as secretary of the Interior, signed a joint agreement that the property would be used as a National Sculpture Garden, operated by the National Gallery. John Woodbridge, then working for Skidmore, Owings, and Merrill on the Pennsylvania Avenue Commission, proposed a circular pool, to mirror the circular form of the Hirshhorn building across the Mall. But the question remained of how to design

a suitable pavilion. The first schematic designs suggested a Miesian branch bank in suburbia, and the outdoor rooms for the sculpture were disproportionately small in relation to the pool (figs. 6, 7).

8. Skidmore, Owings, and Merrill and Dan Kiley, National Sculpture Garden site, 1990
National Gallery of Art

9. James Urban, National Sculpture Garden, an approved plan, rendering by Urban and Associates, 1986
Photograph by Celia Pearson

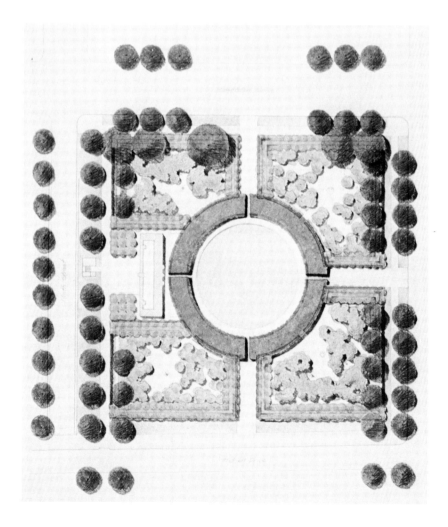

It occurred to me, however, that since the Commission prohibited skating on the big reflecting pools on the Mall's main axis, it would be wonderful to have skating here, giving the place a purpose during the winter. It would begin to reduce the scale of the space and make it more appealing. I remember taking Joseph Albers around Washington when he was here for a stamp design competition. He said to me, "Washington is a city of space and no spaces." He was so right: the Mall's scale is so grand that one of our greatest efforts should be to try to break down the scale. With the National Sculpture Garden plans, we have sought to achieve this through a variety of devices, such as the existing double ring of trees around the pool (fig. 8). Here we have waged a long battle with the Park Service, reminding them that these trees are to grow together finally as an architectural band. Eventually the Park Service consulted Dan Kiley, who was involved in the scheme, for specifications for their tree trimmers. Soon, the trees will grow into a solid visual mass, and it will be a beautiful expression of form while providing considerable shade.

In a plan for the Sculpture Garden approved in 1987, space adjoining the pool was divided into four areas (fig. 9). Dan Kiley advised on

10. Skidmore, Owings, and Merrill, National Sculpture Garden, rendering of pavilion by Art Associates Incorporated, 1986
Commission of Fine Arts

various kinds of trees to be planted in each part, as well as on berming and grading to give a sense of setting for the sculpture. As for the restaurant pavilion, a contract was signed with Government Services, Inc., who raised the money from private sources for its construction. The design, by Charles Bassett of the Skidmore, Owings, and Merrill San Francisco office, is in the spirit of art nouveau rather than being rigid and classicizing. The Commission fell in love with the original scheme the minute we saw it (fig. 10). It has, however, been somewhat altered since.

Among other Mall projects of the past two decades, none is more important than the Washington Monument. The monument itself stood unfinished for years in the nineteenth century, and in my opinion, the surrounding area remains incomplete. Perhaps our biggest future problem on the Mall lies with the monument grounds. During the national bicentennial celebration, the Park Service and Eastman Kodak were granted permission to build an orientation pavilion on the condition that it be torn down in a year. Even though Kodak spent over $1 million on the project, the Park Service was exemplary in enforcing the stipulations of the agreement. But problems remain. How do you deal with visitors there? The 1965 Skidmore, Owings,

and Merrill plan calls for the large, open area to be defined by trees, leaving a wide, roughly circular, and much more coherent open space around the monument. It is an admirable design and should be realized.

We also have received a new submission for the monument grounds from the Park Service,

11. National Park Service, proposed design for Washington Monument grounds, 1986
Commission of Fine Arts

12. EDAW, Signers Memorial,
Constitution Gardens,
mid-1980s
National Park Service

of trees is not satisfactory. Set against that sublime obelisk, they would only look like toys.

The lighting of the Washington Monument remains among unfinished business, and we have approved a plan proposed by the National Park Service, which will illuminate the monument in an intelligent and sensitive manner. Using computer studies to control the lighting, it has been possible to illumine one plane slightly more than another, enhancing the monument's three-dimensional quality. When finally installed, the light fixtures will not be visible during the day, and the flags will not cast shadows on the memorial. The plans are complete at this writing except for funding, which seems to be a problem with much that should be accomplished on the Mall.

One of the most successful memorials erected since the early 1970s is the modestly scaled one to the signers of the Declaration of Independence. It is on an island in the Constitution Gardens lake and is approached by a rustic footbridge (fig. 12). The names of the signers are seen in an elegant landscape setting by Joseph E. Brown of EDAW, Inc. I think it is a paragon of how successful memorials can be.

The greensward that we were hoping to protect in Constitution Gardens, however, could not remain completely open (fig. 13). When legislation was passed for a Vietnam memorial on the site, we had no choice but to monitor its design closely. We indicated that if anything were to be built, it ought not extend vertically; the wonderful sense of meadow was to be respected. As it turned out, we got a masterwork. Paul Spreiregen conducted the competition, and the jurors had the wisdom to choose, of 1,421 entries, number 1,026, by Maya Lin, then an undergraduate student at the Yale University School of Architecture (fig. 14). It was a brilliant leap of imagination to warp the ground plane down, to allow the meadow to remain open, and to orient the memorial's walls toward the two great monuments visible from there, the Lincoln and Washington memorials, so that they are incorporated by reference, as it were, allowing them to symbolize the great ideals and traditions for which those in Vietnam fought.

A difficulty following the competition was that nonprofessionals had trouble visualizing Lin's plans. There was a tremendous reaction

which I am not sure gives any more hope than have others. The previous proposal to offer amenity to the visitors waiting in line included a ring of trees (fig. 11). Although eliminating the underscaled flags that encircle the monument would certainly be an improvement, the notion of replacing them by a row

13. View of Vietnam Veterans
Memorial site, showing
Commission of Fine Arts
members on inspection tour,
1981
Commission of Fine Arts

14. Maya Lin, Vietnam
Veterans Memorial, winning
competition entry, 1981
Commission of Fine Arts

15. Vietnam Veterans
Memorial, an axial proposal
for locating flag and sculpture,
1983
Commission of Fine Arts

16. View of Vietnam Veterans
Memorial, looking west from
apex, mid-1980s
National Park Service

against the design in certain very conservative
quarters. Senator John Warner proved adept
at making peace and bringing some of the factions together, but part of the deal struck,
without the Commission's involvement, was
that the memorial could be realized only if
sculpture and a flagpole were added to the
grounds. The crisis came in March 1982. The
granite had been ordered from India, and the
site was ready for groundbreaking so that the
memorial could open by November for Veterans' Day. Then the secretary of the Interior
informed me by letter that unless the Commission could accept the idea of adding sculpture and a flagpole, work would not begin. The
memorial is on Park Service land and the secretary's permission was necessary for a building permit.

Members of the Commission such as Walter Netsch, who believed in the Bauhaus aesthetic, found the memorial's design complete:
nothing should be added. I too thought the
memorial so superb that it should not be altered. On the other hand, if we refused to compromise, there was the risk that the whole
design would be discarded, without knowledge of what would be proposed in its place.
So I persuaded my colleagues to agree unan-
imously to a letter stating that, in principle,
the sculpture and flagpole could be incorporated. Thus, groundbreaking began. The issues remained, however, of where the flag and
statue would go and at what scale they would
be.

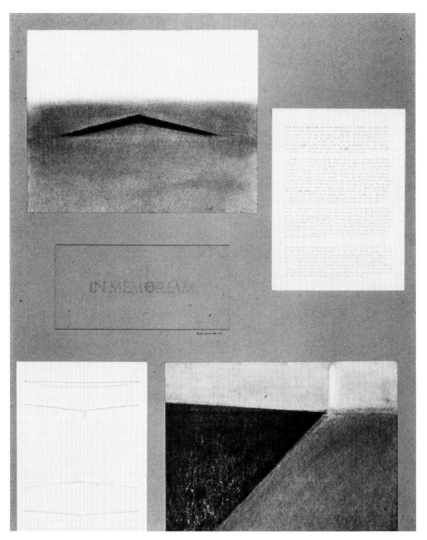

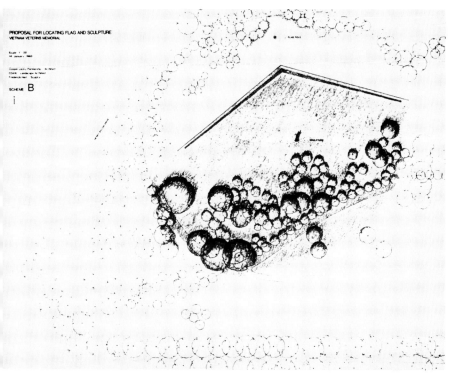

PROPOSAL FOR LOCATING FLAG AND SCULPTURE
VIETNAM VETERANS MEMORIAL

Scale: 1:20
14 January 1983

Cooper-Lecky Partnership, Architect
EDAW, Landscape Architect
Frederick Hart, Sculptor

SCHEME B

The initial scheme for the memorial's modification was highly axial (fig. 15). Proponents of the changes wanted the flagpole on top at the apex, which I felt would look a little like a flag on a golf course. I knew we could always find a place for an American flag, as long as it did not become a precedent for having them scattered all over the Mall above every monument. They also wanted the sculpture placed in front of the apex. I have had some experience installing sculpture outdoors, and I did not think it was fair to the piece, on its own merits, to place it in the middle of a great space. It would be diminished, and it would compromise the very essence of Lin's design. Furthermore, this use of axiality was absurd, because one approaches the memorial either from the east or from the Lincoln Memorial and the southwest. So in the letter to the secretary we had hinted at a solution incorporating both pieces as part of the entrance.

In October of 1982 so many people signed up for the hearing on the proposed additions that it could not be held at our own quarters on Lafayette Square. The Commission had to borrow room in the Treasury Department to accommodate all the network coverage and those who came to state their views. Among them was Maya Lin, who eloquently expressed why she had designed the memorial as she did, so that the names would commemorate the fallen in the order in which they fell — a brilliant aspect of the design (figs. 16, 17). But the business at hand was deciding whether to approve the sculpture, the flagpole, and their proposed location. Testimony lasted four hours. We approved the sculpture and the flagpole at that meeting but not their proposed locations. Not until the following meeting, in February 1983, was the matter resolved.

Interestingly enough, Spreiregen's jury for the original competition had awarded third place to Frederick Hart, who made the sculpture now in question. Hart understood that his new work should not take the central position, but have an adjunct relationship to the wall. As sited at the entrance, his figures contemplate the wall. In the surrounding grove of trees the sculpture, I believe, really works, engaging in a dialogue with the memorial, but not detracting from it when one reaches the wall itself. The whole experience brings people to tears. It has become our most heavily visited memorial after the Lincoln Memorial, at times surpassing even that.

Controversy over the Vietnam memorial seemed to be past until October 1987, when yet another addition was proposed. A group convinced the secretary of the Interior that a sculpture of a woman should be part of the ensemble. Now, the memorial is already explicitly dedicated by Congress to the men and women who served in Vietnam, and this purpose is heralded by an inscription at the apex of the wall. The added sculpture could not literally represent everyone. The wall records the names of all the fallen: some 58,156 names, eight of which (or seventeen hundredths of one percent), duly record the women who died. The total number of women who served there in uniform (the law limits the memorial to the uniformed) was some ten thousand of the total three million. This represents thirty-three hundredths of one percent. The proposal for a statue of a white Army nurse (which itself fails to represent literally many women participants) bore little or no relationship to the existing sculpture vis-à-vis placement. It was submitted as an amendment to the original memorial, but the quality of the sculpture as art, its symbolic deficiencies, and the proposed quasi-axial location, did not strike us as a satisfactory solution. What the scheme did accomplish was to open the door to other groups not incorporated in Hart's realistic sculpture, which we recognized from the beginning as a flaw in the idea of adding *any* sculpture. While sympathetic to the service and suffering of the women involved, we felt that our mandate as a design review body gave us no choice but to discourage future tinkering with a successful memorial. (Since then the Congress has mandated a separate memorial to the women who served, with the hope that it would be built within that precinct.)

How lucky we are that the Mall was situated where it was, nestled into the topographic bowl that rings the federal city (fig. 18). Sweeping down to the foot of majestic Jenkin's Hill on which the Capitol was built, the Mall has scale and monumentality. But is it a place for people?

The point that Norma Evenson has made in her essay, elsewhere in this volume, about the relation of such great spaces to the cities around them I believe is vitally important.

However, a great deal has been happening to Washington since she moved from Capitol Hill. Extraordinary development is taking place on our "main street" along Pennsylvania Avenue. Twelve hundred housing units are planned around that street and close to the Mall. Almost one thousand units are currently scheduled to be built. Construction has been completed on Market Square, and three other projects which incorporate housing are in progress. The revitalization of the whole area, the advent of retail businesses, theaters, art galleries, restaurants, and hotels, should en-

17. View of Vietnam Veterans Memorial, looking east toward Washington Monument, mid-1980s
National Park Service

18. Topographical map, District of Columbia, detail
Commission of Fine Arts

19. Fourth of July celebration on Mall, looking west from Fourth Street vicinity, 1976
Author photograph

hance the interaction of the national Mall, and its tens of millions of visitors a year, with a vibrant city.

The Mall is a people space, even when one is not there for fireworks. I can remember going out on the Fourth of July in 1976, the day of the Bicentennial (fig. 19). One had to climb among the spectators, but I was determined to find the exact spot where the two principal axes of L'Enfant's plan cross, over four hundred feet northwest of the Washington Monument. From there one senses the full impact of the history, the planning, and the majesty that is the national Mall of the United States.

EDITOR'S NOTE

Additional material on the Commission of Fine Arts can be found in Sue Kohler's *The Commission of Fine Arts: A Brief History, 1910–1976, with Additions, 1977–1984,* (Washington, 1985).

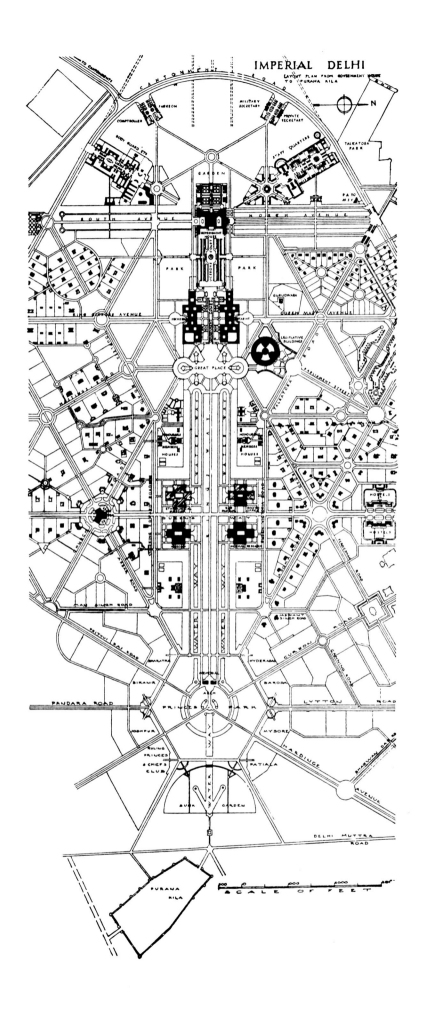

ROBERT A.M. STERN
Columbia University
with RAYMOND W. GASTIL

A Temenos for Democracy:

The Mall in Washington and Its Influence

At the turn of the twentieth century, the Mall in Washington, D.C., was reconceived as a new kind of governmental complex, a combined civic and cultural center that is at once a national front lawn and an imperial forum. This long, wide swath of open space — something between a park and a boulevard — and the buildings along its edges have long served, in effect, as a sacred enclosure, a temenos for a democracy. A calculated expression of centralized power, the Mall nonetheless represents a fundamentally optimistic vision of democracy. This essay will consider the reconstituted Mall's pervasive influence, an influence that has lasted through modernism's hegemony to the present.

To understand the impact of the Mall, it is necessary to begin with Pierre Charles L'Enfant's vision and the reinterpretation of that vision by the Senate Park Commission in 1901–1902.[1] L'Enfant identified the Mall as a four-hundred-foot-wide "Grand Avenue" one and one-half miles long, leading the eye westward toward what seemed the near-infinity of the American continent. Almost certainly he intended for it to be lined by important buildings (pls. V, VII, XI, XIII).

In reality, L'Enfant's vista was all too abruptly terminated by topography, coming to a dead halt at the swampy shores of the Potomac River. The L'Enfant plan was also significantly modified by numerous nineteenth-century projects, including those of James Renwick, Andrew Jackson Downing, and the railroads. When the idea of the Mall was reinstituted by the Senate Park Commission, Daniel H. Burnham, Charles F. McKim, Frederick Law Olmsted, Jr., and Augustus Saint-Gaudens did more than restore L'Enfant's plan, they transformed it conceptually and physically. In extending the east-west and north-south axes over the silted-up riverbed, they greatly increased the size of the federal precinct. At the same time, they punctuated the two principal vistas while blocking out undesirable features with architectural icons, later realized as the Lincoln and Jefferson memorials (pls. LXXVII–LXXXIV).

Such a revision of L'Enfant's plan was a direct result of several factors including a knowledge of historic precedent, a sense that it was possible for American civilization to realize more in a material sense than L'Enfant could have imagined, and the commission members' experience with the World's Columbian Exposition of 1893 (fig. 1). Perhaps most important, the new vision for the Mall can be interpreted not just as a formal descendant of the Chicago fair, but rather as the reflection of the new understanding of American experience that the fair crystallized. By decisively closing down the lens through which the Mall looked across the Potomac toward what had once been frontier, Burnham and McKim expressed the emerging realities of twentieth-century America which were artic-

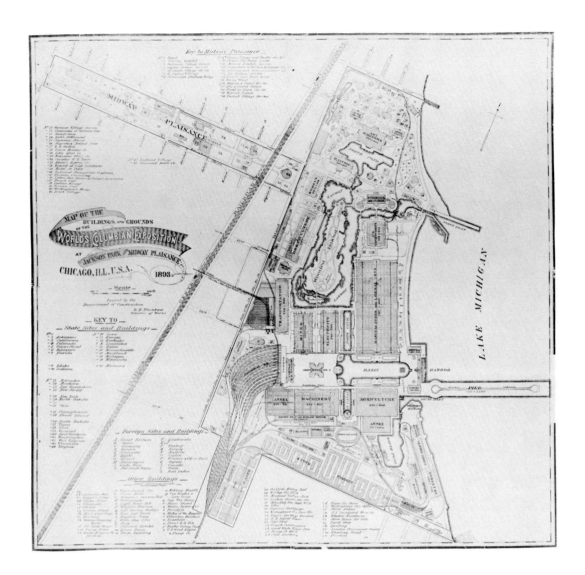

ulated at the fair in Frederick Jackson Turner's famous address, "The Closing of the American Frontier."

For the designers of the Mall, like those of the fair, the closing of the frontier was not necessarily a bad thing, but rather the key to the nation's maturity. With the end of expansion came the opportunity to tend more carefully to the land which had been so hastily colonized and so frequently brutalized. The commission members were determined to give architectural expression to America's self-conception as the inheritor of Western civilization. The reconstituted Mall would render permanent the fair's ideal of America as a new, democratic Rome.[2]

There were several differences between the fair and the Mall, however, which would become increasingly significant as the ideal of Chicago's "White City" developed into the City Beautiful elsewhere. Not included in Washington, at least not by design, was the Midway, the Chicago fair's nearly mile-long, block-wide strip of honky-tonk which the fair's planners provided as a relief from the pretensions of the Court of Honor and the Lagoon. In Washington, and in the cities inspired by the McMillan Plan, it was clear that there was no need to impose honky-tonk. The Main Streets, Broadways, Market Streets, and Pennsylvania Avenues of nineteenth-century American towns already supplied more than

1. World's Columbian Exposition, Chicago, 1893, site plan
Chicago Historical Society

2. Group Plan Commission (Daniel H. Burnham, John M. Carrère, and Arnold W. Brunner), proposed Civic Center, Cleveland, 1903, general view
From Werner Hegemann and Elbert Peets, *The American Vitruvius: An Architect's Handbook of Civic Art* (New York, 1922)

3. Group Plan Commission, proposed Civic Center, Cleveland, 1903, plan
From Hegemann and Peets 1922

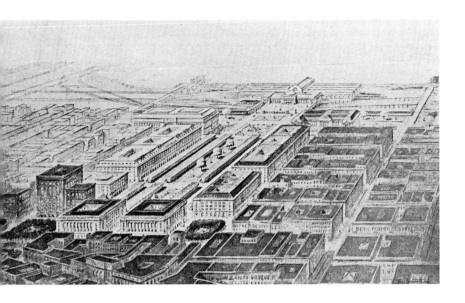

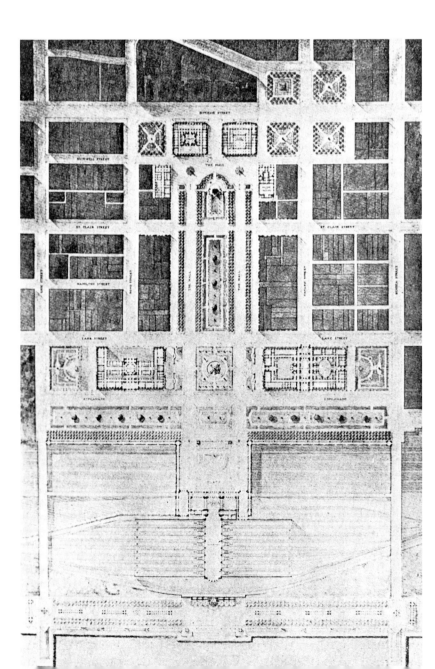

enough true grit. At the same time, deleting the midway from the overall urban vision often showed a disregard for more modest civic amenities — not necessarily honky-tonk — provided by smaller scale, less monumental planning, a disregard that was revealed in the wholesale destruction of downtown neighborhoods in cities such as Cleveland, Saint Louis, and Albany.

After 1902, the Mall was equally if not more influential than the Chicago fair. The Mall's effect on city planning was first felt in Cleveland, where in June 1902, the Group Plan Commission was appointed by Governor Nash of Ohio.[3] The makeup of the commission, consisting of Daniel H. Burnham, John M. Carrère, and Arnold W. Brunner, demonstrates how close fair planning and city planning had become. While Brunner had not worked on the Chicago fair, Burnham had. And Carrère, a leading New York architect, had just shown his planning skills at the 1901 Pan-American Exposition held in Buffalo, the first significant American fair inspired by Chicago's example.

Cleveland's never fully realized Civic Center, which encompassed a forty-four-acre site between Superior Street and the lakeside railroad tracks, had as its main axis a mall leading from the proposed station on the lake to the post office and public library, with a strong cross-axis formed between the complementary city hall to the east and the courthouse to the west (fig. 2). Aesthetic uniformity was considered essential to the success of the design, and it was the "Roman" architecture of the fair and of Washington that was deemed appropriate. In its report, the commission recommended that "the designs of all the buildings of this group plan should be derived from the historic motives of the classical architecture of Rome; that one material should be used throughout and that a uniform scale of architecture should be maintained in their design . . . the general height and mass of all the buildings on the east and west of the Mall should be the same, in fact, these buildings should be of the same design and as uniform as possible" (fig. 3).[4]

As a model for the transformation of the American city, the Cleveland plan set the questionable precedent of "slum clearance," which would come to typify the plans for malls, both in the City Beautiful period and in later, post-World War II schemes. In Chicago's Jackson Park, there previously had been nothing but swamp; the Mall in Washington likewise was realized on mostly open land; but in Cleveland, as in many other cities that would be influenced by the Mall, the grand axial vision required the razing of block after block of housing and commercial buildings, blocks that today we might recognize as viable neighborhoods and even historic districts.

Cleveland was followed by San Francisco, where in 1905 Burnham and his partner Edward H. Bennett proposed an alternative to the mall arrangement by offering a plan in which civic buildings were used to fix key intersections of a new plan (fig. 4).[5] Where the Cleveland mall had been conceived as a monumental set piece, Burnham and Bennett saw the San Francisco Civic Center as a collection of focal points for Haussmannesque diagonal avenues radiating out to the city. The San Francisco plan was accepted the day before the great earthquake and fire of 1906. Ironically, though the calamity resulted in the leveling of 512 central city blocks, it did not in the end create a golden opportunity to rebuild along the new lines proposed by Burnham and Bennett. After the fire San Francisco rebuilt itself in much the same urban pattern as had existed before the disaster. A new civic center was created, however, as a monumental set-piece with a strong, mall-like axis.[6] In 1912, John Galen Howard, Frederick H. Meyer, and John Reid, Jr. offered their plan of a concentrated group of buildings which, like the malls in Cleveland and Washington, included both governmental and cultural facilities (fig. 5). Bakewell and Brown's City Hall, completed in time for the 1915 Panama-Pacific Exposition, is the focus of the composition and one of the glories of American classicism. The building is set at the center of an east-west axis running toward the broad diagonal of Market Street. To the west, the City Hall overlooks a long, rectangular court between the Opera House and the War Veteran's Memorial Building (1931–1932), designed by Arthur Brown, Jr., this time in collaboration with theater architect, G. Albert Lansburgh, to the north, and the State Office Building (1926), designed by Bliss and Faville, to the south. To the east, toward Market Street, the City Hall commands a square as wide as its facade (flanked by two more civic buildings); the

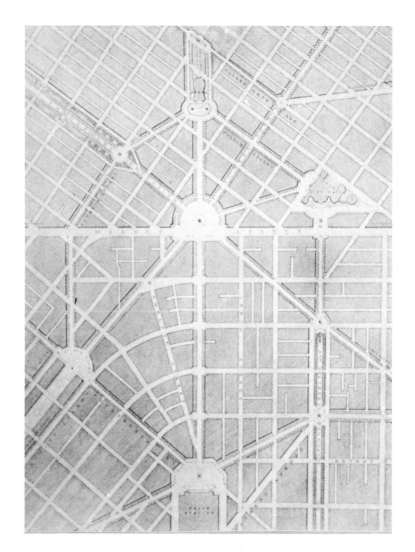

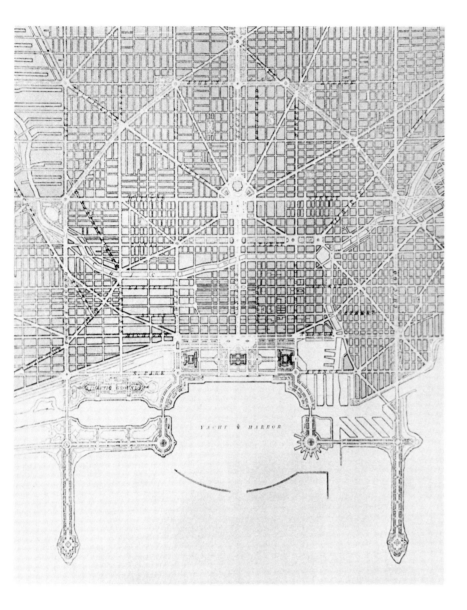

ington's Mall and the World's Columbian Exposition and expanded and rearranged them to suit the problem of an entire city (fig. 6).[8] While the Paris of Napoleon III was repeatedly cited as an example of how to organize a great metropolis and give it elegant details, the heart of the new Chicago city plan followed the lead of the fair and the Mall. Once again, a monumental civic center, with a domed city hall, was proposed. Vaster than the one realized in San Francisco, Burnham's proposal was for a site across the Chicago River at the end of a broad axis which was not a mall but a widened version of the existing Congress Street. Burnham's City Hall plaza was to be the hub of a wheel of avenues radiating into the suburbs.

At the lake, a powerful cross-axis was proposed in the form of a series of parks to be laid out once the site was cleared of railroad tracks, just as Washington's Mall had been. Significantly, Burnham's Chicago plan, unlike the Mall, separated the government buildings from the cultural institutions, placing the former along the east-west axis of Congress Street and the latter along the north-south axis of the parks. Despite its grand forms, parts of the Chicago plan point to the obsessively diagrammatic land-use planning of the mid-twentieth century.

The ideal of the Mall captured the imagination of innumerable smaller communities from Springfield, Massachusetts, to Atascadero, California. It was carried abroad as part of our imperialist baggage, as occurred in Manila (1905), where Burnham proposed an administrative and cultural center, built around a mall, near the bay and south of the old walled Spanish city (fig. 7).[9]

Of all these provincial efforts, the civic center developed in Pasadena, California (begun 1923), is the most compelling and best resolved.[10] In 1921, George Hale led a drive to give Pasadena, then a city with a population of forty-five thousand, a civic center befitting its self-conception as the "Athens of the West." The Pasadena plan, despite its elegant formality, was better integrated into the existing city fabric than most other Mall-inspired efforts. In his master plan, Edward H. Bennett placed the city hall at the intersection of two streets, Garfield and Holly, to take advantage of two buildings already in place, both in terms of location and, to some degree, in terms of stylistic affinity: the Renaissance palazzo Post

4. Daniel H. Burnham and Edward H. Bennett, plan for San Francisco, 1905, proposed street configuration of Civic Center area
From John W. Reps, *The Making of Urban America: A History of City Planning in the United States* (Princeton, 1965)

5. John Galen Howard, Frederick H. Meyer, and John Reid, Jr., master plan for Civic Center, San Francisco, 1912
From Hegemann and Peets 1922

6. Daniel H. Burnham and Edward H. Bennett, *Plan of Chicago*, 1909, general plan
From Burnham and Bennett, *Plan of Chicago* (Chicago, 1909)

square then narrows to the "mall" formed by Fulton Street, extending two blocks to Market Street.

Recently, Skidmore, Owings, and Merrill has attempted to enlarge the Civic Center's domain with an addition to the western end of the Opera House (1979), which replicates the scale and details of the original, replacing terra cotta with precast concrete panels; and with the addition of the new Davies Symphony Hall (1981), which offers a very loose interpretation of the scale, forms, and materials of the earlier buildings, on a site directly south of the Opera House.[7]

Burnham and Bennett's *Plan of Chicago* of 1909 took the planning principles of Wash-

Office (Oscar Wenderoth, 1913) and the Spanish colonial YWCA (Julia Morgan, 1920–1922).

The city hall was designed by Bakewell and Brown, the firm that had worked its magic in San Francisco. Once again there is a magnificent dome, but this one is more Spanish than French, and it is open as well. Amazingly, Pasadena's civic center is low-key without seeming suburban. Garfield Street, the cross-axis, has the Spanish Renaissance Public Library (Hunt and Chambers, 1927) at one end and the Italian Renaissance Civic Auditorium (Bergstrom, Bennett, and Haskell and J.G. Stanton, 1932) at the other.

Sure testimony to America's coming of age as an international political and cultural power was the Mall's impact on the design of cities in the British Empire and Commonwealth. Washington's Mall may be counted high among

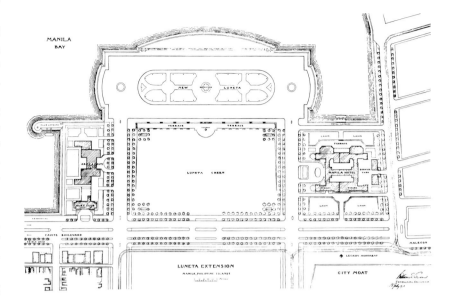

the precedents for Aston Webb's reconfiguration of The Mall in London, in which he provided the city with an imperial core running from Trafalgar Square to Buckingham Palace (fig. 8).[11] The existing Mall, a route without a direct connection to Trafalgar Square, was first laid out by Charles II in 1660–1662, according to a design credited to André Le Nôtre. The space was transformed in Webb's original proposal (1901) into a broad avenue lined by commemorative monuments, punctuated by triumphal arches, and ending in a large, semicircular arcade, framing the east front of Buckingham Palace and focusing on a memorial to Queen Victoria, who had died

earlier that year. Owing to the constrictions of budget, the severe criticism of the architectural community, and perhaps Webb's own change of heart, the design was simplified and the colonnade deleted, making The Mall a less bombastic approach to the Victoria Memorial and the palace. In the end, Webb was able to extend his original proposal, taking responsibility for the design of the Admiralty Arch (1906–1909), which joined Trafalgar Square to the east terminal of The Mall, completing the Processional Way; and designing the new cladding for Buckingham Palace (1913) at the opposite end point.

Herbert Baker and Edwin Lutyens' plan for

7. Daniel H. Burnham and William B. Parsons, proposal for Luneta Extension, Manila, 1910, plan based on Burnham's general plan for Manila, 1905
From *Western Architect* (January 1911). Avery Architectural and Fine Arts Library, Columbia University

8. Aston Webb, proposal for Buckingham Palace, Victoria Memorial, and The Mall, 1901
From *American Architect and Building News* (1901). Avery Architectural and Fine Arts Library, Columbia University

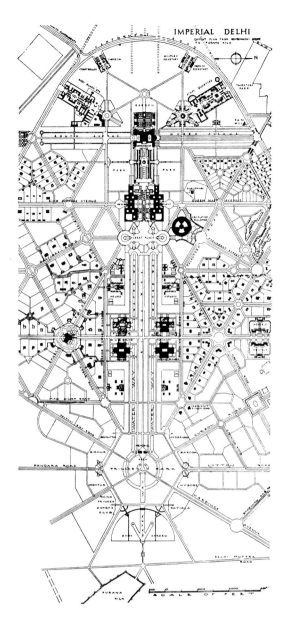

IMPERIAL DELHI

9. Herbert Baker and Edwin
Lutyens, plan of New Delhi,
1912–1931
From *Architectural Review* (London,
January 1931)

New Delhi (1912–1931) also bears witness to the Mall's influence (fig. 9).[12] This was grudgingly recognized when Baker, in an architect's characteristic disregard for immediate precedent, overlooked the McMillan Plan as well as the Chicago fair, and described New Delhi's layout as "a noble development of the germ of L'Enfant's plan of Washington and Wren's rejected design for the City of London."[13] Lutyens, too, credited L'Enfant, explaining that the plan for New Delhi had been criticized by shortsighted observers: "[the plan for New Delhi was] a sorry nuisance to those whose thoughts could not merge beyond the right angles of New York, nor embrace the intel-

ligence of L'Enfant at Washington."[14] But clearly the recent work of McKim and Burnham was on the minds of New Delhi's designers as well. The main axis of the Baker-Lutyens plan for New Delhi runs east-west, sweeping the length of the wide, canal-bordered King's Way, from the All-India Memorial Arch to the governmental acropolis of Baker's twin Secretariats (1913–1928), which frame the climactic finish of Lutyens' Viceroy's House (1912–1931). Like the Capitol in Washington, the Viceroy's House is set on the highest point, at the end of a mall, and like the Capitol it is domed.

In 1912, the same year Baker and Lutyens began their work at Delhi, Walter Burley Griffin of Chicago, won the international competition for the design of Canberra, the new capital of the new Australian nation (fig. 10).[15] Working with his wife, Marion Mahoney Griffin, whose magnificent renderings surely helped capture the commission, Griffin developed a plan which sought to be both grand and suburban. Canberra's neighborhood sectors reflect Garden City ideals. But its superscaled institutional sector is clearly a descendant of plans for Washington.

Like L'Enfant, Griffin used topography as the basis for geometric organization, laying out two major axes, which are parks rather than roads, oriented to natural landmarks. Like L'Enfant, Griffin designed diagonal avenues to connect the groupings of buildings set on these axes. There was also a triangle of power similar to Washington's. Three hills, denoting the capitol, the civic center, and the market center, are connected by long, straight streets to form an equilateral triangle. The capitol is treated as the vertex, and a straight line, the land axis, runs from the capitol, bisecting the triangle, crossing the municipal axis, which forms the base of the triangle, and extending to Mount Ainslie, three miles away. Halfway between the vertex and the base of the triangle is the water axis, running through a basin formed by damming up the Molonglo River.

In Griffin's vision, the capital city was at once a fairground, a sacred center of parliamentary democracy, and a suburb; it was the Chicago fair, the Washington Mall, and Welwyn Garden City rolled into one. Along the north shore of the "ornamental waterway," and within the parliamentary triangle, Griffin placed the "public gardens," which included such cultural institutions as the stadium, national theater, and opera. At the end of the land axis, at the foot of Mount Ainslie, he placed a casino, an incredibly grand site for an institution of leisure, denoting once again how important the fair and the Mall's combination of government, culture, and entertainment were to the image of the twentieth-century city. Regrettably, the realized scheme lacks the architectural force needed to match the splendid scale of the site and the plan.

The Mall proved an appealing model to the ambitious regimes of less-than-democratic powers as well. The Esposizione Universale di Roma (EUR) (begun 1938) was conceived as both a fairground for "The Olympics of Civilization," an international exposition which was intended to prove that Italy had led the way in every scientific and cultural endeavor, and as a permanent civic and cultural center for Rome.[16] Mussolini wanted this world's fair to celebrate two decades of his rule, and he desired the new civic and cultural center as a monument to the "Third Rome," which in his vision would expand toward Ostia and the sea. Given Mussolini's politics as well as the example of the Roman Forum, which is the ultimate source of much of the Mall ideal and only a few miles from the EUR site, it is not surprising that American models proved important as modern illustrations of that ideal's continuing validity, and at the same time as work that had to be surpassed.

The EUR is perhaps distinct, at least before Brasilia, in its conception of the mall as an aggrandized highway (fig. 11). Via Imperiale was to lead from the Forum in Rome to the EUR and on to Ostia and the sea. As a result the axes have greater impact, helped as they are by strongly rhetorical architecture such as the Hall for Receptions and Congresses, designed by Adalberto Libera in 1938, and the Palace of Italian Civilization (now the Palace of Italian Civilization and Labor) designed by Guerrini, La Padula, and Romano in 1939, which stand as terminal features of a cross-axis immediately within the north entrance, the Porta Imperiale.

At the other end of the Fascist power axis, Albert Speer's master plan for Berlin (begun 1937) was probably influenced by Washington, but given Hitler's well-known admiration for Haussmann's Paris and Vienna's Ringstrasse, the American prototype was not

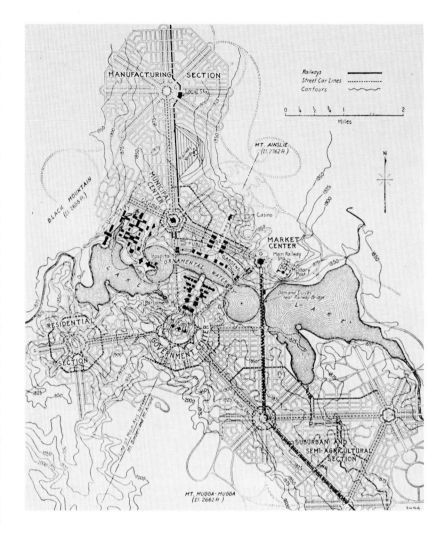

likely to have been uppermost in the architect's mind.[17] Nonetheless, in some ways, Speer's Berlin is akin to the Mall, especially along the five-kilometer stretch from the domed Great Hall south to the Sud-Bahnhof (1937–1943), where governmental and corporate administration buildings were to be located.

After World War II, many believed that once tarred by the brush of fascism, the monumental planning ideal of the Mall would be discredited forever, but in fact it has flourished, proving its validity as an expression of institutional power and not of any single political system. Struggle though the modernists of the mid-twentieth century did to find another expression for the polis, as Le Corbusier sought at Saint Die[18] and Chandigarh,[19] the classical ideal of temenos and forum that the

10. Walter Burley Griffin, plan of Canberra, 1912, winning competition entry
From Hegemann and Peets 1922

11. Universal Exposition of Rome (EUR), final plan, 1938
Architettura (December 1938)

12. Frank Lloyd Wright and Taliesin Associates, Marin County Civic Center, San Rafael, California (1957–1969)
Robert A.M. Stern Architects

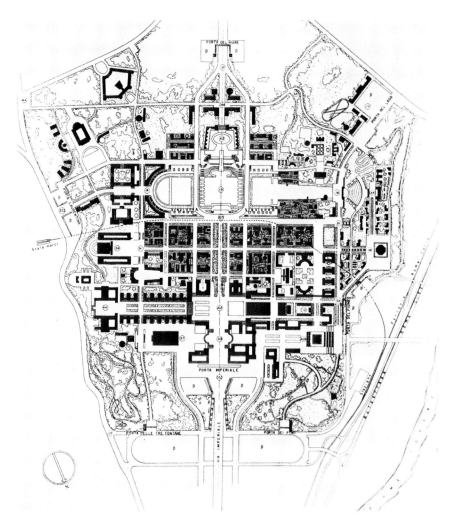

Mall represents remained a powerful guiding premise for most designers.

Even the vehemently anticlassical Frank Lloyd Wright could not avoid the compelling power of the Mall in conceiving his great public projects. At the Marin County Civic Center (1957–1969), Wright took the ideal of the Mall and internalized it (fig. 12).[20] His mall is virtually airborne, becoming a glazed galleria in which the traditional hierarchy of the mall is inverted: along its sides there are government offices, while a cultural institution, the shallow-domed library occupies the dominant position in the composition usually reserved for the capitol or administration building. Earlier Wright's attachment to axial planning was clear in his 1895 design for an amusement center for E.C. Waller on Wolf Lake, near Chicago, which is a bold interpretation of the Chicago fair.[21] More than four decades later the idea still haunted Wright, when he advanced a series of proposals for a civic center in Madison, Wisconsin, first in 1938, and again in 1955, placing the civic buildings on the lakefront beneath a broad, semicircular landscaped terrace, with a great axial swath running down its center.[22]

The search for a modernist equivalent to classical monumentality has almost always led back to the Mall. In many instances, the

Mall ideal has been quite destructive to American urbanism, as has been the case in Saint Louis.[23] By the end of the nineteenth century, the city had a civic, commercial, and cultural spine running from the banks of the Mississippi straight west along Olive Street and Lindell Boulevard to the domed Old Courthouse (1839–1864). There was, however, no mall, no grand open space of representation. Before the decline of river trade the Mississippi itself had played this role, achieving, in effect as well as symbolically, a link for virtually all the important cities of the Midwest. By the end of the nineteenth century, the effort to reinforce Saint Louis' independent identity led to proposals for a mall toward the courthouse, first in 1904 by John Mauran, William Eames, and Albert Groves, at the time of the Louisiana Purchase Exposition, and again in 1907 as part of a larger scheme for urban regeneration, *A City Plan for Saint Louis*, by the Civic League of Saint Louis.[24] The project never came to pass, and in 1933 it was decided that Saint Louis' commercial waterfront should be replaced with a park, thereby dooming the city's oldest district, which contained numerous superb cast-iron and other commercial buildings. Beyond restoring the courthouse, the planners proposed that the most important job was not to build up a civic center but to tear down and clear the ground to prepare the site for whatever would be built following an international competition. It is ironic that this destructive project was undertaken in the name of history; it was one of the first historic preservation projects to come into the National Park System under the Historic Sites Act of 1935. As Charles B. Hosmer, Jr. has written: "It was an urban renewal project with a veneer of history used to coat an expenditure for unemployment relief."[25] By 1942, forty blocks of buildings had been razed (fig. 13).

In 1948, Eero Saarinen won the competition for the park with his design for the Gateway Arch as a memorial to Thomas Jefferson and the Louisiana Purchase. The arch was completed in 1968 (fig. 14). Fearing that it would lead not to the West but to a ragged downtown, city leaders once again agreed that the park should be linked to a mall penetrating the city's interior, following the existing spine of the city and ripping apart the very tissue of buildings and activities that had given Saint Louis vitality. Now Saint Louis has its mall,

13. Aerial view of Jefferson National Expansion Memorial site, Saint Louis, c. late 1930s
National Archives

14. Gateway Mall, Saint Louis, view from building now demolished looking east toward Old Courthouse (1839–1845 et seq.) and Gateway Arch (1963–1965), late 1960s
National Park Service

but all the action is miles to the west in the suburbs.

Despite the failure of the Saint Louis mall, the Mall ideal continues to flourish as the model for cultural centers, such as Lincoln Center for the Performing Arts, designed by a team of architects including Wallace Harrison, Max Abramovitz, and Philip Johnson. Lincoln Center, spearheaded by Robert Moses and John D. Rockefeller III, was a latter-day but unfulfilled version of the Chicago fair. The architects and their sponsors were never really satisfied with the arrangement of travertine-clad buildings set around a Chicago fairlike court of honor – with the maverick Eero Saarinen treated like Louis Sullivan had been at the Chicago fair, relegated to a site to the side of the main court. In an effort to mirror fully the sweep of Burnham and Bennett's 1909 Chicago plan as well as that of Washington's Mall, they considered extending the center's grounds east in the form of a mall leading into Central Park. The opportunity almost came in 1966, when William F. R. Ballard, a former chairman of the City Planning Commission,

with the support of the coordinating architect of Lincoln Center, Wallace Harrison, prepared designs for a traditional tree-lined mall running to the park. Mayor John Lindsay's administration at first seemed to respond positively, but times were changing and the proposal, which called for the demolition of several venerable buildings, met with a public uproar which ended the project.[26]

The Mall ideal has also provided the basis for capitals in Brasilia, whose basic cross-axial plan was designed by Lucio Costa (1957),[27] and in Albany, New York, where Governor Nelson Rockefeller did his best to bring Washington's architectural grandeur to the Empire State.[28] Rockefeller's plateaulike South Mall (1963–1978), designed by Wallace Harrison, adorned with basins and fountains and bordered by *allées* of trees and buildings, stretches south from the New York State Capitol (1867–1899). Modernist and monumental, a Sixth Avenue on the back forty, its principal elements are four identical twenty-two-story office buildings, a forty-four-story tower, and a concrete egg on a pedestal, the Performing Arts

Center—all lifted on a six-story plinth beneath which lie the buried foundations of the low-income housing razed to make way for all this splendor. The complex events surrounding the Empire State Plaza's construction have so preoccupied most commentators that the project's inherent qualities have gone largely unnoticed. In its own mad way it is a splendid vision, a marbleized aircraft carrier, a ship of state, misguidedly launched into a hostile sea of 1960s social activism.

Washington's Mall has survived the design polemics of the twentieth century to remain compelling as a type not only for governmental and cultural centers but also for the very building problem that triggered its reinvigoration a hundred years ago—the world's fairs that are regularly organized to create temporary, representative models of environmental excellence combining aesthetics, culture, and government. In 1984, Bruce Graham of the Skidmore, Owings, and Merrill Chicago office, together with William E. Brazley and Associates, led a team of architects including myself, Thomas Beeby, Charles Moore, Jaquelin Robertson, and Stanley Tigerman, in developing a master plan for the then projected, and later abandoned, 1992 Chicago world's fair, intended to celebrate the five-hundredth anniversary of Columbus' discovery of the New World (figs. 15, 16).[29] Like the 1893 Columbian Exposition, the 1992 fair was to take place on the lakefront and was to create an urban model. The theme was to be the varieties of urban experience, the complexity of cities as a measure of culture and human activity. In the new fair, the court of honor was to be an homage to the designers of the previous century's fair, an aggressive declaration that representative, scenographic—and classical—architecture had returned in strength to play time-honored roles in the public arena of American democracy.

It has and it has not. In June 1985, the Illinois General Assembly voted not to renew the fair project's funding, and the project that had begun in 1978 was dead. Gone it seems was the confidence and the courage of 1890. Perhaps society has lost its taste for the grand gesture. But if that is so, why do so many people visit the Mall in Washington, Lincoln Center, and even Empire State Plaza?

A final word. Throughout this symposium on the Mall, there was precious little atten-

tion paid to the buildings that line it. The vital lesson of the Mall must include the architecture as well. The recent buildings along the Mall are little more than mute containers. To make new enclaves of government and culture, we must renew our pact with architecture as a powerful instrument of communication.[30] Perhaps we need not only the grand axes, but also the grand classical architecture that goes with them. Jefferson, McKim, and Burnham understood this. Do we?

15. Thomas Beeby, Charles W. Moore, Jaquelin Robertson, Robert A.M. Stern, and Stanley Tigerman, with Skidmore, Owings, and Merrill, Chicago, and William E. Brazley and Associates, proposed 1992 Chicago world's fair, 1984
Chicago Historical Society

16. Thomas Beeby et al.,
proposed 1992 Chicago
world's fair, 1984
Chicago Historical Society

1. Recent scholarly discussions that influenced this essay include: John W. Reps, *The Making of Urban America: A History of City Planning in the United States* (Princeton, 1965), 240–262, 497–526; John W. Reps, *Monumental Washington: The Planning and Development of the Capital Center* (Princeton, 1967); Mel Scott, *American City Planning since 1890* (Berkeley, 1969), 47–57; Thomas S. Hines, *Burnham of Chicago: Architect and Planner* (New York, 1974), 139–157; Mario Manieri-Elia, "Toward an 'Imperial City': Daniel H. Burnham and the City Beautiful Movement," in Giorgio Ciucci et al., *The American City: From the Civil War to the New Deal* (Cambridge, Mass., 1979), 1–142; Jon A. Peterson, "The City Beautiful Movement," in Donald A. Krueckeberg, ed., *Introduction to Planning History in the United States* (New Brunswick, N.J., 1983), 40–57; Jonathan Barnett, *The Elusive City* (New York, 1986), 28–29; David Schuyler, *The New Urban Landscape: The Redefinition of City Form in Nineteenth-Century America* (Baltimore, 1986), 180–195.

2. For a discussion of the American Renaissance, see Richard Guy Wilson et al., *The American Renaissance, 1876–1917* [exh. cat., Brooklyn Museum] (New York, 1979), 11–70, 75–109; Robert A.M. Stern, *Pride of Place: Building the American Dream* (Boston and New York, 1986), 306–310.

3. Board of Supervision for Public Buildings and Grounds, *The Group Plan for Public Buildings of the City of Cleveland* (New York, 1903); Werner Hegemann and Elbert Peets, *The American Vitruvius: An Architect's Handbook of Civic Art* (New York, 1922), 139; Scott 1969, 61–63; Hines 1974, 158–173; Geraldine Kiefer, "Back to the Future," *Inland Architect* 30 (November–December 1986), 82–85, 88; Eric Johannesen, "Cleveland's Group Plan," *Inland Architect* 31 (November–December 1987), 30–35.

4. Board of Supervision 1903, n.p.

5. Daniel H. Burnham and Edward H. Bennett, *Report on a Plan for San Francisco* (San Francisco, 1905); Herbert Croly, "The Promised City of San Francisco," *Architectural Record* 19 (June 1906), 425–436; Hines 1974, 174–196; Judd Kahn, *Imperial San Francisco: Practice and Planning in an American City, 1897–1906* (Lincoln, Neb., 1979), 80–102; Joan E. Draper, *Edward H. Bennett: Architect and City Planner, 1874–1954* [exh. cat., Art Institute of Chicago] (Chicago, 1982), 11–13.

6. "Plan of San Francisco's Civic Center," *American City* 7 (July 1912), 13; Hegemann and Peets 1922, 141; Henry Hope Reed, Jr., *The Golden City* (New York, 1959), 92–95, 100–103; Vincent Scully, *American Architecture and Urbanism* (New York, 1969), 140–141; David Gebhard, "Civic Presence in California's Cities: Where and How?" *Architectural Design* 57 (September–October 1987), 74–80; Donlyn Lyndon, "Public Buildings: Symbols Qualified by Experience," in Nathan Glazer and Mark Lilla, eds.,

The Public Face of Architecture: Civic Culture and Public Spaces (New York, 1987), 155–176.

7. Albert Bush-Brown, *Skidmore, Owings, and Merrill: Architecture and Urbanism, 1973–1983* (New York, 1983), 31–33, 64–73.

8. Daniel H. Burnham and Edward H. Bennett, *Plan of Chicago* (Chicago, 1909); Sybil Moholy-Nagy, *Matrix of Man: An Illustrated History of the Urban Environment* (New York, 1968), 238–240; Scully 1969, 140; Harold M. Mayer and Richard C. Wade, *Chicago: Growth of a Metropolis* (Chicago, 1969), 274–282; Carl W. Condit, *Chicago, 1910–29: Building, Planning, and Urban Technology* (Chicago, 1973), 59–85; Hines 1974, 312–345; Draper 1982, 14–25; Robert L. Wrigley, Jr., "The Plan of Chicago," in Krueckeberg 1983, 58–72; Joan E. Draper, "Paris by the Lake: Sources of Burnham's Plan of Chicago," in John Zukowsky, ed., *Chicago Architecture, 1872–1922: Birth of a Metropolis* (Munich, 1987), 107–119.

9. Daniel H. Burnham and Peirce Anderson, "Report on Improvement of Manila," TS, 1905, Avery Library, Columbia University; Daniel H. Burnham, "The Development of Manila," *Western Architect* 9 (January 1906), 7–8; W.E. Parsons, "Manilla, Old and New," *Western Architect* 17 (January 1911), 9–11; Hines 1974, 197–216.

10. "Pasadena City Hall, Pasadena, California," *American Architect* 134 (5 September 1928), 305–309; Draper 1982, 33–34; Ann Scheid, *Pasadena: Crown of the Valley: An Illustrated History* (Northridge, Calif., 1986), 131–153; Gebhard 1987, 74–80.

11. I am indebted to Richard Guy Wilson for suggesting to me the relationship between the Mall in Washington and The Mall in London. Concerning the latter, see Nikolaus Pevsner, *London: The Cities of London and Westminster*, rev. ed. (Middlesex, 1973), 596; Alastair Service, *Edwardian Architecture* (New York, 1977), 166–167; Elizabeth and Michael Darby, "The Nation's Memorial to Victoria," *Country Life* 164 (16 November 1978), 1647–1648, 1650; Gavin Stamp, "London 1900," *Architectural Design* 48 (May–June 1978), 322–323; Alastair Service, *London 1900* (New York, 1979), 243–244.

12. Herbert Baker, *Architecture and Personalities* (London, 1944), 63–87; A.S.G. Butler et al., *The Architecture of Sir Edwin Lutyens* (London, 1950), 28–44, pls. XXV–LXXXIX, figs. 117–218; Christopher Hussey, *The Life of Sir Edwin Lutyens* (London, 1950), 235–358; Robert Grant Irving, *Indian Summer: Lutyens, Baker, and Imperial Delhi* (New Haven, 1981); Gavin Stamp, "New Delhi," in *Lutyens, the Work of the English Architect Sir Edwin Lutyens (1869–1944)* [exh. cat., Arts Council of Great Britain] (London, 1981), 33–43.

13. Quoted in Irving 1981, 84.

14. Quoted in Stamp 1981, 35.

15. H. Allen Brooks, ed., *Prairie School Architecture: Studies from the Western Architect* (New York, 1983), 38–45; Mark L. Peisch, *The Chicago School of Architecture: Early Followers of Sullivan and Wright* (New York, 1964), 105–124; Donald Les-

lie Johnson, *Austrialian Architecture, 1901–1951* (Sydney, 1980), 20–32; Jaquelin Taylor Robertson, "A Fresh Look at the Future of a Capital Idea," *Inland Architect* 25 (January–February 1981), 4–21; "Parliament House, Canberra, Australia," *Progressive Architecture* 62 (March 1981), 88–90; Roger Pegrum, *The Bush Capital: How Australia Chose Canberra as Its Federal City* (Sydney, 1983); David Van Zanten, "Walter Burley Griffin's Design for Canberra, the Capital of Australia," in Zukowsky 1987, 319–343.

16. Spiro Kostof, *The Third Rome, 1870–1950: Traffic and Glory* [exh. cat., University Art Museum, Univeristy of California, Berkeley] (Berkeley, 1973), 74; Manfredo Tafuri and Francesco Dal Co, *Modern Architecture* (New York, 1979), 290–294; Giorgio Ciucci, "Italian Architecture During the Fascist Period: Classicism between Neoclassicism and Rationalism, the Many Souls of the Classical," *Perspecta* 23 (1987), 77–87.

17. Lars Olof Larsson, *Albert Speer: Le Plan de Berlin, 1937–1943* (Paris, 1983); Leon Krier, ed., *Albert Speer: Architecture, 1931–1942* (Brussels, 1985).

18. Le Corbusier, *Oeuvre Complète, 1938–1946* (Zurich, 1946), 132–139.

19. Among the most important recent discussions of Chandigarh are: Le Corbusier, *Oeuvre Complète,* vols. 5–8; Norma Evenson, *Chandigarh* (Berkeley, 1966); Charles Correa, "Chandigarh: The View from Benares"; and Norma Evenson, "Yesterday's City of Tomorrow Today," in *Le Corbusier,* ed. H. Allen Brooks, (Princeton, 1987), 197–202, 241–255.

20. Vincent Scully, *Frank Lloyd Wright* (New York, 1960); Evelyn Morris Radford, *The Bridge and the Building: The Art of Government and the Government of Art,* rev. ed. (New York, 1974); Charles Jencks, *Kings of Infinite Space: Frank Lloyd Wright and Michael Graves* (New York, 1983), 52–55; Stern 1986, 248–249.

21. Henry-Russell Hitchcock, "Frank Lloyd Wright and the Academic Tradition of the Early Eighteen-nineties," *Journal of the Warburg and Courtauld Institutes* 7 (January–June 1944), 46–63.

22. For the 1955 project, see Frank Lloyd Wright, *A Testament* (New York, 1957), 209; and Robert C. Twombly, *Frank Lloyd Wright: His Life and Architecture* (New York, 1979), 325–327, 373–376. For the 1938 project, see Yukio Futagawa, ed., *Frank Lloyd Wright Monograph, 1937–1941* (Tokyo, 1986), 139–143; and Brendan Gill, *Many Masks: A Life of Frank Lloyd Wright* (New York, 1987), 476.

23. Wolf Von Eckardt, *A Place to Live: The Crisis of the Cities* (New York, 1967), 308–316; Charles B. Hosmer, Jr., *Preservation Comes of Age: From Williamsburg to the National Trust, 1926–1949,* 2 vols. (Charlottesville, 1981), I: 626–649.

24. Hegemann and Peets 1922, 140; Scott 1969. Beginning in 1923, a mall-like space was created as Memorial Plaza between Tucker Boulevard and Twentieth Street; see George McCue, *The Building Art in Saint Louis: Two Centuries,* rev. ed. (Saint Louis, 1981), 53.

25. Hosmer 1981, I:626.

26. Henry Raymont, "Lincoln Center Mall to Central Park Is Proposed," *New York Times* (6 December 1966), I:2, 58:5; Henry Raymont, "New Lincoln Center Plan Offers Buildings Rather than a Mall," *New York Times* (22 December 1966), 49:2; Ada Louise Huxtable, "A Planning Happening," *New York Times* (18 December 1966), II: 35, 37; Thomas P. F. Hoving, "No Official Mall Plan," letter to the editor, *New York Times* (12 December 1966), 32:6; Roy R. Neuberger, "Lincoln Center Park Project Opposed," letter to the editor, *New York Times* (23 December 1966), 24:3; William Schuman, "Center No Sponsor of Mall," letter to the editor, *New York Times* (13 January 1967), 22:4; Robert A. Caro, *The Power Broker: Robert Moses and the Fall of New York* (New York, 1974), 1013–1016.

27. Norma Evenson, *Two Brazilian Capitals: Architecture and Urbanism in Rio de Janeiro and Brasilia* (New Haven, 1973), 145–153. While Evenson refers to ancient Egyptian and Roman precedents, she does not mention Washington, D.C., describing the monumental government axis, a grassy mall lined by federal buildings, only as a "traditional Beaux-Arts composition" (p. 147).

28. Sibyl Moholy-Nagy 1969, 157; Martin Filler, "Halicarnassus on the Hudson: The Governor Nelson A. Rockefeller Empire State Plaza, Albany, New York," *Progressive Architecture* 60 (May 1979), 106–109; Samuel E. Bleecker, *The Politics of Architecture: A Perspective on Nelson A. Rockefeller* (New York, 1981), 221; Stern 1986, 323–324.

29. Catherine T. Ingraham, "Land of No Discovery," *Inland Architect* 30 (May–June 1986), 45–53; Luis F. Rueda, ed., *Robert A.M. Stern: Buildings and Projects, 1981–1986* (New York, 1986), 204–205.

30. See, for instance, Roger Scruton, "Public Space and the Classical Vernacular," in Glazer and Lilla 1987, 13–25. Scruton writes: "But it is important to see that the classical vernacular styles which the Romans perfected, and which have lasted until recent times, were, by their good manners, the greatest single reason for the existence in our cities of genuine public space. Everywhere, in Europe and America, the pedestrian confronts Roman architecture, whose forms and details speak a public language that he understands" (p. 18).

J. CARTER BROWN
National Gallery of Art

The Designing of the National Gallery of Art's East Building

When the National Gallery of Art decided to construct a new building, it faced the problem of how to integrate the structure on a Mall characterized by classical architecture. Although the Gallery's East Building does not employ a classical vocabulary, the design nonetheless attains a classic quality that makes it fully compatible with its more traditional neighbors.

In maps prepared after Pierre Charles L'Enfant's design for Washington, one can see that from an early date some sort of building was conceived as anchoring the convergence of the two axes defined by the Mall and Pennsylvania Avenue (pls. VII, XI). The Senate Park Commission Plan of 1901–1902 called for similar development of the site (pls. LXI, LXVIII).

By the 1960s, the National Gallery had become crowded; some of the galleries had been relegated to office space, and the cafeteria was highly inadequate (figs. 1, 2). The latter facility, installed as a government employees' cafeteria, had grown popular with the public, albeit for the food, not its design amenities!

In planning the new building, space was envisioned for two basic functions. One was a center for advanced study, which would bring with it the library and the archives, the curators and the education department, and therefore the administrators. Thus what was needed, really, was an office building, so that the ground floor of John Russell Pope's West Building could be cleared and on the whole

consummated as the great exhibition facility it was intended to be. The second need was more space for temporary exhibitions, as well as for the growing collections in the twentieth-century field. There was an effort to be far-sighted, to think of the centuries hence, knowing that some art not yet created would become part of the national heritage and that a setting more sympathetic than Pope's highly detailed interiors would be needed for displaying such works.

The West Building, however, was an integral part of this project. Some discussions of the design of the East Building have failed to acknowledge that it is not a wholly independent building. I.M. Pei told me that he never would have designed the project as he did if it had been meant as a museum unto itself. It is an addition to an existing facility, in a sense, a pavilion.

The idea of expanding the museum had been envisioned by Andrew Mellon, who held the bargaining leverage of the largest individual gift ever given by any citizen to any government: his collection, an endowment, and the construction of a building. The collection was enough to fill some five of the 130 galleries that he was presenting to the nation, so he knew an addition would not be needed soon. But Andrew Mellon was a man of extraordinary vision. He believed that the East Building's site should be reserved to provide for the possibility of future expansion, and persuaded

1. National Gallery of Art, West Building, eighteenth-century French decorative arts gallery converted into temporary office space, 1974 view
All illustrations: National Gallery of Art

2. National Gallery of Art, West Building, cafeteria, early 1970s view

3. Eggers and Higgins, proposed east and west additions to National Gallery, 1953, aerial view

4. Pietro Belluschi, proposed East Building, 1967, diagrammatic plan of possible space uses

the Congress to reserve the site in the legislation establishing the National Gallery in 1937.

Eggers and Higgins, the successor firm to John Russell Pope, took the initiative in 1953 to demonstrate the value of such an addition and, in so doing, demonstrated effectively the great problems associated with that undertaking (fig. 3). Their proposed addition bore no relation to the central axis of Pope's building. Furthermore, the configuration and size of this scheme made it out of scale. My father gave me a piece of advice at the East Building project's beginning: "Carter, make sure it doesn't end up looking as if the National Gallery had a pup." If we had built the Eggers and Higgins design, that might have been just the result.

So in 1967 the trustees hired Pietro Belluschi to examine the possibilities of such a project. Belluschi was in partial retirement, and it was understood that he would not be a candidate for the eventual commission. Even then an underground tunnel connecting the two buildings was under consideration for moving

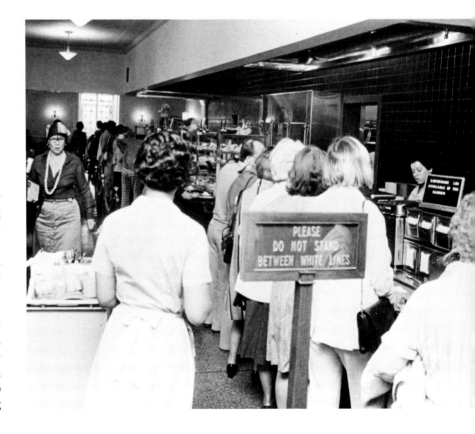

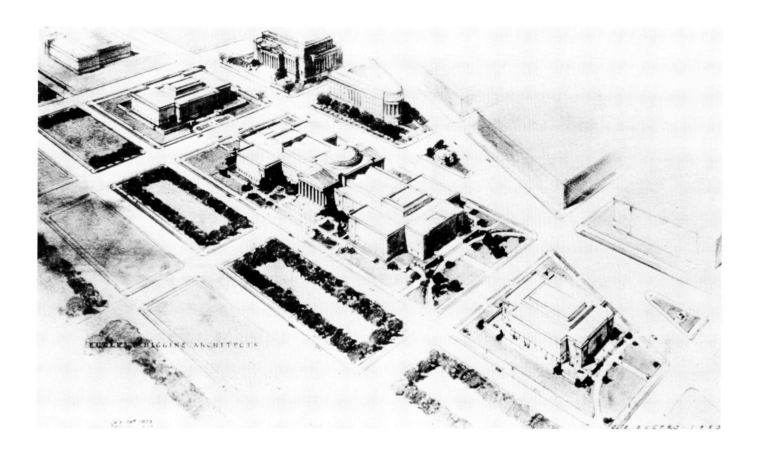

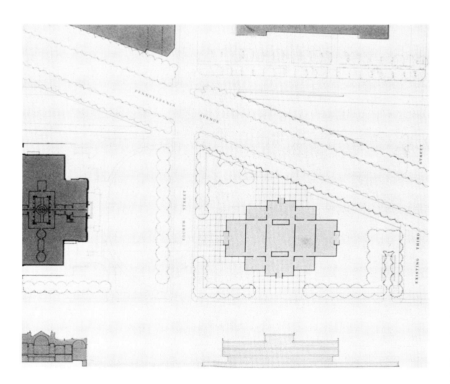

art back and forth in a consistent hygrometric environment, but other problems with this site were immediately manifest. First, a strong axial spine extends east from the original building and meets the adjoining site off center (fig. 4). More space could be attained by filling out the envelope, the area permitted for building on the site; however, just adhering to the setback requirements would have created a very awkward mass. Later, at the outset of his involvement in this project, Pei commented that he could not think of a building in the history of architecture erected on such a trapezoidal plot that was a success.

One possibility explored initially with Belluschi was whether Fourth Street could be closed. We very quickly were assured that it could not be, even though it does not continue immediately north of the site. It does feed into Pennsylvania Avenue, however, and all the traffic engineers and traffic counts we could muster could not change that. In retrospect, leaving Fourth Street open seems absolutely right. There was another option, which never would have passed all the commissions; Bel-

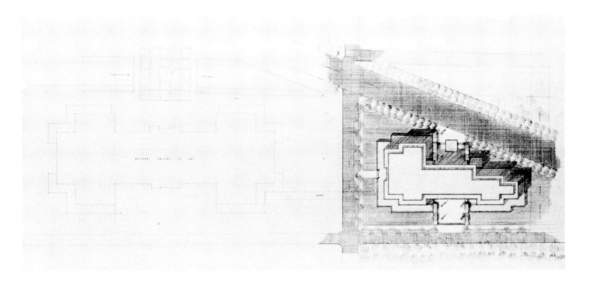

5. Unsolicited proposal for East Building, 1967, site plan

6. Unsolicited proposal for East Building, 1967, south elevation

7. Unsolicited proposal for East Building, 1967, alternative design for south elevation

luschi suggested an air-rights building extending over Fourth Street, since the right-of-way at grade had to remain open.

At about the same time, two proposals arrived over the transom from a California architect who said in effect that he was not sure what we wanted, but that we could work within the footprint two ways (fig. 5). We could have Neiman-Marcus-shopping-center modern (fig. 6), or if the trustees were very conservative, it could be—one might call it—"classical" (fig. 7). The latter perhaps seems more *dernier cri* today, because of postmodernism, though at the time this design recalled the stripped classical work of the 1930s and 1940s. We did not pursue the proposals.

One of the ground rules on which I.M. Pei insisted when he was commissioned to design the project in the following year, 1968, was that the Pope building not be touched. He loved the building, its great interior spaces, and its detailing. He wanted its integrity and form in the green landscape maintained. Pei's early plans even retained the lawn at the east end of the gallery. It was we who asked him to try to develop a visual link at grade, so people would understand that the two buildings were part of the same institution.

Pei was most interested in the project's urban-design implications. I was primarily concerned with how the art would look, and loved small buildings and small spaces that allowed the art to dominate. At Expo '67 in Montreal I had been impressed with Moshe Safdie's Habitat. My favorite museums, even though I work for this one, were the Phillips, the Wallace Collection, the Frick, and other museums in houses, which have a domestic scale and a wonderful sense of humanism to them. As the Senate Park Commission had done in 1901, Pei and I went on a trip around Europe, and I showed him some of my pet museums, including the Poldi-Pezzoli in Milan, and Louisiana, near Copenhagen. The experience was to little avail, because the Mall remained foremost on his mind. The scale of the Mall is its one aspect, I have found from my work on the Commission of Fine Arts, that few people ever fully consider. That scale is huge, and whatever one does there must be done boldly or it will be swallowed up.

Our problem entailed addressing not only the Mall, but also Pennsylvania Avenue. Until the East Building's construction, this space had always "leaked." Pei recognized the situation from the beginning, and in presenting his original plan he had a model made of the whole area. A solution was needed that responded to the cornice heights on the Mall as well as the higher ones along Pennsylvania Avenue. Pei also figured that the only way to enter the new building was opposite the original building's east facade, which had a very handsome door though it had always been closed. Furthermore, the new building would serve two very different kinds of functions: exhibitions and administration. Finally, there was the matter of required setbacks on three sides of the lot, so that there was relatively little space within which to place the building.

The basic design problem can be defined diagrammatically (fig. 8). A sketch made by Pei on an airplane, returning to New York after a meeting with us, reveals his struggle with the east-west axis of Pope's building and other central issues (fig. 9). This sketch is not the final solution of course, but like some old master drawings in which one sees the kernel of another idea, in the upper corner one sees an anticipation of the ultimate design. It is absolutely brilliant. What Pei did, simply by joining two opposite angles, was to produce a ground plan, composed of two classic forms, a right triangle and an isosceles triangle, thereby providing the footprints for the study center and office part (the right triangle) and for the exhibition part (the isosceles) (fig. 10).

8. Diagram of East Building site showing required setback lines from Pennsylvania Avenue and the Mall

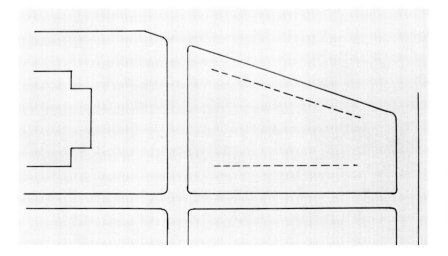

But the problems were far from being solved. In order to respond to the majority of the space on the site lying to the south of the West Building's axis, Pei introduced a third triangle, joining the other two. It constitutes the roof of a major circulation space, and around it he gave us the "house museums" that we had requested in the three parallelogram-shaped towers (fig. 11). The resulting obtuse angles allow wonderful spaces in which to show art. In some ways they are better than right angles, because the pictures speak into the room. But a problem with this geometry is that to gain the open, obtuse angles, it seemed one had to have closed acute ones, which would have yielded very narrow spaces where the walls meet. What on earth, I asked Pei, are you going to do with them? The solution was to cut off the points (fig. 12). That gave the building obtuse angles everywhere—for galleries, stairs, and functions such as air conditioning. It yielded hexagons, each one identical, as forms to be adjoined vertically or horizontally to provide a variety of configurations.

In the research facility, the Center for Advanced Study in the Visual Arts, we wanted to bring a large amount of natural light into the middle of the area, and this became the germ of the idea of the reading room, which I find one of the wonderful spaces in the United States. It draws from the tradition of the great reading rooms in Europe. Providing sufficient floor space was achieved simply by making the height between each level relatively small, which is desirable for office space anyway (fig. 13). The solution includes open-chase "computer floors" with space for future wiring, and innovative concrete ceilings with air-delivery systems integrated with the light fixtures for maximum flexibility in moving partition walls. I knew that staff would change and grow over time, and we wanted to integrate the Center for Advanced Study with the spaces for other scholars, altering specific configurations as needs warranted.

Three towers accommodate varied ceiling heights for different kinds of gallery spaces. To my mind, the most dramatically deft of the many architectural solutions the overall design offers is the way in which the three towers respond precisely to the east-west axis of the Pope building, even though the mass in its entirety is not centered on that axis (fig. 14).

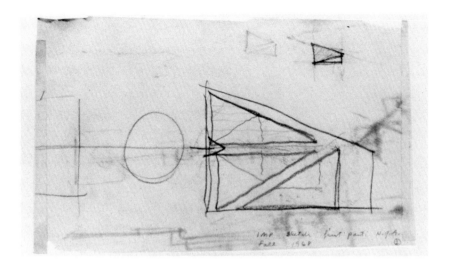

9. I.M. Pei, National Gallery of Art East Building (1971–1978), early conceptual sketches, 1968

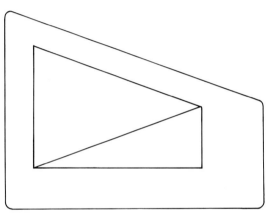

10. Diagram showing basis Pei employed for developing ground plan of East Building, with trapezoidal perimeter suggested by setback lines divided into two triangles

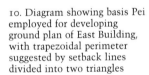

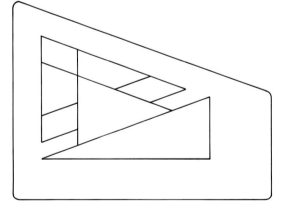

11. Diagram of East Building plan showing the two triangular segments joined by large triangular roof

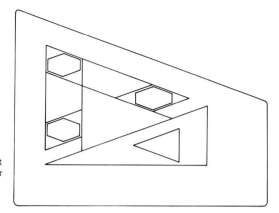

12. Diagram of East Building plan showing hexagonal gallery spaces created in the three tower areas

13. I.M. Pei and Partners, East Building, model showing floor levels in exhibition and administrative-study center areas, 1969

14. East Building, ground floor plan showing alignment with east-west axis of West Building

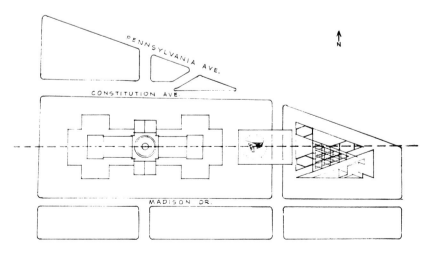

Numerous problems persisted in resolving the museum interior, particularly the great entry hall. Pei said that designing a triangular space was a challenge he had never tackled before. Such spaces, he pointed out, appear vertical at one end and horizontal at the other and never appear the same from any two vantage points. Paul Stevenson Oles, a draftsman in Boston, made renderings to suggest what it would be like. After exhaustive study, the great triangular space acquired the necessary refinements. A whole series of studies was made as to how one could have circulation up an escalator alongside one wall, how one could have good views out to the Mall, and how one could have some sense of transparency (figs. 15, 16). To achieve the necessary amount of unsupported roof, a reinforced concrete truss, even with skylights between the modules, would have appeared so muscular and three-dimensional that I was afraid the results would overwhelm whatever art was displayed in the space.

Pei's breakthrough was creating a glazed space frame (fig. 17). The nodes were connected so that there could be a clear-span over this extraordinary space. The tetrahedrons that result from this essentially triangular geometry are glazed on their sloping sides—to my knowledge, a unique solution at that time. I know that space frames hold up bubble skylights or other solutions in the horizontal plane, but here they become integral, sculptural forms. The leitmotif of triangles, based on L'Enfant's geometry of the intersection of Pennsylvania Avenue with the Mall, is found not only in the space frame overhead, where they become tetrahedral forms, but in the great reinforced concrete coffered trusses, in the shape of the marble floor slabs, and even in the configuration of the elevators.

The glass roof still presented a problem from a curatorial point of view, in that too much light would cause difficulties associated with conserving works of art; and it presented the even greater problem of visitors' eyes adjusting to lower light levels once they entered the other exhibition spaces. How could the space be darkened? Pei refused to put in gray glass, which he said would make it always seem inside like a cloudy day. And so he came up with an idea that was absolutely brilliant, and for once not expensive: opaque slats, such as those found in conservatories without glass

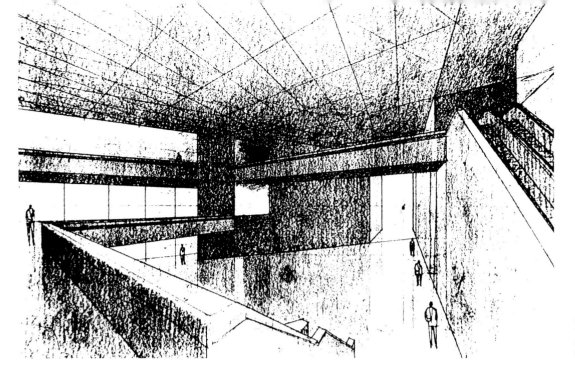

15. East Building, preliminary design showing interior court with solid concrete ceiling, rendering by Paul Stevenson Oles, 1971

16. East Building, preliminary design showing interior court with combination of skylights and areas of solid concrete ceiling, rendering by Paul Stevenson Oles, 1969

that reduce the direct light reaching the plants. Pei said that as long as some real sky were visible, opaque and transparent areas could alternate. But in order to avoid a too-insistent pattern, like lattice, the slats are tubular and made of brushed chrome, so the light can slip around a smooth surface (fig. 18).

The result works marvelously. The transparent ceiling allows one to see the towers extending through the roof, with the result that, paradoxically, the view to the sky brings the scale down. Because the sky is infinite, one then looks for something else to give scale, and the trees provide the needed element. While the glass roof has given the interior a play of light that makes the building so rewarding at all times of the day, it also has allowed us to grow trees, which help create a quasi-parklike extension to the Mall. This great concourse mediates between interior and exterior spaces,

17. East Building, exterior detail of glazed space frame spanning interior court, with tubular slats to reduce intensity of natural illumination

18. East Building, interior view of glazed space frame

suggesting an agora or even a Mediterranean hill town square—a space with a sense of nature. Functionally, the arrangement allows visitors to enter, orient themselves, and decide which part of the building they wish to see.

The stonework was very carefully detailed. For elements such as the escalator in the main space, Pei was able to imbue the marble with a sense of sculpture, even though it is all, actually, veneer. There is circulation of many different kinds. Pei hid the elevators so that people would be motivated to walk the grand stairs. Within the towers are circular stairs. The one detail from the Poldi-Pezzoli that captured Pei's eye was the staircase. His is a free adaptation, but it begins to convey a sense of domestic architecture (fig. 19).

The Commission of Fine Arts granted their approval of the design originally proposed (fig. 20). But the chairman, who was then William Walton, wrote a letter saying that, as a minority opinion, he still was uncomfortable with the south facade. I must confess that the original scheme for this elevation was marginal; it risked looking somewhat like an overgrown motel. Pei had insisted that if offices were to face the Mall, which is such a symbolic place, the usual office clutter could not be visible at night. He wanted a kind of Oriental inscrutability, a screen. And to his credit, he was not satisfied with commission approval by majority vote. He wanted total unanimity, and opted to design a new facade.

Pei's solution on this second round was splendid (fig. 21). The curtain wall defines circulation spaces, so that no offices can be seen. The wall is cantilevered to increase interior space, but basically the window wall is angled back to correspond to the trapezoid's governing geometry and is visually anchored by a bold, horizontal course of reinforced concrete near the top.

One final matter remained to be addressed: space for a new cafeteria and for some of those functions that provide the infrastructure of a museum. These functions were accommodated in the concourse, actually a third building roofed by the plaza, which connected the two main buildings underground at two levels. The structure's lower level provided workshops, a television studio, and parking. Pei placed the garage entry ramp, which also leads to a loading dock, in Pope's building, so

that this potentially awkward feature does not mitigate the pristine, sculptural qualities of his addition. Above the parking lies a public concourse, on a bent axis, with visitors coming from the older building and the adjacent cafeteria entering a long, low tunnel (fig. 22). On reaching the East Building, the space explodes. One can look up and see the two bridges

19. East Building, one of three circular staircases connecting levels of tower galleries

20. East Building, preliminary
design, 1969, model showing
grilled window treatment on
south elevation

21. East Building, south
elevation showing cantilevered window wall

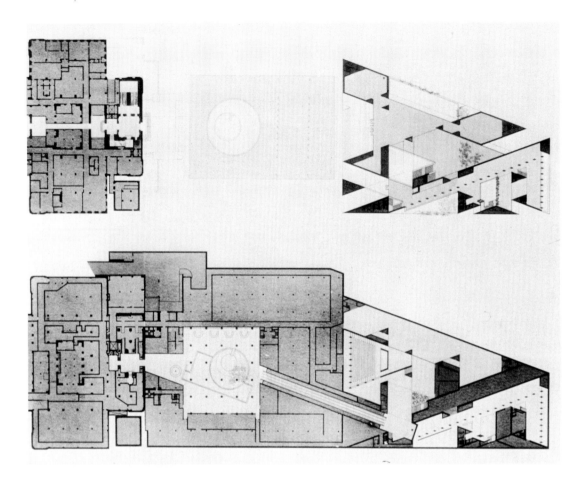

22. East Building, penultimate design of floor plans at ground and subterranean concourse levels

23. East Building, Cascade Café, detail showing tetrahedral skylights

24. East Building, special exhibition of *European Terra Cottas from the Arthur M. Sackler Collection*, 1980, entry view

25. East Building, top floor of tower gallery, showing adjustable laylight ceiling

echoing each other, and the skylight. Outside, the structure's roof forms the plaza, a carpet of stone, achieving a sense of continuity to the two buildings.

Pei called the plaza in its final form only an eighty-percent solution, but I think it works. The tetrahedrons that appear to have been scattered like crystals across the space are, in a sense, leitmotif precursors of the experience one will have of the great space frame inside. They are also functional, bringing light to the concourse and cafeteria below (fig. 23). The waterfall is, in fact, yet another tetrahedron, but a "negative" one — turned upside down. It is faced with rough granite on one side; against it water cascades, bringing light and activity to that key underground space. After the Lincoln Memorial, perhaps more film has been expended there than at any site in Washington, to photograph friends and family in front of this *chadar*. It is a lively place, with lots

of daylight entering halfway between the two buildings so that the effect is not at all that of a subway.

As for the exhibition spaces, we insisted that the museum staff have control as needs changed. There could not be a lot of daylight in them. We wanted variety, even flexibility in ceiling heights. We would need intimate spaces, say, for a show of Persian miniatures or small scale-terra cottas (fig. 24). Therefore, even in the few galleries with natural light, we asked for adjustable ceiling heights (fig. 25). That is not a cheap wish, but it has given us an extraordinary instrument which permits, for example, recreating the Spoleto installation of David Smith's *Voltri* series when the ceiling is at its full height of over thirty feet (fig. 26).

The East Building contains much more exhibition space than is generally realized. It is, for example, a larger museum than the Whit-

ney in this respect. The first impression may be that the whole building is consumed by a central space that is wasteful: big, empty, and of no practical value. The space actually serves a variety of purposes. Primarily this grand public space welcomes visitors to the East Building, as the rotunda does in the West Building. At busy times, it is invaluable in accommodating great numbers of people waiting to see a show. It also has been enormously useful as a place to hold gatherings and celebrations, particularly to thank lenders and to try to make friends who can help an institution that receives no government money for art acquisition and must rely heavily on the private sector for support of its exibition program. We even have found ways of displaying art in the space, though this must be done with great care. Devices are needed to bring the scale down. Nature can assist in many ways to make a kind of sculpture garden out of the space, emphasizing its interaction with the Mall (fig. 27).

The interior spaces are highly varied, but the external form is very powerful in several respects, including the way it relates to the urban context. The building anchors the Mall end of Pennsylvania Avenue, which no longer terminates with a whimper. The tops of the towers align exactly with the cornice heights along that avenue and read as strong forms; the horizontal connectors relate to the Mall buildings and bespeak the lower heights inside. The use of visible concrete as lintels makes the marble veneer convincing. Marble blocks imply compression: when they are visually supported by other blocks beneath, we feel viscerally that it is right, even if those supposed "blocks" are very thin. When it comes to spans, however, something has to seem to be holding the marble up. This Pei invariably does in the East Building by providing reinforced concrete lintels.

I.M. Pei's early experiences are expressed in the East Building. He grew up in China. I have seen the house in Suchow in which he was raised, and think he is much more influenced than he recognizes by concepts of indoor-outdoor interplay, typical of a Ming house and its interior garden. Furthermore, when Pei was at Harvard, he received a fellowship for travel in Europe, and he spent it in France. I also believe that the East Building feels right because it reflects Pei's formative experiences

26. East Building, tower gallery, showing special installation of David Smith's *Voltri* sculpture, with ceiling height at more than thirty feet, 1978

27. East Building, interior court, detail of landscaping

28. Aerial view of National Gallery, West and East buildings, looking east with Capitol in background, 1980

of French cathedrals. When you think of it, there are the twin towers on the west facade, with an entrance porch, or exonarthex, leading to a low entrance space (that traditionally supported a choir loft), and then opening up into a great central nave whose roof utilizes the most advanced technology of the day. As the site is not rectangular, the analogy must end, and yet from the outside, there is the third tower, to the east, that traditionally would have marked the transept crossing (fig. 28).

The East Building uses the same marble from the same quarry as the Pope building; it observes the Pope building's axis and relates to its eastern entrance; it respects the Mall's geometry and its neighbors' heights. I.M. Pei's building may not, technically, be classical. But in a recent poll of its membership by the American Institute of Architects, the East Building was voted one of the ten most architecturally admired buildings in America of all time. Classical? No. A classic? Some of us think so.

EDITOR'S NOTE

Much has been written about the National Gallery of Art's East Building since its inception. An extensive list of sources on the building is contained in James Carlton Starbuck, *Pei's East Building Addition to the National Gallery of Art*, Architecture Series: Bibliography A–123 (Monticello, Ill., 1979).

Additional articles include:

J. Carter Brown, "A Step-by-Step Guide to Designing a New Arty Neighbor for the Mall," *Washington Post, Potomac Magazine*, 16 May 1971, 10–13, 62.

"Pei Addition to Mall," *Architectural Forum* 134 (June 1971), 20–21.

"National Gallery of Art de Washington va bientôt s'agrandir," *Gazette des Beaux Arts* s6 78 (July–September 1971), supp. 8.

Michael Webb, "Purity and Logic of the National Gallery Extension," *Museum News* 50 (September 1971), 10–12.

"National Gallery of Art: Acquisitions, Exhibits, New Addition," *Art Journal* 31 (fall 1971), 81.

William Martin, "The National Gallery of Art, Washington – The Founding Benefactors," *Connoisseur* 178 (December 1971), 248.

J. Carter Brown, "What Is to Become of the National Gallery of Art?" *Connoisseur* 178 (December 1971), 259–262.

Anthony Betts and Joseph Welsh, "Grouted Anchors Solve Hydrostatic Uplift Problems," *Foundation Facts* 8:1 (1972), 3–6.

J. Carter Brown, "The Building Starts with a Programme – But Where Does the Programme End?" *Museum* 26:3–4 (1974), 277–279.

Paul Richard, "The Mellon Mark: 'Dignity, Permanence,'" and Phil Casey, "Monuments and a Man of Marble," *Washington Post*, 14 February 1975, B1, B3.

"Steel Trusses Make Three Galleries One," *Electrical News Record* 194 (13 March 1975), 22–23.

"I. M. Pei and Partners," *Architecture and Urbanism* 61 (January 1976), 110–113.

"National Gallery: Trapezoid Troubles," *Art in America* 64 (January–February 1976), 148.

"The Impossible May Take a Little Longer," *Rambusch Reports* 10 (February 1976).

"Anbau National Gallery, Washington," *Baumeister* 73 (April 1976), 306–307.

Wolf Von Eckardt, "Space, Time, and Architecture," *Washington Post*, 27 June 1976, E1, E3.

Marian Burros and William Rice, "Munchtime on the Mall: Meals and Mounuments," *Washington Post*, 22 July 1976, F8.

Benjamin Forgey, "Mellons, Money, and a National Gallery," *Washington Star*, 24 December 1976, C1–C2.

Grace Glueck, "Moving In on the Met," *New York Times Magazine*, 27 February 1977, 20–23.

Ada Louise Huxtable, "A Spectacular Museum Goes Up in Washington," *New York Times*, 22 May 1977, D1, D29–D30.

Paul Richard, "A New Angle on the Mall," *Washington Post*, 18 December 1977, L1, L12.

"Letters to the Editor," *Washington Post*, 3 April 1978, A17.

Wolf Von Eckardt, "The Gallery's Soaring Symphony of Light and Marble," *Washington Post*, 7 May 1978, L1, L3.

Jo Ann Lewis, "The National Gallery of Art East Building," *Washington Post Magazine*, 21 May 1978, 20–27.

Phyllis Richman, "National Gallery Buffet and Concourse Café," *Washington Post Magazine*, 21 May 1978, 68–69.

Grace Glueck, "Washington's Bold New Showcase for Modern Art," *New York Times*, 28 May 1978, D1, D25.

Paul Goldberger, "New Washington Gallery a Palace," *New York Times*, 30 May 1978, C3.

"Pope and Pei," *Skyline* 3 (1 June 1978), 6.

Diana Loercher, "National Gallery's Soaring Showcase," *Christian Science Monitor*, 9 June 1978, 16–17.

Carleton Jones, "Washington's New Geometric Fantasy: A Dissenting View," *Baltimore Sunday Sun*, 18 June 1978, K1–K2.

Ada Louise Huxtable, "Washington Elitism vs. Paris Populism," *New York Times*, 18 June 1978, D1, D27.

"Pei's Triangular Solution for a New Museum," *Industrial Design* 25 (July 1978), 18.

"National Gallery of Art: A Triumphant New Landmark on the Washington Architectural Scene," *Interior Design* 49 (July 1978), 42–43.

Christian Laine, "Architecture as Self Image: Two National Galleries of Art," *New Art Examiner* 10 (July 1978), 1, 10.

Franz Schulze, "The East Building: Trapezoid Triumphant," *Art in America* 66 (July–August 1978), 55–63.

"Washington Goes Wild about Pei's Triangles," *Design* 356 (August 1978), 19.

J. Jodidio and G. Neret, "Un Temple Americain consacré à l'art," *Connaissance des Arts* 319 (September 1978), 54–63.

Paul Richard, "This Bomb That Is Art," *Washington Post*, 20 November 1978, D15.

Lazlo Glozer, "Der Neue Monumentalismus," *Süddeutsche Zeitung* 290 (16–17 December 1978), 91–92.

Peter Blake, "A Lot of People Think This Is a Beautiful City," *Washingtonian* 14 (December 1978), 144–151.

N. Calavita, "L'East Building della National Gallery of Art di Washington: Un Nuovo Tempio dell'arte?" *Casabella* 43 (January 1979), 34–37.

W. Oechslin, "Pei's Neubau der National Gallery in Washington," *Werk* 66 (January 1979), 33–36.

Benjamin Forgey, "Design Process of East Building Seen in Sketches," *Washington Star*, 6 January 1979, C2.

"I.M. Pei: East Building of the National Gallery of Art, Washington, D.C., U.S.A.," *Architecture and Urbanism* 103 (April 1979), 29–44.

Antoine Blanchette, "Washington: L'Agrandissement du Musée National des Etats-Unis," *Vie des Arts* 23 (spring 1979), 78–79.

David W. Scott, "The New Building of the National Gallery of Art, Washington, D.C.," *Museum* 31:2 (1979), 110–115.

Peter Blake, "Devil's Advocate and the Diplomat," *AIA Journal* 68 (June 1979), 76–77.

Andrea O. Dean, "Conversations: I.M. Pei," *AIA Journal* 68 (June 1979), 60–67.

Benjamin Forgey, "The Gallery's Year: Triumph and Flaws," *Washington Star*, 3 June 1979, B1–B2.

Patsy Rogers, "Talking with I.M. Pei," *Washington Star, Homelife*, 29 June 1979, 24–27.

Robert Bates, "I.M. Pei Speaks Out for Concrete," *Concrete International* 1 (August 1979), 25–27.

James Mann, "An Adventure in Architectural Concrete," *Concrete International* 1 (August 1979), 18–24.

"Extension de la National Gallery, Washington, U.S.A.," *Techniques et Architecture* 326 (September 1979), 56–57.

"Sulla National Gallery di Pei . . .," *Architettura: Cronache e Storia* 25 (November 1979), 648–649.

"National Gallery Public Cafeteria: A Fine Blending of High Art and Design," *Kitchen Planning* 17 (January–February 1980), 6–15.

"National Gallery of Art East Building . . . Washington, D.C./Case Study," *Building Operating Management* 27:4 (April 1980), 106–107.

Wolf Von Eckardt, "Half of a Good Thing," *Washington Post*, 5 April 1980, E1–E2.

Benedetto Gravagnuolo, "L'East-Building della National Gallery of Art di Washington," *Museologia* 7 (January–June 1980), 90–96.

"Art Gallery Geometry Poses Installation Problems," *Electrical Construction and Maintenance* 79 (June 1980), 114, 116.

Lori Simmons Zelenko, "What Is the National Gallery of Art Doing Today, and What Are Its Plans for the Future?" *American Artist* 45 (May 1981), 10, 79, 84–85.

Jean Houdart, "Washington Capitale Culturelle," *Le Monde* (27–28 December 1981), x.

Nancy Love, "Museums on the Mall," *Signature* 17 (March 1982), 52–55, 127–128.

Peter Blake, "Best Building," *WETA* magazine 2:9 (June 1989), 8–9.

Carter Wiseman, "The East Building of the National Gallery (1968–78): The Power of Art, Taste, and Money," in *I.M. Pei: A Profile in American Architecture* (New York, 1990), 155–183.

DANIEL URBAN KILEY
Office of Dan Kiley

A Critical Look at the McMillan Plan

Washington is our sacred precinct; the Washington Monument the lodgepole, the *axis mundi*, which centers our universe. A center such as this should draw us magnetically and majestically toward itself while relating us outwardly to what is beyond. Pierre L'Enfant's plan of 1791 fulfills such an expectation. It is a powerful vision of Washington and one befitting a nation's capital (pls. IV–XIV). The L'Enfant design emerged from a basic understanding of the broad features of the land surrounding the city and an attempt to relate the city to the region. Foremost in the scheme was the recognition of the city's location on the banks of the Potomac River. L'Enfant's plan developed a fundamental dynamic between the city and the river — a design of both land and water (fig. 1; pls. LI, LII).

The Senate Park Commission of 1901–1902 failed to appreciate the power and significance of L'Enfant's original scheme (pls. LXIV–LXVII). Its most controversial contribution was to create the Tidal Basin and the Lincoln Memorial with its reflecting pool. The result was to sever the city from the river, and from its connection with the region.

There exists no grander axis than that between the Capitol and the Washington Monument. The McMillan Plan's continuation of the Mall axis beyond the monument was redundant and inappropriate (fig. 2). Originally the Potomac River lapped the lawn of the monument. Constitution Avenue, with the water along its edge, was a grand and splendid entry into the city, leading directly to the Tiber Canal. The canal, with its marketplace, issued into the city along the base of the Ellipse, from Seventeenth Street to Fourteenth Street, continuing the line of Constitution Avenue. From the White House one looked over a broad expanse of river to the hinterland beyond; from the Capitol the vista was of the river in the foreground and the hills of Virginia in the background. L'Enfant's vision of a Venice-like Washington, bequeathed to the city by nature and extending outward to the region, was defeated and replaced by a closed, insular design. The Senate Park Commission, as Edmund Bacon rightfully states in his *Design of Cities*, "desired a contained, self-completing, and comfortably inward-looking idea, rather than a dynamic interrelationship with the region." [1]

It would be most ideal, although impracticable, to restore Washington to L'Enfant's original plan. Yet perhaps it would be possible to restore the bay and make of the Lincoln Memorial an island connected to the land by the Memorial Bridge and Twenty-third Street (fig. 3). Along Constitution Avenue the perpendicular streets, terminating the orthogonal grid, could end in a series of docks and ramps lined with cafés (fig. 4). Recreating the Tiber Canal also would provide a historic recall of early Washington. I would suggest further that Constitution Avenue cross the Potomac via the Roosevelt Island connection

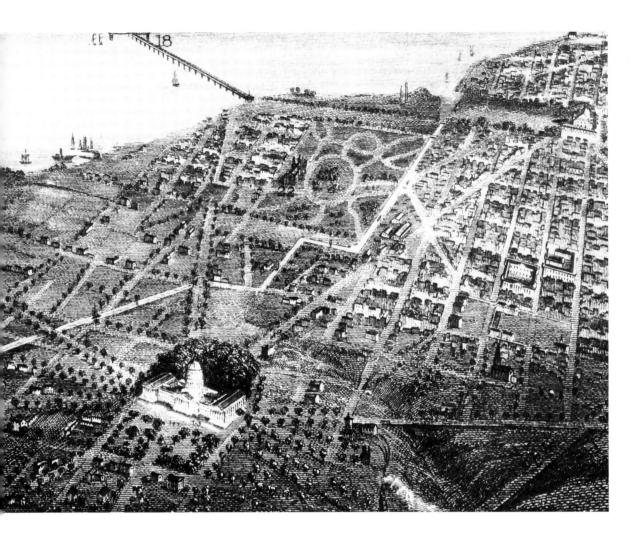

1. *Washington, D.C., and Its Vicinity*, lithograph by W. Ridgway, 1862, after drawing by J. Wells, looking southwest, detail
Library of Congress

2. Current United States Geological Survey map of Washington showing McMillan Plan's continuation of Mall axis to the west of Washington Monument

3. Modified United States Geological Survey map of Washington showing the restoration of Potomac Bay and Lincoln Memorial on an island connected by Memorial Bridge and bridge from Twenty-third Street

4. Lori Hey, proposed treatment of Potomac Bay area, prepared in author's studio, Graduate School of Design, Harvard University, 1987. Washington Monument shown on a rectangular island, Lincoln Memorial on a promontory, and orthogonal street pattern terminating at cafés and boat docks

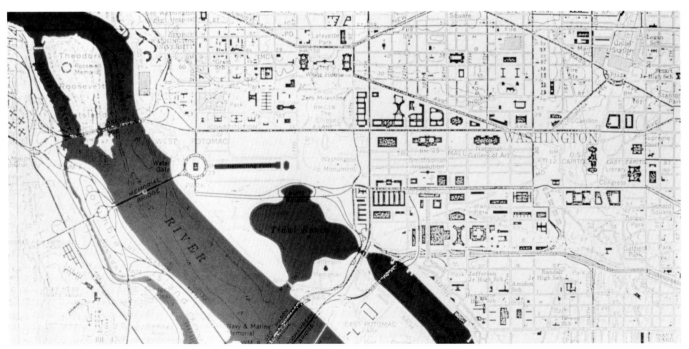

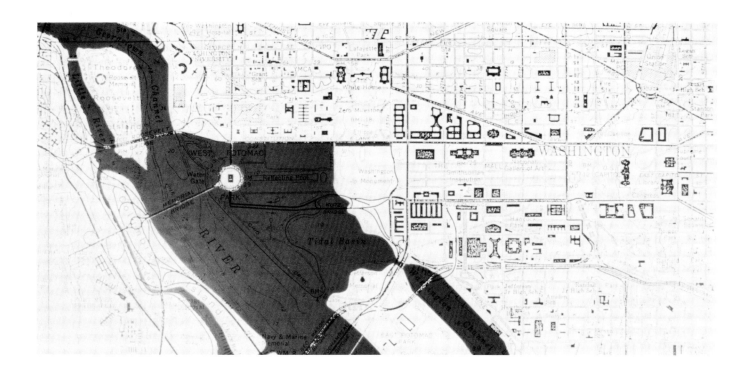

and issue directly into the city. The Memorial Bridge approach, making of the Lincoln Memorial a traffic circle, was ill-conceived.

The Senate Park Commission's greatest achievement was to restore the Mall from Andrew Jackson Downing's incomprehensible forest of wiggly paths to an approximation of L'Enfant's original plan (pls. XXVIII, LVI, LVII).

Yet I should like to recommend several changes in the ground disposition of the Mall with a view to strengthening the structure of the Mall and humanizing it.

The central opening of the Mall is too wide in relation to its sides, especially given the relatively open spacing of the oaks and elms along its sides. By adding a row of trees ad-

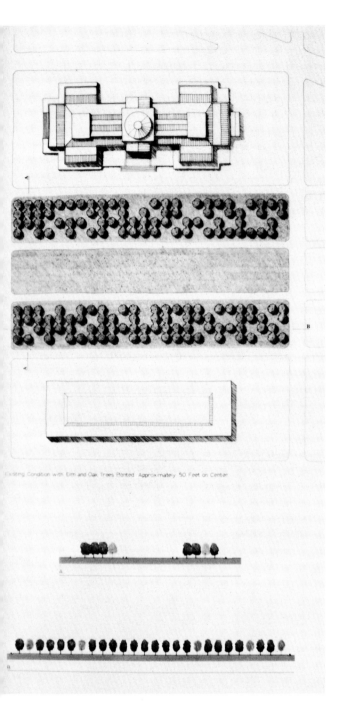

Existing Condition with Elm and Oak Trees Planted Approximately 50 Feet on Center

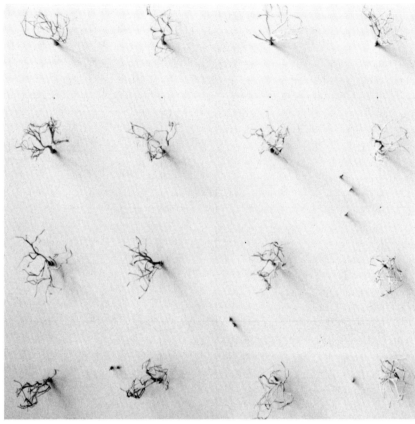

significantly strengthen the Mall (figs. 8–10). Although the Senate Park Commission spent three months abroad studying the avenues and malls of Europe, especially the Tuileries Gardens in Paris, they seemed to have missed the source of their power. Before the commission was established, Frederick Law Olmsted, Sr. had exclaimed that the Tuileries was the most beautiful space he had ever experienced. The horsechestnut trees of the Tuileries are spaced twelve feet on center (fig. 11)! In 1967, as a consultant to Skidmore, Owings, and Merrill, I sought to correct the spacing of the trees on the Mall by recommending that they be planted twenty-five feet on center. Ideally, I now think they should be planted twelve feet six inches on center. The heavier planting would give density to the sides and more force to the central opening. It also would diminish the effect of the haphazard arrangement of buildings along the Mall. (Elbert Peets' fear of a series of disorganized and unrelated structures, expressed in his *Civic Art*, apparently

5. Sectional plan and elevations of Mall in its current state, showing trees spaced fifty feet on center

6. Model of existing arrangement of trees on Mall showing weak effect of spacing fifty feet on center

jacent to the central space on both sides, thereby narrowing the opening, a much stronger thrust toward the Capitol would be achieved. As it is, the Mall is divided into thirds without dominance in the center.

In general, the wide spacing of the trees, fifty feet on center, renders the Mall weak and inconclusive (figs. 5–7). Heavier planting would

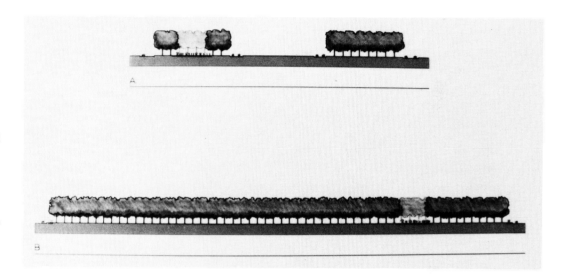

7. Model of existing arrangement of trees on Mall showing scattered effect of elms and oaks spaced fifty feet on center

8. Sectional elevations of Mall showing effect of proposed tree spacing twenty-five feet on center with an added row of trees on either side of Mall's open center

9. Sectional plan of Mall, with proposed increased tree density and addition of a row of trees to each side of Mall's open center

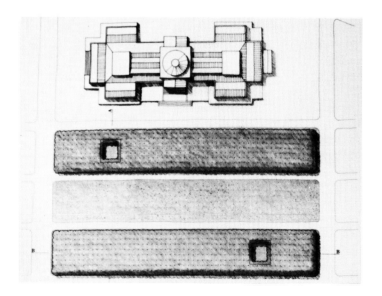

was justified, at least on the south side of the present Mall, despite the Senate Park Commission's assurance that the buildings would "hang together."[2]

The Mall needs to be humanized and diversified, I believe, with more activities and facilities to make it a livelier and more comfortable place for visitors. The millions of people who stroll along the Mall each year need places to sit and rest, in and out of the sun; they need places where they may have a drink or a snack, and they need rest rooms. As in the Tuileries, there could be occasional open spaces within the Mall's rows of trees to accommodate a diversity of uses, such as play areas, water or sculpture gardens, and concessions (fig. 12). The Mall also needs a convenient, pleasant transportation system — along the lines of the Elephant Train in Florida's

10. Model showing effect of proposed dense tree spacing twenty-five feet on center on Mall

11. View of Tuileries Gardens, Paris, with horsechestnut trees spaced twelve feet on center and open spaces that provide areas for snack bars, cafés, and gardens
Author photograph

Fairchild Gardens — to help the weary and those with children. Such facilities can be incorporated without destroying the classic dignity and continuity of the Mall.

In addition, I should like to make the following recommendations. First, I believe that the Capitol ought to be linked to the Mall in a stronger way. L'Enfant's suggestion of a cas-

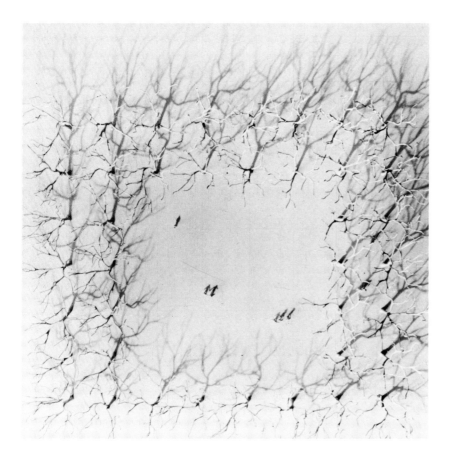

12. Model of proposed arrangement of trees on Mall, showing open areas that could be used for a variety of purposes to diversify activities on the Mall

cade with broad steps was a good one. The Capitol grounds themselves also could be improved with better planting—the present planting is confused (too many species), lacks unity, and does not have the classic arrangements to be in keeping with the Capitol. Second, at the Fourteenth Street crossing, I believe that the Mall should terminate with a raised architectural terrace overlooking the Washington Monument grounds. Pedestrian overpasses could link this terrace with the grounds of the monument. It would be better, of course, to lower Fourteenth Street to accommodate a Mall-level pedestrian crossing. Finally, I suggest that the monument grounds be cleared of trees and that the hill be shaped to form a cone, appropriately scaled to the grandeur of the monument. A grassy lawn would then slope to meet the waters of the bay.

NOTES

1. Edmund M. Bacon, *Design of Cities* (New York and London, 1976), 223.

2. Werner Hegemann and Elbert Peets, *The American Vitruvius: An Architect's Handbook of Civic Art* (New York, 1922; reprint 1972), 289.

Editor's Note:
Daniel Kiley's work on federal projects on or near the Mall has been extensive. It includes: the Pennsylvania Avenue redevelopment plan (1964), the Skidmore, Owings, and Merrill plan for the Mall (1965), the Tenth Street Overlook (1969), the Victorian garden for the Smithsonian Institution (1976, destroyed), and the National Gallery of Art, East Building (1978). For further reading see:

President's Council on Pennsylvania Avenue, *Pennsylvania Avenue* (Washington, 1964).

"Pennsylvania Avenue," *Architectural Forum* 121 (July 1964), 65–75.

Frederick Gutheim, *The Grand Design* [exh. cat., Library of Congress] (Washington, 1967).

"Landscape Design: Works of Dan Kiley," *Process Architecture* 33 (1982), 55, 80–83, 101–105.

The Work of Dan Kiley: A Dialogue on Design Theory, Proceedings of the First Annual Symposium on Landscape Architecture, University of Virginia School of Architecture (Charlottesville, 1983).

Concerning the student projects for the Mall cited in the article, see "Redesign of the Washington Mall," *GSD News* (Graduate School of Design, Harvard University), May-June 1987, 4–5.

Issues Relative to the Mall in Designing the National Air and Space Museum

As with any commission, this project, begun in 1964, presented certain unique challenges. First, it was necessary that so prominent a building would respond sensitively to the physical and symbolic constraints of the site. In addition, the building would accommodate a wide range of exhibits and at the same time serve as host to vast numbers of visitors. The budget allocated was $40 million.

Central to our objectives was the desire for continuity with the rest of the Mall. Harmony with the surrounding buildings, their monumental scale and their geometry of large, bold, yet simple shapes, was essential (fig. 1; pls. CXIX, CXX). The site, on the south side of the Mall between Fourth and Seventh streets, was the last major space remaining for a building on the Mall, as stipulated by the McMillan Plan and its successors.

We recognized that the museum's strongest relationship would be with the National Gallery of Art directly across the Mall and that a symmetrical relationship with the National Gallery was necessary. Thus we took care to match the buildings' center lines and conducted studies of the two buildings as a framing element for the Capitol. The National Gallery also influenced the geometry and exterior materials of our building. Furthermore, we had to consider the strong form of the Hirshhorn Museum to the west; an open site to the east, similar to that occupied by the National Gallery's East Building; and a range of federal office buildings to the south along Independence Avenue.

The site was very long and narrow: about twelve hundred feet east to west and only three hundred feet north to south (fig. 2). In addition, it was required that the building be set back some forty feet from Independence Avenue to the south, and it could project no farther north than the Hirshhorn Museum. The National Capital Planning Commission also stipulated a height limit of eighty-three feet.

The National Air and Space Museum organization was headed by Michael Collins, the former astronaut, and much of the museum's success is a result of his vision and the dedication of his staff members. We worked closely with them to determine what sort of place the museum should be. We agreed that the building should be a place of excitement (figs. 3, 4). It should celebrate an age that is still young, an age that we see not just as historians but as participants. We wanted a museum that would say as much about the present and the future as it would about the past. It would inspire as well as educate.

Members of the museum staff gave us a number of functional requirements as well. First, they wanted the maximum volume of space in order to house as many of their important air and space vehicles as possible. They also wanted an environment that would accommodate a variety of exhibits, from tiny models to large relics (figs. 5, 6). To their credit,

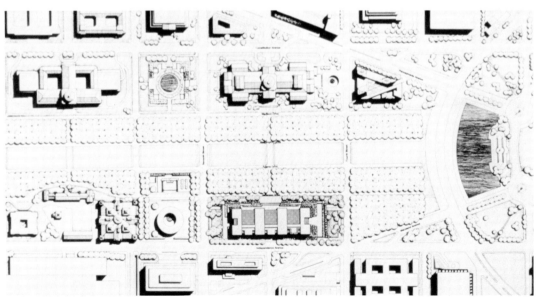

1. View of Mall, looking east
from Washington Monument;
National Air and Space
Museum on right, below
United States Capitol, 1977
Photograph by George Silk

2. Hellmuth, Obata, and
Kassabaum, National Air and
Space Museum (1971–1975),
site plan showing Mall from
Union Square to Twelfth
Street
Hellmuth, Obata, and Kassabaum

3. View of Capitol from
Rocketry and Space Flight
Hall, National Air and Space
Museum, 1977
Photograph by George Silk

4. National Air and Space
Museum, central atrium
housing Milestones of Flight
exhibition, 1977
Photograph by George Silk

5. National Air and Space
Museum, Rocketry and Space
Flight Hall, 1977
Photograph by George Silk

6. National Air and Space
Museum, exhibit of astronauts
in space working environ-
ment, 1977
Photograph by George Silk

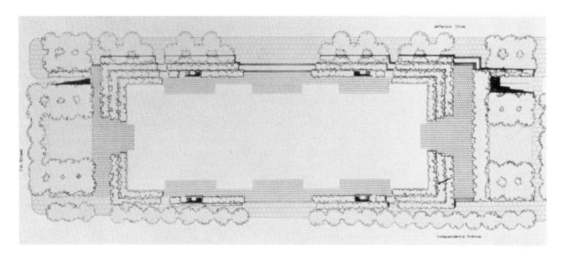

7. National Air and Space
Museum, site plan, 1972
Hellmuth, Obata, and Kassabaum

8. National Air and Space
Museum, preliminary design,
1964, north elevation,
architects' rendering
Hellmuth, Obata, and Kassabaum

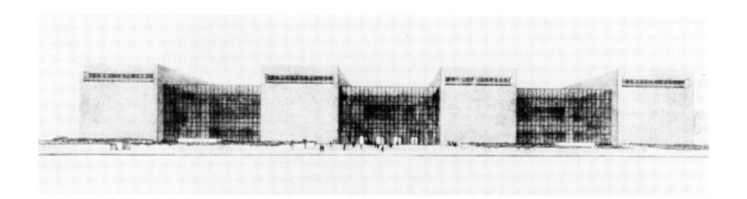

9. National Air and Space Museum, final design, 1972, north elevation, architects' rendering
Hellmuth, Obata, and Kassabaum

10. National Air and Space Museum, central atrium, 1977
Photograph by George Silk

the staff was open to ideas about how to create the exhibit space. But the final requirement, that the museum be completed within its budget, was not open to negotiation.

All these constraints affected the form of the museum, the materials used, and the ways they were used. The constraints shaped the

scheme. The narrow site limited the dimensions of the museum to 225 feet from north to south and about 685 feet from east to west (fig. 7). To use as much of this area as possible, many solutions were considered. One design, featuring an overhanging roof, was completed and approved in 1964, but it was shelved owing to the expenditures of the Vietnam War (fig. 8). When the project was revived in 1970, the original budget of $40 million remained in effect. The original design, however, could no longer be built within that budget, so we began again from scratch.

The second, and final, design approved by the museum board and the Commission of Fine Arts consisted of a series of four enclosed blocks alternating with three glass galleries to form a geometrically simple, monumental elevation facing the Mall (fig. 9). At the same time, the variation in the blocks prevented an overly monolithic effect. Although the Mall is a place of monumental buildings, a sense of scale needed to be maintained.

The north elevation's glass bays are shorter than the enclosed blocks, and recessed so as not to dominate. Their recesses align with projecting portions of the National Gallery's south elevation as if the buildings might fit together like two pieces of a puzzle. This correspondence further strengthens the relationship between the two structures.

The glass galleries have skylights and, below them, trusses from which aircraft and spacecraft are suspended, an arrangement that allows many exhibits to be viewed against the sky, suggesting their natural environment (fig. 10). It also allows visitors to maintain visual contact with the Mall. The glass bays are no

less important as windows into the museum, affording glimpses of the exhibits from the Mall. Smaller glazed galleries in the middle of the east and west elevations, each with a skylight, provide more gallery exhibition space with natural light and enhance an overall feeling of openness (fig. 11).

This blending of indoors and outdoors contributes to a more pleasant interior environment, creating a sense of enticement and welcome. It also strengthens the relationship between the museum and Mall, intensifying the building's sense of belonging on this site.

Fortunately, one side of the museum faces north, an orientation that permitted opening the building onto the Mall without the problems of direct exposure to the sun (fig. 12). Had the site been on the Mall's north side, our design would have been quite different. As it stands, the south elevation is almost entirely enclosed so as to avoid excessive sunlight (fig. 13).

While the open galleries allow some exhibits to be viewed against the sky, the enclosed galleries are more theaterlike. They offer the exhibit designers a chance to use props, painted backgrounds, and artificial lighting to create settings appropriate to the artifacts displayed. One can see, for example, scenes of Navy planes from the deck of an aircraft car-

11. National Air and Space Museum, Rocketry and Space Flight Hall, detail of window wall, 1977
Photograph by George Silk

12. National Air and Space Museum, north elevation seen from across Mall, 1977
Photograph by George Silk

13. National Air and Space Museum, south elevation, 1977
Photograph by George Silk

14. National Air and Space Museum, detail of enclosed gallery showing simulation of World War I fighter planes in France, 1977
Photograph by George Silk

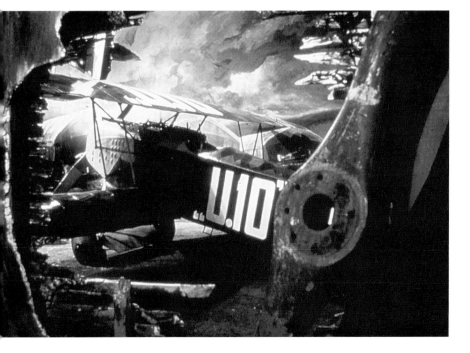

rier and World War I fighters over a depiction of the fields of France (fig. 14). The two primary levels in the museum contain several dozen separate exhibit areas varying from expansive to intimate.

Unifying all the exhibit areas, the main circulation paths were designed to be simple and easy to understand (fig. 15). Running east and west through the museum, parallel to the Mall, is a two-level central circulation spine resembling that of a shopping mall, which leads through the galleries to the exhibit areas and an auditorium. From both levels of the central spine, the Mall almost always can be seen through one of the open galleries. This ongoing experience reinforces the relationship between indoors and outdoors, facilitating visitors' orientation. Although walkways branch off to allow further exploration, they invariably return to the main circulation area. The movement of people through the building

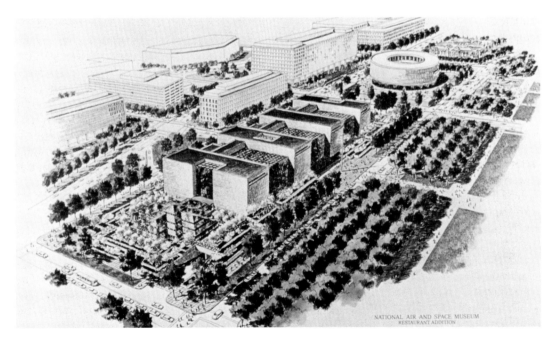

15. National Air and Space
Museum, central atrium, 1977
Photograph by George Silk

16. National Air and Space
Museum, central atrium, 1977
Photograph by George Silk

17. Hellmuth, Obata, and
Kassabaum, National Air and
Space Museum, restaurant
addition (1986–1988), archi-
tects' rendering, 1986
Hellmuth, Obata, and Kassabaum

was one of our first considerations during the design process: we wanted to provide an enjoyable experience that would minimize "museum fatigue."

When visitors enter the central open gallery, they are immediately greeted with a view of some of the most significant artifacts, such as the Wright brothers' plane and Charles Lindbergh's *Spirit of Saint Louis* (fig. 16). In a brief time visitors can see these exhibits and browse the rest of the museum. Those who are less hurried can visit the theater and explore displays on both levels. Up to sixty thousand people pass through the building in a single day, many more than originally expected. But because of the central spine, the circulation has worked well.

In addition to the exhibit areas, the top level of the museum houses all staff and administration areas, plus a small dining room. The original public food service area proved inadequate for the immense crowds, and in 1988 we added a new dining facility to serve thirteen hundred at the east end on the ground level (fig. 17). The addition, a glass pavilion, provides a panoramic view of the Mall's east end and the Capitol. The interior is ornamented with plants and trees. Since the addition is low and visually reads as an independent structure, the basic symmetry of the museum and its complementary relationship with the National Gallery of Art are preserved.

As for structure, the museum is basically a steel cage or latticework (fig. 18). The enclosed galleries are supported by simple steel frames. In the open galleries a more complex system of tubular steel trusses was used in the form of an L to span the skylight roofs and give lateral support to the glass walls facing the Mall. To support the suspended exhibits, the

truss system was designed for a hanging load of about four tons at various points in the skylight structures. The skylights at the east and west ends of the building are supported by pipes that also serve as air ducts. The structure of the new dining pavilion is a light-weight steel truss system. Its skylight glass contains screening dots to minimize the sun's glare.

The Commission of Fine Arts, which played a major role in the evolution of the museum's design, requested the use of pink Tennessee marble on the exterior (fig. 19) to match the marble of the National Gallery of Art. The hue of the marble also complements the brick of the Smithsonian Arts and Industries Building and the stone of the Smithsonian Institution Building nearby. The marble panels were to be installed in the conventional manner on precast panels, but that method would have exceeded the budget. Instead, we designed a steel latticework on which the marble panels — five feet by two and a half feet, and one and a half inches thick — were attached. The marble exterior is a curtain wall, as is the bronze-tinted acrylic plastic in the bays. The marble paneling is repeated on the interior walls at the entries and in the large, open exhibit halls, again reflecting a desire to blend indoor and outdoor aspects.

The National Air and Space Museum was dedicated on 4 July 1976. Despite the fact that the museum has become more popular than anyone had imagined, with ten to twelve million visitors a year, it accommodates crowds very well. I am grateful to have participated in the project and to share in its success.

19. National Air and Space Museum, north elevation, looking east at night, 1977
Photograph by George Silk

EDITOR'S NOTE

For further discussion of the building, see: "Rejuvenated Architecture for Washington," *Progressive Architecture* 46 (March 1965), 188–195.

"Luft- und Raumfahrtmuseum, Washington," *Baumeister* 72 (October 1975), 877–879.

William Marlin, "Stately Setting for U.S. Air and Space History," *Christian Science Monitor*, 14 May 1976, 19.

Benjamin Forgey, "Air and Space Museum," *Washington Star*, 25 June 1976, C1, C2.

Wolf Von Eckardt, "Space, Time and Architecture," *Washington Post*, 27 June 1976, E1, E3.

Jean M. White, "A Bicentennial Blastoff for a Wonder of Marble and Glass," *Washington Post*, 27 June 1976, E1, E3.

"Modernism and the Monolith," *Progressive Architecture* 57 (July 1976), 70–75.

Gyo Obata, "The National Air and Space Museum," *Military Engineer* 68 (July–August 1976), 279–281.

"National Air and Space Museum," *Architecture and Urbanism* 68 (August 1976), 63–70.

"Recent Works by Hellmuth, Obata, and Kassabaum," *Space Design* 145 (September 1976), 4–56.

Jack Eisen, "Air and Space Museum a Hot Tourist Draw," *Washington Post*, 20 September 1976, C1, C3.

Michelle Morgan, "Evaluation: The National Air and Space Museum as Barrier Free Design," *AIA Journal* 65 (December 1976), 34–37.

"National Air and Space Museum," *Print Casebooks: The Best in Environmental Graphics* 2 (1976–1977), 28–32.

Susan Braybrooke, "A Monumental Conquest of Space," *Industrial Design* 24 (January-February 1977), 30–39.

Irene Preston, "Where Dreams of Flight Hang Intact," *Southern Living* 12 (July 1977), 40–43.

"Display Space," *Building* 230 (1 April 1979), 72–76.

Andrea O. Dean, "Evaluation: The World's Most Popular Museum," *AIA Journal* 67 (November 1980), 36–45.

Stephen Trowbridge, "HOK: An American Recipe for Success," *RIBA Journal* 89 (March 1982), 31–35.

Walter McQuade, *Architecture in the Real World: The Work of HOK* (New York, 1984), 132–137.

JEAN PAUL CARLHIAN
Shepley, Bulfinch, Richardson, and Abbott

Smithsonian Institution: South Quadrangle Project

quiet oasis shaded by a great tree, created as a gesture toward the national bicentennial celebration and cherished by the citizens of our capital, became a *cause célèbre* when it was designated the site for a new museum complex of the Smithsonian Institution. In addition to the aesthetic, technological, and functional issues always involved in the design of a new building, our project had to honor the context of the surrounding, highly varied architecture and create an atmosphere appropriate for the serious museum visitor despite a bustling thoroughfare, Independence Avenue, and a dreary concrete monolith across the street, while retaining the well-loved, ancient tree and its garden (fig. 1). From its inception, this project acquired special significance due to the importance of its location, the nature of its site, and the presence of three buildings momentous enough to have been designated National Historic Landmarks.

The four-and-one-half-acre site adjoins the Mall, the greatest space in the national capital. The surrounding setting includes the Victorian Smithsonian Institution Building, referred to as the Castle (1847–1855), the Arts and Industries Building (1879–1881), initially designed as an exhibition facility, and one reminiscent of a classical palazzo, the Freer Gallery of Art (1913–1923) (figs. 2–4). Thus the architectural problem was of inserting a new building in such a historic context.

The program called for a set of facilities covering 350,000 square feet and consisting of two museums, the Arthur M. Sackler Gallery of Asiatic art and the National Museum of African Art, as well as the S. Dillon Ripley Center and an array of separate administrative offices of various Smithsonian agencies.

The overall bulk mandated by such program requirements would have resulted in an aboveground structure so large as to overpower the existing adjoining buildings. Early in the process the decision was made to place the facility underground so that the existing structures would not be compromised and the open space would be retained.

The new complex further had to be designed to support an array of full-grown plant specimens at ground level, creating a heavy burden for its structural system and a delicate waterproofing problem. Access points to the various elements of the complex had to be restricted to three discreet entrance structures endowed with architectural features sympathetic to a set of landmarks of widely different styles.

In accordance with an initial design concept provided by the Japanese architect Junzo Yoshimura, our firm embarked on a three-year development phase under the scrutiny of seven government agencies with an array of regulatory powers. The process called for a step-by-step development devised to establish, first, an acceptable footprint, then a desirable bulk, followed by an appropriate skyline silhouette and facade design, including architectural de-

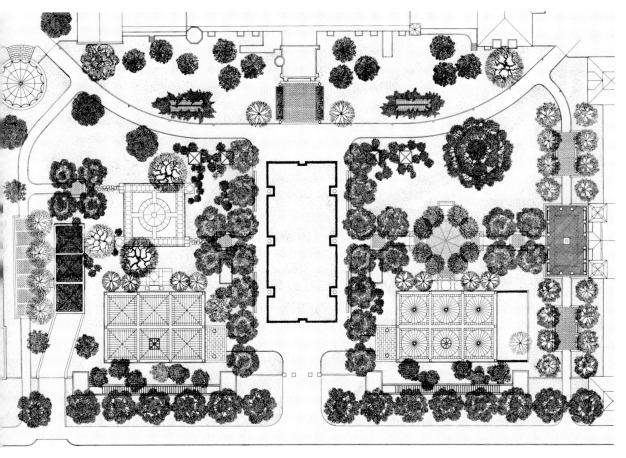

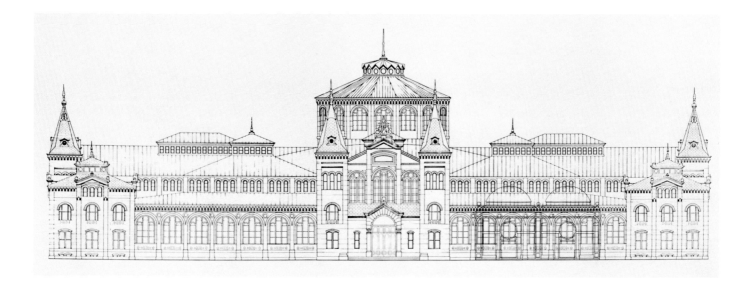

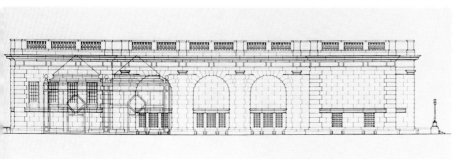

3. Smithsonian Institution, Arts and Industries Building, west elevation, showing elements of Museum of African Art entrance pavilion superimposed
Shepley, Bulfinch, Richardson, and Abbott

4. Freer Gallery of Art, east elevation, showing Sackler Gallery entrance pavilion superimposed
Shepley, Bulfinch, Richardson, and Abbott

tailing and materials selection. Footprints were limited to a rectangular area sixty-four by ninety-four feet for each of the twin museum pavilions and a circle forty-two feet in diameter for a kiosk serving as an entrance to a third basement level, the first two levels being devoted to the museums (fig. 5).

The location of the twin pavilions was dictated by the desire to preserve an unimpaired view of the south facade of the Castle from the north sidewalk of Independence Avenue and the wish to rely on the kiosk as a means of partially closing the northwest opening of the quadrangle site, thus contributing to its sense of enclosure. The existing Forrestal Building, stretching its long and gloomy north facade along the south boundary of the site, was deemed to affect adversely the setting as a whole and the garden in particular. The placement of the twin pavilions generated by

such a consideration was intended to soften the building's impact by providing distracting foreground elements of interest to visitors entering the garden from northern access points (figs. 6–8).

The overall height of the twin pavilions was determined by significant features of the surrounding existing buildings: the main cornice of the Freer Gallery established their maximum height, and the location of the main belt courses on the Castle and the Arts and Industries Building set their cornice level. Rich skyline characteristics of the Victorian landmarks yielded clues to the treatment of the twin pavilions' roofs. The pitched shapes of the Arts and Industries Building inspired the pyramidal treatment of the Sackler Gallery roof, while the arcaded feature of the Freer Gallery served as a motive for the arched openings of the Museum of African Art, engendering a domed treatment of its roof. Likewise, the Sackler Gallery's pyramidal roof forms generated the diamond-shaped openings of its facade. These solutions embodied a determination to achieve not only a harmonious relationship between old and new, but a unifying cross-fertilization of styles and forms by bringing Victorian characteristics to the Sackler Gallery and classical features to the Museum of African Art.

Pink granite from Texas was selected as a material for the Museum of African Art as compatible with the brick and tile facing of the Arts and Industries Building, while a warm

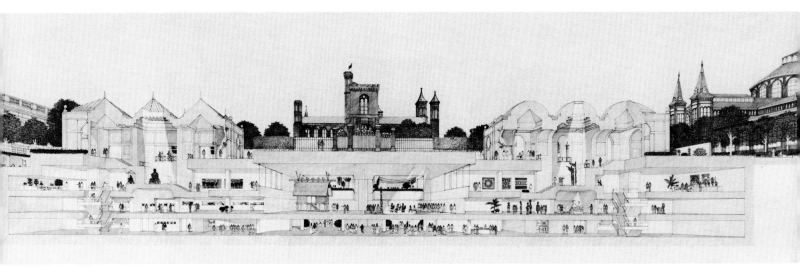

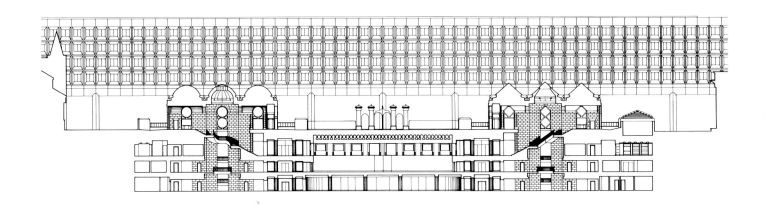

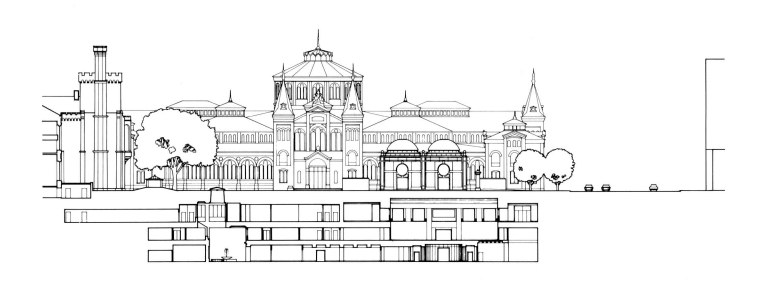

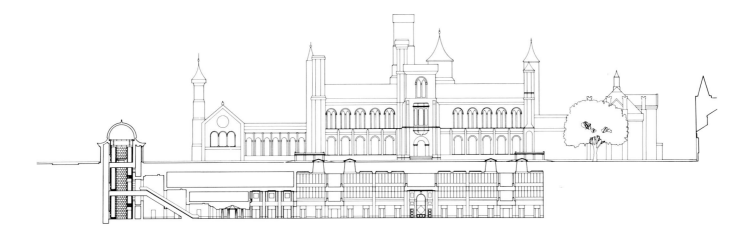

gray granite from Minnesota was chosen for the Sackler Gallery as a pleasant accompaniment to the granite facade of the Freer Gallery. Limestone was specified for the kiosk as most befitting a structure directly on the Mall. Copper was elected for all the roofs for its lasting value, but also for its colorful aging characteristics, bringing a note of polychromy to the new structures in keeping with the richness of their Victorian neighbors. The overall size and proportions of the window openings were modeled on those of the adjoining structures. Facade elements were articulated and modulated through the application of various finishes to the single type of granite chosen for each pavilion.

The very importance and singular characteristics of the site remained among our primary concerns. The orthogonal relationship of existing surrounding structures, the size of the open spaces between them, and the presence of a century-old European linden became determining factors. The understated treatment and judicious placement of the twin pavilions on the one hand and the kiosk on the other freed an open area large enough to be treated as a garden, and one of exceptional quality. An entity unto itself, this space, the Enid A. Haupt Garden, was conceived as a private retreat rather than a public space; a garden simple, noble, and grand rather than complicated, fussy, and pretty. Featuring open vistas and secluded glens, the area is divided in three parts, each one designed as a miniature theme-garden closely related to the building for which it is providing a setting.

The Castle is announced by a *parterre de broderie* adorned with urns and benches designed in a Victorian manner (fig. 9). The Spring and Fall Garden is entered through a modern version of a Chinese moon-gate and features a circular island in a square reflecting pool, all acknowledging its oriental inspiration (figs. 10–11). This garden's counterpart on the African side recognizes elements of those of the Alhambra and Shalimar as precedents (fig. 12). It is a Summer Garden — a diamond-shaped enclosure featuring a jet and a cascade surrounded by granite seats adorned with runnels fed by miniature fountains. The entire space is punctuated by eight structures housing emergency exit stairs required by law. Four of these, organized as pairs of bookends, frame 117-foot-long skylights over exhibition galleries. Two others, on account of their presence in front of the Castle's south facade, were enriched with a special treatment featuring Seneca sandstone elements salvaged from a nearby structure (fig. 13). They came from the same quarry as the stone for the Castle. (The quarry is now on the National Register, prohibiting further exploitation.) The plant material was selected for its impact as accompaniment to the architecture — occasionally as a simple statement, sometimes for its symmetrical impact, and often for its participation in an overall grouping.

In each of the twin pavilions, which serve as entrances to the museums, an open porch leads to a grand vestibule from which garden views are to be enjoyed, and to a monumental staircase descending to the exhibition galler-

9. South Quadrangle, Victorian parterre, looking south from Smithsonian Institution Building
Photograph by Robert C. Lautman

10. South Quadrangle, Spring and Fall Garden, looking east to Arts and Industries Building, through moon-gate
Photograph by Robert C. Lautman

11. South Quadrangle, Sackler
Gallery and Spring and Fall
Garden
Photograph by Nick Wheeler/
Wheeler Photographics

12. South Quadrangle,
Museum of African Art and
Summer Garden, looking
southeast
Photograph by Robert C. Lautman

ies laid out on two lower floors (fig. 14). The circular kiosk, which provides access to the third underground level harboring various Smithsonian agencies, was derived from a drawing by George Stanley Repton (fig. 15). Visitors descend via a winding stairway to a vestibule marking the start of a long, moving stairway bypassing, for reasons of security, two levels of museum facilities. A circular rotunda serves as an introduction to a top-lighted, 280-foot-long concourse terminating at an evocative mural by the artist Richard Haas.

13. South Quadrangle, emergency exit-stair housing, Smithsonian Institution Building in background
Author photograph

14. South Quadrangle, Sackler Gallery entrance pavilion, stairhall
Photograph by Robert C. Lautman

15. George Stanley Repton,
design for a conservatory
Royal Pavilion, Art Gallery and
Museums, Brighton

EDITOR'S NOTE

For further discussion of the complex, see: "Buried Treasure," *Architectural Record* 172 (February 1984), 112–121.

Paul Richard, "The Smithsonian's Mystery Building," *Washington Post*, 30 August 1987, G1, G4.

"Underneath a Garden," *Architectural Record* 175 (September 1987), 112–121.

"Masterful Placemaking Beside the Mall," *Architecture* 76 (November 1987), 43–47.

Edwards Parks and Jean Paul Carlhian, *A New View from the Castle* (Washington, 1987).

Contributors

J. Carter Brown has been the director of the National Gallery of Art since 1969 and chairman of the Commission of Fine Arts since 1971. He is a member of the President's Committee on the Arts and Humanities, is treasurer of the White House Historical Association, and an honorary member of the American Institute of Architects. He serves ex-officio as a trustee of the National Trust for Historic Preservation and on the boards of the Federal Council on the Arts and Humanities and the Pennsylvania Avenue Development Corporation.

Born in Paris, Jean Paul Carlhian graduated from the Ecole des Beaux-Arts. He completed his education at the Harvard Graduate School of Design and has taught there and at Yale University. After working as a designer for Harrison and Abramovitz on the United Nations Headquarters, he joined the office of Shepley, Bulfinch, Richardson, and Abbott, where he became a partner in 1963. His projects include Mather House and the Executive Development Complex for Harvard University, the Christian A. Johnson Music and Art Center at Middlebury College, the Graduate Center at Brown University, the College Center at Vassar College, and a student center for the University of Vermont.

Norma Evenson is professor of architectural history at the University of California, Berkeley. Her research has focused extensively on the design of capital cities. Major publications include *Chandigarh*; *Two Brazilian Capitals: Architecture and Urbanism in Rio de Janeiro and Brasilia*; *Paris: A Century of Change, 1878-1978*; and *The Indian Metropolis: A View toward the West* (1990).

Professor at the University of California, Los Angeles, Thomas S. Hines holds a joint appointment in the Department of History and the Graduate School of Architecture and Urban Planning. He is the author of *Burnham of Chicago: Architect and Planner* (1974) and *Richard Neutra and the Search for Modern Architecture* (1982). He was also co-curator, with Arthur Drexler, of the Neutra retrospective at the Museum of Modern Art, New York (1982) and has published articles in such journals as *American Quarterly, Journal of Urban History, Places,* and *Journal of the Society of Architectural Historians*. He has been the recipient of Guggenheim, Fulbright, and National Endowment for the Humanities fellowships. He is working on a book to be called "Modernism and Regionalism: A History of Los Angeles Architectural Culture."

Daniel Urban Kiley was at the Harvard Graduate School of Design from 1936 to 1938, and is a registered architect and landscape architect. In a professional career spanning fifty years, he has worked on some of this country's major commissions with its leading architects. Recipient of many awards and honors, Kiley has had his work widely published in professional and technical periodicals in the

United States and abroad. He has served on President Kennedy's Advisory Council for Pennsylvania Avenue, the National Council for the Arts and Government, the Boston Redevelopment Authority, the Washington, D.C., Redevelopment Land Agency, and the Vermont Council for the Arts. Kiley is president of the Office of Dan Kiley and currently a member of the Cambridge Redevelopment Authority.

Richard Longstreth is associate professor of architectural history and director of the graduate program in historic preservation at George Washington University. His writings include *The Buildings on Main Street: A Guide to American Commercial Architecture* (1987) and *On the Edge of the World: Four Architects in San Francisco at the Turn of the Century* (1983). Currently he is completing a book on retail development in southern California from the 1920s to the 1950s.

Gyo Obata was born in San Francisco in 1923, the son of distinguished Japanese-born artists. In 1945 he received his bachelor's degree in architecture from Washington University in Saint Louis. The following year, after studying under Eliel Saarinen, Obata received a master's degree in architecture and urban design from the Cranbrook Academy of Art in Michigan. Obata is chairman and chief executive officer of Hellmuth, Obata, and Kassabaum (HOK), which he helped found in 1955. He has participated in the design and planning of buildings of nearly every type and scope.

A specialist in American garden history of the eighteenth and nineteenth centuries, **Therese O'Malley** is assistant dean of the Center for Advanced Study in the Visual Arts at the National Gallery of Art. She received the Ph.D. from the University of Pennsylvania for which she wrote a dissertation on the early landscape and urban planning history of the national Mall in Washington between 1791 and 1852.

Jon A. Peterson teaches a variety of courses on American urban history and is working on a history of the origins of modern American city planning before World War I. He is chair of the Department of History at Queens College of the City University of New York.

Pamela Scott has been researching and teaching the history of Washington architecture for the last fifteen years. Her publications include editorship of the microfilm edition of *The Papers of Robert Mills*, "Robert Mills and American Monuments," and "Stephen Hallet's Designs for the U. S. Capitol." She will be coauthor of the Washington volume in the *Buildings of the United States* series sponsored by the Society of Architectural Historians. Currently she is working on a major study of Pierre Charles L'Enfant's design of Washington and a monograph on Robert Mills.

Robert A.M. Stern, a practicing architect, writer, and teacher, is a principal in the firm of Robert A.M. Stern Architects in New York. He is a professor of architecture at Columbia University and the author of many books on architectural subjects, including *New York 1900, New York 1930,* and *Pride of Place,* the companion to his documentary television series on American architecture. **Raymond W. Gastil** assisted Stern with *New York 1930* and *Pride of Place* and collaborated on Stern's most recent book, *Modern Classicism.*

David C. Streatfield is associate professor of landscape architecture and interior design and planning at the University of Washington. He was educated in England, where he practiced as an architect before coming to the United States in 1962. His research interests focus on modern landscape design from the eighteenth century to the present, and he has published numerous articles on the history of landscape design. Now working on a history of garden design in California and a history of modernism in landscape architecture, he also is actively involved in historic preservation.

A frequent lecturer and contributor to journals, **Richard Guy Wilson** specializes in modern and American architecture, city planning, decorative arts, and art. Among his books are *McKim, Mead, and White, Architects* (1983) and *The AIA Gold Medal* (1984); as a guest curator for museum exhibitions he contributed to *The American Renaissance, 1876–1917* (1979), *The Machine Age in America, 1918–1941* (1986), and *The Art That is Life: The Arts and Crafts Movement in America* (1987). He teaches and is chair of architectural history at the University of Virginia.

CORRIGENDA

page 177:   XII. *Plan of the City of*
Washington . . . , engraving by
Thackara and Vallance, fall
1792, probably based on
March 1792 plan (pl. x)
Library of Congress

XIII. Detail pl. XII

page 193:   pl. XXXVIII should
be reversed